Wrongful Convictions and Miscarriages of Justice

This innovative work builds on Huff and Killias' earlier publication (2008), but is broader and more thoroughly comparative in a number of important ways:

- while focusing heavily on wrongful convictions, it places the subject of wrongful convictions in the broader contextual framework of miscarriages of justice and provides discussions of different types of miscarriages of justice that have not previously received much scholarly attention by criminologists;
- it addresses, in much greater detail, the questions of how, and how often, wrongful convictions occur;
- it provides more in-depth consideration of the role of forensic science in helping produce wrongful convictions and in helping free those who have been wrongfully convicted;
- it offers new insights into the origins and current progress of the innocence movement, as well as the challenges that await the exonerated when they return to "free" society;
- it assesses the impact of the use of alternatives to trials (especially plea bargains in the U.S. and summary proceedings and penal orders in Europe) in producing wrongful convictions;
- it considers how the U.S. and Canada have responded to 9/11 and the increased threat of terrorism by enacting legislation and

adopting policies that may exacerbate the problem of wrongful conviction; and

- it provides in-depth considerations of two topics related to wrongful conviction: voluntary false confessions and convictions which, although technically not wrongful since they are based on law violations, represent another type of miscarriage of justice since they are due solely to unjust laws resulting from political repression.

C. Ronald Huff is Professor of Criminology, Law and Society and of Sociology at the University of California, Irvine. He is a Fellow and Past-President of The American Society of Criminology. His publications include more than 100 journal articles and book chapters and 12 other books. His current research focuses on wrongful convictions and gangs.

Martin Killias is Professor of Criminal Law, Procedure and Criminology at the University of Zurich. Over 25 years, he directed the Institute of Criminology at the University of Lausanne and served as a part-time judge at the Federal Supreme Court of Switzerland. His research has focused on comparative and experimental studies.

Huff and Killias provide a groundbreaking, comprehensive and innovative collection of top-notch research on wrongful convictions from a cross-national perspective. The book deserves to be in the personal libraries of all criminal justice scholars and should be required reading for students taking courses on topics such as comparative criminal justice or wrongful convictions.

> – **Talia Harmon**, *Criminal Justice, Niagara University*

Extensive in its scope and coverage, this book provides a valuable extension to the scholarship on how wrongful convictions and miscarriages of justice are to be understood and responded to. A must read for all those interested in the debate about public protection and public policy when justice goes wrong.

> – **Michael Naughton**, *Sociology and Law, University of Bristol, Founder and Director, Innocence Network UK (INUK).*

Wrongful Convictions and Miscarriages of Justice is masterful in adding new material that broadens the wrongful convictions critique of the delivery of justice in the U.S. It draws from U.S. and Canadian experience to expand the possibilities for reform and includes especially strong chapters that deal with legal mechanisms found in court settings.

> – **Cathleen Burnett**, *Criminal Justice and Criminology, University of Missouri–Kansas City*

An essential read for anyone interested in wrongful convictions in the global context. This book does a particularly good job of helping the reader understand the difference between adversarial and inquisitorial systems of justice, and how each system contributes to or effectively combats wrongful convictions. The new edition includes many important updates, including the role of forensic science in causing, and then correcting, miscarriages of justice.

> – **Mark Godsey**, *Law, University of Cincinnati College of Law*

 **Routledge**
Taylor & Francis Group

Also from Routledge:

A Theory of African American Offending: Race, Racism, and Crime by Shaun L. Gabbidon and James D. Unnever

Voices from Criminal Justice: Thinking and Reflecting on the System ed. by Heith Copes and Mark Pogrebin

Crime and the Life Course by Michael Benson

Social Statistics: The Basics and Beyond by Thomas J. Linneman

Applied Statistics for the Social and Health Sciences by Rachel A. Gordon

Regression Analysis for the Social Sciences by Rachel A. Gordon

Corrections: Foundations for the Future by Jeanne B. Stinchcomb

Lifers: Seeking Redemption in Prison by John Irwin

When Crime Appears: The Role of Emergence ed. By Jean Marie McGloin, Christopher J.

Sulliva, and Leslie W. Kennedy

Forthcoming:

Race, Law and American Society: 1607-Present, 2nd Edition by Gloria J. Browne-Marshall *Human Trafficking: Interdisciplinary Perspectives* ed. by Mary C. Burke

Research Methods in Crime and Justice by Brian Withrow

GIS and Spatial Analysis for the Social Sciences: Coding, Mapping, and Modeling, 2nd Edition by Robert Nash Parker and Emily K. Asencio

Wrongful Convictions and Miscarriages of Justice: Causes and Remedies in North American and European Criminal Justice Systems

Edited by C. Ronald Huff, University of California, and Martin Killias, University of Zurich

Routledge
Taylor & Francis Group

NEW YORK AND LONDON

First published 2013
by Routledge
711 Third Avenue, New York, NY 10017

Simultaneously published in the UK
by Routledge
2 Park Square, Milton Park, Abingdon, Oxon OX14 4RN

Routledge is an imprint of the Taylor & Francis Group, an informa business

Library of Congress Cataloging-in-Publication Data
Wrongful convictions and miscarriages of justice : causes and remedies
in North American and European criminal justice systems / edited by
C. Ronald Huff and Martin Killias.
   p. cm.
   Includes bibliographical references and index.
   1. Criminal justice, Administration of—North America.   2. Criminal
justice, Administration of—Europe.   3. Judicial error—North
America.   4. Judicial error—Europe.   I. Huff, C. Ronald.   II. Killias,
Martin.
   HV9960.N7W76 2013
   345′.0122—dc23

                                                                        2012033099

ISBN: 978-0-415-53993-7 (hbk)
ISBN: 978-0-415-53995-1 (pbk)
ISBN: 978-0-203-59728-6 (ebk)

Typeset in Adobe Caslon
by RefineCatch Limited, Bungay, Suffolk, UK

To our grandchildren, Skylar ("Sky") Mills Connor and Lena and Flavio Clavel, whose smiles, laughter, and personalities bring great joy to our lives, as well as to a forthcoming grandchild (on the Killias side) who will enter the world at about the same time that this book is published. May they all live in nations, and in a world, that work to improve the quality of justice for all.

CRH and MK

TABLE OF CONTENTS

ACKNOWLEDGMENTS   XIII

FOREWORD   XV
MICHAEL L. RADELET

CHAPTER 1   WRONGFUL CONVICTIONS AND MISCARRIAGES OF
            JUSTICE IN COMPARATIVE PERSPECTIVE: PREFACE
            AND INTRODUCTION   1
            C. RONALD HUFF AND MARTIN KILLIAS

PART I: WRONGFUL CONVICTIONS AND MISCARRIAGES
OF JUSTICE: CAUSES AND FREQUENCY

CHAPTER 2   WRONGFUL CONVICTIONS IN A WORLD OF
            MISCARRIAGES OF JUSTICE   15
            BRIAN FORST

CHAPTER 3   HOW MANY FALSE CONVICTIONS ARE THERE?
            HOW MANY EXONERATIONS ARE THERE?   45
            SAMUEL GROSS

CHAPTER 4   ERRORS OCCUR EVERYWHERE—BUT NOT AT THE
            SAME FREQUENCY: THE ROLE OF PROCEDURAL
            SYSTEMS IN WRONGFUL CONVICTIONS   61
            MARTIN KILLIAS

CHAPTER 5   TRIAL AND ERROR   77
            BRANDON L. GARRETT

CHAPTER 6 THE PROSECUTOR AND WRONGFUL CONVICTIONS: MISPLACED PRIORITIES, MISCONDUCT, IMMUNITY, AND REMEDIES 91
JIM PETRO AND NANCY PETRO

CHAPTER 7 FORENSIC SCIENCE AND WRONGFUL CONVICTIONS 111
SIMON A. COLE AND WILLIAM C. THOMPSON

CHAPTER 8 THE IMPORTANCE OF HAVING A LOGICAL FRAMEWORK FOR EXPERT CONCLUSIONS IN FORENSIC DNA PROFILING: ILLUSTRATIONS FROM THE AMANDA KNOX CASE 137
JOËLLE VUILLE, ALEX BIEDERMANN, AND FRANCO TARONI

CHAPTER 9 TUNNEL VISION, BELIEF PERSEVERANCE AND BIAS CONFIRMATION: ONLY HUMAN?
CHRISJE BRANTS 161

CHAPTER 10 "VOLUNTARY" FALSE CONFESSIONS AS A SOURCE OF WRONGFUL CONVICTIONS: THE CASE OF SPAIN 193
MARCELO F. AEBI AND CLAUDIA CAMPISTOL

CHAPTER 11 THE CHANGING FACE OF MISCARRIAGES OF JUSTICE: PREVENTIVE DETENTION STRATEGIES IN CANADA AND THE UNITED STATES 209
KATHRYN M. CAMPBELL

CHAPTER 12 THE RISKS OF SUMMARY PROCEEDINGS, PLEA BARGAINS, AND PENAL ORDERS IN PRODUCING WRONGFUL CONVICTIONS IN THE U.S. AND EUROPE 237
GWLADYS GILLIÉRON

PART II: WRONGFUL CONVICTIONS AND MISCARRIAGES OF JUSTICE: CONSEQUENCES AND REMEDIES

CHAPTER 13 LIFE AFTER EXONERATION: EXAMINING THE AFTERMATH OF A WRONGFUL CAPITAL CONVICTION 261
SAUNDRA D. WESTERVELT AND KIMBERLY J. COOK

CHAPTER 14 MORE PROCEDURE AND CONCERN ABOUT INNOCENCE BUT LESS JUSTICE?: REMEDIES FOR WRONGFUL CONVICTIONS IN THE UNITED STATES AND CANADA 283
KENT ROACH

CHAPTER 15 THE ROCKY ROAD TO REFORM: STATE INNOCENCE
            STUDIES AND THE PENNSYLVANIA STORY   309
            SPERO T. LAPPAS AND ELIZABETH F. LOFTUS

CHAPTER 16 EDWIN BORCHARD AND THE LIMITS OF
            INNOCENCE REFORM   329
            MARVIN ZALMAN

CHAPTER 17 WRONGFUL CONVICTIONS, MISCARRIAGES OF
            JUSTICE, AND POLITICAL REPRESSION:
            CHALLENGES FOR TRANSITIONAL JUSTICE   357
            C. RONALD HUFF

PART III: WRONGFUL CONVICTIONS AND MISCARRIAGES
OF JUSTICE: CONCLUSIONS AND RECOMMENDATIONS

CHAPTER 18 WRONGFUL CONVICTIONS, AND MISCARRIAGES
            OF JUSTICE – WHAT DID WE LEARN?
            MARTIN KILLIAS AND C. RONALD HUFF   373

ABOUT THE CONTRIBUTORS   397

INDEX   407

Acknowledgments

First, we wish to thank all of those colleagues who so readily agreed to contribute chapters to our book and whose work is represented in this volume. Without their scholarship, this book would obviously not exist. We also appreciate the many colleagues of ours, in both North America and Europe, who encouraged us to produce this book, bringing together recent scholarship by some of the world's leading scholars addressing wrongful convictions and other miscarriages of justice. We also appreciate Stephen Rutter at Routledge for approaching us and expressing his interest in this book project and for bringing it to fruition; to Joseph Parry, our editor during part of this project; and to the editorial and production staff at Routledge, who have assisted in the production of the book. Finally, of course, we are indebted to our families and close friends for their continual support and encouragement throughout this project, despite the demands on our time—and their patience!

FOREWORD
Michael L. Radelet

The problem of "miscarriages of justice" has attracted an explosion of attention in the past three decades. When Ron Huff and I started to publish our studies in this area a quarter of a century ago, we could review much of the 20th-century research on the subject in one article (Huff, Rattner, and Sagarin, 1986; Bedau and Radelet, 1987). Almost all the research on erroneous convictions prior to the mid-1980s followed closely in the footsteps of Edwin Borchard (see Zalman, Chapter 16), consisting mainly of descriptions of cases in which innocent people had been convicted. With few exceptions, all the work on the issue had been done in the U.S. or England. Even the terminology was crude, with authors using terms such as "miscarriages of justice," "erroneous convictions," "wrongful convictions," "convictions of the innocent" (among others) pretty much interchangeably. Today, young scholars in this area have available two dozen or more scholarly books, scores of articles and chapters, and shelves full of case studies discussing erroneous convictions as a foundation for their work.

The growing number and quality of studies on erroneous convictions is not all that has changed in the past 25 years. Younger criminologists who wonder if their scholarship can have any influence on public opinion (and maybe even public policy) can look at the literature on erroneous convictions and see an area where criminological research has indeed had major impacts. Indeed, Frank Baumgartner and his colleagues (2008) have argued that concern about erroneous convictions has been the most important factor explaining the recent declines in death penalty support. In 1985, Gallup found that 72 percent of Americans supported the death penalty, and only 15 percent of those standing opposed mentioned "wrongful convictions" as a reason for their position (Gallup, 1986). Twenty-four years later, 59 percent of the respondents in the 2009 Gallup Poll said that they believed that an innocent person had been executed in the preceding five years (Gallup Report, 2010). Perhaps not coincidentally, by 2011 support for the death penalty had dropped to 61 percent, a 39-year low (Newport, 2011). When support for the death penalty given the option of life imprisonment without parole ("LWOP") was last measured in October 2010, Gallup found that support for the death penalty outweighed support for LWOP by a slim 49–46 margin (Gallup Report, 2010). Empirical research by criminologists and legal scholars on erroneous convictions (and other issues related to the death penalty) has undoubtedly been a major catalyst for this public opinion shift.

One of the most significant changes over the past 25 years is that virtually all scholars, and even many politicians and participants in the criminal justice system, have grown to realize that erroneous convictions do occur, throughout the world,[1] at least on occasion. It is also more difficult to justify the errors, at least in the way Ernest van den Haag did in 1985 when commenting on a draft of a study that identified 25 20th-century cases in which executed defendants were possibly innocent (Bedau and Radelet, 1987).[2] Van den Haag found that number of erroneous executions:

> if true, a very acceptable number . . . All human activities—building houses, driving a car, playing golf or football—cause innocent people to suffer wrongful death, but we don't give them up because on the whole we feel there's a net gain. Here, a net gain in justice is being done.
>
> (Margolick, 1985)

Today, given the extensive publicity attached to erroneous convictions and the opportunities that people have had to study the cases or even meet the wrongly convicted, it is doubtful that many would agree that the death penalty offers a "net gain" that outweighs the horror of wrongful executions.

The chapters in this book, taken as a whole, leave the reader wondering not only about cases where factually innocent defendants are convicted, but also about related errors that lead to imperfect outcomes in the criminal justice system. In the case of homicide, for example, we know of all sorts of cases where defendants argued that they did indeed kill someone, but did so by accident, in self-defense, or because of insanity. Some might argue that they were guilty of second-degree murder or manslaughter, but not of first-degree murder. How many cases are there annually where a juvenile defendant's mental status is misjudged, and she or he is erroneously waived into our adult courts? But we make these godlike decisions with less than perfect skills, and sometimes we err. Once we realize that we occasionally convict defendants who are totally innocent, we can use the realization as a window through which we can see all sorts of other errors—or potential errors—that can be made and are being made when dividing the line between the innocent and the guilty.

Perhaps the most important effect of the growing attention to wrongful convictions is that it opens (or reopens) the door for research and debate about other imperfections in the criminal justice system. If we can convict defendants who are totally innocent, can we have faith in the idea that most prison sentences are proportionate to harm and culpability? Are the harshest sentences arbitrarily imposed, or, worse yet, systematically predictable by legally irrelevant variables such as race and gender? How prevalent is prosecutor overzealousness or incompetent defense counsel, even with defendants who are unquestionably guilty? How common are departures from judicial neutrality, and are these departures influenced by judicial elections? In the end, we can use erroneous convictions as a window through which we can detect and examine all sorts of imperfections in criminal justice systems around the world, and focus our efforts on eradicating them.

Perhaps the most amazing thing about this area of research over the past 25 years is that it has attracted such an unusually dedicated and creative group of scholars. For this book, Professors Huff and Killias have brought together the very best of these scholars in a way that far surpasses any collection heretofore available. Readers will marvel at Samuel Gross' struggle for precision (Chapter 3), the awakening of Jim and Nancy Petro (Chapter 6), and the compassion of Saundra Westervelt and Kim Cook (Chapter 13). There is not a chapter in this book that can be skipped.

Given the evolution of the study of erroneous convictions over the past quarter century, one can only imagine what scholars in the area will be studying and writing about 25 or so years in the future. We have learned quite a bit, but the most important thing these authors teach us is that we have just scratched the surface.

Notes

1 Although the problem is universal, Martin Killias shows in Chapter 4 that the frequency of erroneous convictions varies between countries and types of justice systems.
2 When published, this paper included 23 such cases. Originally we included the cases of Ethel and Julius Rosenberg, but in the end restricted our inventory to what we believed were erroneous convictions for homicide and erroneous death sentences for rape.

References

Baumgartner, Frank, Suzanna L. DeBoef, and Amber E. Boydstun. 2008. *The Decline of the Death Penalty and the Discovery of Innocence*. New York: Cambridge University Press.

Bedau, Hugo Adam and Michael L. Radelet. 1987. Miscarriages of Justice in Potentially Capital Cases, *Stanford Law Review* 40: 21–179.

Gallup Report, 1986. The Death Penalty. *Gallup Report* 244–245 (Jan.–Feb. 1986), 10–16.

Gallup Report, 2010. *Gallup News—Death Penalty (as of Jan. 22, 2010)*, available at http://www.deathpenaltyinfo.org/documents/Gallup.pdf.

Huff, C. Ronald, Arye Rattner, and Edward Sagarin. 1986. Guilty Until Proven Innocent: Wrongful Conviction and Public Policy, *Crime and Delinquency* 32: 518–44.

Margolick, David. 1985. 25 Wrongly Executed in U.S., Study Finds. *New York Times*, Nov. 14.

Newport, Frank. 2011. *In U.S., Support for the Death Penalty Falls to a 39-year Low* (Oct. 13, 2011), available at <http://www.deathpenaltyinfo.org/documents/Gallup.pdf>.

1

WRONGFUL CONVICTIONS AND MISCARRIAGES OF JUSTICE IN COMPARATIVE PERSPECTIVE

PREFACE AND INTRODUCTION

C. Ronald Huff and Martin Killias

When we published an earlier book[1] on wrongful convictions with a cross-national, comparative focus, we noted that the extant literature on wrongful convictions seldom included cross-national perspectives. That book included a number of "nation reports," describing and analyzing wrongful convictions in the context of an array of different criminal justice systems in the U.S., Canada, a number of European nations, and Israel. It stimulated considerable discussion concerning topics such as the causes of wrongful convictions; the respective advantages and disadvantages of the adversarial and continental/inquisitorial systems of justice; how the incidence of wrongful convictions might best be reduced; and other important topics. In the United States, the International Division of the National Institute of Justice, acting in part in response to the book, held a conference on this important subject, bringing together scholars and policymakers from a number of nations on several continents to discuss the challenges posed by wrongful convictions and how we might learn from each other's experiences. The conference included a keynote address and resulted in a comprehensive report.[2]

While also incorporating cross-national perspectives, this book's focus is broader in a number of ways:

(1) while focusing heavily on wrongful convictions, it places the subject of wrongful convictions in the broader contextual framework of miscarriages of justice and provides discussions of different types of miscarriages of justice that have not previously received much scholarly attention by criminologists;

(2) it addresses, in much greater detail, the questions of how, and how often, wrongful convictions occur;

(3) it provides more in-depth consideration of the role of forensic science in helping produce wrongful convictions and in helping free those who have been wrongfully convicted;

(4) it offers new insights into the origins and current progress of the innocence movement, as well as the challenges that await the exonerated when they return to "free" society;

(5) it assesses the impact of the use of alternatives to trials (especially plea bargains in the U.S. and summary proceedings and penal orders in Europe) in producing wrongful convictions;

(6) it considers how the U.S. and Canada have responded to 9/11 and the increased threat of terrorism by enacting legislation and adopting policies that may exacerbate the problem of wrongful conviction;

(7) it provides in-depth considerations of two topics related to wrongful conviction: voluntary false confessions and convictions which, although technically not wrongful since they are based on law violations, represent another type of miscarriage of justice since they are due solely to unjust laws resulting from political repression.

In Part I, we focus on issues concerning the causes of wrongful convictions and the frequency with which these errors occur. We begin with Chapter 2, in which Brian Forst correctly places the problem of wrongful conviction in the larger context of miscarriages of justice. Arguably, no one has done this better than Forst who, in an award-winning book,[3] focused extensively on both Type I and Type II errors and their consequences for public safety and for society. In this chapter, Forst acknowledges the serious impact of wrongful convictions on the lives of offenders and their families, as well as on public respect for the criminal justice system. He notes, however, the large disparity between Type I and Type II errors, arguing that the data suggest that for every wrongful conviction, there may be more than 1,000 "failures to convict" in felony level cases. There are also other miscarriages of justice, including wrongful arrests made by the police; violence against unarmed, innocent people; and other injustices. He then focuses on how we might better manage our errors, drawing on lessons from statistical inference and on examples of how product defects are addressed. Noting that reducing either false positives or false negatives can have an adverse impact on the other type of error, he focuses on reducing the social costs of miscarriages of justice, including recommendations for the police, prosecution, courts, and corrections regarding how we might begin to manage wrongful convictions "mindfully."

Perhaps no one has devoted more time and effort than Samuel Gross in attempting to estimate the frequency of wrongful convictions and exonerations. How many of these errors do we make and how often do we discover those errors and exonerate the innocent? In Chapter 3, Gross argues that no one knows the exact answers to these questions. He reviews recent efforts to estimate the frequency of wrongful conviction. He then discusses the use of inferential methods of arriving at an estimate without having adequate direct information versus using actual exonerations in cases involving rape or homicide (where DNA is likely to be present) as another basis for estimation. He notes, however, that even the recent National Registry of Exonerations, which he co-founded, represents only a small percentage of the total. The rate of exonerations in states having the death penalty far exceeds the comparable rate in non-death penalty states, for example, and exonerations are far more likely in cases where DNA evidence is available for post-conviction appellate review. He concludes that about 2%–3% of death sentences since 1973 have ended in exoneration and that a reasonable estimate of wrongful convictions appears to be 1%–5% for serious felonies in the United States. Similar error rates involving airplane crashes, for example, would clearly be unacceptable, but what is our tolerance for wrongful convictions? And, of course, the questions posed by Gross relate to those posed by Forst in Chapter 2, as well, since reducing one type of error (wrongful convictions) can also increase the other type of error (failures to convict the guilty). Both have serious consequences for public safety and for public confidence in the criminal justice system.

While we know that human decision-making and human behavior are both prone to errors, and that those kinds of errors clearly contribute to wrongful convictions and other miscarriages of justice, what about systemic errors, those that are endemic to both adversarial and inquisitorial criminal justice systems? In Chapter 4, Martin Killias describes, summarizes, and compares these two types of systems that characterize North American and European criminal justice. He analyzes the comparative merits, as well as problematic aspects, of these two systems with respect to their systemic contributions to wrongful conviction errors. His discussion focuses especially on six key aspects of these systems:

(1) the comparative emphasis placed on the search for the truth versus procedural justice;
(2) the role of the defense counsel;
(3) different functions of the trial;
(4) different forms of "plea bargaining";
(5) different styles of police interviews/interrogations;
(6) the role of confessions.

Killias concludes by making a number of recommendations designed to reduce systemic errors, thus reducing the number of wrongful convictions that occur in each type of system.

What can trial transcripts tell us about the factors that help generate wrongful convictions? In Chapter 5, Brandon Garrett summarizes what he found when he analyzed the trial transcripts of the first 250 DNA-based exonerations in the United States. For him, careful analysis of those transcripts raised a number of critical questions. For example, when jurors hear "evidence" about alleged confessions or hear testimony from eyewitnesses or from jailhouse informants, how can they tell if it has been compromised in some way? Garrett's chapter focuses on those three types of evidence, while noting that other factors also contributed significantly to the production of wrongful convictions and subsequent exonerations in those 250 cases, including flawed forensic evidence; incompetent defense counsel; prosecutorial and police misconduct; and judicial error due to inadequate oversight related to the tendency to afford prosecutors undue deference.

As Garrett mentions in Chapter 5, prosecutorial misconduct is one of the frequent factors related to wrongful convictions in the U.S., where prosecutors are ethically bound to pursue justice but too often seem intent on defending convictions instead—even when confronted with clear evidence that some of those convictions were erroneous, often sending innocent people to prison for many years. In Chapter 6, Jim Petro (a former prosecutor and former Ohio Attorney General who recently received the Champion of Justice Award from the Innocence Network) and Nancy Petro (his co-author on this chapter and on their recent book[4]) note that U.S. prosecutors are arguably the most powerful officials in the criminal justice system and argue that their power has increased even further as the proportion of convictions via plea bargains has increased. This chapter recounts Jim Petro's awakening as a prosecutor due to the wrongful conviction and subsequent exoneration of Clarence Elkins, who had been convicted almost exclusively on the erroneous testimony of his traumatized six-year-old niece, who had been raped by another man; examines the role of the prosecutor; discusses prosecutorial misconduct, including *Brady*[5] violations related to the withholding of potentially exculpatory evidence; reviews recent court rulings on prosecutorial immunity; and offers potential wide-ranging remedies designed to reduce wrongful convictions. The Petros raise an important question: Given that we are aware of the role that prosecutorial misconduct has played in known cases of wrongful conviction that went to trial, how extensive might this problem be when well over 90% of convictions never go to trial but are, instead, arrived at through plea bargains? It is a troubling question, indeed.

As Simon Cole and William Thompson point out in Chapter 7, forensic science was not mentioned prominently as a possible contributor to wrongful convictions until the past two decades. After all, how could "science" help *cause* such terrible errors? Today, most of us think of forensic science as a tool to help free the wrongfully convicted but, as Cole and Thompson note, that perspective emerged primarily in the 1990s as the use of DNA testing became more widely employed and may have accounted for more than one-third of all wrongful convictions that have been exposed since 1989. This chapter points out that forensic science can contribute to both Type I and Type II errors and provides an in-depth analysis and discussion of how we might think about forensic science's role. How good a job does it do in providing scientific support for correct hypotheses and failing to support the kinds of incorrect hypotheses that can result in wrongful convictions? How does it sometimes contribute to the conviction of innocent defendants? The authors argue that this may be an appropriate "window of opportunity" to carefully assess forensic science as an institution and consider reforms that go beyond the usual focus on individual errors, since broader reforms are likely to have far greater impact.

Of course, forensic science plays a critical role in both adversarial and inquisitorial criminal justice systems, and it is often given even heavier weight in the latter, where greater deference is generally granted to experts. Nowhere has that been more apparent than in the recent case of Amanda Knox, the American student studying in Italy who was convicted of murdering her British roommate. In Chapter 8 Joëlle Vuille, Alex Biedermann, and Franco Taroni provide a detailed and careful analysis of the role that forensic science played in that case, re-examining the way in which the forensic scientists interpreted the results of the DNA testing that was subsequently introduced as evidence by the prosecution in convicting Knox. How did they interpret the results? Since inferences can vary, what inferences did they draw? How should one decide the probative value of such evidence? Should such forensic evidence be viewed as definitive or only in probabilistic terms? How did they frame their findings? The Knox case provides an excellent exemplar on which to base the kind of reconsideration of the role of forensic science that was suggested by Cole and Thompson in Chapter 7. Vuille et al. argue that forensic scientists and legal actors need to work together toward a common and logical framework for communicating the strength of forensic examinations to assist the triers of fact in reaching accurate conclusions regarding competing hypotheses.

Chapter 9 shifts our focus to another type of error that frequently contributes to the conviction of innocent persons—confirmation bias and related cognitive factors. Chrisje Brants provides a careful re-examination of four cases of wrongful conviction in the Netherlands. These cases illustrate a number of errors, including police incompetence and misconduct; unethical prosecutors and experts; failure to disclose potentially exculpatory evidence; misunderstandings about expert evidence; false confessions; and courts that believed "improbable theories." Brants takes the reader on a guided tour inside the cognitive world of tunnel vision, belief perseverance, and confirmation bias as they affect cases in both the adversarial and inquisitorial systems of justice. She describes these errors and analyzes them in the context of the Dutch system, while also revealing the vulnerability of both kinds of systems due to human cognitive biases. She notes, ironically, that the legal cultures that surround both types of criminal justice systems also produce tunnel vision of their own, making it nearly impossible to effectuate any reforms that are not based on their existing fundamental characteristics.

While we have long known that false confessions are an important cause of wrongful convictions, Marcelo Aebi and Claudia Campistol introduce us, in Chapter 10, to another important subtype of false confession—voluntary false confessions that are motivated by a desire to obtain personal intangible benefits. Relying on press reports in Spain, they compile a database of reports involving such cases, and they conclude that such false confessions can be categorized into two subtypes of motivation: (1) false confessions designed to pressure legislators for changes in the law (for example, expanded decriminalization in cases involving abortion or euthanasia); and (2) false confessions intended to protect actual offenders by accepting responsibility for crimes that were actually committed by others (thus demonstrating loyalty to the group, for example). Aebi and Campistol also consider claims that the latter type of false confessions have frequently been employed by the ETA terrorist group, by juveniles, and by members of the Roma minority group, especially women, but they found no convincing empirical evidence to support those claims. The analysis presented by Aebi and Campistol raises interesting questions that one might contemplate, however, and that were raised in an earlier paper by Aebi.[6] For example, what if a member of a terrorist group, such as the ETA, falsely confesses to a crime in order to divert attention from another active member of a terrorist cell, who may be planning major terrorist incidents? In his earlier paper, Aebi referred to such an act as a "voluntary wrongful conviction" and wondered if the police might drop their investigation due to such a false confession. Given the greater weight placed on confessions in the U.S. adversarial system, compared with the inquisitorial system, one might be concerned that closing the case and adding to the "clearance rate" in such a case might soon be followed by a major terrorist incident committed by persons who should have been suspects in a continuing investigation if the evidence did not correspond with the confession.

This mention of terrorism provides a convenient segue to Chapter 11, in which Kathryn Campbell focuses on U.S. and Canadian responses to the September 11 terrorist attacks on the United States. She asks whether, in attempting to deter such attacks in the future, these two neighboring countries might have adopted legislation and policies that have led to new forms of miscarriages of justice that have not received much scholarly attention in criminology. Post-9/11 examples of such legislative and policy initiatives include increasingly harsh immigration policies, preventive detention without charges or trials, and the increased use of deportation based on unsubstantiated allegations. What has been the impact of these policies on the presumption of innocence and on respect for due process in these two democracies? Campbell argues that the preventive detention policies in both the U.S. and Canada have created new forms of miscarriages of justice. She poses the important question of how such democratic societies should balance their understandable security concerns with the respect for individual rights that is so central to free democracies.

As Jim and Nancy Petro noted in Chapter 6, the ever-expanding reliance on plea bargains in the U.S. raises serious questions about how they might be contributing to wrongful convictions, given what we know about the serious ethical violations committed by some prosecutors in cases that went to trial and were, presumably, subjected to greater scrutiny. In Chapter 12, Gwladys Gilliéron expands that discussion by linking it to the increased use of summary proceedings, penal orders, and other alternatives to trials in European nations. It is clear that: (1) convictions are increasingly being obtained via non-trial alternatives in both adversarial and inquisitorial systems of justice; and (2) such alternatives have far fewer safeguards built in to protect the rights of the defendants. Gilliéron argues that most of our research and our concerns about wrongful convictions have been focused on those discovered after trials, but given the growth in non-trial convictions, more attention should be paid to the miscarriages of justice that result from the latter. She describes and discusses these alternatives to trial in both adversarial and inquisitorial systems of justice and raises important questions concerning how these systems might reduce the use of coercion in inducing guilty pleas and thereby reduce the risks of wrongful convictions.

Part II shifts our focus to the consequences of wrongful convictions and other miscarriages of justice and remedies that might be considered to reduce such errors and mitigate their impact on the victims of these injustices. Such considerations begin in Chapter 13, wherein Saundra Westervelt and Kimberly Cook take us inside the lives of 18 death row exonerees. What happened *after* they passed through those prison gates for the final time? Were they truly "free?" Free from what? Free from prison, certainly, but perhaps not free from the imprisonment of poverty, joblessness, isolation, and/or homelessness. Westervelt and Cook correctly note that most of our attention has focused on the causes of wrongful conviction and how to reduce such errors. But, they ask, is exoneration really the end of the story? Are they truly free or are they free only to be re-victimized by an unfair society and its criminal justice system? Based on their in-depth interviews with 18 death row exonerees, the authors help us understand the strategies that they used to cope with these challenges and the unmet needs that remain to be addressed by an inadequate system of criminal and social justice.

In Chapter 14, Kent Roach questions whether merely providing more procedural rights, coupled with growing public concern about wrongful convictions, automatically translates into more justice for the wrongfully convicted. He compares and contrasts the U.S. and Canadian systems' respective approaches to dealing with wrongful convictions. Although these two nations are geographic neighbors and although both have documented concerns about wrongful convictions, their approaches to designing remedies for this problem are quite different. Roach discusses each nation's legal system and legal culture and how those factors affect their respective approaches to this problem. He argues that although the Canadian system provides far fewer formal legal remedies than does the U.S., in practice the Canadian system has thus far proved to be more flexible and generous in providing relief to those who were wrongfully convicted. This is due, at least in part, he argues, because the Canadian system seems to evaluate new evidence on its merits, has been less concerned about the finality of convictions, and has imposed fewer rigid requirements and barriers for obtaining relief. Much of the difference, he posits, is related to the contrast between the resistance to post-conviction relief exhibited by U.S. prosecutors and courts compared with their Canadian counterparts. That resistance is, of course, a central concern expressed elsewhere in this book, as well, including the very next chapter.

Prosecutorial resistance to post-conviction relief is further highlighted by Spero Lappas and Elizabeth Loftus in Chapter 15, via their detailed account and analysis of Pennsylvania's efforts to address actual innocence. The authors help us vicariously experience some of the major battles that go on when a state decides to look into wrongful convictions and how they might be prevented. Lappas and Loftus document, through this case study, the efforts by prosecutors, especially, to "delegitimize" the critics of false convictions and discredit reform efforts by redefining what "innocence" means, including challenging the validity of exonerations; asserting their role as the sole "guardians" of the criminal justice system's integrity; and arguing that reform efforts are either unmanageable, dangerous to public safety, or both. This detailed case study and their analysis of the legislative attempt to establish an innocence commission (which was also met with further demonization of the reforms and the reformers) leads the authors to conclude that some prosecutors, even when faced with overwhelming evidence of actual innocence, appear to believe that once convicted, a defendant is "never innocent again."

Despite the barriers to reform discussed in the previous chapter, the innocence movement has indeed made much progress in the U.S. and in other nations. Marvin Zalman argues, in Chapter 16, that Edwin Borchard, often cited as the first wrongful conviction scholar, may also be regarded as the "patron saint" of the U.S. innocence movement, even though Borchard clearly could not have foreseen many of the modern reforms that have occurred. Zalman fills a void in the scholarly literature via his careful study of Borchard's career, which has not been fully understood or appreciated. Through an exploration of the intellectual and ideological roots of Borchard's seminal book, *Convicting the Innocent,*[7] Zalman reveals the dedicated activism exhibited by Borchard in advocating legislation to compensate the wrongfully convicted. The modern innocence movement, however, has progressed far beyond what Borchard might have envisioned, although some of his early ideas can certainly be connected to some of these reforms. Zalman provides a careful assessment of the innocence movement's progress and offers a realistic appraisal of current reforms and impediments to reform in policing, prosecution, courts, law schools, cognitive psychology, and forensic science. He concludes that meaningful innocence reform requires complex changes in polices and practices that will necessitate changes in political and institutional cultures—a conclusion echoed elsewhere in this book.

In Chapter 17, Ronald Huff notes that although the term "wrongful conviction" has come to be defined, by general consensus, as requiring proof of "actual innocence," it also belongs to a larger category of injustices known as "miscarriages of justice." After considering the Council of Europe's convention (Protocol 7 to the European Convention of Human Rights and Fundamental Freedoms) concerning the responsibility of member nations to compensate those who have been wrongfully convicted, he introduces another type of miscarriage of justice that he calls "convictions based on political repression" and argues that such convictions, while not technically "wrongful" in the sense of actual innocence (since, after all, the defendant did violate the laws on the books), are certainly miscarriages of justice. The chapter discusses the impacts of wrongful convictions on the lives of those convicted and their families; on public safety (since the actual offender usually remains free to commit more crimes); and on public confidence in the criminal justice system. Next comes a consideration of the obligation of nation states to address the problem of wrongful convictions. These obligations pose special challenges for emerging democracies in their periods of "transitional justice," since they must decide whether to address the "wrongs of the past" or focus on current reforms only. These challenges are among those confronted by formerly Communist nations in Eastern Europe and by South Africa in the post-apartheid era, for example. Huff's discussion cites the legislative efforts of two such nations, Poland and Hungary, to address these issues. He notes that these challenges could soon face some additional nations following the recent revolutions and protests in a number of Middle Eastern nations that have been ruled by repressive regimes.

The book concludes with Chapter 18, in which we summarize the major findings that are collectively represented in this book and offer recommendations that are based on the contributions of our contributors as well as our own research. Consideration is given to the similarities and differences between the two dominant systems of criminal justice, adversarial and inquisitorial, and what we might learn from the strengths, deficiencies, and reform efforts that characterize each of those systems. In the end, the issue cannot be what system we adopt or prefer, but instead how we build into both accusatorial and inquisitorial systems the safeguards that may help to prevent wrongful convictions in the future. Many of the proposals that are advanced in this book do not even require legislative change. In many instances, reforming daily practices and routine procedures can result in significant progresss in reducing wrongful convictions, protecting public safety, and enhancing public respect for our systems of justice.

Notes

1   Huff, C.R., and M. Killias (eds.), *Wrongful Conviction: International Perspectives on Miscarriages of Justice*. Philadelphia, PA: Temple University Press, 2008.
2   Huff, C.R. "Conclusions from an International Overview." Pp. 39–48 in M. Jolicoeur, *International Perspectives on Wrongful Convictions*. Washington, DC: National Institute of Justice, International Center, 2010.
3   Forst, B., *Errors of Justice: Nature, Sources and Remedies*. New York: Cambridge University Press, 2004.
4   Petro, J., and N. Petro, *False Justice: Eight Myths that Convict the Innocent*. New York: Kaplan Publishing, 2010.
5   Brady v. Maryland, 373 U.S. 83 (1963).
6   Aebi, M. "Thinking About Wrongful Convictions in Spain." Unpublished paper presented at the International Workshop on Wrongful Convictions. Breil/Brigels, Switzerland, August 2003.
7   Borchard, E.M., *Convicting the Innocent: Errors of Criminal Justice*. New Haven: Yale University Press [with the collaboration of E. Russell Lutz], 1932.

Part I

Wrongful Convictions and Miscarriages of Justice

Causes and Frequency

2

WRONGFUL CONVICTIONS IN A WORLD OF MISCARRIAGES OF JUSTICE

Brian Forst

One of the virtues of our system of justice is that it is largely insulated from popular trends in the wider society. Occasionally, however, this insulation interferes with the ability of the system to achieve its goals of justice with effectiveness, efficiency, and celerity. One prominent example is the failure of criminal justice agents to apply important developments in the management of errors and assurance of quality systems—widely used now for decades throughout the public and private sector—to the problem of miscarriages of justice. This oversight is not that alone of criminal justice agents. Criminologists and criminal justice scholars as well are often inclined to restrict their analyses of miscarriages of justice to frameworks that ignore miscarriages other than wrongful convictions. Any comprehensive assessment of miscarriages of justice should also include wrongful police intrusions against the public and failures to bring offenders to justice. Moreover, it should weigh the social costs associated with each type of error and assess criminal justice policies considering all these types of miscarriage of justice and their social harms. Some attempts to reduce wrongful convictions may impose greater harms on society than those associated with the problem itself.

This chapter will address these issues. It will begin by distinguishing the major types of miscarriage of justice from one another and provide rough estimates of the magnitude of each. It will then distinguish miscarriages along a spectrum from bad luck and insufficient resources, on one end, to negligence and venal acts of misbehavior by criminal justice agents on the other, and along another dimension that distinguishes laws, policies, and the exercise of discretion as primary sources of miscarriages of justice. Next, we consider frameworks for assessing alternative interventions for reducing miscarriages of justice. Then we examine options for reducing wrongful convictions available to the police, prosecutors, and judges, and the prospective consequences of achieving reductions in wrongful convictions at each stage, in terms of resource expenditures and increases in failures to convict culpable offenders and the associated social costs. We conclude with a consideration of viable options for managing wrongful convictions, mindful of the impacts of these options on other types of miscarriage of justice and on criminal justice legitimacy.

Wrongful Convictions and Other Miscarriages of Justice

Miscarriages of justice are often defined or characterized as serious departures from due process, rather than as departures from just outcomes. In this chapter we focus on outcomes and the associated costs rather than on legal process, following the logic that unless a departure from proper process creates harm to victims, defendants, or others, it is benign.[1]

Wrongful convictions, the central focus of this book, are serious departures from just outcomes. They are among the most serious of all miscarriages of justice. They violate the most fundamental principle of justice: people shall not be punished for crimes they did not commit. They violate the rights of the innocent and those who care about them. They impose both immediate and long-term costs[2] not only on those wrongfully convicted, but on people who depend on them for financial and emotional support as well. They waste criminal justice resources that could be productively applied elsewhere. They are a miscarriage of justice that creates a second type of miscarriage of justice: when the wrong person is arrested and convicted, justice is not done *and* the real offender remains free to commit further crimes. They undermine criminal justice legitimacy. When revealed as routine, they diminish the willingness of ordinary citizens to support the system as reporters of crime, witnesses, and conscientious jurors (Tyler, 2006). They are especially egregious in cases that send the defendant to death row. The alternative of convictions that put innocent people in prison for life is arguably little better, and for some wrongfully convicted people possibly worse, but they are at least reversible.

It turns out, however, that wrongful convictions are neither the only type of miscarriage of justice nor the most serious. The most severe miscarriage of justice is the case in which the police kill an innocent person—an act that amounts roughly to capital punishment of the innocent without due process. Such cases are rare, but usually avoidable— the product of lapses in training, supervision, and policies, especially those involving police accountability. One prominent example of these extreme miscarriages of justice is the 2005 killing of two unarmed and innocent men—James Brissette and Ronald Madison—on the Danziger Bridge in New Orleans by officers of the New Orleans Police Department, six days after Hurricane Katrina (an episode that also involved the wounding of four other unarmed men). Another such example is the notorious killing of Amadou Diallo, an unarmed, innocent man, by New York Police Department officers in 1999. These cases involve the ultimate harm by criminal justice officials against innocent people, and they deprive suspects of their day in court. Many more miscarriages of justice exist in the form of police brutality, corruption, and other misbehaviors that go unreported and unsanctioned.

A much more pervasive miscarriage of justice consists of cases of wrongful arrests that do not end in conviction. These too impose needless harms on innocent people. Let us not forget: wrongful convictions begin with wrongful arrests, even when the police follow the rules of legal procedure. Regardless of whether or not wrongful arrests end in conviction, however, they are very costly. They are stimulated largely by police incentive systems, both formal and informal, that induce the police to weigh incriminating evidence much more heavily than exonerating evidence. Police are typically rewarded for making arrests regardless of what happens afterward in court. An officer's prospects for promotion are not likely to be diminished, in contrast, if he or she brings arrests to the prosecutor that rarely end in conviction.[3] Police departments usually do not know who these officers are, since feedback about the results of adjudication is not routinely provided to the police in most jurisdictions (Forst et al., 1977, 1982).

An even more pervasive miscarriage of justice is the failure to hold culpable offenders accountable for the crimes they commit. These are not ordinarily classified as miscarriages of justice, but there are good reasons to do so. They are lapses that compromise public safety and quality of life, and they undermine the credibility of deterrence. When the public perceives widespread injustices to victims of crime, they are likely to be less inclined to report crimes to the police and come forth as witnesses. Tom Tyler (2006) has found that people are less likely to obey the law and respect governmental authority when they regard the criminal justice system as lacking in legitimacy (see also Tyler, Schulhofer, and Huq, 2010). Failure to convict the culpable thus threatens the integrity of the justice system through both the reality and the perception of ineffectualness. In weakening the ability of the police, prosecutors, and courts to bring offenders to justice in the future, these lapses can bring about a vicious cycle in which lost legitimacy and reduced public support feed one another.

All failures to convict are not created equal. Some offenders are less culpable than others. Juveniles, emotionally disturbed offenders, and people who commit crimes in a state of diminished capacity beyond their ability to control are examples of marginal cases of "errors of impunity"— false negatives of justice—criminal acts that go unpunished despite the fact that the other elements of a crime have been met (Forst, 2004). These are not bona fide miscarriages of justice. They are more akin to car accidents or tornadoes than to crimes in which culpable offenders go free. The community may be able to do more to prevent them, but these crimes are beyond the reach of the adult criminal justice system to do so.

Other cases involving adult criminal offenders who evade conviction are less ambiguous. These are miscarriages of justice following crimes by willful adult offenders that impose serious harms on victims and the community. When these offenders avoid arrest and conviction, or are released from the physical constraints of the justice system prematurely, public safety and quality of life are threatened and often violated; the credibility of deterrent effectiveness is lost; and citizens may perceive an injustice and become alienated from the police and courts. These miscarriages of justice threaten criminal justice legitimacy. They can run through the entire criminal justice system, from victimization through policing, prosecution, and adjudication.

How widespread are failures to convict? Felony offenses committed by adults that do not end in conviction number well over ten million annually.[4] This is a large number when compared with the approximately one million felony convictions annually. It looms even larger when viewed against Blackstone's (1769) famous rule, "better that ten guilty persons escape than that one innocent suffer." Available estimates of wrongful convictions run in the neighborhood of 0.5 to 1% of all convictions (e.g., Huff et al., 1996; Gross, Chapter 3, this volume), amounting to some 5,000 to 10,000 wrongful felony convictions annually. This boils down to a number between 1,000 and 2,000 failures to bring felony offenders to justice for each person wrongfully convicted of a felony offense. One cannot help but wonder whether Blackstone would have approved of such a number.

Failures to bring offenders to justice thus endangering the community have many sources: skillful offenders; a public unwilling to report crimes and come forth as witnesses; ineffective police; laws that allow offenders to go free following official violations of due process (usually Fourth or Fifth Amendment violations); lapses in prosecution and adjudication; weak sanctions; and flawed parole release decisions. It is not unreasonable to regard as a miscarriage of justice the meting out of a lenient sentence that permits an active offender to reoffend, particularly when the harms imposed on the victims of the subsequent crimes are substantial. (In recent years the larger problem appears to have been overly punitive sentences, but it is worth taking a longer view in this discussion.) Nor does it stretch conventional notions of justice to consider the failure of an individual officer to act prudently in a particular case as a miscarriage of justice, especially when such failure allows subsequent identifiable crimes to occur.

Sources of Miscarriages: Benign and Malignant

Most miscarriages of justice are fairly benign, the product of too many crimes and too few resources to deal with them adequately. This is probably the primary explanation for the several millions of felony crimes that fail to result in arrest and conviction each year. Even in affluent jurisdictions, however, where crime loads tend to be smaller and resources more abundant, miscarriages of justice can occur just due to misfortune: innocent bystanders, sometimes with prior records, who fit the general description of the offender, happen to be in the wrong place at the wrong time, are arrested and then identified in a line-up, and are then either found guilty at trial or plead guilty because they face overwhelming odds against acquittal and a lighter sentence for pleading guilty.

Other miscarriages of justice are more troublesome. These include training and supervision lapses that render police officers unprepared quickly to find and build strong cases for arrest and filing with the court and to recognize that some people first identified as suspects are not really the offenders in the case at issue. Worse than training and supervision lapses are instances in which police officers, laboratory technicians, or prosecutors knowingly violate rules of criminal procedure in order to bring about arrest and conviction. These may be more common in especially serious cases, in which the agent may gain political support and public acclaim for arrest or conviction.

Another important dimension along which miscarriages of justice should be assessed and dealt with is more basic. Miscarriages of justice may be either systematic—a product of ill-conceived laws, policies set by criminal justice executives, and rules—or random, associated with disparity in the exercise of discretion by criminal justice agents. The exercise of discretion may produce both random disparities in outcomes and systematic errors of justice. Both types of disparity may originate with variation in practitioner views of appropriate courses of action for individual cases.[5] The exercise of discretion is likely to be heavily influenced as well by systems of accountability, such as those that induce the police to clear crimes by arrest and prosecutors to increase conviction rates. Regardless of their sources, both systematic and random errors impose costs on society that can be profound.

Systematic miscarriages of justice often begin with draconian laws. Legislators may feel pressure to secure re-election by promoting dubious laws accompanied by get-tough slogans such as "three-strikes-and-you're-out" laws and "drug kingpin" laws. When public fear and political pandering overwhelm reason, draconian mandatory sentences often follow, as legislators may tend to be all-too-willing to put political self-interest above the public interest. The sentences that result may be technically in accordance with Eighth Amendment protections against cruel and unusual punishments, but they may nonetheless be excessive under any coherent rationale for sentencing. They not only worsen matters associated with wrongful convictions, but impose needless costs on all who receive them, whether wrongfully convicted or not, and ultimately on all of society.

Frameworks for Assessing Miscarriages of Justice

The criminal justice system manages wrongful convictions largely by setting a high standard of evidence for a jury to convict: proof beyond a reasonable doubt. This standard is mindful of the need to convict the culpable; it discourages but nonetheless allows for the erroneous conclusion that an innocent person is guilty. In an unreasonably defense-minded world, the standard would be higher: proof beyond *any* doubt. Few people would care to live in such a world. It would enable, if not encourage, criminal behavior. It would be a world in which the responsibility for justice would shift from our system of public courts to private citizens, one in which we would all spend substantially more time and money protecting ourselves, with considerably more serious miscarriages of justice as a consequence.

Still, the standard of proof beyond a reasonable doubt is not without serious flaws. Before examining these flaws, let us see how this standard of evidence is conventionally defined in the courts:

> Proof beyond a reasonable doubt is proof that leaves you firmly convinced of the defendant's guilt. There are very few things in this world that we know with absolute certainty, and in criminal cases the law does not require proof that overcomes every possible doubt. If, based on your consideration of the evidence, you are firmly convinced that the defendant is guilty of the crime or crimes charged, you must find him guilty. If, on the other hand, you think there is a real possibility that he is not guilty, you must give him the benefit of the doubt and find him not guilty.[6]

This is a noble attempt to bring clarity to an inherently difficult concept. It is simply impossible to pin down what it means precisely in such a way that any two "reasonable" people would agree in its application in particular cases.

All standard definitions of "proof beyond a reasonable doubt" are limited only partly in their subjective ambiguity.[7] They are limited more significantly in their failure to include essentials that are routinely incorporated in systems of error management used in other settings, particularly those pertaining to the prevalence of each major type of error and the respective costs of each type. Prominent examples of such error management systems include quality control programs designed to reduce irregularities and maximize quality in the production of goods and services, subject to budget constraints, throughout the private sector and in much of the public sector (Evans and Lindsay, 2010); bridge maintenance and public safety management (Frangopol et al., 2010); systems designed to manage diagnosis and treatment errors in medical settings, using signal detection technology (Leape, 1994; Akay, 1996); algorithms designed to balance investment yields against the risk of losses in financial portfolios (Drake and Fabozzi, 2010); and systems created to manage the exercise of discretion in applying instruments of monetary policy (McCallum, 2004).[8]

Even rudimentary systems of quality control recognize the need to manage both false positives (Type I errors—errors of rejecting research hypotheses when they are true) and false negatives (Type II errors—errors of accepting research hypotheses when they are false).[9] Reducing either error alone can produce unacceptable increases in the other type of error. The criminal justice system could eliminate the risk of wrongful convictions altogether only by making it impossible to convict anyone. Blackstone recognized that both types of errors must be considered, but he did not say precisely how many more than ten culpable offenders should be freed to prevent the conviction of an innocent person.

One can imagine reducing wrongful convictions with jury instructions that raise the standard of proof for conviction higher than the "reasonable doubt" standard but short of the "any doubt" standard. What effect would such an increase have on the error of failure to convict culpable offenders? Under a large variety of assumptions, it has been found that raising evidentiary standards to an extent that produces a ten percentage point reduction in the conviction rate from current margins approximately doubles the number of true offenders set free per innocent person convicted and increases the total error rate by about ten percentage points (Forst, 2004).[10]

Fortunately, raising the evidentiary standard for conviction is not the only way to reduce wrongful convictions. Advances in forensic technology, most notably DNA evidence, allow the police and prosecutors to reduce wrongful arrests and convictions and failures to convict culpable offenders simultaneously.[11] Strengthening the quality of arrests by the police, with associated increases in conviction rates, other factors constant, reduces both the number of offenders freed per innocent person convicted and the total percentage of cases erroneously decided (Forst, 2004).

Reducing the Social Costs of Miscarriages of Justice: From Victimization to Corrections

Nor did Blackstone speak to the respective costs of each type of error. Attempts to manage miscarriages of justice should account not only for how alternative interventions influence the rate of occurrence of each type of miscarriage, but also for the harms each intervention imposes on victims, offenders, and their families, the costs of the resources consumed in the process, and the costs imposed on witnesses and the community at large. All miscarriages of justice are not equal.

While the social costs associated with miscarriages of justice are empirically elusive—involving both tangible and intangible costs and the costs of future crimes prevented by a sanction—we should attempt to assess them nonetheless because they are important in the real world and significantly larger than zero, which is the value imputed to them when they are ignored. Social costs in the present context have two basic components: costs associated with crimes and costs associated with interventions, public and private, to prevent and respond to crime. The crime costs include the costs of property stolen or damaged, injury or death (including medical expenditures and the costs of pain and suffering), and lost income. Most of these costs are borne by the victim, sometimes over a lifetime; other crime costs are borne by those who cover insurance claims for medical costs and property losses, job productivity losses borne by employers, victim service agency costs, and psychic costs associated with fear of crime.[12] The public intervention costs include expenditures for police, prosecutors, courts, and corrections. Private intervention costs include those for private security personnel; security and surveillance systems (locks and alarms, bullet-proofing, protected parking facilities, cameras, security lighting, movement sensors, and so on); costs incurred by dependents of incarcerated offenders;[13] by witnesses who give time to police, prosecutors, and trials; and costs associated with community crime prevention activities.

One of the most elusive of all social costs is that related to the asymmetry of legitimacy in failures to convict and wrongful convictions. This asymmetry derives from what Max Weber and Egon Bittner characterize as the state's monopoly on the authority to use force in invoking criminal sanctions. The state has a responsibility to use this monopoly power with humility; the requirement that the state must prove guilt beyond a reasonable doubt reflects this concern. Failure to convict a culpable offender does not carry the same weight of responsibility. This important consideration defies measurement, but it should not be ignored.

It is common to take a less nuanced approach and assert that all miscarriages of justice are simply unacceptable. Such a position is unsustainable, like attempting to mandate for perfect weather. Many miscarriages of justice are the product of unpreventable random errors. The costs of attempting to manage the errors that result from these uncontrollable forces can easily exceed the costs associated with the random errors themselves. They should be accounted for.

Following the conventional social welfare calculus, a criminal sanction—from the time of the first contact with the police through the sentencing process—will be excessive when a decrease in the sanction from a given level would reduce the associated social costs. It will be insufficient when an increase in the sanction would reduce the total social costs of crime and sanctions (Forst, 2004). The social cost of a miscarriage of justice is the difference between the total cost borne by society under the sanction given and the smaller social cost associated with an optimal sanction.[14]

One way to deal with the costs of miscarriages of justice is to start with what appear to be the most serious errors on both plates of the balance scale of justice—such as those involving malfeasance of criminal justice agents and the most serious crime categories—and work our way in from these endpoint extremes toward the less serious errors. At some margin the cost of attempting further to reduce the rate of a particular miscarriage of justice will exceed the social benefit of doing so. In our complex world, we are not likely to eliminate either wrongful convictions or other miscarriages of justice entirely. We would be remiss nonetheless in failing to work diligently to reduce the combined social costs of all miscarriages of justice, starting with the most serious miscarriages, and to use coherent frameworks for resolving the tensions among them.

Let us now consider briefly how the police, prosecution, courts, and correctional sectors might each be reformed to reduce the social costs of miscarriages of justice.

Police. Law enforcement is the engine of miscarriages of justice. Wrongful convictions rarely occur without lapses in policing. The police are usually the citizen's first point of contact with the criminal justice system; they can do much to reduce the social costs associated with wrongful convictions and other miscarriages of justice. The opportunities lie at several stages: crime prevention, the initiation of contacts with the community, the use of ethnic and racial profiling, techniques for witness identification of offenders, the use of force, and systems of accountability.

Good policing starts with crime prevention; solving crimes can be enhanced in the process. The police prevent crimes largely by building and maintaining mutually supportive relations with the community. One can argue whether it is a miscarriage of justice when a crime occurs that the police could easily have prevented. It is more difficult to argue that police failure to solve a crime due to a lapse in good, standard policing practice is not a miscarriage of justice. Solving crime is, after all, what the police are supposed to do. Community policing can help the police both to prevent and solve crimes.

But closing a case by arresting the wrong person is no solution at all; it only compounds the error of the unsolved crime. Traditional policing has relied on systems of accountability that put great pressure on crime solving and case closing and little on reducing errors of justice. The police can reduce these errors by doing thorough crime scene investigations and interviews to ensure that the collection of pertinent information—both incriminating and exculpatory—is comprehensive and objective, with follow-up interviews as needed. In building better relations with the community, the police can reduce both wrongful convictions and failures to convict offenders by encouraging witnesses to report crimes and accurately identify offenders.

The police can reduce errors of justice further by eliminating racial and ethnic profiling practices. Usually justified on grounds that offenders are disproportionately from certain ethnic groups—black drug traffickers and Muslim terrorists are common examples—these involve proactive stops and interrogations without behaviors that might warrant reasonable suspicion for such police actions. They may succeed in bringing some offenders to justice and deterring others, but these fishing expeditions do so at a high cost to innocent people whose rights are violated in the process. The rate of false positives in these operations can be extremely high. This combination of costly intrusions and high false positive rates is difficult to justify in terms of the expected social costs of the crimes prevented in the process.[15]

Racial and ethnic profiling would be a dubious practice even if the social benefits of the practice exceeded the social costs. Race is a socially constructed variable, in the eyes of the beholder—unlike age and gender. It is measured less precisely than such crime-related variables as the number of prior felony convictions. Moreover, two profilers might not agree about the ethnicity of a given person, and both may disagree with the ethnic self-designation used by the person in question. People often re-think their own racial and ethnic identities over time; they may change their self-designations from one census to the next, sometimes in the spirit of assimilation, sometimes in the spirit of group identity (Skerry, 2000; Etzioni, 2000).[16] Basing profiling policies on statistical associations between race or ethnicity and crime in the absence of other factors implicating a particular individual is, in short, both morally and methodologically dubious, even when it improves predictions of crime, except under extraordinary circumstances (see also Kennedy, 1997, 1999).

Other factors are likely to be much more important, especially when terrorists can and do recruit individuals who do not fit ethnic and gender stereotypes. Airline screeners, for example, give extra scrutiny to passengers based on whether they purchased a one-way rather than a round-trip ticket; if purchased with cash rather than a credit card; if purchased just before the flight; and if they appear nervous, regardless of their ethnicity.

Subjecting people to close scrutiny solely because of their race or ethnicity violates basic notions of due process. As false positive errors associated with factors over which a person has no control accumulate, the people targeted are bound to become more alienated. The vast majority of Muslims are, after all, not terrorists, and the vast majority of black males are not drug runners. Many have suffered the indignities of profiling with grace and dignity. As false positive errors accumulate, however, the patience of a few could reach a breaking point. We can expect minority moderates to police their own extremists when they see that the system is legitimate (Tyler, 2006; Tyler, Schulhofer, and Huq, 2010). Ethnic and racial profiling undermine this sense of legitimacy.

When the police screen people, they have a responsibility to inform them why they were selected, for the sake of transparency, common courtesy, and legitimacy. When the factors used to screen are valid and the citizens inconvenienced by such screening are thus informed, they are likely to be more supportive of the police, building a potentially virtuous cycle of police–community relations.

The police can further reduce the social costs of miscarriages of justice by improving the methods used for witness identification of offenders. Erroneous witness identification has been found repeatedly to be the most common source of wrongful convictions (Donigan and Fisher, 1980; Huff, Sagarin, and Rattner, 1996; Connors, Lundregan, Miller, and McEwen, 1996; Scheck, Neufeld, and Dwyer, 2001; Garrett, 2011, 2012). The errors fall into two primary categories: victims and witnesses who fail to get a good look at the offender at the time of the crime and misidentification in lineups due to faulty police procedures, sometimes induced by police with a strong interest in solving the crime and closing the case (Loftus and Burns, 1982; DNA Testing, 1995). Witnesses fail frequently as well to identify the actual offender, leading to false negative errors. These are sometimes intentional, as when the witness is intimidated by the offender, fearing reprisal if they help the police and prosecutor.

Both false positives and false negatives associated with mistaken witness identification have been found to increase as the time between the offense and the witness identification grows long (Baddeley, Thompson, and Buchanan, 1975). They are more common as well when the crime was violent (Clifford and Scott, 1978; Loftus and Burns, 1982). Even in nonviolent crime, witnesses commonly experience fear, stress, and anxiety that clouds perceptions and memories (Huff et al., 1996).

Lineups can be useful for validating a witness's identification of the offender, but they too can contribute to false positives and false negatives. Both types of errors can be reduced when the procedures are valid, designed to maximize accuracy rather than maximize arrests and convictions.[17]

We have noted that incidents of police use of force are among the most flagrant miscarriages of justice. The Bureau of Justice Statistics reports about 370 killings by the police annually from 1976 to 1998 (Brown and Langan, 2001). Many of these are justifiable, but many more may be avoidable; a few are sheer acts of brutality (Skolnick and Fyfe, 1993). It turns out that some police departments are much more trigger-happy than others. A survey of the 51 largest police departments by Whitlock and Fallis (2001) produced data for the period 1990 to 2000, from which one could establish that Los Angeles County, Washington (DC), San Diego,

Phoenix, Denver, and Prince Georges County, Maryland had particularly high rates of these killings, adjusting for the crime rates and other pertinent factors.[18] At the low end were Dallas, Chicago, San Antonio, New Orleans, Suffolk, NY, and Fairfax, VA. This is a limited sample, covering just 20% of the U.S. population, but it suggests possibilities for the routine and much more extensive collection and analysis of pertinent data elements on the use of deadly force in police departments throughout the country. Routine accounting of this sort could help substantially to reduce what may be the most serious justice error of all.

These are the tip of the iceberg of excessive force cases, the most serious of many more cases in which the police use greater force than needed to deal effectively with suspects of crimes and, in too many cases, people are simply viewed as undesirable and in need of "curbside justice." While improvements have been made to reduce them, more can yet be done. Among the more promising of the proposals that have been offered to reduce the problem of excessive use of force are the following: guidelines that inform officers on the appropriate level of force for a variety of common real-world situations (Skolnick and Fyfe, 1993); training that includes extensive situational role-playing and violence avoidance exercises (Fyfe, 1986); more rigorous screening of officers; better supervision; clearer and more thoughtfully crafted policies; stronger systems of accountability, both internal and external (e.g., civil suits, civilian review boards, and the media); and the replacement of guns with the use of nonlethal weapons (batons, chemical sprays, electronic devices, capture nets, and so on) in a variety of situations calling for the use of force. These proposals are complementary; each could reduce the use of deadly force, and collectively they are more likely to be effective than if a department is deficient in any one of them. Used collectively, they could also improve the ability of the police to solve and prevent crimes.

One factor could be the most important of all to reduce these and other police-induced miscarriages of justice: leadership. Jerome Skolnick and James Fyfe (1993) observed that until Patrick Murphy became commissioner of the New York Police Department in the early 1970s, nothing was effective in repairing decades of recurring waves of brutality and corruption in the 40,000-officer NYPD. His integrity and intolerance of police misbehavior changed the culture of the department.[19] Some 20 years later, an equally transformative and more polarizing figure,

William J. Bratton, built on the foundation laid by Murphy by introducing a program of accountability that reduced police misbehavior and crime simultaneously.[20]

Unfortunately, transformational leaders come along maybe once in a generation. In the meantime, police departments can put in place a set of policies for reducing excessive force and other miscarriages of justice. Genuine commitment to both the ideals and methods of community policing may be an essential element of such policy reform. The federal government can provide additional support by tracking more systematically fatal and nonfatal shootings by police officers on a comprehensive, department-by-department basis. Such tracking would not only serve as an additional accountability system, but would also permit research on the sources of variation across departments, to establish why some departments do significantly better, or worse, than others.

Prosecution. The prosecutor has been called the most powerful person in America (Jackson, 1940; Reiss, 1974).[21] Whether true or not, there can be little question that the prosecutor has more control over wrongful convictions and several other miscarriages of justice than anyone else in the criminal justice system. Prosecutors are the official external reviewer of police arrests, with the power to decide whether to file an arrest brought by the police as a criminal matter and which charges cited in the arrest documents are worthy of prosecuting in court. They exercise discretion over whether to screen arrests more carefully and thus reveal lapses in police work; determine what further evidence is needed to prosecute the case; and resolve discrepancies between incriminating and exculpatory evidence, thus shaping post-arrest investigations.

There is considerable opportunity for prosecutors to err in making these determinations. They can over-allocate resources to cases involving innocent suspects and minor offenders and under-allocate to others; they can give excessive concessions to serious offenders for providing evidence against low-level, less culpable collaborators or worse: innocent people. They also set policy over how decisions are to be made generally from screening to indictment, in plea negotiations and trial preparation, and in recommending a sentence to the judge in court.

Prosecutors rarely make public their priorities in making these decisions and setting policy, or the principles that govern them. Nor is it common for them to acknowledge making errors in managing their operations or contributing in any way to wrongful convictions or other miscarriages of justice. We can understand why in remembering that local prosecution in the United States is the work of the district attorney, usually elected at the county level. To secure re-election, the DA will typically promote his or her accomplishments in fighting crime and securing convictions, not in minimizing miscarriages of justice, as reflected, for example, by low rates of appellate review or reversal. Research focusing on prosecution has tended also to ignore miscarriages of justice, leaving it to scholars of wrongful conviction to cover prosecutors along with police, judges, legislators, and others.[22]

One might expect prosecutors to be more careful to avoid error in cases eligible for capital punishment, but even for those, an astonishingly large number of defendants have been exonerated of all charges, based largely on DNA evidence (Liebman et al., 2000). Wrongful conviction rates may even be higher in capital cases than in others to the extent that prosecutors place a higher premium on winning the big cases than on avoiding wrongful convictions. Prosecutor misconduct has been cited in nearly 20% of those cases (Liebman et al., 2000; see also Bedau and Radelet, 1987; Gershman, 1999; Huff et al., 1996; Scheck et al., 2001).

Appellate review helps to control prosecutorial excesses that lead to wrongful convictions, but prosecutors are overruled in just a very small percentage of convictions. In a landmark case, Supreme Court Justice George Sutherland wrote: "While [the prosecutor] may strike hard blows, he may not strike foul ones. It is as much his duty to refrain from improper methods calculated to produce a wrongful conviction as it is to use every legitimate means to bring about a just one."[23] This observation does not appear to have left much of an impression on prosecutors in the nearly 80 years since. In a sample of 350 potentially capital cases involving "wrong-person" conviction errors, Hugo Bedau and Michael Radelet (1987) found 35 cases of prosecutors suppressing exculpatory evidence, and 15 other errors attributable to "overzealous prosecution" (p. 57). Bedau and Radelet's findings are not unique; others have found convictions of innocent people following prosecutor withholding of exculpatory evidence from the defense (Gershman, 1997; Huff et al., 1996; Scheck et al., 2001).

Prosecutors sometimes combine plea bargaining with the concealment of exculpatory evidence to secure convictions. They may do so convinced that the person is the actual offender, sometimes based on a prior record, but these are wrongful convictions nonetheless. Brad Heath and Kevin McCoy (2010) found that prosecutors in the District of Columbia secured no fewer than ten convictions against persons charged with murder from 2000 to 2010 after concealing exculpatory evidence, via plea bargains to shorten terms of sentencing. Draconian sentencing laws that became especially popular since the 1980s have given prosecutors throughout the land greater leverage to engage in such acts, and wrongful convictions are likely to have increased as a by-product of this legislation (Bjerk, 2007), either to induce a wrongfully arrested person to plead guilty or a culpable offender to provide false, incriminating information against an innocent person. Plea bargaining can be effective for bringing offenders to justice, but it also raises the risks of wrongful convictions and distortions associated with more serious offenders getting lighter sanctions in exchange for evidence against less serious offenders.

One of the most important and least understood sources of wrongful convictions is the prosecutor's preference for more convictions rather than stronger ones. The prosecutor is free to choose any evidentiary standard between "probable cause" and "beyond a reasonable doubt" in deciding whether to accept an arrest for prosecution and how to process the case. In lowering the standard at the pretrial stages of prosecution, the prosecutor raises the certainty of punishment, but also raises the wrongful conviction rate, mostly by way of plea bargaining, and lowers the average severity of punishment from levels ordinarily given in trials. In the process, the prosecutor also elects to take on more cases and increase the ratio of pleas to trials; preparing cases for trial is much more time-consuming than negotiating pleas (Boland and Forst, 1985; Wright and Miller, 2002).

Prosecutors, in fact, vary substantially in their preference for either more convictions with higher plea-to-trial rates and more wrongful convictions, on the one hand, or fewer convictions with lower plea-to-trial rates and more failures to convict culpable offenders on the other. Prosecutors' offices that accept a higher proportion of arrests for prosecution tend to have higher plea-to-trial ratios than offices that are more selective in deciding which arrests to file in court (Boland and Forst, 1985; Wright and Miller, 2002). This has been found to be true regardless of office size and crime rate, raising serious questions about the common refrain that plea bargaining is driven primarily by resource scarcity.[24]

The practice of placing more, or less, emphasis on case screening and trials rather than on plea negotiations has strong implications for miscarriages of justice. Offices that choose to be more selective in screening cases and then putting more time into preparing cases for trial increase errors of impunity, allowing more culpable offenders to go free who would otherwise plead guilty if threatened with the prospect of a trial, and increase the total error rate as well (Forst, 2004). The number of additional false negatives (offenders freed) per false positive (wrongful conviction) depends on the quality of police arrests and wrongful arrest rate. A more selective arrest screening policy is more clearly warranted when the quality of arrests is low and the wrongful arrest rate high.[25]

Prosecutors can err in other ways as well: in assessing criminal liability (e.g., whether an adult has a serious mental impairment or emotional illness, whether a defendant acted in self-defense), determining how much time and energy to put into each case from screening to final disposition, based on strength of evidence, offense seriousness, role of the defendant in the alleged crime, and the dangerousness of the defendant. They may also make tactical errors, as when Los Angeles Assistant District Attorney Christopher Darden asked defendant O. J. Simpson to try on a pair of shrunken, bloody gloves in trial, contributing to what most authorities regard as a wrongful failure to convict a culpable offender. Empirical analysis of prosecutor operations could help to identify prosecution policies and practices that are most, and least, effective in achieving the goals of justice and minimizing the social costs of miscarriages of justice.

But the opportunities to take advantage of these prospects are elusive, and they will remain so as long as comprehensive data on prosecution remain unavailable and the operations remain opaque. This lack of transparency of the central component of the criminal justice system has no parallel elsewhere in the system or, for that matter, in the entire public sector. Until this problem is solved, the improvement of prosecution will be a dream, which limits the legitimacy not only of prosecution, but our entire system of criminal justice.

Adjudication and Sentencing: Judges, Juries, and Legislators. Miscarriages of justice can originate in the courtroom, a product of decisions made by judges and juries. Judges can err in deciding which cases to dismiss, in managing the trial proceedings, in giving instructions to the jury, and in exercising discretion in sentencing convicted defendants. Appellate judges occasionally correct these errors, but given the limited resources of appellate courts, most of these miscarriages of justice are bound to go uncorrected.

Even when given proper instructions, juries too make errors of justice, convicting the innocent and freeing the culpable. Here is what former Supreme Court Justice Sandra Day O'Connor (1997) says about how this happens:

> Too often, jurors are allowed to do nothing but listen passively to the testimony, without any idea what the legal issues are in the case, not allowed to take notes or participate in any way, and finally to be read a virtually incomprehensible set of instructions and sent into the jury room to reach a verdict in a case they may not understand much better than they did before the trial began.

Other miscarriages of justice associated with the jury have been well documented. Juries frequently misunderstand legal and scientific complexities, even when clearly presented (Frank, 1973; Eisenberg and Wells, 1993; Garvey, Marcus, and Johnson, 2000). They often forget what was said, a problem exacerbated by jurisdictions that forbid note taking (ForsterLee et al., 1994; O'Connor, 1999; Vidmar, 1989). When note taking is permitted, the notes are typically less than comprehensive and accurate, and one juror's notes can be used to bully other jurors, regardless of the accuracy of the information (Heuer and Penrod, 1994). Jurors have been characterized as highly fallible and often unreliable arbiters, sometimes renegades, and too often incompetent, despite having been empanelled (Kersch, 2003). One such juror can nullify the competency and diligence of the other 11. They can be easily seduced, especially when their senses are overwhelmed by extremely brutal crimes with unattractive defendants and victims with whom the jurors identify (Borchard, 1932; Penrod and Cutler, 1987; Scheck et al., 2001).

Even when juries are competent and do their work diligently, what happens afterward—at the sentencing stage—can undo this good work. Sentencing policy is a product of the boundaries set by legislation and the discretion exercised by judges (and occasionally juries). They are typically justified in terms of serving any or all of several purposes: to deter the individual from subsequent acts of crime; to deter others; to incapacitate; to satisfy a public demand for retribution; to rehabilitate; and to provide restorative justice for the victim.

Sentencing policy has varied substantially over the past 50 years, more so than other aspects of the justice system. It swung from a system that relied heavily on judicial and parole board discretion in the 1960s and 1970s to one more structured, under systems of guidelines ranging from advisory to mandatory, and with sanctions for any particular offense ranging from moderate to draconian. Sentencing policy then swung back to a more flexible system following three landmark decisions from 2000 to 2005: *Apprendi v. New Jersey* (530 U.S. 66 [2000]), *Blakely v. Washington* (542 U.S. 296 [2004]), and *United States v. Booker* (543 U.S. 220 [2005]).[26] These decisions were instrumental in correcting a system that relied largely on fallible yet unchallenged information contained in presentence investigation reports prepared by probation officers.

The shift to tougher, more rigid sentencing in the 1980s surely contributed to an unprecedented explosion in prison and jail populations in the United States, from 503,600 in 1980 to 2,304,000 by 2008, a period that witnessed an equally unprecedented decline in crime (the number of homicides dropped from 23,000 in 1980 to 16,000 in 2008, despite a 34% increase in the resident population, from 228 million to 305 million). Sentencing laws became especially draconian in the 1990s, with a sharp rise in mandatory minimum sentences—attributable largely to the politicization of sentencing, in which the strategy of attacking incumbents for being weak on crime became highly successful and widespread.

An important aspect of this legislation is "drug kingpin" laws, which mete out tough sentences to drug traffickers, many of whom are low-level sellers rather than anyone resembling a kingpin. Such laws have contributed substantially to the large run-up in prison populations since 1990. Another aspect is "three strikes and you're out," which assigns long terms of incarceration to offenders convicted of a third felony offense. The popularity of these laws is rooted in commonsense notions of retributive justice, but the effectiveness of the laws is contradicted by a large and growing body of evidence documenting that offenders tend to commit fewer crimes as they age, and offenders with more prior convictions tend to be older (Blumstein et al., 1986; Sampson and Laub, 1993). The expensive and often tragic consequence is that U.S. prisons became overloaded with people given long sentences just as they were about to end their criminal careers. Taxpayers might be more willing to tax themselves to reduce crime than to achieve other government services, but they ought to know that many billions of dollars have been wasted on the warehousing of middle-aged and older people who are well beyond their years of danger to the community. Alternatives such as intermediate sanctions and programs of restorative justice are likely to be more fair and efficient than the draconian alternatives that have been so politically popular and exorbitantly costly, both financially and in terms of human suffering.

Lawmakers could fix the problem. They could, conceivably, appeal to the voters' sense of fiscal austerity and compete politically by pointing out the colossal waste associated with prison and jail costs, if not the burdens borne by families of the incarcerated, especially for offenders who are not dangerous. One might expect that voters would like to know how much they pay, per voter, for this waste. With crime rates near all-time lows, one might imagine that the public would be open to this sort of dialogue. Scary stories about crime have always played well politically, but so have facts about billions of wasted taxpayer dollars.

Correctional Officials. Miscarriages of justice often occur after sentencing. Miscarriages can occur in dealing with either incarcerated or non-incarcerated populations. Correctional officials can inflict needless harm on convicted defendants, typically by neglecting their oversight responsibilities to protect inmates from violence among themselves. Lapses in security can compromise the public's safety by allowing inmates to escape. Prison parole authorities may err in deciding when an inmate eligible for parole release is ready for release, imposing costs on society when releasing either prematurely or belatedly. Probation officers can err in deciding whether to revoke a probationer's probation term.

Millions of people are directly affected in the United States by such errors of justice. Over seven million were under correctional authority in 2008—more than 2% of the U.S. population. Over two million of these were in prison or jail (about two-thirds in prison), the rest on probation (over four million) or parole (one million) (Glaze et al., 2009).

Prisons are the most expensive component of the correctional system. Charles Logan (1993) has observed that prison authorities are capable of committing a variety of errors:

We ask an awful lot of our prisons. We ask them to correct the incorrigible, rehabilitate the wretched, deter the determined, restrain the dangerous, and punish the wicked. We ask them to take over where other institutions of society have failed and to reinforce norms that have been violated and rejected. We ask them to pursue so many different and often incompatible goals that they seem virtually doomed to fail. Moreover, when we lay upon prisons the utilitarian goals of rehabilitation, deterrence, and incapacitation, we ask them to achieve results primarily outside of prison, rather than inside. By focusing on external measures, we set prisons up to be judged on matters well beyond their direct sphere of influence.

(pp. 23–4)

His solution to this constellation of problems is to employ a "confinement" model, under which "the mission of a prison is to keep prisoners . . . in, keep them safe, keep them in line, keep them healthy, and keep them busy—and to do it with fairness, without undue suffering, and as efficiently as possible" (p. 25). Logan proposes to monitor the success of prison administrators in achieving these goals with specific prison performance measures in each of eight corresponding areas: security, safety, order, care, activity, justice, conditions, and management. Under any such system of performance assessment, it would be especially helpful to estimate the social costs associated with errors in each of the domains, to provide a basis for prioritizing them. In the meantime, Logan's system provides a potentially useful starting point for identifying and managing errors in corrections.[27]

Managing Wrongful Convictions Mindfully

Wrongful convictions are an abomination of justice. They violate not only innocent defendants, but their friends, families, and all who depend on them for support. They violate victims too, as they allow actual offenders to go free. Wrongful convictions seriously undermine criminal justice legitimacy. They warrant more attention than they have received.

But they are a small share of all miscarriages of justice. Focusing on wrongful convictions as though they can be treated in a vacuum may be a serious problem when reforms designed to reduce them come at the expense of increasing other miscarriages of justice. We could eliminate wrongful convictions altogether only by banning all convictions, but few people would care to live in a society of anarchy and vigilante justice. Wrongful arrests that do not end in conviction warrant more attention too, as do incidents of police brutalization and failures to convict offenders. Wrongful arrests that do not end in conviction could be reduced if prosecutors provided more systematic information about the reasons for rejecting arrests at the screening stage, and by incorporating in police officer assessment systems inducements to improve the quality of police arrests and reduce the number of arrests rejected by the prosecutor at screening. Police brutalization is a criminal offense that warrants prevention through closer scrutiny of police operations and tough sanctions when such violations are uncovered. Failures to convict offenders—the most pervasive of all errors of justice—can be reduced through better police work, improved use of technology, more criminal justice resources, and with community justice programs that leverage the small numbers of police and other justice resources by enlisting the support of private citizens to report crimes and come forth as witnesses as needed.

Perhaps the greatest opportunities for reducing miscarriages of justice and the associated social costs lie in making greater use of tools of error management used in other domains, as suggested earlier. This can begin without giving up any of the fundamental principles of justice, through better documentation of both false positives (wrongful arrests and convictions) and false negatives (failures to arrest and convict) by the police and prosecutors. This means putting in place systems that answer the following questions: In which offenses are these errors of justice most prevalent? What are the most common sources of each type of error? When and where does each occur most often? When we have made the reforms and installed the programs that provide answers to these questions, we will be on the road to a system that is more transparent, more just, and more legitimate than we have today.

Notes

1 Of course, we may wish to focus policy reform on sanctions against officials who violate due process even when the violations create no harm in a particular case, to deter harm over the long term.
2 The most prominent of these long-term costs are income lost due to a decline in job skills and stigma associated with a criminal record.
3 It is common to hear the complaint from the conservative community that our police are hamstrung by constitutional protections that are weighted too heavily in favor of offenders.

One rarely hears, from any community, the complaint that police incentive systems are biased toward arrests without convictions.

4   In 2007, 12.7 million felony crimes were committed against individuals in the U.S., including almost 5.2 million violent incidents, 3.2 million household burglaries, almost 1 million motor vehicle thefts, and 3.4 million larcenies involving thefts of amounts exceeding $250. Several million more felonies were committed against commercial establishments. Bureau of Justice Statistics, U.S. Department of Justice, Criminal Victimization in the United States, 2007 Statistical Tables 96 (2010), *available at* http://bjs.ojp.usdoj.gov/content/pub/pdf/cvus07.pdf.

5   Dworkin (1977) further distinguishes between "weak" and "strong" discretion. Weak discretion refers to the need for judgment in the face of vague rules; for umpires, judges, and other interpreters of rules, it is the fairly mechanical and uncontroversial work that comes with the job. Strong discretion, on the other hand, is neither mechanical nor trivial, involving judgments supported by principles and invoked under a duty that is larger than that ordinarily associated with the problem at hand, involving an "ultimate social rule or set of social rules" (p. 69). Both types of discretion are likely to manifest differently from official to official.

6   133 Sample Jury Instructions [18 U.S.C. §§ 241 (1997)].

7   For one thing, variation in the perceptions of jurors about precisely where in the conventional definition of proof beyond a reasonable doubt the line is drawn between "firmly convinced of the defendant's guilt" and "less than firmly convinced" is itself less than firm. This complicates the task of finding a proper balance between the error of convicting an innocent person and that of failing to convict a true offender.

8   The tools for reducing errors in the management of discretion in these several domains are not always used, especially in settings in which the incentives to take conflicting errors seriously are weak. Improvements traceable to these tools are nonetheless unmistakable.

9   Statisticians have developed numerous refinements on these basics. One such refinement is *statistical power analysis,* which assesses the effect of sample size on the risk of a Type II error (β), with power defined as the probability of accepting the research hypothesis when it is true ($1-\beta$). The result is commonly presented in the form of a graph depicting the relationship between $1-\beta$ and the value of the parameter tested, for a wide array of sample sizes. Another variant is *receiver operating characteristic* analysis, which traces the relationship between the rate of true positives (positives accurately identified as positive as a percentage of total actually positive) and the false positives rate (negatives falsely identified as positive as a percentage of total actually negative).

10 These estimates were based on a wide variety of assumptions about the proportion of arrests brought to the prosecutor involving factually innocent persons, the proportion of arrests accepted for prosecution, and plea-to-trial ratios.

11 However, as Cole and Thompson (2012) observe, this technology can and has been misused against innocent suspects.

12 Mark Cohen (2000) and others have estimated the major elements of these costs, with convergent assessments using a variety of imputation methods: declines in property values associated with crime rate increases, jury verdicts, and surveys on willingness to pay to prevent and avoid crime.

13 A large share of these costs are associated with lost parenting services. Most inmates are parents; some 65% help to support at least one dependent at the time of arrest (Piehl et al., 1999).

14 Estimating the social costs of individual crimes is especially difficult for crimes involving large intangible costs, such as rape. It is no less difficult for crimes without immediate victims, such as crimes involving drugs, prostitution, and many white-collar offenses. Since drug crimes account for a larger percentage of correctional populations than any other crime, it could be especially important to estimate the social costs associated with these

crimes. Our drug laws are justified largely on the grounds that drugs harm society by producing higher levels of street crime, due in part to drug users committing crimes to support drug habits, in part to pharmacological effects of drugs, and in part to complex drug-crime culture effects. These various effects vary substantially by drug type (Boyum et al., 2011). Drug laws have been justified also because of the costly health problems drugs impose on society, as well as lost productivity and well-being, and the effects of having drugs in more homes and thus more accessible to children if legalized.

15 Some types of profiling other than racial or ethnic profiling are less objectionable. "Profiling" has several different connotations: It can be used to prevent further crimes committed by a serial offender; to develop a psychological picture of a particular offender; or to fit a particular pattern of offending with a more general criminal archetype, a process conducive to empirical analysis. Profiling originated with the work of Howard Teten, sometimes referred to as the "grandfather" of profiling, although essentials of contemporary profiling were used in the 19th century murders committed by Jack the Ripper (Turvey, 2001). The non-psychological essentials of profiling can be traced largely to Cesare Lombroso's development of criminal archetypes, based on physical characteristics. Teten developed profiling in 1962 at the FBI as an investigative tool for homicide cases, in collaboration with colleague Pat Mullany. Teten regarded profiling as "applied criminology" (Forst, 2004).

16 The U.S. Census Bureau offered five categories for race/ethnicity on the 1990 census form and 20 in 2000, allowing respondents to check as many boxes as they like. In the 2010 census, the Bureau included changes designed to clarify that Hispanic ethnicity is not a race, noting that all the categories in survey are social-political constructs rather than scientific. Etzioni (2000) argues that the Census should allow Americans to classify themselves as multiracial to account for people of mixed racial backgrounds who do not self-identify with any particular racial category.

17 The police violate these principles when they ask the witness to find the person in a file of mug shots, and then put the person selected by the witness in the lineup, or when they give nods or other cues to the witness as he or she goes through a file of pictures (Eysenck and Eysenck, 1994). Errors can occur also when the lineup consists largely of people who do not fit the description of the offender, increasing the risk of selecting a particular person in the lineup who is in fact innocent of the crime in question but who fits the description approximately, unlike the others in the lineup. Defense counsel, especially those appointed by the court, are not always diligent about catching these various types of improper witness identification procedures.

18 Overall, more killings occurred in larger jurisdictions, jurisdictions with more homicides, and jurisdictions with relatively few sworn officers. The regression result produced by the author based on the data provided by Whitlock and Fallis is:

Killings = 0.5021 + .00000394*Population - .00075*Cops + .0161*Homicides, with all three independent variables significant at .01 (t = 4.87, -3.84, and 7.30, respectively), and with R^2 = .893 (adjusted R^2 = .886; F = 131, significant at a level arbitrarily close to zero). Whitlock and Fallis reported Prince Georges County as highest rated, based on the number of killings per officer, under the headline, "County Officers Kill More Often Than Any in U.S." However, the county has a higher than average homicide rate and lower than average number of officers per resident population, so the number of killings per officer will be artificially high both because the killings in the jurisdiction are spread over a smaller base and because of the inverse regression relationship between officers and killings generally. Prince Georges County ranked high, nonetheless, under any reasonable accounting.

19 Skolnick and Fyfe single out as the most essential factor Murphy's "genius . . . to put in place fundamental structural reforms and redundant checks on integrity and abuse in every part of the department" (p. 185).

20 Bratton's approach was more controversial than Murphy's. Appointed by Mayor Rudolph Giuliani to serve as NYPD commissioner from 1994 until Giuliani fired him two years later, Bratton is widely credited for reducing New York's homicide level from 1,997 in 1993 to fewer than 1,000 by the end of his term. Some of this reduction would surely have occurred without him, however, and the rest may have come at an unacceptable cost to civil liberties. Under Bratton's "zero tolerance" policing philosophy, the number of citizen complaints jumped by about 60%, from 3,500 citywide in 1993 to 5,500 in 1996 (Davis and Mateu-Gelabert, 1999).

21 During the ten-year period from 1992 to 2002, marked by an unprecedented decline in crime, the prison population increased by 61%. An analysis of data on offenses, arrests, convictions, incarcerations, and sentence terms by Bushway and Forst (2012) identified prosecutorial discretion as a primary source of the problem.

22 An important exception is Petro and Petro (2012), this volume.

23 *Berger v. United States* (295 U.S. 78, 1935). The case involved a federal prosecutor who grossly overstepped the bounds of proper behavior in order to win a conviction.

24 Examples of jurisdictions in the former category, with higher screening standards and fewer pleas per trial in the early 1980s, include New Orleans, Portland (OR), and Washington (DC). Examples in the latter camp include Manhattan (NY), Geneva (IL), and Cobb County (GA) (Boland and Forst, 1985, p. 11). Unfortunately, the data series on which this analysis was based was discontinued a few years after the study using those data was conducted. If data were available to replicate the research reported here, the lists could well be different, but I have yet to hear a compelling reason to expect that the extent of variation in plea-to-trial rates and arrest screening practices across district attorneys' offices would have changed over the ensuing years.

25 These findings were based on extensive simulations under a wide range of assumptions about the rate of true offenders brought to prosecution, the rates of wrongful convictions in pleas and trials, and office-wide conviction rates in trial. The increases in the number of offenders set free under a more selective prosecution strategy are also accompanied by longer prison terms, often with social costs well in excess of the benefits.

26 In *Apprendi*, the Court ruled, five to four, that the Sixth Amendment right to a jury trial prohibited judges from enhancing criminal sentences beyond statutory maximums based on facts other than those decided by the jury beyond a reasonable doubt. In *Blakely*, the Court ruled, five to four, that the Sixth Amendment right to a jury trial prohibited judges from enhancing criminal sentences based on facts other than those decided by the jury or confessed to by the defendant. In *Booker*, the Court ruled, six to three, that the federal sentencing guidelines violate the Sixth Amendment right to a jury trial by requiring judges to determine facts for criminal sentencing, and so should be made advisory rather than mandatory. Prior to these decisions, defendants could be sentenced under guidelines to crimes for which they had been acquitted in court.

27 Joan Petersilia (1993) has offered a parallel system of performance measurement for the larger pool of non-incarcerated persons under correctional authority. She identifies the following as the primary goals of community corrections: 1. Assess the offender's suitability for placement; 2. Enforce court-ordered sanctions; 3. Protect the community; 4. Assist offenders to change; and 5. Restore crime victims.

References

Metin Akay, *Detection and Estimation Methods for Biomedical Signals* (Academic Press, 1996).

Alan D. Baddeley, N. Thompson, and M. Buchanan, "Word Length and the Structure of Memory," *Journal of Verbal Learning and Verbal Behaviour*, Volume 1 (1975), pp. 575–589.

Hugo Adam Bedau and Michael L. Radelet, "Miscarriages of Justice in Potentially Capital Cases," *Stanford Law Review*, Volume 40, Number 1 (November 1987), pp. 21–179.

David Bjerk, "Guilt Shall Not Escape or Innocence Suffer: The Limits of Plea Bargaining When Defendant Guilt is Uncertain," *American Law and Economics Review*, Volume 92 (2007), pp. 305–327.

William Blackstone, *Commentaries on the Laws of England* (Oxford: Clarendon Press, 1765–1769) http://www.lonang.com/exlibris/blackstone/.

Alfred Blumstein, Jacqueline Cohen, Jeffrey A. Roth, and Christy A. Visher, eds., *Criminal Careers and Career Criminals*, Volume 1 (Washington, DC: National Academy of Sciences, 1986).

Barbara Boland and Brian Forst, "Prosecutors Don't Always Aim to Pleas," *Federal Probation*, Volume 49 (June 1985), pp. 10–15.

Edwin M. Borchard, *Convicting the Innocent* (New Haven, CT: Yale University Press, 1932).

David A. Boyum, Jonathan P. Caulkins, and Mark A. R. Kleiman, "Drugs, Crime, and Public Policy," in *Crime and Public Policy*, James Q. Wilson and Joan Petersilia, eds. (New York: Oxford University Press, 2011).

Jodi M. Brown and Patrick A. Langan, *Policing and Homicide, 1976–98* (Washington, DC: Bureau of Justice Statistics, 2001).

Shawn D. Bushway and Brian Forst, "Studying Discretion in the Processes that Generate Criminal Justice Sanctions," *Justice Quarterly*, Volume 29 (2012).

Brian R. Clifford and Jane Scott, "Individual and Situational Factors in Eyewitness Testimony," *Journal of Applied Psychology*, Volume 63 (1978), pp. 352–359.

Mark A. Cohen, "Measuring the Costs and Benefits of Crime and Justice," *Criminal Justice*, Volume 4 (2000), p. 263. http://www.ncjrs.gov/criminal_justice2000/vol_4/04f.pdf.

Simon A. Cole and William C. Thompson, "Forensic Science and Wrongful Convictions," (2012). Chapter 7, this volume.

Edward Connors, Thomas Lundregan, Neal Miller, and Tom McEwen, *Convicted by Juries, Exonerated by Science: Case Studies in the Use of DNA Evidence to Establish Innocence After Trial* (Washington, DC: National Institute of Justice, 1996).

Robert C. Davis and Pedro Mateu-Gelabert, *Respectful and Effective Policing: Two Examples in the South Bronx* (New York: Vera Institute of Justice, 1999).

"DNA Testing Turns a Corner as Forensic Tool," (no author) *Law Enforcement News* (October 15, 1995), p. 10.

Robert L. Donigan and Edward C. Fisher, *The Evidence Handbook*, 4th edition (Evanston, IL: Traffic Institute, Northwestern University, 1980).

Pamela Peterson Drake and Frank J. Fabozzi, *The Basics of Finance: An Introduction to Financial Markets, Business Finance, and Portfolio Management* (New York: John Wiley & Sons, 2010).

Ronald Dworkin, *Taking Rights Seriously* (Cambridge, MA: Harvard University Press, 1977).

Theodore Eisenberg and Martin T. Wells, "Deadly Confusion: Juror Instructions in Capital Cases," *Cornell Law Review*, Volume 79 (1993), pp. 1–17.

Amitai Etzioni, "A New American Race?" *The Responsive Community*, Volume 10 (2000). http://www.gwu.edu/~ccps/etzioni/M37.pdf.

James R. Evans and William M. Lindsay, *The Management and Control of Quality*, 8th edition (Southwestern College Publishing, 2010).

Hans J. Eysenck and Michael W. Eysenck, *Mind Watching: Why We Behave the Way We Do* (London: Multimedia Books, 1994).

Brian Forst, *Errors of Justice: Nature, Sources and Remedies* (New York: Cambridge University Press, 2004).

Brian Forst, Frank Leahy, Jean Shirhall, Herbert Tyson, Eric Wish, and John Bartolomeo, Arrest Convictability as a Measure of Police Performance (Washington, DC: U.S. Department of Justice, 1982).

Brian Forst, Judith Lucianovic, and Sarah Cox, *What Happens After Arrest?* (Washington, DC: Institute for Law and Social Research, 1977).

Lynne ForsterLee, Irwin A. Horowitz, and Martin Bourgeois, "Effects of Notetaking on Verdicts and Evidence Processing in a Civil Trial," *Law and Human Behavior*, Volume 18 (1994), pp. 567–578.

Dan M. Frangopol, Richard Sause, Chad S. Kusko, eds., *Bridge Maintenance, Safety, Management and Life-Cycle Optimization* (Boca Raton, FL: CRC Press, 2010).

Jerome Frank, *Courts on Trial: Myth and Reality in American Justice* (Princeton, NJ: Princeton University Press, 1973).

James J. Fyfe, "The Split-Second Syndrome and Other Determinants of Police Violence," in *Violent Transactions*, Anne Campbell and John Gibbs, eds., (New York: Basil Blackwell, 1986).

Brandon Garrett, *Convicting the Innocent: . . .* (Cambridge, MA: Harvard University Press, 2011).

Brandon Garrett, "Trial and Error," (2012). Chapter 5, this volume.

Stephen P. Garvey, Sheri Lynn Johnson, and Paul Marcus, "Correcting Deadly Confusion: Responding to Jury Inquiries in Capital Cases," Cornell Law Review, Volume 85 (2000), pp. 627–655.

Bennett L. Gershman, *Prosecutorial Misconduct*, 2nd edition (St. Paul, MN: West, 1999).

Lauren Glaze, Todd Minton, and Heather West, *Correctional Populations in the United States* (Washington, DC: Bureau of Justice Statistics, 2009), file corr2.csv.

Samuel R. Gross, "How Many False Convictions are There? How Many Exonerations are There?" (2012). Chapter 3, this volume.

Brad Heath and Kevin McCoy, "Prosecutor Misconduct Lets Convicts Off Easy," *USA Today* (December 28, 2010).

Larry Heuer and Steven Penrod, "Trial Complexity: A Field Investigation of Its Meaning and Effects," *Law and Human Behavior*, Volume 18 (1994), p. 29.

C. Ronald Huff, Arye Rattner, and Edward Sagarin, *Convicted But Innocent: Wrongful Conviction and Public Policy* (Sage, 1996).

Robert H. Jackson, "The Federal Prosecutor," *Journal of the American Judicial Society*, Volume 24 (1940).

Randall Kennedy, *Race, Crime, and the Law* (New York: Random House, 1997).

Randall Kennedy, "Racial Profiling May Be Justified, But It's Still Wrong," *The New Republic* (September 13, 1999), pp. 30–35.

Ken I. Kersch, "Juries on Trial," *The Public Interest*, Issue 150 (2003), p. 121.

Lucian L. Leape, "Error in Medicine," *Journal of the American Medical Association*, Volume 272 (1994), pp. 1851–1857.

James S. Liebman, Jeffrey Fagan, Valerie West, and Jonathan Lloyd, "Capital Attrition: Error Rates in Capital Cases, 1973–1995," *Texas Law Review*, Volume 78 (2000), p. 1839.

Elizabeth F. Loftus and T. E. Burns, "Mental Shock Can Produce Retrograde Amnesia," *Memory and Cognition*, Volume 10 (1982), pp. 318–323.

Charles H. Logan, "Criminal Justice Performance Measures for Prisons," in *Performance Measures for the Criminal Justice System* (Washington, DC: Bureau of Justice Statistics, 1993), pp. 19–60.

Bennett T. McCallum, "Misconceptions Regarding Rules vs. Discretion for Monetary Policy," *Cato Journal*, Volume 23 (2004), p. 365.

Sandra Day O'Connor, "Juries: They May Be Broke, But We Can Fix Them," *The Federal Lawyer*, Volume 44 (1997), p. 22.

Steven D. Penrod and Brian L. Cutler, "Assessing the Competency of Juries," in *The Handbook of Forensic Psychology*, Irving Weiner and Allen K. Hess, eds. (New York: Wiley, 1987).

Joan Petersilia, "Measuring the Performance of Community Corrections," in *Performance Measures for the Criminal Justice System* (Washington, DC: Bureau of Justice Statistics, 1993), pp. 61–86.

Jim Petro and Nancy Petro, "The Prosecutor and Wrongful Convictions: Misplaced Priorities, Misconduct, Immunity, and Remedies," (2012). Chapter 6, this volume.

Anne Morrison Piehl, Bert Useem, and John J. DiIulio, Jr., *Right-Sizing Justice: A Cost-Benefit Analysis of Imprisonment in Three States* (New York: Manhattan Institute Center for Civic Innovation, 1999). http://www.manhattan-institute.org/pdf/cr_08.pdf.

Albert J. Reiss, Jr., "Discretionary Justice in the United States," *International Journal of Criminology and Penology*, Volume 2 (1974).

Robert J. Sampson and John N. Laub, *Crime in the Making: Pathways and Turning Points Through Life* (Cambridge, MA: Harvard University Press, 1993).

Barry Scheck, Peter Neufeld, and Jim Dwyer, *Actual Innocence: When Justice Goes Wrong and How to Make it Right* (New York: Penguin Putnam, 2001).

Peter Skerry, *Counting on the Census? Race, Group Identity, and the Evasion of Politics* (Washington, DC: Brookings, 2000).

Jerome H. Skolnick and James J. Fyfe, *Above the Law: Police and the Excessive Use of Force* (New York: Free Press, 1993).

Brent E. Turvey, *Criminal Profiling: An Introduction to Behavioral Evidence Analysis*, 2nd edition (San Diego, CA: Academic Press, 2001).

Tom R. Tyler, *Why People Obey the Law* (Princeton University Press, 2006).

Tom R. Tyler, Stephen Schulhofer, and Aziz Huq, "Legitimacy and Deterrence Effects in Counter-Terrorism Policing: A Study of Muslim Americans," *New York University Public Law and Legal Theory Working Papers*, Paper 182 (2010). http://lsr.nellco.org/nyu_plltwp/182.

Neil J. Vidmar, "Is the Jury Competent?" *Law and Contemporary Problems*, Volume 52 (Autumn 1989).

Craig Whitlock and David S. Fallis, "County Officers Kill More Often Than Any in U.S.," *Washington Post* (July 1, 2001), pp. A1, A8–9.

Ronald Wright and Marc Miller, "The Screening/Bargaining Tradeoff," *Stanford Law Review*, Volume 55 (2002), pp. 116–117.

3

HOW MANY FALSE CONVICTIONS ARE THERE? HOW MANY EXONERATIONS ARE THERE?

Samuel Gross

Our [criminal] procedure has always been haunted by the ghost of the innocent man convicted. It is an unreal dream.

> Judge Learned Hand, United States District Court
> Southern District of New York
> *United States v. Garsson (1923)*

DNA testing [has] established conclusively that numerous persons who had been convicted of capital crimes (by 'proof beyond a reasonable doubt') were, beyond any doubt, innocent.

> Judge Jed Rakoff, United States District Court
> Southern District of New York
> *United States v. Quinones (2002)*

The most common question about false convictions is also the simplest: How many are there? The answer, unfortunately, is almost always the same, and always disappointing: We don't know. Recently, however, we have learned enough to be able to qualify our ignorance in two important respects. We can put a lower bound on the frequency of false convictions among death sentences in the United States since 1973, and we have some early indications of the rate of false convictions for rape in Virginia in the 1970s and early 1980s. These new sources of information suggest—tentatively—that the rate of false convictions for serious violent felonies in the United States may be somewhere in the range from 1%–5%. Beyond that—for less serious crimes and for other countries—our ignorance is untouched.

The Nature of the Problem

The very occurrence of false convictions is a reflection of our ignorance. If we know that a defendant is innocent, he is not convicted in the first place, and we are not likely to do better later on. The essence of the problem is that we are trying to count events we can't observe. There are other unknown quantities in criminal justice: for example, the number of crimes that are not reported to the police. That one, however, can be estimated by a comparatively straightforward method, the victimization survey: a representative sample of the general population is contacted and asked how often members of their households were victimized in the past year, and in what manner (e.g., Rand and Catalano, 2007). This is an imperfect but serviceable tool. We don't know the exact number of unreported robberies, rapes, and assaults, but we can estimate approximately how many occur, and where, and who the victims are. We have no comparable estimates for false convictions.

False convictions are not merely unobserved—like unreported crimes—but in most cases they are unobservable. The problem is not simply that we don't know whether a particular prisoner is innocent. We also may not know whether he is HIV positive, but we can test him for that condition, or the prison population as a whole, or a random sample. We can't do anything like that for false convictions, so we're left with two strategies: (1) we can attempt to infer the frequency of false convictions without direct information, or (2) we can try to use the false convictions we do know about—exonerations—as a basis for estimates about the entire category.

Indirect Measures

Judge/Jury Disagreement

Several researchers have developed a clever indirect measure of the frequency of false convictions. Surveys of judges who presided over criminal trials reveal that sometimes these judges disagree on the correct verdict with the juries that actually decide the cases. When that happens, one side or the other must be wrong, and sometimes it will be a jury that convicted the defendant. Using data on such disagreements, these researchers have constructed statistical models that indicate that up to 10% of criminal convictions in jury trials are erroneous (Baldwin and McConville, 1979; Gastwirth and Sinclair, 1998; Spencer, 2007).

The technical details of these judge/jury disagreement studies are beyond the scope of this chapter, but three structural limitations are noteworthy. First, these studies cannot pick up false convictions in cases in which judges and juries agree that the defendant is guilty, but he is not. Many exonerations fit that description. Second, these models are not able to estimate separately the proportion of convicted defendants who are factually innocent, as opposed to those who may be guilty but should not have been convicted under the law, given the evidence presented. In at least some cases it is clear that the judges involved thought juries should have acquitted under the law, even though the judges also believed that the defendants were factually guilty. Third, at best this research provides information on false convictions at jury trials. But about 95% of defendants who are convicted of felonies in the United States—and a higher proportion of those who are convicted of lesser crimes—plead guilty.

Despite these limitations, this line of research establishes an important point. Judges and juries are the two types of tribunals we trust to determine guilt or innocence. The rate of disagreements between them shows that there must be a substantial number of errors among criminal convictions, even if we cannot estimate that number directly.

Opinion Surveys

A second set of researchers have surveyed police officers, prosecutors, defense attorneys, and judges, and asked them how often they believe false convictions occur. The earliest such survey, in 1986, produced a summary estimate of the respondents' views: approximately 0.5% of serious felony convictions in the United States are erroneous (Huff et al., 1986). In two recent replications the consensus of criminal justice professionals has shifted, probably as a result of the large number of widely publicized exonerations in the past 25 years. The modal and mean responses now reflect the view that 1%–3% of serious felony convictions are errors (Ramsay and Frank, 2007; Zalman et al., 2008).

These results are interesting, but it's hard to attach much weight to them one way or the other. The lawyers, police officers, and judges who participated in these surveys had no systematic information on the frequency of false convictions; most of them probably gave the matter very little thought. They were guessing with little to go on, and aggregating their guesses doesn't make them more valid. These surveys, however, do reveal something about the biases of the respondents. All three surveys found that defense lawyers estimate higher rates of false conviction than judges, who estimate higher rates than police officers and prosecutors. The two more recent surveys also found that all categories of respondents think that false convictions are much less likely in their own jurisdictions than in the country as a whole. In other words, everybody thinks errors are more likely to happen on someone else's watch. Defense lawyers, who have relatively little power over criminal cases, see more errors than police and prosecutors, who have the primary responsibility and control. And everybody agrees that the problem is mild where they work and worse in other places, where cases are handled by strangers on all sides.

There has been one similar survey of a sample of the general population, respondents who have both less information about the criminal justice system and less personal investment in its accuracy. Their average estimate of the rate of error (for what it's worth) is considerably higher than that of the professionals: 4%–5% (Zalman et al., 2011).

Estimates Based on Exonerations

How Many Exonerations are There?

The false convictions we know about are those that are identified at some time after the innocent defendant is convicted. For our purposes, that means that new evidence of innocence emerged that was powerful enough to persuade a court or a prosecutor to vacate the conviction and dismiss the charges, or a governor to pardon the defendants. We call false convictions that have come to light and been remedied to this extent "exonerations" (Gross et al., 2005).

In 1923 Judge Learned Hand wrote that false convictions are "an unreal dream" (United States v. Garsson, 1923). This was a common, but by no means universal, view in the early twentieth century when exonerations were not widely publicized. In 1932 Edwin Borchard, in the preface to his classic book *Convicting the Innocent*, quoted a Massachusetts prosecutor who said: "Innocent men are never convicted. Don't worry about it, it never happens in the world. It is a physical impossibility." Borchard's book was a response, documenting 65 of these cases that never happened.

Several similar compilations with varying numbers of exonerations appeared in the 1950s and 1960s: 13 cases in Erle Stanley Gardner's *The Court of Last Resort* (1952); 34 in Jerome and Barbara Frank's *Not Guilty* (1957); 80 in Edward Radin's *Innocent* (1964); and 85 exonerations in Hugo Bedau's *Murder, Errors of Justice, and Capital Punishment* (1964). In the 1980s more comprehensive databases began to appear. Bedau and Radelet (1987) published a collection of 350 cases of innocent defendants who had been convicted of homicide or of non-homicidal capital crimes. Their article was expanded to a book in 1994 (Radelet, Bedau & Putnam) including 417 cases. Gross (1987) compiled a set of 97 false convictions caused by eyewitness misidentifications, from 1900 to 1982; Huff, Rattner, and Sagarin (1996) described a set of 205 exonerations; and Gross et al. (2005) published a compilation of 340 exonerations in the United States from 1989 through 2003.

Finally, in the last 20 years, on-going lists of exonerations have replaced scattered one-shot studies. Starting in 1993 the Death Penalty Information Center has maintained a list of American defendants who were sentenced to death and then exonerated after the beginning of 1973; as of December 2012, that list included 141 exonerations (Death Penalty Information Center, 2012). The Innocence Project maintains a similar list of all DNA exonerations in the United States; it included 301 cases as of December 2012 (Innocence Project, 2012). The most comprehensive list is the most recent one. In May 2012, the University of Michigan Law School and the Center on Wrongful Convictions at the Northwestern University School of Law inaugurated the National Registry of Exonerations, which reports all known exonerations in the United States since January 1989. The Registry had 1032 cases as of December 2012 (National Registry of Exonerations, 2012). An initial report by the Registry described an additional 1,100 "group exonerations" that occurred in the aftermath of the discovery of ten different police scandals around the country in which officers systematically framed innocent defendants for crimes that never occurred, mostly drug crimes (Gross and Shaffer, 2012).

Plainly, the harder researchers look for exonerations, the more they find. The initial report by the National Registry of Exonerations was based on 873 cases as of March 1, 2012; nine months later, the Registry had added more than 150 exonerations—mostly old cases that were not previously identified—with no end in sight. That report also describes how known exonerations are concentrated in cities and states where the media are most likely to notice them, and how some exonerations are deliberately concealed. The authors conclude that most exonerations are not widely known and have not been identified by researchers (Gross and Shaffer, 2012).

In sum, we know of at least a couple of thousand exonerations in the United States since 1989 (including the group exonerations), and of hundreds that occurred earlier—and there are probably at least as many, and perhaps several times more, that are not generally known.

Meaningless Estimates Based on Known Exonerations

By now there should be no doubt that innocent people are convicted of serious crimes in the United States on a regular basis. Still, some prominent lawyers and judges try to wish the problem away. In 2006 Justice Antonin Scalia, quoting Oregon prosecutor Joshua Marquis, wrote in a concurring opinion in the Supreme Court that American criminal convictions have an "error rate of .027 percent—or, to put it another way, a success rate of 99.973 percent" (*Kansas v. Marsh*, 2006). In other words: Not to worry, we get it right more than 99.9% of the time.

Unfortunately, these reassuring words are nonsense. Here's how Scalia and Marquis arrive at their numbers. You start with 340 known, proven exonerations from 1989 through 2003 (Gross et al., 2005). You multiply that number by ten "to be safe." Then you take that product, divide it by an estimate of the millions of all criminal convictions over time, and end up with something less than one-tenth of 1%. This makes no sense. Imagine that a car company gets reports that 65 of its 2010 sedans have faulty steering columns which sometimes lock up. What if the company said: "That's no big deal. We have 10 million cars on the road, so that's a defect rate of less than one-thousandth of 1%. Even if there are ten times as many, the number is trivial." Needless to say, that would be ridiculous. The total number of defects could be ten or 100 or 1,000 or 10,000 times greater than the first batch that came to light. Unless we investigate systematically, we just don't know—not for steering columns and not for criminal convictions. For steering columns, of course, we can recall the cars and check. Such recalls sometimes reveal hundreds of thousands of defects. For convictions there is no direct check for accuracy.

The essential error in these estimates is the assumption (typically unstated) that exonerations are a substantial fraction of false convictions. But why, except as an article of faith, would anyone suppose that the small number of miscarriages of justice that we happen to learn about years later—like the handful of fossils of early hominids that we have discovered—is anything more than an insignificant fraction of the total?

In any event, the exonerations we know about tell us a lot about the ones we have missed. The rate of exoneration from death sentences, as we'll see, is nearly 140 times greater than from felony convictions in general (Gross and O'Brien, 2007; Gross and Shaffer, 2012). Does this mean that false convictions are 140 times more likely in death cases than in other felony convictions? I think not. It must mean (at least in large part) that errors in capital cases are more likely to be *detected*. In other words, this extraordinary concentration of exonerations among death sentences tells us that the vast majority of false convictions for non-capital felonies remain undetected.

Overall, 83% of the exonerations in the National Registry are in rape and homicide cases (Gross and Shaffer, 2012), which together constitute about 2% of felony convictions (Durose and Langan, 2003), but the problems that cause false convictions are hardly limited to rape and murder.

For example, in 47 of the exonerations in the Registry the defendants were convicted of robbery compared to 203 convictions for rape, (Gross and Shaffer, 2012) even though there is every reason to believe that there are many more false convictions for robbery than for rape (Gross et al., 2005). For both rape and robbery, the false convictions we know about are overwhelmingly caused by mistaken eyewitness identifications—a problem that is almost entirely restricted to crimes committed by strangers—and arrests for robberies by strangers are at least several times more common than arrests for rapes by strangers. Why are there so comparatively few robbery exonerations? Because DNA evidence is the factual basis for the great majority of rape exonerations, but DNA is hardly ever useful in proving the innocence of robbery defendants. And beyond robbery, we know of hardly any exonerations in convictions for other common felonies: burglary, assault, auto theft, and so forth—and essentially none at all for misdemeanors. Are we supposed to believe that these unexamined convictions are all accurate?

The sunny logic of Scalia and Marquis could be applied to all sorts of public issues. For example: Why worry about juvenile drug use? Sure, over 130,000 were arrested for drug offenses in 2009 (U.S. Census Bureau, 2012), but that's only 0.17% of the 74 million plus kids under 18 (Puzzanchera et al., 2012), a trivial number. Multiply it by ten, and it's still less than 2%. No need to worry.

That would be silly, of course. We know better.

Genuine Estimates Based on Known Exonerations

Actually to use exonerations to estimate the proportion of erroneous convictions, we need a well-defined group of cases within which we identify all convictions that are in error, or at least a substantial proportion of them. It's hard to imagine how that might be done for criminal convictions in general, but it may be possible, at least roughly, for two types of cases for which exonerations are comparatively common: death sentences and rapes. For death sentences we know enough about the entire universe of convictions to be able to produce meaningful estimates. For rape we may be able to do the same for what amounts to a random sample in at least one state.

Death Sentences Since 1973

Murder cases receive far more attention than other criminal prosecutions, both before conviction and after, and as a result, a higher proportion of false convictions are brought to light. That is especially true for death sentences, which represent less than one-tenth of 1% of prison sentences (Gross and O'Brien, 2007), but account for about 12% of known exonerations from 1989 through February 2012 (Gross and Shaffer, 2012), a disproportion of more nearly 140 to 1. This suggests that a substantial proportion of innocent defendants who are sentenced to death are ultimately exonerated, perhaps even a majority. If so, we can use capital exonerations to try to estimate the false conviction rate among death sentences.

Death sentences and capital exonerations in the United States are both carefully tracked, the former by the Bureau of Justice Statistics of the Department of Justice; the latter by the Death Penalty Information Center.

As a result we know that 111 of the 7,534 death sentences pronounced from 1973 through 2004 ended in exoneration, or 1.5% (Gross and O'Brien, 2007). That figure—1.5%—is not the final word on exonerations for those defendants who've been sentenced to death since 1973. As time passes, some defendants in this group who have not yet been exonerated will be; others who are innocent will never be identified. But it's a starting point for calculating a lower bound for the rate of exoneration in capital cases.

The death sentenced defendants who have been exonerated since 1973 spent an average of nine-and-a-half years in prison, and some much longer than that (Death Penalty Information Center, 2012). Many defendants still on death row have been there for much shorter periods. Some of them will yet be exonerated, but this process tapers off over time. Eighty-one percent of the capital exonerations between 1973 and 2004 occurred within 15 years of conviction, and 95% occurred within 20 years of conviction. If we consider only those death sentences that were at least 15 years old by 2004—those that were pronounced through 1989—we find an exoneration rate of 2.3% (86/3792). If we look at those cases that were at least 20 years old by 2004 (judgments entered through 1984) we also find an exoneration rate of 2.3% (Gross and O'Brien, 2007). This figure—2.3%—is the actual proportion of exonerations for death sentences imposed in the United States between 1973 and 1989. It is a good estimate of the proportion of all death sentences since 1973 that will eventually result in exonerations, which means that it is an underestimate of the true rate of false capital convictions.

Convincing courts, prosecutors, or governors not merely to commute death sentences but to release a defendant from death row is very difficult. It may be that a few of these released prisoners are guilty, but not many. On the other hand, there must be a considerable number of innocent capital defendants who are not exonerated, even after 15 years or more, in prison. Some may yet be cleared and freed, most probably will not. That is particularly true for innocent capital defendants who were removed from death row but not released from prison, which ultimately happens to most death sentenced defendants.

The reason that exonerations are so comparatively common among death sentences is that huge amounts of resources—by prosecutors, defense attorneys and courts—are devoted to reviewing and evaluating the evidence in cases of defendants who may be put to death. Once that threat is removed, however, innocent defendants no longer benefit from the special attention and resources that are devoted to prisoners under sentence of death. The focus and urgency of a possible execution are removed, and they are far less likely to be exonerated than if they had remained on death row. For example, 41% of all defendants sentenced to death between 1973 and 2004 had been removed from death row because their capital sentences or their convictions were reversed by the courts by the end of 2004. The great majority of them remain in prison, for life. But only 15% of the capital exonerations in that period (17/111) involved defendants who had been sentenced to death but were no longer on death row (Gross and O'Brien, 2007).

A second study also bears on this issue. Professor Michael Risinger (2007) examined capital rape-murder cases from 1982 through 1989. Using DNA exonerations as his measure of innocence, Risinger estimates that at least 3.3% of defendants sentenced to death for rape-murder in that period were innocent, and perhaps as many as 5%. Since Risinger's study is limited to DNA exonerations there is little doubt that all the exonerated defendants are innocent, but for the same reason his estimates are based on a total of 11 exonerations, and therefore inevitably imprecise.

Rapes (and Some Homicides) in Virginia, 1973–1987

Rape is a partial exception to the general background problem of studying false convictions: If semen from a rape was recovered from the victim, was not tested before trial, and is available now, there is a highly reliable test for the identity of the rapist. That is why we have had 193 DNA exonerations in rape and sexual assault cases from 1989 through February 2012, and another 92 in murder cases that also included rapes or sexual assaults (Gross and Shaffer, 2012). In themselves, however, these exonerations tell us little about the rate of false convictions for rape.

Many innocent defendants who have been convicted of rape have not had post-trial DNA testing. Some never ask because they haven't heard of that possibility or don't care enough to try for one reason or another— perhaps because they received comparatively light sentences long ago and don't want to revisit that part of their past, or because they have also been convicted of other crimes and will remain in prison one way or the other. Some innocent rape defendants will have died without DNA testing;

others will have been deported. Some have asked for testing and are waiting in the long queues at innocence projects and crime labs, and many cases might have been tested but the biological evidence was lost or destroyed.

To get a reasonable estimate of the proportion of wrongful convictions we need to test a reasonably representative sample of all rape convictions in a particular jurisdiction and time period. This might just be possible.

Starting in 2001, the Virginia Department of Forensic Science (DFS) discovered several hundred boxes containing closed rape and homicide files from 1973 through 1987—before pretrial DNA testing was done in that laboratory—many of which contained biological evidence that was never tested for DNA. In late 2005, tests on a small preliminary sample found two previously unknown false convictions out of 22 cases—a false conviction rate of 9% within that tiny sample (Shear and Stockwell, 2005).[1] This initial testing led Virginia Governor Mark Warner to order DFS to test all DNA samples in those files and identify any additional defendants who were wrongfully convicted (Shear and Stockwell, 2005). As of this writing, in the summer of 2012, that project is still under way.

As far as we know, the cases in the DFS project are reasonably representative of all rape and homicide cases from 1973 through 1987 for which biological evidence was sent to the Virginia Department of Forensic Science. This study may provide uniquely valuable data on the frequency of false convictions among such cases in Virginia in the 1970s and 1980s.

As of June 2012, we know of 715 cases that have had DNA testing as part of this project, but 465 of those tests were "indeterminate"—that is, useless as data either because no DNA profile could be developed, or because there were no reference DNA profiles for the convicted defendant or the victim with which to compare a profile that was developed. That leaves 250 completed tests in the sample, of which 227 included a sexual assault (Roman et al., 2012). To date, the DNA tests in these 250 cases have produced eight exonerations, or 3.2%. An additional five cases are known to be under re-investigation by prosecutors. If they all become exonerations, the known rate will rise to 5.2% (Green, 2012(a)).

The Urban Institute has released a preliminary study of the DFS project (Roman et al., 2012). The researchers identified 56 cases in which the DNA did not match the convicted defendant, including 38 in which, in their judgment, the results are "exculpatory supporting exoneration." The Urban Institute study focuses on cases in which there was a sexual assault, even if the main conviction was for murder. This makes sense. Almost all the cases with complete DNA testing include sexual assaults, so this is the group for which a meaningful false conviction rate might be developed. The study identifies 33 "likely exonerations" in this group, 15% of those with useable DNA tests (33/227).

It's hard to know what to make of the Urban Institute's estimates of the rate of false conviction among sexual assault cases in Virginia. Fifteen percent is a far higher figure than any comparable ratio, estimate, or guess. As the study notes (Roman et al., 2012, p. 10), the researchers frequently had insufficient information about the context of the crimes to determine the "probative value of DNA testing results." For example, in three cases from Richmond, Virginia, for which the Urban Institute claims that DNA tests "support exoneration," local prosecutors have said that the facts of the crimes make DNA results irrelevant to the defendant's guilt (Green, 2012(b)). Despite these qualifications, the data reported by the Urban Institute are startling. Even if they have misclassified two-thirds of their cases, the remaining error rate for the sexual assault cases would be 5%.

In any event, the actual rate of accomplished exonerations from the entire DFS sample is already 3.2%, and likely to rise to 5% or higher as more cases are finalized.

Conclusion

So where does that leave us? I'll summarize briefly:

- We know of at least 2,000 exonerations in the United States since the beginning of 1989, and there have been many others that are not known to researchers—very likely more than those that are known.
- These exonerations cannot be used to estimate the rate of false conviction directly because the great majority of erroneous convictions are never detected.
- We do know, however, that 2.3%–3.3% of death sentences in the United States since 1973 have ended in exoneration. This is not a complete count. Some innocent defendants who were sentenced to death have not been exonerated – mostly, I expect, defendants who have been removed from death row but remain in prison.

- We also know that among convicted defendants in rape (and a few homicide) cases for which physical evidence was sent to the Virginia Department of Forensic Science from 1973 through 1987, at least 3.2%–5% were innocent, and probably quite a few more.

The information at hand is still very limited, and generalizations are difficult. There are strong theoretical reasons to believe that the rate of false convictions may be higher for murders in general, and for capital murders in particular, than for other felony convictions (Gross, 1998). The rape cases for which biological evidence was submitted to the Virginia Department of Forensic Science in the 1970s and 1980s may not be representative of rape cases in the United States generally, let alone other felony cases. We don't know.

Still, this is a start—considerably better than total ignorance. It's enough to make some initial and tentative estimates. Marvin Zalman (2012) makes what he calls a very general "intelligence estimate" of the rate of false convictions in the United States, from 0.5%–1.0% at the low end to 2%–3% at the high end. In light of the new information from Virginia, my own tentative estimate would be a similar but somewhat higher range: 1%–5% of convictions for serious felonies in the United States are erroneous.

Is that a lot or a little? That depends on your point of view. If as few as 1% of serious felony convictions are erroneous, that means that perhaps 10,000–20,000 or more of the nearly 2.3 million inmates in American prisons and jails (Glaze, 2011) are innocent, and thousands of new innocent defendants are locked up each year. If the rate is higher, these numbers will go up.

If as few as one-tenth of 1% of jetliners crashed on takeoff, we would shut down every airline in the country. That is not a risk we are prepared to take—and we believe we know how to address that sort of problem. Are 10,000 to perhaps 50,000 wrongfully imprisoned citizens too many? Can we do better? How? There are no obvious answers. The good news is that the great majority of convicted criminal defendants in America are guilty. The bad news is that a substantial number are not.

Note

1   The state tested 31 cases in that initial batch (Shear and Stockwell, 2005) but completed the testing in only 22. In four cases, no DNA was detected; in one case there was insufficient DNA for analysis; and in four cases there were no DNA samples from the defendants for comparison (Rudin and Eisenberg, 2008).

References

Baldwin J, McConville M. 1979. *Jury Trials*. Oxford: Clarendon Press, p. 41.

Bedau HA. 1964. Murder, Errors of Justice, and Capital Punishment, in *The Death Penalty in America*, HA Bedau (Ed.), pp. 434–52.

Bedau HA, Radelet ML. 1987. Miscarriages of justice in potentially capital cases. *Stanford Law Rev.* 40: 21–179.

Borchard EM. 1932. *Convicting the Innocent: Errors of Criminal Justice*. New Haven: Yale University Press.

Death Penalty Inf. Cent. 2012. *Innocence: List of Those Freed From Death Row*. Washington, DC: Death Penalty Information Center. Available at: http://www.deathpenaltyinfo.org/innocence-list-those-freed-death-row.

Durose MR, Langan PA. 2003. *Felony Sentences in State Courts, 2000*. Washington, DC: U.S. Dept. of Justice, Bureau of Justice Statistics.

Frank J, Frank B. 1957. *Not Guilty*. Garden City, NY: Doubleday.

Gardner ES. 1952. *The Court of Last Resort*. New York: William Sloane Associates.

Gastwirth JL, Sinclair MD. 1998. Diagnostic test methodology in the design and analysis of judge–jury agreement studies. 39 *Jurimetrics* 59.

Glaze LE. 2011. *Correctional Population in the United States, 2010*. Washington, DC: U.S. Department of Justice, Bureau of Justice Statistics.

Green F. 2012(a) DNA tests prompt review of four possible wrongful convictions. *Richmond Times-Dispatch*, July 6. Available at: http://www2.timesdispatch.com/news/news/2012/jul/06/dna-tests-prompt-review-5-possible-wrongful-convic-ar-2038311/.

Green F. 2012(b). Richmond DNA cases show not all reports prove innocence. *Richmond Times-Dispatch*, June 24. Available at: http://www2.timesdispatch.com/news/state-news/2012/jun/24/tdmain12-richmond-dna-cases-show-not-all-reports-p-ar-2009815/.

Gross SR. 1987. Loss of innocence: eyewitness identification and proof of guilt. *J. Legal Stud.* 16: 395.

Gross SR. 1998. Lost lives: miscarriages of justice in capital cases. *Law Contemp. Probl.* 61(4): 125.

Gross SR, O'Brien B. 2008. Frequency and predictors of false conviction: why we know so little, and new data on capital cases. *J. Empirical Legal Stud.* 5: 927–62.

Gross SR, Shaffer M. 2012. *Exonerations in the United States 1989–2012*, Univ. Mich. Public LawWork. Pap. No. 277, Ann Arbor. Available at: http://papers.ssrn.com/sol3/papers.cfm?abstract_id=2092195.

Gross SR, Jacoby K, Matheson DJ, Montgomery N, Patil S. 2005. Exonerations in the United States, 1989 through 2003. *J. Crim. Law Criminol.* 95: 523.

Huff CR, Rattner A, Sagarin E. 1986. Guilty until proven innocent: wrongful conviction and public policy. *Crime & Delinquency*. 32: 518–44.

Huff CR, Rattner A, Sagarin E. 1996. *Convicted but Innocent: Wrongful Conviction and Public Policy*. Thousand Oaks, CA: Sage.

Innocence Project. 2012. *Know the Cases*. New York: Innocence Project. Available at: http://www.innocenceproject.org/know/.

Kansas v. Marsh, 548 U.S. 163 (2006).

National Registry of Exonerations. 2012. Available at: http://www.law.umich.edu/special/exoneration/Pages/about.aspx.

Puzzanchera C, Sladky A, Kang W. 2012. *Easy Access to Juvenile Populations: 1990–2010*. Washington, DC: National Center for Juvenile Justice. Available at: http://ojjdp.gov/ojstatbb/ezapop/asp/comparison_display.asp.

Radelet ML, Bedau HA, Putnam C. 1994. *In Spite of Innocence*. Boston: Northeastern University Press.

Radin, E. D. 1964. *The Innocents*. New York: Morrow.

Ramsay RJ, Frank J. 2007. Wrongful conviction: perception of criminal justice professionals regarding the frequency of wrongful conviction and the extent of system errors. *Crime & Delinquency* 53(3): 436–70.

Rand M, Catalano S. 2007. *Criminal Victimization, 2006*. Washington, DC: U.S. Department Justice, Bureau Justice Statistics.

Risinger DM. 2007. Innocents convicted: an empirically justified factual wrongful conviction rate. *J. Crim. Law Criminol*. 97(7): 61–807.

Roman J, Walsh K, Lachman P, Yahner J. 2012. *Post-Conviction DNA Testing and Actual Innocence*. Washington, DC: Urban Institute, Justice Policy.

Rudin N, Eisenberg A. 2008. *Addendum to Scientific Advisory Committee Meeting Minutes: Report to the Commonwealth of Virginia Scientific Advisory Committee by the DNA Subcommittee on confirmation bias and "inconclusive" conclusions*. Richmond, VA: Dep. Forensic Sci., Jan. 7. Available at: http://www.dfs.state.va.us/about/minutes/saCommittee/20080108.pdf.

Shear MD, Stockwell J. 2005. DNA tests exonerate 2 former prisoners; Va. governor orders broad case review. *Washington Post*, Dec. 15, p. A1.

Spencer, BD. 2007. Estimating the accuracy of jury verdicts. *J. Empirical Legal Stud*. 4: 305.

U.S. Census Bureau, *Statistical Abstract of the United States: 2012, Table 326*. Available at: http://www.census.gov/compendia/statab/2012/tables/12s0326.pdf.

Zalman, M, 2012. Qualitatively estimating the incidence of wrongful convictions. *Criminal Law Bulletin* 48(2), forthcoming.

Zalman M, Larson MJ, Smith B. 2011. Citizens' attitudes toward wrongful convictions. *Criminal Justice Rev*. 37: 51–69.

Zalman M, Smith B, Kiger A. 2008. Officials' estimates of the incidence of "actual innocence" convictions. *Justice Quarterly*. 25: 72–100.

Cases

United States v. Garsson, 291 F. 646 (SDNY 1923).
United States v. Quinones 205 F.Supp.2d 256 (SDNY 2002).

4

ERRORS OCCUR EVERYWHERE—BUT NOT AT THE SAME FREQUENCY

THE ROLE OF PROCEDURAL SYSTEMS IN WRONGFUL CONVICTIONS

Martin Killias

Obviously, errors are universal. Wrongful convictions can, therefore, occur anywhere at any time and independently of the procedural system in place. Evidence assembled over the last years suggests, however, that the frequency of wrongful convictions varies considerably across systems. Despite the formidable difficulties in assessing the odds of innocent defendants being convicted, illustrated by Zalman (2012), some indications point to the possibility that exonerations, at least in serious crimes, are substantially more frequent in the United States compared to Europe. For example, Gross et al. (2005) found 328 exonerations of defendants sentenced to death or very long prison terms in the United States over a period of 15 years (also see Gross, Chapter 3, this volume). This represents about 20 exonerations per year. Translated into the relative proportions in Germany, this would equal about seven exonerations each year for inmates serving life or very long sentences; about five in France; and roughly one every second year in Switzerland. The actual figures for these three countries fall far short of such proportions (Kessler, 2008; Dongois, 2008;

Killias, 2008). The lower frequency of exonerations in Europe may be related to a number of characteristics of the criminal justice systems that will be described in the following section. Of course, all systems are vulnerable to errors committed by forensic experts, eyewitness testimony and, most of all, the ever-increasing use of summary proceedings. Errors are further increased if courts have to assess evidence concerning facts that occurred decades ago, or if one-sided media publicity in high-profile cases pushes toward a conviction. Possible remedies are being presented, ranging from making appeals more efficient, restricting the use of summary proceedings, developing a culture of error management among forensic experts, and making systems less vulnerable to false confessions and insufficient defense counsel. The basic argument is that wrongful convictions are the result of certain features of criminal justice systems that increase such risks, rather than merely a matter of incompetent actors.

Accusatorial and Inquisitorial Systems Compared

It is obviously beyond the scope of this essay to give a full account of the differences between accusatorial and inquisitorial systems, let alone that there exist many variants across Anglo-Saxon countries on one hand and European nations on the other. However, the common origins in common law and the extensive standardization of procedural practices under the European Convention of Human Rights (ECHR) there allow drawing a few characteristic features of both systems of criminal procedural law (van Koppen and Penrod, 2003).

The Focus on Material Truth vs. Procedural Justice

European and American courts consider it to be their role to establish, beyond reasonable doubt, whether the defendant is guilty or not. The way in which this is accomplished differs, however. In Europe, the police, prosecutors and courts are discouraged from bringing unreasonable charges against any defendant, and they are obliged also to consider evidence that is in his or her favor. In establishing material truth, all actors of the criminal justice system, including judges, play a far more active role than under the accusatorial system, where establishing the facts and collecting as well as presenting the evidence is seen as the parties' responsibility. Many consequences derive from this fundamental difference in approach. One is that confessions (as with any declarations by the defendant, such as a guilty plea) never have the same binding character in Europe as in the United States, although in more pragmatic terms, a confession obviously makes an acquittal far less likely. In practice, most defendants confess at some point during the investigation or during the hearing in court. The focus in a European trial typically is not on the question of guilt or innocence, but on the sentence that is meted out by the same court in the same hearing. In the same vein, lie detectors are not allowed under the ECHR, nor are "accusatorial methods of police interrogations." This bans manipulative techniques of interviewing, including confronting the defendant with closed-ended (confirmatory) questions, anxiety cues, or deception (for example, by presenting false evidence). Of course, violations of such standards certainly occur and it would be naïve to claim that they are uniformly respected across the continent, but this is obviously true with respect to due process rules in the United States.

The Role of the Defense Counsel

These differences in the assessment of material "truth" by the court give the defense counsel a substantially different role in the European context. Whereas American defense lawyers are expected to conduct their counter-investigation, often involving substantial investments in time and resources, European defense counsels have access to the file of the prosecution at an early stage of the investigation. Whenever they believe that certain factual circumstances need to be investigated more thoroughly, they can require the prosecutor (or, indirectly, the police) to extend the investigation in certain directions before the file is sent to the court, along with the indictment. In that case, the prosecutors usually accept all reasonable inputs because, otherwise, they risk that the court may interrupt the trial and order the investigation to be completed. As European defense counsels usually do not like contesting facts that establish that the defendant is manifestly guilty, they usually concentrate on mitigating circumstances and try to obtain, whenever possible, a suspended sentence. Under the relatively mild sentences that are common practice in Europe,[1] this strategy is often successful.

Different Functions of the Trial

In sum, both the prosecution and the defense counsel are far more controlled by the court under the European system than in the United

States. Although the disclosure of evidence before trial is an obligation for the prosecution (in the sense that the defense counsel has free access to the entire file from an early stage of the procedure and long before the indictment), the defense counsel could, theoretically, keep secret "his" file until the trial. In practice, he or she is discouraged from doing so because the court usually will, after being confronted with a new "story," interrupt the hearing and order a complementary investigation of the new facts by the prosecutor (and, in practice, the police). Delaying the disclosure of critical evidence would be considered unprofessional, however, and the counsel might be subject to disciplinary sanctions. In sum, the European system pushes both parties to "clarify" the "truth" before the case comes to trial. Unlike the American model, the court hearing serves not so much to find the relevant facts, but rather to assemble all circumstantial evidence in order to arrive at a fair sentence that will be meted out at the end of the trial. Of course, there are contested verdicts where prosecution and defense fight hard in court to convince the judges (jurors are an exception nowadays in Europe), but these instances are rare exceptions now. Confronted with rather compelling evidence, most defense lawyers convince their clients to confess (and plead "guilty," at least in general terms) and to concentrate their efforts on obtaining a moderate sentence.

Different Forms of "Plea Bargaining"

The fact that both the prosecution and the court have no discretion to decide what kind of "truth" they are going to present to the court, there remains less room for negotiated pleas. This seems at odds with common knowledge that "negotiations" occur everywhere and under all systems. Although negotiated pleas exist on both sides of the ocean, there are important differences regarding the kinds of cases that can be settled informally and the extent to which this can be done. Whereas American prosecutors and defense counsels can agree on any plea to any offense at any stage of the procedure, European actors have far less discretion in this respect. The most common form of "guilty plea" that is known throughout Europe is the so-called "penal order," a decision by the prosecutor by which he or she "offers" the defendant a verdict and a sentence without any further hearing. If the defense counsel (or the defendant) does not insist on a court hearing within a fixed deadline (usually from 10 to 30 days), the "penal order" becomes final and takes the place of a verdict and sentence imposed by the court. If it is contested by the defendant, the case goes to court, and the penal order takes the place of an indictment.

There are two noteworthy differences between "penal orders" and "American style" negotiated pleas. Americans use plea bargaining for all kinds of offenses, from the most trivial to the most serious, whereas European "penal orders" allow only short sentences, usually ranging from a few days to six months or one year at most. Thus, "penal orders" are not an available option for more serious offenses. Further, European procedure does not allow prosecutors (and courts) to "threaten" the defendant with a much harsher penalty if he insists on his case being heard in court (rather than being settled out of court), a practice the U.S. Supreme Court did not find unconstitutional in *Bordenkircher v. Hayes* (1978). Under continental law, where the prosecutor is legally expected to behave "reasonably," to present the case in court in a "balanced" way and to give due consideration to mitigating and exculpatory circumstances, no prosecutor could, after issuing a penal order (with a sentence of, say, six months) in the first place, recommend a sentence of, say, two years based on the same facts, if the case goes to court. This would be considered unjustifiable retaliation against a defendant who did not accept the penal order, and could expose the prosecutor to criminal liability for "abuse of powers".[2] Indeed, either the six months initially imposed or the two years recommended in court for the same facts would be far below or above, respectively, what an "objective" assessment of the case would suggest. Even the confession that goes along with a guilty plea would, in Europe, not allow mitigating the sentence by more than one third, and even less in many countries (see Gilliéron, Chapter 12, this volume). Under the continental system, obtaining a verdict does not require the same investment of time and resources as it often does in the United States (Pizzi, 1999) and, therefore, a confession has a lower bargaining value in Europe compared to the United States. The other side of the coin is that a defendant in Europe is less pressured to enter a guilty plea. Whenever he accepts an "offer" made by the prosecution, his advantage will be in avoiding a public hearing (with extensive press coverage), in having his case settled within a reasonable time with a foreseeable outcome, and in saving costs that otherwise might need to be spent in his defense.

The two systems of plea bargaining differ further in the extent to which they allow "negotiation" of the facts. Of course, penal orders, "patteggiamento" or "Absprachen" (agreements) all allow streamlining the factual basis of a case to some extent, but only within the limits of plausibility (that is, what an initial assessment of the evidence would suggest to be true). If the defendant accepts the arrangement (the penal order or any other out-of-court settlement), but claims innocence, European law would not allow the court to ignore this fact. Any verdicts without hearing in the court are explicitly available only if the defendant admits the relevant facts, and certainly not if he claims innocence (Gilliéron, 2010). Ignoring his claim would be in flagrant contradiction with the presumption of innocence stipulated in Article 6 § 2 ECHR. In other words, "Alford" pleas (where the defendant claims being innocent of a crime to which he formally pleads guilty; *North Carolina v. Alford, 1970*) are not possible under European law. Recent reforms have extended plea bargaining in Europe to some cases of medium severity (with sentences of up to five years in exceptional cases), such as the "patteggiamento" in Italy and similar settlements ("Absprachen") in Germany and Switzerland (see Gilliéron, Chapter 12),[3] but have left these features basically unchanged.

In sum, and contrary to American law, European systems allow plea bargaining only in cases of minor severity, even if "penal orders" and negotiated pleas represent a substantial proportion of all case disposals by prosecutors. Since wrongful convictions often occur as a result of summary proceedings (Gilliéron, 2010), this difference may explain why exonerations in Europe more often occur in cases involving minor offenses and less so in those involving serious crimes (Killias, 2008).

Does the Difference Make a Difference?

Two Forms of "Plea Bargaining"

Do the described legal differences between the accusatorial system, as it exists in the United States, and the continental style of inquisitorial procedure really make a difference with respect to convicting innocent defendants? With respect to plea bargaining, some empirical data exist that were collected in Switzerland for the period 1995 to 2004 (Killias, Gilliéron, and Dongois, 2007). Reviewing all cases of exonerations over a period of ten years, it turned out that exonerations of factually innocent defendants almost exclusively concerned penal orders (petty offenses, mostly traffic violations) that were summarily handled by prosecutors without a hearing. In such cases, defendants with similar names sometimes got mixed up and were convicted of the "wrong" offense, or labs attributed the results of blood analysis to the "wrong" person. Another frequent source of error occurred when the defendants' mental health problems were not discovered during a summary proceeding, but only when, in connection with a later offense, the person's mental condition was examined more thoroughly. On the other hand, exonerations in more serious cases were very rare in Switzerland or Germany (where some data exist for the 1960s and before; Peters, 1970–1974). This suggests that errors are heavily related to summary proceedings, an argument further developed by Gilliéron using American data (Gilliéron, 2010 and Chapter 12, this volume). Summary proceedings may indeed be more vulnerable to errors in the assessment of facts because of bureaucratic routines, especially if no hearing with the defendant takes place, or because of strong pressure on the defendant to admit to acts that he actually did not commit, in order to avoid the risk of being convicted, after trial, for a far more serious crime entailing a far longer sentence or even the death penalty. Not surprisingly, many exonerations in America concern cases where the defendant pled guilty after a negotiation where he faced serious threats of going to prison for a far longer period of time.

Two Different Styles of Police Interviews

Another area where the two systems differ substantially is in police interviewing. A recent systematic review of studies on the impact of interrogation styles on confessions in police interviews showed that more neutral methods of questioning (the "information-gathering approach") preserved and, in some cases, even increased the likelihood of true confessions, while simultaneously reducing the likelihood of false confessions (Meissner, Redlich, Bhatt, and Brandon, 2012). This form of police interrogation is the standard in continental Europe (Slobogin, 2003; Vrij, 2003). In America, however, the accusatorial style approach prevails, whereby the defendant is hard pressed to confess, with threats of harsher treatment in case of continued denial; many leading or closed-ended questions; and alleged evidence that the police claim to have obtained (for instance, from co-defendants). Although the 12 randomized trials located and meta-analyzed by Meissner et al. (2012) were all laboratory-based, rather than field experiments, the differences obtained are impressive. In line with the few eligible field studies, the laboratory trials showed that both accusatorial and information-gathering methods increase confessions. However, the probability of ending up with a true confession increased significantly under the information-gathering approach, while the risk of obtaining a false confession decreased. Compared to the accusatorial style, it turned out that the information-seeking method elicited significantly more true confessions and substantially reduced the risks of false confessions.

Therefore, accusatorial styles of questioning defendants that remain popular in American police work may be responsible for many false confessions and, indirectly, many convictions of factually innocent defendants. Since interview methods differ substantially across nations and systems, these differences may well explain why wrong confessions differ so much across countries. Under the ECHR (article 6 § 2), threats or deception during police interviews, such as confronting the defendant with lies about already obtained evidence or confessions by co-defendants, is considered unfair and may later be a reason to quash the conviction. Most codes of criminal procedure have provisions outlawing constraint as well as "unfair" or unfaithful behavior during investigations. Misbehavior of police officers and prosecutors may, however, be more efficiently discouraged by provisions in the criminal codes that make "abuse of power" a criminal offense in several European nations.[4] As observed above, confessing and entering a guilty plea is not the exception, but the rule, in daily routine in Europe, since most defendants (and their lawyers) consider denial as counter-productive in the face of strong evidence.

The Role of Confessions

Many exonerations in America over the last 20 years involved convictions that were obtained after false confessions. This in itself may possibly explain the higher rate of exonerations in the United States. The problem is likely to be exacerbated, however, by the role confessions play under the accusatorial, compared to the inquisitorial, system. Certainly, there are examples of false confessions and their fatal role in Europe as well (Brants, 2008), but overcoming a false admission of guilt is far more complicated under the American system. The American plea bargaining system is based on the admission of guilt which, in the daily routine, is not questioned any further by the court. In other words, facts are established in an American criminal procedure in a way that resembles civil procedures anywhere in the Western world. In lawsuits related to damages, for instance, any party's declarations concerning his/her fault or the amount of losses is not further questioned, but instead is taken for granted, and plaintiffs as well as defendants find it very difficult to repeal such "unfortunate" admissions later. In a continental criminal procedure, however, a confession may obviously greatly help the police to close a case, but it is not legally binding on the court in its mission of finding the "truth". In practice, the police will try to use a confession as a basis for finding as much corroborating evidence as possible. Many of the important reforms brought about by the U.S. Supreme Court in the 1960s were probably motivated, in part, by the cardinal role of confessions in the American system. If a defendant's declarations can make such a difference, it is crucial that they are obtained after due warnings and in the presence of his defense counsel (Zalman, 2011: 293; Neubauer, 2007). In Europe, such reforms have now also been adopted in many countries, obviously owing to the prominent influence of American law on European minds. So far, Europeans have paid very little attention to undesirable side effects of such reforms (as described by Stuntz 2012: 216–236), as raising the costs of convictions, increasing social inequality and extending plea bargaining. Alternatively, control over police behavior during interrogations might also have been achieved by recording interviews on videotape and making this a condition for establishing the validity of interrogations. In sum, the role of confessions and the degree to which they can be questioned later in the procedure is another important element that may make a difference between accusatorial and inquisitorial systems.

How Could Systems Reduce the Risks of Convicting the Innocent?

Obviously, defendants and witnesses may lie anywhere, and under all systems; experts may draw erroneous conclusions based on the material at hand all over the world; and there may be incompetent legal staff anywhere and at any time. It would be wrong, however, to conclude from this obvious state of affairs that wrongful convictions have to be accepted as part of a risky world. Indeed, systems also differ in how they deal with errors and in how they act in order to control such risks.

Make Prosecutorial and Police Officers Accountable for Unethical Behavior

Under the continental system, prosecutors and police officers are obliged to seek the "truth" and to behave, in pursuit of that purpose, with fairness and without preconception. Of course, the world never is as ideal as such principles may suggest, but it is a fact that prosecutors often initiate exonerations when they discover, years later and in relation to a different case, that a former conviction was wrong (Killias, Gilliéron, and Dongois, 2007; Killias, 2008). Similarly, they do a lot to prevent wrongful convictions through avoiding one-sided investigations. This outlaws (and, eventually, even makes an offense) the intentional ignorance (or suppression) of possibly exculpatory evidence and almost necessarily imposes what Meissner et al. (2012) call an "information-gathering interviewing method." As a side effect, these rules and practices mean that the defense counsel plays a less decisive role under the continental system. Thus, an innocent defendant has a better chance of being acquitted even if his counsel is poorly motivated, incompetent, or lacking resources. In sum, a crucial step in reducing the risk of errors would be to make police and prosecutorial services less one-sided, and to make them criminally liable in cases involving intentional misbehavior.

Restrict Plea Bargaining and Summary Proceedings

A next step could be to increase safeguards to plea bargaining. Of course, the safest way may be to reduce summary proceedings in general and to ban them completely from cases where the defendant risks a long custodial sentence. But even if one agrees that plea bargaining should continue to be used even in capital cases, it would be advisable to consider certain safeguards. For instance, prosecutors could be banned from requiring longer sentences following a trial if their earlier offer of a "deal" is rejected by the defendant. The continental experience shows that defendants widely accept deals even if they know that by going to court they do not risk a substantially different sentence. In other words, the "bargaining power" of prosecutors may not fade away if they no longer can threaten defendants with long sentences as a response to the rejection of their offer. Under the European "penal order" system, an urgent reform would be to oblige prosecutors to hear the defendant before the case is closed (Thommen, 2010).

Adopt More Neutral Interrogation Methods

A further step that would not require deep rearrangements could be the adoption of the "information-gathering" approach in police interviews. As observed by Meissner et al. (2012), accusatorial interview methods significantly increase the odds of false confessions, but do not produce more confessions overall. Therefore, by banning accusatorial methods, the risk of false confessions and, indirectly, of wrongful convictions might be reduced without any loss in the efficiency of police interrogations. Given that false confessions often help produce wrongful convictions in America, this measure alone might significantly reduce the odds of innocent defendants being wrongfully convicted.

Make Appeals Work

A further step might be to make appeals to higher courts more efficient. In many ways, the mere availability of appeals can work as a sort of "quality control," comparable to what has been designed over the last decades in medical and other fields. A former study (Killias, 2008) came to the conclusion that in Switzerland, about one decision in four is brought before a higher court, and that one appeal in three is successful. These rates vary considerably across Europe, as do the powers of higher courts. In some countries (for example, France and England), the powers of higher courts are limited to legal issues and do not allow for the review of facts or sentences. In Germany, Switzerland, the Netherlands, Austria, Italy, and other countries with courts of appeal having wide powers to re-examine all relevant issues, decisions are often overturned for reasons that concern the sentence, rather than the verdict. Even so, lower courts may act more cautiously when they anticipate a high rate of successful appeals. Therefore, a well-developed system of appeals may act as a strong incentive to avoid judicial errors of all kinds.

Introduce or Generalize Quality Control Among Forensic Experts

Sometimes, experts are also a source of error in finding the relevant facts. Many observers suggest that experts should be "independent" of the police and/or the prosecution. Of course, it is unacceptable that prosecutors, for example, suppress unfavorable findings or oblige experts to streamline their conclusions in a way that suits their case. Beyond this independence (that should be self-evident), errors committed by experts are rarely the result of intentional manipulation, but rather of human error in the treatment of materials or in the statistical interpretation of the evidence (see Vuille, Biedermann, and Taroni, Chapter 8, this volume). How often do such errors occur? Schiffer (2009) reports the findings of an experimental test conducted with Bachelor's and Master's degree students of forensic science who were in their final year of studies at the University of Lausanne (Switzerland)—the people who will soon play the role of forensic expert in any of the police laboratories. The test included interpreting fingerprints. Among the 48 students, six erroneously excluded the person from whom the fingerprints had been taken and five identified an incorrect person as being the "suspect." The latter error obviously can have dramatic consequences. False exclusions can be just as devastating if, for example, a third party becomes the focus of investigators as a result. Obviously, confirmatory testing (and quality control) should become the routine procedure whenever the results of a forensic science expert are contested by the defendant or are otherwise inconsistent with the known facts of the case. Interestingly, coroners have far more thoroughly developed systems of quality control, pushed perhaps by similar trends in their medical environment, whereas police laboratories and forensic scientists have not yet fully embraced this trend (Schiffer, 2009). Finally, the physical evidence should be conserved for many years beyond the final settlement of the case. It has been noticed that the lower rates of exonerations in Europe might also be due to the fact that physical evidence often is destroyed once the case is definitively settled in court.

Allow Exonerations Whenever a Serious Error is Detected

The way in which systems deal with wrongful convictions—once it is discovered that an error has occurred—should also receive attention. Many countries, such as France (Dongois, 2008) are extremely restrictive as far as the admission of errors committed by the judicial system is concerned, whereas others—the United States, Germany (Peters, 1970–1974), and Switzerland are good examples—more generously grant exonerations. Obviously, errors occur under both the accusatorial and the inquisitorial systems, and legislators should anticipate this risk by making effective redress available. Once an exoneration is achieved, governments should obviously also provide fair compensation (see Zalman, Chapter 16, this volume) for the undue loss of liberty over many years, let alone all the other human costs produced by unjustified detention.

Reconsider Removing Statutes of Limitation

A final word of warning concerns the making of criminal law. In recent decades, statues of limitation have increasingly been challenged for a number of reasons. Whereas Anglo-Saxon law has always been skeptical about the mere idea of prescription, European legislators have, over the last decade, removed or restricted statutes of limitation to allow criminal prosecutions of more and more offenses decades after the relevant facts occurred. One argument is that with the introduction of DNA evidence, the guilt of a person can "eternally" be established and there is, therefore, no reason to limit criminal prosecutions to a certain number of years after the facts. Another concern is that many victims of crimes may, at the time of the offense, not be aware of what happened to them, and may, therefore, reach the point where they can file a complaint only years after the fact. This reason is invoked by victims of sexual abuse by former authority figures, but also increasingly by victims of diseases (for example, asbestos-related diseases) that break out years (or decades) after having been exposed to certain health risks. In such cases, there is good reason to presume a higher than usual risk of convicting factually innocent defendants. Years or decades after the alleged misbehavior, it often is still possible to establish that the defendant was in contact with the victim, or that the victim was exposed to certain health risks, whereas potentially exculpatory evidence may no longer be available. For example, the defendant may be innocent in the sense that he never engaged in reprehensible conduct toward the victim, but peers or other potential witnesses may no longer be available to testify in his favor. Similarly, the defendant may have taken all the precautions that were required by the circumstances 30 or more years ago, but it may no longer be possible to prove what he actually did. Beyond this, the conceptions about what constitutes appropriate or inappropriate behavior toward children, or how much is to be done to control certain health risks to employees, vary over time. This easily leads to a situation where the defendant's behavior will be assessed according to current knowledge and standards, rather than those that were considered adequate at that time. Unfortunately, legislators seldom consider the risks of wrongful convictions when changing statutes of limitation.

Conclusions

As we have seen, the risk of wrongfully convicting innocent defendants varies across systems. The observation that this risk may be higher under the accusatorial, compared to the inquisitorial system, obviously may not be very helpful. Defenders of both systems will react strongly to suggestions to "replace" one system with the other one, let alone that the substitution of one system by another one would represent a formidable task that would absorb a huge amount of energy for years to come. Why not try, therefore, to identify a number of features of both systems that contribute disproportionately to the risk of wrongful convictions? This has been suggested by Givelber (2001) when he advocated extending the rules of disclosure or to stop "penalizing" defendants for insisting on a trial. We can add to this list recommendations to change the style of police interrogations; restrict the scope of plea bargaining to cases of minor importance; hear defendants in all cases; and extend appeals to include both factual and sentencing issues. All these reforms seem to be feasible under both the accusatorial and the inquisitorial systems. In sum, the measures proposed here are likely to make criminal procedures less vulnerable to the defects of individual actors. There are and always will be incompetent defense lawyers, aggressive police officers, and ambitious prosecutors. The best we can do under both systems is to make them less critically important.

It is true that this list includes more suggestions on how the American (accusatorial) system might be amended than how Europeans might improve their inquisitorial approach. European nations have, much to the advantage of their systems, adopted many of the innovations of the Earl Warren Court era, such as the Miranda warnings, the right to counsel, and excluding evidence based on the "fruit of the poisonous tree" concept—a trend that has not changed the continental inquisitorial into an accusatorial system. Asking Americans to consider more thoroughly certain features of European criminal justice systems may, in the end, help to reduce wrongful convictions in the United States without harming due process rules. Preventing convictions of innocent defendants is, in the end, a valuable goal to pursue in itself, no matter where the ideas for improvement actually originated.

Notes

1   See the sentences meted out in Europe for the most common crimes in the *European Sourcebook of Crime and Criminal Justice Statistics 2010*, Tables 3.2.5.1–3.2.5.21.
2   Many European criminal codes provide for sanctions against this form of misbehavior by police officers, prosecutors, judges et al. (§§ 339–345 German Criminal Code, Art. 432–4 to 432–9 French Criminal Code, Art. 312 Swiss Criminal Code).
3   See Art. 438–443 of the Italian, § 257c of the German, and Art. 358–362 of the Swiss Code of Criminal Procedure as well as Art. 167 of the Dutch Law on Criminal Procedure. Most European countries have introduced similar "simplified" procedures over the last 20 years.
4   See the references in Footnote 2.

References

Brants C. (2008). The Vulnerability of Dutch Criminal Procedure to Wrongful Conviction. In C.R. Huff and M. Killias (Eds.), *Wrongful Conviction. International Perspectives on Miscarriages of Justice*, Philadelphia: Temple University Press, 157–182.

Dongois N. (2008). Wrongful Convictions in France: The Limits of "Pourvoi en Révision". In C.R. Huff and M. Killias (Eds.), *Wrongful Conviction. International Perspectives on Miscarriages of Justice*, Philadelphia: Temple University Press, 249–261.

European Sourcebook of Crime and Criminal Justice Statistics (2010). 4th edition. The Hague: Boom Juridische Uitgevers. www.europeansourcebook.org.

Gilliéron G. (2010). *Strafbefehlsverfahren und plea bargaining als Quelle von Fehlurteilen*. Zurich: Schulthess.

Givelber D. (2001). The Adversary System and Historical Accuracy: Can we do better? In S.D. Westervelt and J.A. Humphrey, *Wrongly convicted. Perspectives on Failed Justice*, New Brunswick/New Jersey/London: Rutgers University Press, 253–268.

Gross S.R., Jacoby K., Matheson D., Montgomery N., Patel S. (2005). *Exonerations in the United States 1989 through 2003*. University of Michigan, (unpublished paper).

Kessler I. (2008). A Comparative Analysis of Prosecution in Germany and the United Kingdom: Searching for Truth or Getting a Conviction? In C.R. Huff and M. Killias (Eds.), *Wrongful Conviction. International Perspectives on Miscarriages of Justice*, Philadelphia: Temple University Press, 213–247.

Killias M. (2008). Wrongful Convictions in Switzerland: The Experience of a Continental Law Country. In C.R. Huff and M. Killias (Eds.), *Wrongful Conviction. International Perspectives on Miscarriages of Justice*, Philadelphia: Temple University Press, 139–155.

Killias M., Gilliéron G., Dongois N. (2007). A survey of exonerations in Switzerland over ten years. Report to the Swiss National Science Foundation, Lausanne and Zurich: Universities of Lausanne and Zurich.

Meissner C.A., Redlich A.D., Bhatt S., Brandon S. (2012). Interview and interrogation methods and their effects on true and false confessions. www.campbellcollaboration. org.

Neubauer D.W. (2007). *Judicial Process: Law, Courts, and Politics in the United States*. Boston: Wadsworth.

Peters K. (1970–1974). *Fehlerquellen im Strafprozess. Eine Untersuchung der Wiederaufnahmever-fahren in der Bundesrepublik Deutschland*. (Sources of errors in criminal proceedings, A study of cases of successful petitions of revision in the Federal Republic of Germany.) 3 volumes, Karlsruhe: C. F. Müller 1970, 1972, 1974.

Pizzi W.T. (1999). *Trials without Truth*. New York/London: New York University Press.

Schiffer B. (2009). The relationship between forensic science and judicial error: A study covering error sources, bias and remedies. University of Lausanne, PhD dissertation.

Slobogin C. (2003). An Empirically Based Comparison of American and European Regulatory Approaches to Police Investigation. In P.J. van Koppen and S.D. Penrod (Eds.), *Adversarial versus Inquisitorial Justice. Psychological Perspectives on Criminal Justice Systems*, New York/Boston/Dordrecht/London/Moscow: Kluwer Academic, 27–54.

Stuntz W.J. (2011). *The Collapse of American Criminal Justice*. Cambridge (Mass.): Harvard University Press.

Thommen M. (2010). Unerhörte Strafbefehle. *Swiss Criminal Law Review* 128 (4), 373–393.

Van Koppen P.J., Penrod S.D. (2003). Adversarial or Inquisitorial. Comparing Systems. In P.J. van Koppen and S.D. Penrod (Eds.), *Adversarial versus Inquisitorial Justice. Psychological Perspectives on Criminal Justice Systems*, New York/Boston/Dordrecht/London/Moscow: Kluwer Academic, 1–19.

Vrij A. (2003). "We Will Protect Your Wife and Child, but Only if you Confess. Police Interrogations in England and the Netherlands." In P.J. van Koppen and S.D. Penrod (Eds.),

Adversarial versus Inquisitorial Justice. Psychological Perspectives on Criminal Justice Systems, New York/Boston/Dordrecht/ London/Moscow: Kluwer Academic, 55–79.

Zalman M. (2011). *Criminal Procedure. Constitution and Society*, Boston etc.: Prentice Hall.

Zalman M. (2012). Qualitatively Estimating the Incidence of Wrongful Convictions. *Criminal Law Bulletin* 48 (2), 221–277.

5
TRIAL AND ERROR
Brandon L. Garrett[1]

The Supreme Court has emphasized that "the trial is the paramount event for determining the guilt or innocence of the defendant." (Herrera v. Collins, 1993). On the other hand, the Court has noted that in our adversarial system, "the Constitution entitles a criminal defendant to a fair trial, not a perfect one" (Delaware v. Van Arsdall, 1986). While no trial may be completely "perfect," some trial errors are more harmful than others. With the benefit of modern DNA tests, we know that even at a seemingly "fair trial," an innocent person can be convicted. Every few weeks another innocent person is walked out of prison, freed by DNA testing on old evidence.

Looking back at the criminal trials of those innocent people, one might expect to find out that weak evidence was used to convict them, since, after all, they were not actually guilty. Perhaps jurors were swayed by sinister details of the rapes and murders with which the defendants were charged. However, when I read the transcripts of the trials of the first 250 people exonerated by DNA tests, while writing my book, *Convicting the Innocent*, I came to the conclusion that jurors were not always so wrong to convict based on the seemingly solid evidence that they heard (Garrett, 2011). Only years later did DNA tests show that this trial evidence was in fact deeply flawed. In retrospect, we can unravel how what the jurors saw was misleading. Grave errors were cemented before trial, during the criminal investigation, and crucial evidence was contaminated or even concealed, making cases seem far stronger than they should have been to the jurors.

Even seemingly powerful testimony by a trial witness—an informant recalling the defendant's confession, a detective describing a confession in custody, and an eyewitness pointing out the defendant from the stand—can be tainted by unreliable procedures commonly used by police across the country. A few representative examples from wrongful conviction cases illustrate flaws in our criminal procedure and how states can effectively reform criminal procedure to make our criminal trials less error prone.

Jailhouse Informants and Prosecutorial Misconduct

Jerry Watkins served 13 years for a murder he did not commit. In November 1984, an 11-year-old girl was found stabbed to death in a partially wooded field in Hancock County, Indiana. The autopsy indicated that she had been raped. She was Watkins's sister-in-law, and, despite a strong alibi, he was a suspect early on for a reason: He had been previously charged with molesting her. He had pleaded guilty to molestation, and a year later was in a holding cell, facing sentencing in nearby Marion County, Indiana.

There, a jailhouse informant was placed in Watkins's cell. The informant had just been convicted of forgery and burglary, but police apparently asked that sentencing be postponed pending his cooperation. The informant had a long list of aliases, prior convictions, and escapes from prison. He had a history of cooperating with the police in multiple states (Watkins Trial Transcript, 1987). At Watkins's criminal trial, he testified that he hadn't yet received any money from police in Indiana, but in Florida he was paid "by the kilo" in cocaine he helped police seize (*Id.* at 1076). He testified so frequently that he had hangers and clothes in his cell. He commented: "No one else has had clothes to wear to Court" (*Id.* at 1102).

He was placed in Watkins's cell and claimed he heard Watkins confess in detail to the murder. He described at trial how Watkins "was upset real bad, he was cryin'. He was holdin' the bible in his hands" (*Id.* at 1053). More powerful were the details about the crime. He said the victim was Watkins's "sister's little girl." "He said that he'd cut her throat. That he'd left her in some bushes in Hancock County." More specifically, he said "her jugular vein was cut"(*Id.* at 1058). The informant said that he had no prior knowledge of these details: "I hadn't heard anything about it either" (*Id.* at 1062).

The informant also denied that prosecutors made him any promises of leniency. He said: "They didn't promise to do anything. They said that after the trial was over . . . that they would talk to the people in Indianapolis and if there was any consideration or anything—it would be done" (*Id.* at 1065). The prosecutors denied at trial that there had been any deal. The informant had by the time of trial been sentenced, and a prosecutor testified that there was no consideration "whatsoever" given to the informant's cooperation in the Watkins case (*Id.* at 1921).

No other evidence connected Watkins to the crime. In fact, blood typing excluded him. The prosecution theory was that one man raped and killed the victim. The forensic analyst inaccurately suggested to the jury that the serology might be inconclusive, speculating that the blood group substances that excluded Watkins might be "erratic" or "spurious" or the result of bacterial contamination. Watkins also presented a detailed alibi at trial, and several alibi witnesses testified on his behalf. However, since the time of death could not be pinned down, he had to account for his whereabouts over several days.

Watkins also took the stand. He admitted to molesting the victim in the past, but denied committing a murder. He denied that he had ever confessed in jail, but recalled that "a man he did not know had been in the holding cell the day of his sentencing and had asked him lots of questions about his case." Watkins recalled that the informant "just kept buggin' me and buggin' me and buggin' me trying to see what he could get out of me," and that he finally "got tired of him askin' me so I told him" nothing more than "what charge I was in for" (*Id.* at 1737).

The jury also had more cause to doubt the informant's story. The defense presented another inmate at trial, who heard the informant describe "a scheme for getting out of jail. The plan was to find an unsolved crime, have a confederate research the newspaper coverage," and then tell police he heard the culprit confess. Prosecutors responded by introducing newspaper articles into evidence, and pointing out that none of them included details about how the victim was killed or the vegetation where her body was found.

During the closing arguments, the prosecutor admitted that the informant had testified for the police many times before, but insisted that in this case, "we've promised him nothing." He had argued: "Did he research it in the paper as has been intimated? I don't think so . . . it just couldn't happen." The prosecutor noted that the informant "knew about the jugular vein—something that was never in the paper." In addition, the informant had said Watkins admitted that he "left this little girl in the bushes, which was certainly an accurate statement" (*Id.* at 2172). This was information that the "public could not know, the public did not know" (*Id.* at 2224).

The defense lawyer in response agreed that the "jugular vein is a bombshell in this case," but countered that he could have heard that information from multiple sources or just assumed a fatal stabbing to the neck would have severed the jugular (*Id.* at 2189). The defense added that the informant "goes around the land peddling perjury," and was "a master of misinformation" who would "turn in his own mother if he thought he could get out of jail a day early" (*Id.* at 2190–91).

Jurors were clearly focused on the testimony of the jailhouse informant. During their deliberations, they asked to read his testimony again (*Id.* at 46). They found Watkins guilty, though the jury recommended against a death sentence. Watkins was sentenced to 60 years in prison for murder. After the trial, the defense introduced affidavits from two more men in the jail who said the informant had told them how police fed him the details about the crime. The court denied the motion for a new trial and Watkins's appeals were dismissed.

In 1992, Jerry Watkins obtained DNA testing that excluded him as the rapist. Remarkably, the Indiana Court of Appeals concluded that the DNA results were not sufficient to order his release, stating that they only "suggest the possibility" of another perpetrator and were merely "cumulative" of the trial evidence (Watkins v. State, 1996). In fact, the DNA conclusively showed that someone else, not Watkins, had raped the victim.

Meanwhile, a host of evidence of prosecutorial misconduct mounted. The jury had not heard the whole story—not even close. Evidence about other suspects had been concealed. So had evidence about a witness who gave a detailed and accurate description of what the victim was wearing and saw the victim abducted from a park in a black Camaro; Watkins had no such car. Several others gave statements that the informant admitted to making up his statements.

Watkins filed a federal habeas petition, again seeking to have his conviction overturned. The federal judge described how it had been uncovered that placing the informant in Watkins's cell had been contrary to a direct and "emphatic" order from the jail commander that this informant was not to be allowed outside his own cellblock (Watkins v. Miller, 2000). The informant had also recanted in an affidavit in which he said:

> That the State of Indiana did in fact pay (with promises) for this petitioner's testimony, and did in fact show him not only the "deathsite," but "grizzely" [sic] pictures of the murder in order to inflame this petitioner's feelings towards the defendant (Jerry Watkins), and thus secured (for the state) a statement from this petitioner that could, and was used to obtain a conviction (*Id.* at 852). He went on to say that he was cheated and that "the Courts [of] the (State of Indiana) and (Jerry Watkins) were cheated as well"(*Id.*). If it was true that police had shown the informant photographs of the dead victim and had taken him to the field where she had been killed, then they would have suborned perjury and actively participated in fabricating false testimony against Watkins.

The federal judge concluded that if this statement was true, it was "explosive" (*Id.* at 853). Records that the defense had never seen showed police had met with the informant several times at the jail just before Watkins was in the holding cell with him—and had taken the informant out of the jail, perhaps to see the "deathsite." If the informant had, in fact, received the "detailed information" about the murder from police or a prosecutor, "that information utterly destroys the state's case against Watkins" and it "described an intentional corruption of the criminal justice system." The judge noted that the prosecution had at trial brought in newspaper articles about the case to show that the jailhouse informant had "specific, correct knowledge that he could not have derived from newspaper articles" (*Id.*).

Although the court granted Watkins's habeas petition, the federal judge failed to ensure that the prosecutors who allegedly fed facts to the informant were appropriately sanctioned. The judge decided not to address whether the police and prosecutors had concealed the fact that they had offered the informant a deal and had fed him specific details of the crime. Although the judge concluded that the "prosecution's failure to disclose such information would amount to suborning perjury and corrupting the judicial process," he declined to investigate further.

Because the prosecutors had also concealed a host of other evidence (a *Brady* violation), the judge decided to reverse on that ground alone. He said that "[a] finding of such subornation of perjury would require more extensive proceedings and evidence than have been submitted here." He declined to investigate much less recommend that the prosecutor suffer any sanction for potentially grave ethical violations (*Id.*).

Meanwhile, prosecutors sought to appeal, and pushed for another round of more modern STR DNA tests. In 1999, Watkins had asked for STR DNA tests but prosecutors had said the evidence could not be found. In 2000, the materials were found and were tested. The results again excluded Watkins. Prosecutors finally dropped all charges against him and he was released. But the DNA did more. A DNA profile was entered into the Indiana State Police database. It matched another man who pled guilty to the sexual assault after prosecutors agreed to drop murder charges.

Watkins was far from the only person exonerated by DNA tests who was convicted based on false informant statements. Informant statements of several different kinds, including cellmates, codefendants, or cooperating witnesses, played a role in 20 percent of the first 250 DNA exoneration cases. These incentivized witnesses were concentrated in the murder cases. Just like in Watkins's case, almost all of the jailhouse informants claimed that exonerees admitted details about the crime that only the true culprit could have known. Many informants admitted receiving rewards from prosecutors for these lies, but in some cases it came to light years later that deals with the prosecution had been concealed from the defense.

Jailhouse informant testimony in particular is inherently suspect. If informant testimony is to be used as evidence in criminal trials, it should be carefully regulated to make sure that deals are not hidden, prior statements are carefully documented, and judges instruct jurors about the potential unreliability of informant testimony. Judges could also assess the reliability of informants before permitting them to testify. Prosecutors can themselves adopt guidelines requiring the careful use of informants and careful documentation of their statements and of any consideration to be provided in exchange for their cooperation. However, very few jurisdictions have adopted any of those protections (Williams, 2011).

Contaminated Confessions

In 1988, an elderly woman was killed in Rochester, New York, while out for a walk. The crime remained unsolved. Frank Sterling became a suspect and was interrogated alone, without a lawyer. Sterling waived his *Miranda* rights; when asked whether he agreed to waive, he answered "yeah" (Sterling Trial Transcript at 618–19, 1992). The interrogation began at 7 a.m and continued for 12 hours.

To try to get more out of him, an officer used a hypnotic-type "relaxation" technique where he lay down beside Sterling, held his hand, and they breathed deeply (*Id.* at 649–52). Sterling for the first time supposedly told the officer that the victim was wearing "a purple top, maybe two-toned, and dark pants" (*Id.* at 655). The officer also testified at trial that at the interrogation he had not yet looked at the photos and did not know what the victim was wearing (*Id.* at 658). But the other officer recalled they had already showed Sterling photos of the crime scene (*Id.* at 769).

In the last 20 minutes of the interrogation—the only portion that was video-recorded—Sterling appears utterly exhausted and distraught. It is difficult to watch that video with the knowledge that he is innocent. In the recorded portion of the questioning, he mentions three details that became crucial at trial: the location of the murder in brush by the side of a jogging trail, the victim's clothing and her purple jacket, and a BB gun found at the scene. Could Sterling, who we now know is innocent, have guessed those details?

Sterling later told *New York Magazine*, "They just wore me down . . . I was just so tired . . . It's like, 'Come on, guys, I'm tired—what do you want me to do, just confess to it?'" Sterling recalls he was never asked an open-ended question about what happened. Instead, he was asked leading questions and asked to answer "yes." "'Yes' and grunts—that's basically what the whole confession is about" (Kolker, 2010).

There were also inconsistencies that should have been a red flag to the detectives. For example, Sterling said the victim fell in the brush. Yet the crime scene evidence indicated that she was dragged a long distance to the place where her body was found. Sterling had an alibi; he was at work much of the day in question.

Sterling's defense lawyer asked the jury: "And do you feel in your stomach that this is reliable? That this is free of suggestion? That this is voluntary?" Prosecutors responded: "Truthful? How does the defendant know it's a purple jacket or purple top? A guess? [The police] never released to the media . . . the purple jacket."

Sterling tried to appeal, arguing another man had committed the crime. The judge rejected his motion. "Only Sterling confessed to authorities," read the judge's decision. "Only Sterling had a motive . . . Only Sterling knew facts that had not been publicized." Sterling spent nearly 19 years in prison before DNA exonerated him and inculpated another man (Kolker, 2010).

Frank Sterling was not alone. In 26 percent of the first 250 DNA exonerations, innocent defendants made incriminating statements, delivered outright confessions, or pleaded guilty. In 16 percent (40 cases) of the exonerations, innocent defendants falsely confessed. All but two of the 40 DNA exonerees who falsely confessed were said to have confessed in detail. As in Sterling's case, 23 of those 40 false confessions were recorded, but only in part, usually just a confession statement at the end of a long interrogation. What the jurors heard was seemingly irrefutable evidence that those individuals had confessed when they offered police details that only the true culprit could have known. In eight cases, the confessions were thought to be such powerful evidence of guilt that the defendants were convicted despite DNA tests at trial that excluded them.

Police are supposed to be carefully trained never to contaminate a confession by disclosing key details to the suspect. During the interrogation "[w]hat should be sought particularly are facts that would only be known by the guilty person." Thus police are trained to ask open questions, like "What happened next?" And "the truthfulness of a confession should be questioned, however, when the suspect is unable to provide any corroboration beyond the statement, 'I did it'" (Inbau et. al., 2001). However, detectives may themselves lose track of who said what during complex interrogations lasting many hours and using psychologically coercive tactics. Absent a recording of the entire interrogation, it may be impossible to unravel what transpired.

Perhaps because of the way that detailed facts were incorporated into the confessions, judges rejected challenges to the confessions at trial. Of those 40 exonerees who falsely confessed, 14 were mentally retarded or borderline and three more (at least) were mentally ill. Thirteen were juveniles. All but four were interrogated for more than three hours. Seven described their involvement as coming to them in a "dream" or "vision." Seven were told they failed polygraph tests. Several described threats or physical force. In addition, like Sterling, all waived their *Miranda* rights. Despite the long interrogations they endured and the heightened vulnerability of those who were juveniles or mentally disabled, judges rejected motions to suppress the confessions.

Recording of interrogations should be mandatory. A record of who said what during an interrogation can help prevent wrongful convictions like that of Frank Sterling. Recording can also increase the reliability of confessions as evidence. More than 750 law enforcement jurisdictions across the United States are voluntarily recording interrogations. Studies have shown that once recording becomes standard practice, police officers and prosecutors become strong supporters of the reform. After all, a taped record can mean fewer motions to suppress and fewer claims that suspects were unduly deceived or abused. In addition to requiring recording of interrogations, judges should also conduct hearings to carefully evaluate those recordings to assess the reliability of interrogations before allowing them in court. Recording interrogations protects the innocent, aids police and prosecutors, and provides judges and jurors with the clearest evidence of what transpired during the interrogation process. Still more should be done to regulate confessions. We should carefully examine some of the psychologically coercive techniques used to interrogate suspects in the United States, and improve screening of psychologically vulnerable individuals at police stations, and reconsider the role of judges when reviewing the admissibility of confession evidence.

The New Jersey Supreme Court and Eyewitness Misidentifications

McKinley Cromedy's case would, in its way, lead to the most thorough reconsideration of the rules surrounding eyewitness identifications in the United States. At his trial, Cromedy's defense lawyer argued that his client had been misidentified by the victim of a rape, telling the jury in the opening statement that "the evidence will show, not that she's a liar, but that she's mistaken, that her identification is wrong and it's a misidentification" (Cromedy Trial Transcript, 182, 1994).

The victim, a white college student, had been raped by a black man in her apartment. A few days later, she had helped a police artist draw a composite sketch of a black man with a full face and a moustache, and she looked at thousands of photos of black men who had been arrested. One of those photos was of Cromedy. In fact, the police had him in mind as a suspect because he had been seen in the area, but she did not identify him.

Almost eight months after the rape, she saw Cromedy crossing the street. She thought he was her attacker because of his appearance, but also because of his unusual way of walking due to a limp—"a swagger," as she put it (*Id.* at 104). She called the police, who called her back 15 minutes later to say that they had picked up a man matching her description. She then went to the police station and positively identified Cromedy as her attacker. The police officer explained, "I've had a lot of experience with identifications and I'm not going to lead somebody. I asked her to see if she recognized this person" (*Id.* at 142). Yet she was not given a lineup to test her memory. She was asked to identify Cromedy by viewing him one-on-one from behind one-way glass—a show-up.

Cromedy's lawyer argued that the identification was improper, saying that the show-up was "like true or false, and to me that is about as suggestive as a procedure you can have . . . She knows somebody was picked up. What could be more suggestive?" However, the judge ruled that the identification was admissible, emphasizing that "she was very certain of her identification"(*Id.* at 164, 168). Following the U.S. Supreme Court's ruling in *Manson v. Brathwaite*, an eyewitness identification that was the product of suggestive procedures, such as this one, may still be admitted based on a set of "reliability" factors, including the apparent confidence of the eyewitness (Manson v. Brathwaite, 1977). That test has been discredited by decades of social science research demonstrating that factors such as confidence do not correspond with reliability at all. The memory of an eyewitness must be handled sensitively because it is highly malleable. In fact, the apparent confidence of an eyewitness may be just a byproduct of suggestive police procedures.

Moreover, psychologists have long found that eyewitnesses have particular trouble identifying persons of the opposite race. The defense lawyer asked for a special jury instruction, asking the jury to consider "whether the cross-racial nature of the identification has affected the accuracy of the witness's original perception and/or accuracy of a subsequent identification." The trial judge denied the request (State v. Cromedy, 1999).

The jury saw the victim describe her ordeal on the stand and, finally, point to Cromedy in the courtroom and agree she was "absolutely sure" he was her attacker. The jury convicted Cromedy and he was sentenced to 60 years in prison. On appeal, though, the New Jersey Supreme Court reversed his conviction. The court ruled in 1999 that "forty years" of empirical studies documented a heightened risk of error when white eyewitnesses try to identify black subjects. The court noted that some courts, such as in California, Massachusetts, and Utah, had permitted such instructions. The court ruled that under the facts of Cromedy's case, it was reversible error not to instruct the jury about "the possible significance of the cross-racial identification factor" (*Id.* at 120, 132).

The court reversed Cromedy's conviction without knowing that he was innocent. After the ruling, however, the prosecution agreed to conduct DNA tests. The results excluded him and he was exonerated. The victim later commented, "I couldn't believe that I was wrong" (Avril, 2006).

What made the response to the wrongful conviction of McKinley Cromedy even more remarkable was that the state of New Jersey then embarked on a project of revamping its criminal procedure rules. The New Jersey attorney general's office issued guidelines to all law enforcement agencies in the state requiring that detailed procedures be followed when eyewitnesses are asked to identify a suspect (Office of the Attorney General, 2001). These guidelines were a landmark reform. New Jersey became the first state in the country to adopt double-blind lineups. No longer would the officer administering the procedure know who the suspect is. Other best practices long recommended by social scientists were adopted. All lineups would use sequential photo arrays, where photos are shown one at a time to prevent "comparison shopping." Eyewitnesses were to be instructed that the perpetrator might not appear in the lineup. The results were to be recorded, including the witnesses' certainty at the time of the identification procedure.

In 2006, the court expanded this rule to require that police similarly record or document all eyewitness identifications. The court noted, "Misidentification is widely recognized as the single greatest cause of wrongful convictions in this country" (State v. Delgado, 2006). In 2007, the court adopted a model jury instruction charging all jurors not to rely on "the confidence level" of an eyewitness, at least not "standing alone." Jurors are cautioned: "Although nothing may appear more convincing than a witness's categorical identification of a perpetrator, you must critically analyze such testimony. Such identifications, even if made in good faith, may be mistaken" (State v. Romero, 2007).

Finally, the court asked that a special master explore something more fundamental: the U.S. Supreme Court's *Manson v. Brathwaite* test for evaluating admissibility of eyewitness identifications. The special master held hearings, with the participation of the New Jersey Office of the Public Defender, the New Jersey attorney general, the New Jersey Association of Criminal Defense Lawyers, and the Innocence Project at Cardozo Law School, and recommended that the court adopt a new test for evaluating eyewitness identification evidence and require pretrial hearings to evaluate all eyewitness identifications. The New Jersey Supreme Court issued its ruling in that case, *State v. Henderson*, in August 2011, and established a comprehensive social science framework for regulating eyewitness identifications in the courtroom (State v. Henderson, 2011). The decision provides a national model for how to ensure that sound lineups are conducted in the first instance, rigorously evaluate the reliability of eyewitness evidence pretrial, and carefully instruct jurors about the factors affecting the reliability of eyewitness evidence at trial.

Most other states have not yet followed suit. For example, in Kirk Bloodsworth's case, the first death row DNA exoneration, the Court of Appeals of Maryland had upheld the trial court's refusal to allow expert testimony on the dangers of eyewitness misidentifications. The trial judge excluded this testimony on the grounds that such evidence would be unnecessary and would "confuse or mislead" the jury (Bloodsworth v. State, 1985). We now know, of course, that the jury was in fact gravely misled when it believed the eyewitnesses in Bloodsworth's case. Other judges have become more open to questioning reliability of eyewitness identifications by providing juries with cautionary instructions concerning eyewitness error, or admitting expert testimony explaining social science research concerning misidentifications.

Seven states—Connecticut, Illinois, Maryland, North Carolina, Ohio, West Virginia, and Wisconsin—have passed statutes in response to these misidentifications. The statutes vary—the North Carolina and Ohio statutes are the most specific in requiring that best practices be adopted for eyewitness identifications. Other states have recommended best practices and studied the problem further, while still more local jurisdictions and departments have adopted voluntary guidelines. All of this marks the beginning of a sea change. Traditionally, police had no written procedures on identifications, and, worse, they routinely used unreliable and suggestive lineups. However, it is police who are harmed most in the first instance when eyewitnesses choose known innocent fillers, which they do more than 30 percent of the time, according to available archival and field studies (Wells et al., 2011). Poor lineup procedures can cause irreparable harm to investigations when eyewitnesses are "burned" or have their credibility damaged by having picked out fillers. In addition, because so many DNA exonerations involve eyewitness misidentifications, and because decades of social science research support the use of double-blind and well-documented lineups, police will likely continue to adopt improved procedures. It is crucial that they do so. Nor should our constitutional criminal procedure permit grossly suggestive procedures so long as the identification appears "reliable." Judges should impose consequences if the police fail to ensure that sound identification procedures are used. Following the New Jersey *Henderson* model, judges can evaluate identifications in pretrial hearings, consider excluding the evidence or part of it, and, when admitting it at trial, they should provide jurors with careful instructions on the relevant factors affecting the accuracy of eyewitness memory, and also permit experts to testify and explain those factors.

Conclusions

Each of the types of evidence discussed—jailhouse informant testimony, confession testimony, and eyewitness testimony—share a common problem. The jury may hear confident witnesses describing seemingly powerful evidence, but they cannot tell how police and prosecutors may have shaped the testimony, even inadvertently. As I describe in *Convicting the Innocent*, other types of trial evidence that contributed to convictions of the innocent, such as forensic evidence, share the same character. Shoddy defense lawyering, prosecutorial and police misconduct, and deferential judicial review can further contribute to such errors. Errors can be introduced early on in the criminal process, and detecting them later is incredibly difficult. Errors may become intertwined and mutually reinforcing. Once an informant statement is contaminated, once facts are disclosed in the interrogation room, or once a suggestion is made to an eyewitness, the opportunity to learn the truth may be lost. These innocent people were the lucky ones in one way, despite the ordeals they suffered, since DNA tests could later be done to free them. That is not true of the vast majority of criminal convictions, which do not involve usable DNA evidence. While these wrongful convictions are the tip of a much larger iceberg, we can learn from patterns of error in these trials to make our criminal justice system more accurate.

Note

1   This chapter is adapted from an article written for the Winter 2012 issue of the ABA's magazine, *Criminal Justice*, which in turn reported some of the data from my book, *Convicting the Innocent: Where Criminal Prosecutions Go Wrong* (Harvard University Press, 2011). A resource website presenting underlying materials and data appendices is available at http://www.law.virginia.edu/html/librarysite/garrett_innocent.htm.

References

Avril, T. (May 22, 2006). Eyewitness' Blind Spot. *Philadelphia Inquirer.*

Garrett, Brandon L. (2011). *Convicting the Innocent: Where Criminal Prosecutions Go Wrong.* Cambridge, MA, Harvard University Press.

Inbau, Fred E. et al. (2001). *Criminal Interrogations and Confessions.* 4th Edn., Sudbury, MA: Jones and Bartlett 367, 425.

Kolker, Roger (October 3, 2010). "I Did It: Why Do People Confess to Crimes They Didn't Commit?," *New York Magazine.*

Office of the Attorney General, N.J. Department of Law and Public Safety (April 18, 2001). *Attorney General Guidelines for Preparing and Conducting Photo and Live Lineup Identification Procedures.*

Trial transcript, Jerry E. Watkins v. State of Indiana, 3CSCC-87C8-CB0764 (Ind. Sup. Ct. Aug. 1987).

Trial transcript, People v. Frank Sterling, Ind. No. 91-0624 (N.Y. County Ct., September 17, 1992).

Trial transcript, State of New Jersey v. McKinley Cromedy, Ind. No. 1243-07-93 (N.J. Sup. Ct., July 27, 1994).

Wells, Gary, Steblay, Nancy K., Dysart, Jennifer E. (2011). *A Test of the Simultaneous vs. Sequential Lineup Methods: An Initial Report of the AJS National Eyewitness Indentification Field Studies,* American Judicature Society, available at www.ajs.org/wc/pdfs/EWID_Printfriendly.pdf.

Williams, Carol (August 1, 2011). "Gov. Brown Signs Law Weakening Testimony of Jailhouse Snitches." *Los Angeles Times.*

Cases

Bloodsworth v. State, 512 A.2d 1056, 1062 (Md. 1985).

Delaware v. Van Arsdall, 475 U.S. 673, 681 (1986).

Herrera v. Collins, 506 U.S. 390, 416 (1993).

Manson v. Brathwaite, 432 U.S. 98 (1977).

State v. Cromedy, 727 A.2d 457 (N.J. 1999).

State v. Delgado, 188 N.J. 48, 62–63 (2006).

State v. Henderson, 2011 WL 3715028 (N.J. 2011).

State v. Romero, 191 N.J. 59, 76 (2007).

Watkins v. Miller, 92 F. Supp. 2d 824, 834 (S.D. Ind. 2000).

Watkins v. State, No. 30A04–9504–PC–118, 1996 WL 42093 (Ind. App. January 29, 1996).

6

THE PROSECUTOR AND WRONGFUL CONVICTIONS

MISPLACED PRIORITIES, MISCONDUCT, IMMUNITY, AND REMEDIES

Jim Petro and Nancy Petro

Many believe that, with regard to responsibility for outcomes in criminal justice, the buck stops with the prosecutor,[1] arguably the most powerful official in the U.S. criminal justice system. Three hundred[2] DNA-proven wrongful convictions have prompted recommended best practices in criminal justice procedures that promise to reduce conviction error. While these important changes will likely impact all players in the system and the entire process from investigation to sentencing, efforts to reduce error and optimize fairness and accuracy in criminal justice must include a comprehensive examination of the prosecutor.

Revelations of prosecutorial overreach and misconduct in wrongful convictions,[3] coupled with perceived growth in the prosecutor's power (as more and more cases are settled in plea bargaining without going to trial)[4] have prompted concern over the rightful role of prosecutors and the doctrine of absolute immunity, the broad liability protection they enjoy.

This chapter will:

(1) share my (Jim Petro's) personal encounter with prosecutorial power;
(2) examine the rightful role of the public prosecutor;
(3) discuss prosecutorial failings and misconduct revealed in wrongful convictions;
(4) review recent court rulings on prosecutorial immunity;
(5) consider remedies to prosecutorial misconduct.

A Personal Encounter with Prosecutorial Power

In 2005, I learned first-hand of the authority of a county prosecutor. I was serving as the elected Attorney General of Ohio. Yet, I could not correct a terrible DNA-proven conviction error. It took more advocacy, irrefutable evidence, and public pressure—resources many convicts cannot muster— before the prosecutor finally recommended that the jurisdiction's judge vacate the verdict and release an innocent man.

My awakening to both wrongful conviction and prosecutorial power came via a phone call received in September 2005 from a respected colleague, State Representative Bill Seitz, a conservative Republican from Cincinnati. He introduced Mark Godsey, a professor at the University of Cincinnati Law School and Director of the Ohio Innocence Project. Godsey was thinking outside the box in seeking my assistance on behalf of his client, an Ohio inmate who had been convicted of murder and child rape. The attorney general is the state's top public lawyer for civil cases against the state and also provides significant prosecutorial and investigative support services for county prosecutors and local law enforcement. Attorneys general are generally viewed as being on the "other side" of criminal defense or innocence attorneys such as Mark Godsey.

However, Representative Seitz knew that I believed that DNA was the most reliable form of evidence. A major initiative of our office was the collection and entry into CODIS, the national database of criminal DNA, of more than 200,000 DNA samples from Ohio convicts. I was not surprised when the effort solved dozens of cold cases and contributed to resolution in hundreds more in the ensuing years. However, I did not anticipate that DNA was about to shake the foundations of my assumptions about criminal justice.

Mark Godsey explained that DNA testing of crime scene evidence had excluded Clarence Elkins, a family man with no prior record, who was serving a life sentence for the rape/murder of his mother-in-law and the rape of his niece. The DNA also identified the true perpetrator, an imprisoned Ohio felon, who had lived a few doors from the crime. Yet, Godsey had no confidence that the jurisdiction's prosecutor, who had inherited the case after Elkins's conviction, would respond with an appropriate new look at the case. In fact, thus far the Innocence Project team had met with only resistance, denial, and opposition in the face of strong evidence of a conviction error.

After thoroughly reviewing the case—and asking the same of my Chief Deputy for Criminal Justice, a seasoned prosecutor—we came to the conclusion that Clarence Elkins was indeed innocent. Because I had been taught as a young prosecutor that my job was to seek the truth, I presumed that a call to the prosecutor would elicit cooperation in getting this matter quickly resolved. However, every attempt we made to discuss the case or meet with the prosecutor or her assistant was rebuffed. The release of Clarence Elkins was delayed by months, because the prosecutor apparently perceived her duty as defending a conviction rather than seeking the truth.

An unnecessary public debate between the prosecutor and our office, the utilization of the bully pulpit of my office, and media attention on this clear miscarriage of justice, eventually prompted the appropriate response, which came in the form of an unannounced fax to my office. A copy of the court's order to vacate Clarence Elkins's conviction appeared with no advance notice or acknowledgment that this battle would have been unnecessary if all in the system had shared the goal of seeking the truth.

In the face of the DNA evidence, the true perpetrator pled guilty, which extended his prison term to life. Tragically, he had been convicted of three child rapes committed while the innocent Elkins languished in prison.

This case was not only my awakening to wrongful conviction but also to the threat to justice posed by prosecutors who place winning and protecting a conviction above seeking the truth.

The Rightful Role of the Public Prosecutor

The prosecutor's role—as both the state's advocate seeking to convict criminals and as our true minister of justice seeking the truth—is only conflicted when one veers from the priority responsibility as defined in this clear dictum from the ABA Standards of Criminal Justice (American Bar Association 3d. ed.): "The duty of the prosecutor is to seek justice, not merely to convict."

The American system of justice challenges prosecutors every day to keep their priorities in the right order. The adversarial system that relies on a competitive presentation by the prosecution and the defense can easily distract advocates from the quest for truth in the courtroom.

Many prosecutors and judges serve at the pleasure of the voting public. The perception that voters want prosecutors and judges to be tough on crime discourages reassessment of a case at every stage of the process and especially post-conviction.

The overarching responsibility of the prosecutor to seek the truth is particularly important in view of the credibility afforded the prosecutor as the state's lawyer. In spite of our system's professed commitment to consider persons innocent until proven guilty, many presume that the state would not bring an action against a person without strong cause. This places a moral obligation on the prosecutor not to permit competitiveness—or strong belief in the guilt of the suspect—to prompt improper leveraging of this public trust or any compromise in fair presentation of the evidence.

I am in the camp of those who believe that much of the responsibility for the accuracy of the criminal justice system rightfully rests with the prosecutor. Equipped with both college and law degrees, the prosecutor must make the first critical decision of whether or not evidence in a case supports a criminal charge.

Both tunnel vision—in criminal justice, the tendency to focus on a particular suspect or crime theory to the exclusion of other suspects, theories, or contradicting evidence—and a rush to judgment have often contributed to wrongful convictions. These human tendencies—to see what we want to see and rush to closure—can prematurely focus an investigation. Prosecutors may be driven to tunnel vision by public pressure to solve cases quickly, by the press of case overloads, and by cynicism born of constant exposure to crime and criminals.

So prevalent are these recognized blinders to truth that numerous cognitive biases have been identified and defined. For example, Keith Findley (Findley, 2010), Clinical Professor of Law at the University of Wisconsin Law School, in his article "Tunnel Vision" describes "confirmation bias" as "the tendency to seek or interpret evidence in ways that support existing beliefs, expectations, or hypothesis" (as cited in Nickerson, 1998; Trope and Liberman, 1996); and "belief perseverance" as the common tendency to be "disinclined to relinquish initial conclusions or beliefs, even when the bases for those initial beliefs have been undermined" (as cited in Burke, 2006; Lieberman and Arndt, 2000).

These human tendencies frequently demonstrated in wrongful convictions are more understandable—although equally worthy of concern—in police officers, who are focused on investigating details and building a case.

As a former prosecutor who had to make the tough decisions of whether or not to pursue a conviction, I believe that the prosecutor's responsibilities include standing back and providing a fresh set of eyes on the collected evidence. The prosecutor must recognize human tendencies to rush to judgment, to have tunnel vision, and to place a higher value on evidence that supports the crime theory. The prosecutor must make an independent evaluation of the reliability of each piece of evidence; insist upon more evidence in a weak case; and question any inconsistencies with the crime theory.

In two cases of wrongful conviction that engaged our office while I was Ohio attorney general, police officers had identified the suspect within a few hours of the crime and appeared to have focused their efforts on building a case for prosecuting this suspect (both were convicted but eventually exonerated through DNA).[5]

Each wrongful conviction provides lessons that can help reduce conviction errors. For example, tunnel vision and a rush to judgment were apparent in hindsight in the Clarence Elkins case. Elkins was arrested within a few hours of the crime and was convicted on the eyewitness testimony of his six-year-old niece. Because the little girl knew her uncle, the evidence at first glance seems conclusive. However, a wrongful conviction may have been prevented if the limited evidence in the case had prompted a pause and questions. How convincing was the young girl's first "identification"? In fact her first reference when reporting the crime in a voice-mail message just after awakening and finding her deceased grandmother was that "someone" killed her grandmother. She did not mention "Uncle Clarence" in this most important first recollection.

How reliable was the identification when made by a little girl who was savagely assaulted in the dark of night, beaten to unconsciousness, and left for dead? Where was the collaborating physical evidence? No blood, semen, hair, or other evidence was found in Elkins's cars or home, which were thoroughly searched within a few hours of the brutal crime. And what about Elkins's alibis that would have made committing the crime nearly an hour's drive away virtually impossible?

While many forces can prompt prosecutors to lose sight of their first obligation to seek the truth, the U.S. Supreme Court has made clear (in *Berger v. United States*, 295 U.S.) the importance of this solemn duty, uniquely imbued in the prosecutor's position of largely unchecked power:

> The United States Attorney is the representative not of an ordinary party to a controversy, but of a sovereignty whose obligation to govern impartially is as compelling as its obligation to govern at all; and whose interest, therefore, in a criminal prosecution is not that it shall win a case, but that justice shall be done. As such, he is in a peculiar and very definite sense the servant of the law, the twofold aim of which is that guilt shall not escape or innocence suffer. He may prosecute with earnestness and vigor—indeed he should do so. But, while he may strike hard blows, he is not at liberty to strike foul ones. It is as much his duty to refrain from improper methods calculated to produce a wrongful conviction as it is to use every legitimate means to bring about a just one.

Prosecutorial Failings and Misconduct

Americans generally assume that prosecutors are well-intentioned public servants who would never knowingly seek to convict an innocent. Historically, wrongful conviction has been considered an extremely rare event, and the occasional conviction error was accepted as unavoidable human error. It has been only through study of DNA-proven wrongful convictions that the commonly held myth—wrongful convictions are the result of innocent human error[6]—has been challenged with the revelation that some police officers and some prosecutors contributed to wrongful convictions through misconduct. The Innocence Project reported (West, 2010) that in 65 of the first 255 DNA exonerations, appeals and/or civil lawsuits alleged prosecutorial misconduct. In 31 of these cases the courts confirmed prosecutorial misconduct or error. In 18 percent of the cases claiming prosecutorial misconduct, courts overturned the conviction or ruled the misconduct harmful.

A report on the National Registry of Exonerations (Gross and Shaffer, 2012) shared data of official misconduct over a larger sampling of wrongful convictions. This included prosecutorial and police misconduct and noted challenges in identifying official misconduct:

> Misbehavior is rarely advertised. If misconduct is not uncovered in litigation or by journalists, we don't know about it. As a result, our data underestimate the frequency of official misconduct, as we've mentioned. The misconduct we do know about occurs in 42% of all exonerations (368/873), including 56% of homicide cases (232/416), 35% of child sex abuse cases (36/102), but only 18% (37/203) of sexual assault cases. It is likely that misconduct by police or prosecutors or both is more common in homicide exonerations than others for reasons we've discussed: Homicides are more important than other crimes, and often also more difficult to investigate and prosecute, so the temptation to lie and cheat is unusually strong. Perjury and false confessions are both more common in homicide cases than sexual assault cases; perjury by government agents *is* official misconduct, and both of these types of false statements may be obtained by misconduct.
>
> (p. 67)

Failure to meet the requirement to share with the defense information that supports the suspect's innocence, as established in *Brady v. Maryland* (1963); knowingly using unreliable snitches; coercing witnesses; knowingly utilizing questionable forensic science or scientists; withholding information from timely delivery to the defense; accepting coerced confessions; purposely misleading jurors; and other unethical, overreaching tactics cannot be classified as "human error."

The temptation to ignore ethical boundaries can be significant not only because prosecutors are encouraged by voters to be tough on crime, but also because they have rarely been held accountable for misdeeds. The doctrine of absolute immunity that protects prosecutors from liability has resulted in very few instances in which prosecutors have been held accountable for wrongful conviction, even in cases in which their actions have been tantamount to framing a person. Sanctions in the form of judicial tongue-lashings and court reversals or other rulings that negatively impact cases are applied unevenly and infrequently enough to discourage hesitation for prosecutors willing to take the risk of overreach.

A landmark study highlighted both the troubling frequency of prosecutorial misconduct and the lack of sanctions to discourage it. *Preventable Error: A Report on Prosecutorial Misconduct in California 1997–2009*, a research project of the Northern California Innocence Project (NCIP), involved a comprehensive analysis of 4,000 publicly available cases of allegations of prosecutorial misconduct in California. Of these, the courts rejected about 75 percent of the misconduct allegations; did not comment directly on misconduct but ruled 282 of the cases had been fair; and identified 707 cases as including prosecutorial misconduct. In 548 of these, courts ruled that the misconduct was "harmless" and that the defendants had received a fair trial. According to the report, in the remaining 159 cases in which the courts deemed the misconduct harmful, "they either set aside the conviction or sentence, declared a mistrial or barred evidence" (Ridolfi and Possley, 2010, p. 3).

And what sanctions did the prosecutors face as a result of identified prosecutorial misconduct? Between January 1997 and September 2009, only 6 disciplinary actions were reported against prosecutors handling criminal cases. The bottom line: "The State Bar publicly disciplined only one percent of the prosecutors in the 600 cases in which the courts found prosecutorial misconduct and the NCIP identified the prosecutor" (Ridolfi, and Possley, 2010, p. 3). The NCIP study identified ways in which prosecutors improperly questioned witnesses or engaged in improper argument, such as:

> eliciting inadmissible evidence in witness examination; vouching for a witness's truthfulness; testifying for an absent witness; misstating the law; arguing facts not in evidence; mischaracterizing evidence; shifting the burden of proof; impugning the defense; arguing inconsistent theories of prosecution; appealing to religious authority; offering personal opinion; engaging in discriminatory jury selection; intimidating a witness; violating the defendant's Fifth Amendment right to silence; presenting false evidence; and failure to disclose exculpatory evidence.
>
> (p. 25)

The NCIP study importantly reported that about 97 percent of California's felony cases were not included in this look at prosecutorial misconduct, because they never went to trial. They were settled primarily by guilty pleas (Ridolfi and Possley, 2010, p. 3).

Many observers have noted that prosecutors have become even more powerful in recent decades as a result of the nation's evolution to more tough-on-crime sentencing mandates and policies such as "three strikes and you're out." Today, plea bargains resolve the vast majority of criminal cases. While plea bargains provide essential efficiency and often a reasonable result, critics note that the prosecutor, with the authority to threaten long sentences and offer shorter ones, has become judge and jury in these cases. We now know that some innocent people plead guilty or confess to crimes they didn't commit rather than risk a draconian sentence. It's illogical to assume that prosecutorial overreach and misconduct in the trial setting doesn't also impact plea negotiations, which are not generally within the purview of the public.

Among intentional abuses is the failure of prosecutors to comply with *Brady v. Maryland* (1963), which is sometimes accompanied by failure of the courts consistently to enforce the *Brady* requirement, namely that prosecutors must disclose to the defense any evidence favorable to the defendant, whether it is material to the question of guilt or to the punishment.

Judges need to put muscle back into *Brady*. As long as courts continue to identify *Brady* violations but then resort to an after-the-verdict, on-appeal, rearview appraisal of whether or not the undisclosed evidence would have been material to the outcome of the trial—often ruling that the error was immaterial or harmless—and as long as bar associations provide virtually no sanctions for prosecutors who violate *Brady*, prosecutors will take the limited risk of non-disclosure or will not feel compelled to characterize evidence conservatively as "significant enough" to be subject to *Brady*.

Recent Court Rulings on Prosecutorial Immunity

As evidence of prosecutorial misconduct has been revealed in wrongful convictions, lawsuit challenges are prompting courts to reconsider absolute immunity. Recent rulings reveal the difficulties in providing absolute immunity for public prosecutors who are acting in good faith while also providing remedy for those citizens who have been victims of intentional prosecutorial misconduct.

On November 9, 2009, the U.S. Supreme Court heard arguments in a case that was detailed in decisions of both the U.S. Court of Appeals and the Iowa Supreme Court. Terry Harrington, 19, a star Nebraska high school football player, lost his shot at an athletic scholarship, a college education, and pursuit of happiness, when he was convicted of the murder of a retired police captain who was working at a car dealership just over the state line in Council Bluffs, Iowa. Harrington and Curtis McGhee, both black, were convicted by an all-white jury on the testimony of a 16-year-old with a criminal record, who may have felt that he was in danger of being charged himself with the crime. His initial testimony was laced with inaccuracies, but with promises that he would not be charged and might receive financial assistance, the teen eventually fingered Harrington and McGhee, who were convicted.

In 2003, after Harrington had served 25 years of a life sentence, his conviction was reversed by the Iowa Supreme Court, which noted that the prosecutor had failed his obligation to reveal to the defense another credible suspect in the case. Numerous reports by Council Bluffs police referenced the alternative suspect, a white man, who had been a suspect in a former homicide and was a relative of the city fire department captain. The court also indicated that the key witness in the case was "a liar and a perjurer" (*Harrington v. State of Iowa*, p. 17).

Eventually, the witnesses recanted their testimony against Harrington and McGhee. The charges against Harrington were dropped and he was released. McGhee, who had recently pled no contest in a plea deal in which he agreed to testify against Harrington in a proposed retrial, was sentenced to time served and also released.

Both men filed a civil lawsuit in which they alleged the prosecutors helped assemble false evidence to convict them. The prosecutors claimed absolute immunity. The district court found, and the Court of Appeals agreed, that absolute immunity does not extend to "the actions of a County Attorney who violates a person's substantive due process rights by obtaining, manufacturing, coercing and fabricating evidence before filing formal charges, because this is not 'a distinctly prosecutorial function'" (*McGhee v. Pottawattamie County Iowa*, Nos. 07-1453, 07-1524, November 21, 2008, US 8th Circuit).

The prosecutors then appealed to the United States Supreme Court, and oral arguments were heard. However, as the *Des Moines Register* reported, before the high court ruled, a settlement was reached in which Pottawattamie County agreed to pay $7.03 million to Terry Harrington and $4.97 million to Curtis McGhee Jr. In exchange, the two men agreed to drop the lawsuit against the county.

While the settlement precluded the Supreme Court from ruling on whether or not prosecutorial immunity extends to conduct prior to trial and to malicious deceit alleged in this case, Rob Warden, executive director of the Center on Wrongful Convictions at Northwestern University School of Law, implied that the case might still send a cautionary message. "This means that prosecutors who step outside their traditional role and who act as investigators can still be subject to civil rights lawsuits just as police would be," he said (Petro and Petro, 2011, p. 133; Rood, 2010).

The question of prosecutorial immunity has been topical recently, in part due to the rash of high-profile DNA-proven wrongful convictions. In her report, "Reconsidering Absolute Prosecutorial Immunity," Margaret Johns (2005) provided clear definition of the historic protection provided prosecutors:

> In litigation under the federal civil rights statute, 42 U.S. C. §1983, two kinds of immunity apply to prosecutors: absolute immunity and qualified immunity. The immunity applied depends on the function the prosecutor was performing at the time of the misconduct. When prosecutors act as advocates, absolute immunity applies. Under absolute immunity, prosecutors are immunized even when the plaintiff establishes that the prosecutor acted intentionally, in bad faith, and with malice. Under qualified immunity, prosecutors are immunized unless the misconduct violated clearly established law of which a reasonable prosecutor would have known.

Johns also commented on the challenge that wrongful conviction poses to prosecutorial immunity:

> This functional approach to prosecutorial immunity has created confusion and conflict in the lower courts. Together, these immunities deny civil remedies to innocent people who have been wrongly convicted of crimes as a result of prosecutorial misconduct. While qualified immunity strikes a balance between providing a remedy for egregious misconduct and protecting the honest prosecutor from liability, absolute immunity should be reconsidered.

Indeed, recent cases have challenged our courts to ponder the boundaries of absolute immunity. *Connick v. Thompson* raised such questions before the U.S. Supreme Court in 2011. John Thompson was convicted of the murder of the son of a prominent New Orleans businessman based on testimony of another suspect in the crime. When Thompson's photo appeared in the newspaper, three suburban white siblings identified him as the man who had carjacked them, a separate crime. District Attorney Harry Connick Sr. of the Parish of Orleans, which includes the City of New Orleans, tried the carjacking case first. The testimony of the eyewitnesses trumped John Thompson's alibi, and he was convicted. That conviction prompted Thompson's decision not to testify in his own defense in the murder trial.

John Thompson was convicted of murder and sentenced to death. Lawyers from the law firm of Morgan Lewis in Philadelphia eventually signed on to his case and the defense team spent the next 11 years attempting to get a new trial for Thompson. The U.S. Supreme Court rejected what was thought to be their final effort in May 1999. However, an investigator then uncovered blood evidence from the carjacking that had never been turned over to the defense. The evidence excluded Thompson from the hijacking. This spectacular *Brady* violation was one of several—including a critically ill prosecutor's confession that he had hidden this evidence from the defense—that led to the reversal of the carjacking conviction. Thompson was then quickly acquitted of the murder at his new trial. Thompson sued District Attorney Connick and his office, and a jury awarded Thompson $14 million for his ordeal in serving 18 years in prison, many on death row, for crimes he did not commit.

However, the U.S. Supreme Court, in a contentious 5-4 decision, overturned the award in the spring of 2011. The ruling that divided the high court also inspired debate nationally. *NPR*'s Nina Totenberg wrote that Justice Ruth Bader Ginsburg's decision to read aloud her dissent was an effort to "underscore her view that the 'deliberately indifferent attitude' in the DA's office had created 'a tinderbox,' where miscarriages of justice were inevitable" (Totenberg, 2011).

Ginsburg may have been referring to the track record of Connick's 30-year prosecutorial career. According to the Innocence Project, 36 men convicted by Connick and his office alleged prosecutorial misconduct, and 19 won conviction reversals. "Many saw Ginsburg's dissent as a call to Congress to change the law," wrote Totenberg (2011).

In January 2012, the U.S. Supreme Court reversed the murder conviction of Juan Smith in an 8-1 decision in *Smith v. Cain*, another case raised on alleged *Brady* violations in the Orleans Parish District Attorney's Office. Smith had been convicted on the testimony of one eyewitness. It was not revealed to the defense that the victim/eyewitness first said that he had not seen the perpetrators' faces and could not identify them.

Other recent rulings have provided cautionary signals to prosecutors. On February 1, 2012, U.S. District Judge Elaine Bucklo ruled that former Cook County Assistant State Attorney Mark Lukanich does not have prosecutorial immunity in a lawsuit that claims that Lukanich was nearby when the plaintiff was beaten by police until he provided a false coerced confession. Ronald Kitchen spent more than two decades in prison, thirteen on death row, before his release and exoneration in 2009.

The judge dismissed Kitchen's claims for malicious prosecution against Lukanich, ruling that "initiating a prosecution and presenting the state's case are prosecutorial acts and are barred from suit by absolute immunity." However, the judge denied prosecutorial immunity for the prosecutor's alleged involvement in the case before arrest. "The facts alleged in the first amended complaint, if true, plausibly show that ASA Lukanich was aware of Kitchen's tortured interrogation and knowingly obtained a coerced and involuntary confession" (Elaine E. Bucklo, *Ronald Kitchen v. Jon Burge*, 2012).

In a similar lawsuit, *Beaman v. Souk*, U.S. District Court Judge Joe Billy McDade ruled in March 2012 that two McLean County judges, James Souk and Charles Reynard, are not immune from claims of alleged misconduct in a lawsuit filed by Alan Beaman, who served 13 years in prison for the murder of his former girlfriend, before the Illinois Supreme Court overturned his conviction. The McLean County state's attorney's office subsequently dismissed the charges against Beaman. The lawsuit alleges that two judges, formerly prosecutors in this case, worked with police officers to frame Beaman for the crime. Judge McDade's ruling was consistent with a recommendation from Magistrate Judge Byron Cudmore that the former prosecutors were immune from claims related to their prosecutorial roles but not for their investigative involvement in the case before the arrest of Beaman.

In May 2012 the federal 7th Circuit Court of Appeals ruled that prosecutors are not immune from alleged constitutional violations. Herb Whitlock and Gordon "Randy" Steidl spent 21 and 17 years, respectively, in prison before key witnesses recanted, important evidence was deemed unreliable, and the two men were released from prison. According to the *Chicago Tribune*, the ruling permits them to sue for what Steidl has alleged was a "17-year conspiracy involving the Paris police department, Illinois State Police, and the Edgar County state's attorney's office" (Sweeney, 2012). Former county prosecutor Michael McFatridge is among those named in the suit.

"If their claims are true, a grave and nearly unbelievable miscarriage of justice occurred in Paris, Ill" (*Herbert Whitlock and Gordon "Randy" Steidl v. Charles Brueggemann, et al.*) opined the court. Meanwhile, attorneys from the office of Illinois Attorney General Lisa Madigan will argue before the Illinois Supreme Court that the state should not have to defend (or pay for the defense of) McFatridge for allegations of "willful and wanton misconduct" (Sweeney, 2012).

We are also observing unprecedented responses and consequences to allegations of prosecutorial misconduct from the public, which indicate growing public awareness of and outrage over the tragic results of prosecutorial misconduct. Michael Morton (Evidence of Innocence, 2012) was released in October 2011 after serving 25 years in prison for the murder of his wife, Christine. He had steadfastly proclaimed his innocence. Williamson County (TX) District Attorney John Bradley fought for six years the Innocence Project's efforts to do DNA testing on a bandana found near the murder scene. When eventually tested, the bandana revealed the DNA of the victim and that of an imprisoned felon. Michael Morton was subsequently released from prison and exonerated. District Attorney Bradley's resistance to the DNA testing became a key issue in his primary re-election campaign. The longtime incumbent Bradley was defeated in the May 2012 primary election by challenger Jana Duty.

Tragically, the felon DNA on the bandana also linked to evidence found at the scene of a similar murder of a young mother two years after Morton's conviction. Public records requests revealed numerous pieces of evidence supporting Michael Morton's innocence that were not shared with the defense by Ken Anderson, who was then prosecutor and is now a district judge. The high-profile case has prompted the scheduling of an unusual formal court of inquiry into allegations that Anderson committed criminal misconduct in the prosecution of Morton. The Court of Inquiry, scheduled to begin in February 2013, promises to put a national spotlight on questions surrounding prosecutorial immunity.

Remedies for Prosecutorial Misconduct

As wrongful convictions focus national attention on failures of our criminal justice system, initiatives to reduce prosecutorial misconduct can come from efforts across the full spectrum of criminal justice and the broader society.

The Supreme Court's ruling in *Connick v. Thompson* (2011) seemed to eliminate the opportunity for remedy through civil lawsuits for the wrongfully convicted alleging prosecutorial misconduct. Following this decision, John Thompson joined with the Innocence Project, Voices of Innocence, and other innocence organizations on a national tour, "Prosecutorial Oversight: A National Dialogue in the Wake of *Connick v. Thompson*." According to Barry Scheck, co-founder and co-director of the Innocence Project, solutions discussed in public forums across the nation have included:

> developing better internal systems to deal with misconduct, greater oversight from the disciplinary arms of state bar associations, better reporting of misconduct from judges with better systems for dealing with their complaints, and the creation of an independent state agency with the authority and resources to investigate allegations of prosecutorial misconduct.
>
> (Scheck, 2012)

To these we would add that the priority of seeking the truth must be elevated in *law schools*, and the lessons of DNA-proven wrongful conviction—the scope, contributors to, and remedies—should be added to the core law school curriculum.

The *legal profession* must lift the professional standards of lawyers by applying meaningful sanctions for violations of legal requirements, standards, and ethical expectations. Bar associations must take stronger action to restore confidence in the integrity of all licensed attorneys, particularly those who represent the state. Continuing legal education courses should include the scope of, contributors to, and remedies for wrongful conviction and provide the latest research on the level of reliability of different forms of evidence.

The highest level of professionalism and ethical standards and a commitment to the overarching goal of seeking the truth must be constantly reinforced in the *culture of every prosecutor's office*. A wrongful conviction should be considered a "never event"[7]—a term borrowed from the healthcare industry—that should require public reporting, public apology, and a comprehensive formal review to identify what went wrong and what adjustments to procedures or oversight can prevent the error from reoccurring. Any prosecutor or prosecutorial office responsible for a second wrongful conviction should be the subject of serious scrutiny.

It is difficult to imagine that the intent of the doctrine of absolute immunity was to include protecting prosecutors from accountability for criminal behavior. Our *judges and courts* need to re-examine criminal and civil absolute immunity for prosecutors and consider a qualified liability protection as more appropriate in light of the lessons of DNA. Disbarment, financial penalty, settlements to the victim, and even prison sentences are reasonable sanctions in the relatively rare cases of intentional misconduct or misconduct with malice that lead to wrongful imprisonment. Intentional injustices perpetrated under color of law should neither be tolerated nor left unanswered.

The propensity of some judges to identify violations and then rule them harmless should be challenged by the *media and voters*. Open disclosure— which removes prosecutorial discretion in sharing evidence—is a recommended option for greater assurance that all pertinent evidence is seen by the defense. This is now utilized in some states and jurisdictions.

The role of citizens in the United States is perhaps the most important in achieving policy change. *Voters* must become critical observers of their local prosecutors, judges, and law enforcement. We must support and elect prosecutors who demonstrate a commitment to seeking the truth. We must urge judges to add muscle to protections such as the *Brady* require-ment. We should encourage and closely follow progress on implementing best practices in criminal justice procedures in our local police departments.

Every responsible citizen should be as informed in judicial and prosecutorial elections as in a presidential election. Arguably, the former can have a greater impact on one's life. Some prosecutors obstruct efforts to utilize DNA testing. Some prosecutorial professional organizations oppose cost-neutral recommended reforms and best practices that reduce conviction errors. Voters can and should voice concern and signal their disapproval at the next election. The "us vs. them" competitive sport mentality in the system must be tempered when new significant evidence requires cooperation to determine truth or when recommended changes in public policy can reduce conviction error.

Conventional wisdom is a powerful force in criminal justice. It has driven tougher sentencing in the past several decades with a resulting explosion in the prison population. In the wake of our new understanding of the role played by prosecutorial misconduct in wrongful convictions, we must send the message to prosecutors that we are less interested in conviction percentages and more concerned about conviction accuracy. Convicting the innocent directly undermines public safety as it enables the guilty to continue acts of crime and violence.

These shifts in professional culture and renewed commitment to fundamental priorities in justice won't just happen. Citizens need to advocate for and support the standard of accuracy, professionalism, and accountability that we seek in other important services, from healthcare to the airline industry. We have learned in the last two decades that accuracy in criminal justice is not what we believed or what it can be. We have discovered abuses of prosecutorial power, arrogance, callousness, stubbornness, laxity, and malice. The integrity of our justice system will rest upon how we respond to the wakeup call of wrongful conviction.

Notes

1. Known in some jurisdictions as County Prosecutor, District Attorney, State's Attorney, or United States Attorney.
2. At this writing, the Innocence Project, the non-profit legal clinic that pioneered using DNA to prove innocence, reports 300 wrongful convictions. However, in May 2012 the University of Michigan Law School and the Center on Wrongful Convictions at Northwestern University School of Law made public the National Registry of Exonerations, a searchable database of prisoners exonerated by DNA and other proofs of innocence in the United States since 1989. At its launch, the database included nearly 900 cases with significant detail. Another nearly 1,100 cases, in which convictions were overturned due to 12 police scandals, were included in numerous media reports of "2,000 false convictions in the past 23 years."
3. Studies of DNA-proven wrongful conviction have determined that government misconduct is a significant contributor to conviction error. The Innocence Project reported (West,

2010, p.1) that 65 of the first 255 DNA exonerees claimed prosecutorial misconduct in appeals or civil suits, and in 18 percent of the cases, the error resulted in reversal of the conviction. The Innocence Project noted this is similar to the 17.6% harmful error rate determined in a larger study in 2003 that included non-innocence cases by the Center for Public Integrity. Retrieved on June 6, 2012, from http://www.innocenceproject.org/docs/ Innocence_Project_Pros_Misconduct.pdf

4. According to the *New York Times* (Oppel, R. A. Jr., 2011), "fewer than one in 40 felony cases now makes it to trial, from data from nine states that have published such records since the 1970s, when the ratio was about one in 12."

5. Clarence Elkins was arrested on the morning of Sunday, June 7, 1998, for murder and rapes that occurred earlier that morning nearly an hour's drive from his home. He served nearly eight years in jail and prison before DNA exonerated him and identified the true perpetrator who is now serving a life sentence for the crimes. Anthony Michael Green was identified as the suspect in a Cleveland rape within fifteen minutes of officers arriving on the scene, according to an officer's testimony at Green's trial. Green was convicted but exonerated after serving 13 years for the rape. The true perpetrator, reading about the crime and exoneration, which was detailed in a comprehensive series written by Connie Schultz in the *Plain Dealer* (Cleveland), turned himself in and proved to be a match with the crime scene DNA. He was sentenced to five years in prison for the crime.

6. This is myth number four in *False Justice—Eight Myths that Convict the Innocent* (Petro, J. and Petro, N., 2011), one of eight widely believed misconceptions regarding the criminal justice system that have been challenged or debunked by DNA-proven wrongful convictions.

7. The National Quality Forum, a non-profit organization with a mission to improve American healthcare, has endorsed a list of serious events—"never events"—that should not happen in a hospital. The events are largely preventable but are serious and some can be fatal. Examples of "never" surgical events are surgeries performed on the wrong body part or the wrong person. (Retrieved on June 7, 2012 from http://www.qualityforum.org/projects/sre2006. aspx.) The Leap Frog Group, a non-profit national volunteer organization that rewards advances in healthcare, suggests that response to a never event should include an apology, reporting of the event, and a root-cause analysis. (From Factsheet on Never Events, retrieved on June 6, 2012, http://www.leapfroggroup.org/media/file/Leapfrog-Never_Events_Fact_ Sheet.pdf.)

References

ABA Standards of Criminal Justice: Prosecutorial Function 2d Def. Function § 3-1.2(c), The Prosecution Function, standard 3-1.2(c), (American Bar Association 3d. ed. 1993).

Brady, E. (March 27, 2012). Judges not immune in Beaman wrongful conviction lawsuit. Panatgraph.com.

Burke, A. (2006). Improving prosecutorial decision-making: Some lessons of cognitive science. *William & Mary Law Review*, 47, 1587–1633.

Chuck, E. (May 21, 2012). Researchers: More than 2,000 false convictions in past 23 years. MSNBC-US News.

Evidence of Innocence: The Case of Michael Morton. (March 25, 2012). 60 Minutes, CBS News.

Findley, K. A. (May 11, 2010). Tunnel Vision, (Book Chapter) Conviction of the innocent: Lessons from psychological research, B. Cutler, (Ed.), APA Press, 2010; Univ. of Wisconsin Legal Studies Research Paper No. 1116. Available at SSRN: http://ssrn.com/abstract= 1604658.

Gross, S., & Shaffer, M. (May, 2012). Exonerations in the United States, 1989–2012, Report by the National Registry of Exonerations. Retrieved from http://globalwrong.files.wordpress.com/2012/05/exonerations_us_1989_2012_full_report.pdf.

Johns, M. (May 11, 2005). Reconsidering absolute prosecutorial immunity. *Brigham Young Law Review.*

Lieberman, J. D. & Arndt, J. (2000). Understanding the limits of limiting instructions: Social psychological explanations for the failures of instructions to disregard pretrial publicity and other inadmissible evidence. *Psychology, Public Policy and Law*, 6 677-711, doi: 10.1037//1076-8971.6.3.677.

Nickerson, R. S. (1998). Confirmation bias: A ubiquitous phenomenon in many guises. *Review of General Psychology*, 2, 175–220.

Oppel, R. A. Jr. (September 25, 2011). Sentencing shift gives new leverage to prosecutors. *The New York Times.*

Petro, J. & Petro, N. (2011). *False Justice—Eight Myths that Convict the Innocent.* New York: Kaplan Publishing.

Ridolfi, K. M. & Possley, M. (2010). Preventable Error: A Report on Prosecutorial Misconduct in California 1997–2009. A VERITAS Initiative Report, Northern California Innocence Project, Santa Clara University School of Law.

Rood, L. (January 5, 2010). $12 million wrongful conviction settlement is hailed. DesMoines.com.

Scheck, B. (May 5, 2012). Errant prosecutors seldom held to account. Statesman.com.

Schwartz, J. (December 19, 2011). Exonerated of Murder, Texan Seeks Inquiry on Prosecutor. *The New York Times.*

Sweeney, Annie. (May 30, 2012). Wrongful conviction case against police, prosecutors wins appeal. *Chicago Tribune.*

Totenberg, Nina (April 2, 2011). Man wrongly convicted: Are prosecutors liable? NPR.

Trope, Y. & Lieberman, A. (1996). Social hypothesis testing: Cognitive and motivational mechanisms. In E. T. Higgens and A. W. Kruglanski (Eds), *Social Psychology: Handbook of Basic Principles* (pp. 239–270). New York: Guilford.

West, E. (August 2010). Court Findings of Prosecutorial Misconduct Claims in Post-Conviction Appeals and Civil Suits Among the First 255 DNA Exoneration Cases. Innocence Project. Retrieved on June 6, 2012, at http://www.innocenceproject.org/docs/Innocence_Project_Pros_Misconduct.pdf.

Cases

Beaman v. Souk, (U.S. District Court for Central District of Illinois) Judge J. B. McDade, March 2012.

Berger v. United States, 295 U.S. 78 (1935).

Brady v. Maryland, 373 U.S. 83 (1963).

Connick v. Thompson, 000 U.S. 09-571 (2011).

Curtis W. McGhee Jr., v. Pottawattamie County, 07-1453 (U.S. District Court for Southern District of Iowa), February 1, 2008.

Herbert Whitlock and Gordon "Randy" Steidl v. Charles Brueggemann, et al. Nos. 11-1059, 11-1060, 11-1061, 11-1068, 11-1069 & 11-1070 (U.S. Court of Appeals, 7th Circuit), May 30, 2012.

Ronald Kitchen v. Jon Burge (U.S. District Court for Northern District of Illinois) Judge Elaine Bucklo, February 1, 2012.

Smith v. Cain, 000 U.S. 10-8145.

State of Ohio v. Anthony Green, transcript of trial proceedings, Court of Common Pleas, County of Cuyahoga, Case No. CR 228250.

Terry J. Harrington v. State of Iowa, No. 122/01-0653, February 23, 2003.

7

FORENSIC SCIENCE AND WRONGFUL CONVICTIONS

Simon A. Cole and William C. Thompson[1]

Introduction

An edited volume on the subject of wrongful convictions published prior to 1990 might not have had a chapter on forensic science. Certainly forensic science has been cited as a contributor to miscarriages of justice since as long ago as the Dreyfus case. But, until the last couple of decades forensic science has tended to take a back seat in discussions of miscarriages of justice, compared to other issues like eyewitness identification, perjury, official misconduct, and interrogation practices (Roberts & Willmore, 1993, p. 1). Although the earliest U.S. study of miscarriages of justice mentioned "[t]he unreliability of so-called 'expert' evidence" as a contributor to wrongful convictions (Borchard, 1942, p. xix), most of the early U.S. studies which attempted systematically to identify causes of wrongful conviction discussed eyewitness identification; false confessions; police and prosecutorial misconduct; bad lawyering; race; failures of the discovery process; and public pressure for a conviction, but made scant mention of forensic science (e.g., Frank & Frank, 1957; Huff, Rattner, & Sagarin, 1996; Radin, 1964). Radelet et al. (1992, pp. 141, 253) was a notable exception, discussing the use of misrepresented serology and hair evidence to leverage false confessions and misleading medical examiner testimony.

This situation led Schiffer and Champod (2008) to comment, in the predecessor volume to this one, "forensic science (to convict and to exonerate) is underrepresented and often wrongly understood in research concerning wrongful convictions."

This disjunction between forensic science and wrongful convictions made intuitive sense because the characteristics popularly associated with "science" would seem to be the antitheses of the characteristics of wrongful convictions. Wrongful convictions were thought to be caused by unclear, misguided, or fallacious reasoning, but science is supposed to embody clear, logical reasoning from valid, empirically demonstrable premises. Wrongful convictions were thought to be caused by unjustified biases against people of certain races or classes, against persons with prior criminal records, or even simply against the police's preferred suspect, but science is supposed to be objective and free of bias. Wrongful convictions were supposed to be caused by deceitful and otherwise unreliable information from witnesses, informants, co-conspirators, and the like, but science, goes the truism, "never lies." Wrongful convictions were supposed to be caused by evidence that was less reliable than it appeared, like eyewitness identification evidence, but the very notion of science is associated, in the popular imagination, with high reliability, indeed often with certainty.

For these reasons the notion that forensic science might contribute to miscarriages of justice is often treated as ironic because of the popular association of science with notions of "truth" and "certainty." Of course, any sober assessment should clearly understand that forensic techniques, like any other detection system, should be expected to yield errors—both "type I" and "type II"—at some rate (see Forst, Chapter 2). And yet, much discourse surrounding forensic science invokes popular stereotypes of science as "certain" in a way that other evidence is not. Science, therefore, would seem to be the antithesis, and indeed perhaps even the antidote, to the causes of wrongful convictions.

Forensic Science as Exposer of Wrongful Convictions

The intuition that forensic science could be the antidote to wrongful conviction seemed to be borne out by the development of forensic DNA profiling in the mid-1980s. The very first use of forensic DNA profiling in a criminal case averted an investigation that, in retrospect, seems quite likely to have resulted in a wrongful conviction: the prosecution of a mentally retarded individual who falsely confessed to the murder and rape of a teenage girl that had been linked to another rape-murder (Wambaugh, 1989). Soon thereafter, as is now well known, two American attorneys, Peter Neufeld and Barry Scheck, realized the potential of forensic DNA profiling to expose wrongful convictions and started the Innocence Project and later the Innocence Network and the innocence movement. Thus, forensic science emerged in the 1990s as perhaps the greatest engine for exposing wrongful convictions ever encountered by criminal justice systems. According to a recent estimate, post-conviction DNA testing was responsible for exposing 37 percent of the wrongful convictions exposed during the period 1989–2012 in the US (Gross & Shaffer, 2012).

Even more important than their number, however, was what we might call their "epistemic hardness"—their imperviousness to the sort of skeptical doubt that had historically prevented the achievement of consensus around the "reality" of wrongful convictions (Aronson & Cole, 2009; Kreimer, 2005). Moreover, in a sort of "halo effect," the "reality" that DNA testing lent to post-conviction DNA exonerations rubbed off on even the non-DNA exonerations. Innocence skeptics' inability to deny the reality of post-conviction DNA exonerations made it difficult to deny the "reality" of exonerations achieved through other means (Scheck, 2006, p. 604). In a very real sense, the notion that there is a wrongful conviction "problem," which has today largely assumed the status of common sense, is a product of forensic science—of post-conviction DNA testing. Without post-conviction DNA testing, we might still be debating the "reality" of alleged wrongful convictions, with innocence skeptics citing trial records in support of the claim that the allegedly wrongfully convicted are in fact guilty. Thus, without dismissing the efforts of those scholars who studied wrongful convictions prior to its development or those who study through other paradigms, such as journalism, forensic DNA profiling can justly be viewed as having played a very large role in ushering in, circa 1990, a new era in the study of wrongful convictions, an "age of innocence" (Rosen, 2006, p. 237; Zalman, 2010/2011, pp. 1484–1498). This "new era" differed from the earlier era in a variety of ways including:

(1) greater attention to wrongful convictions among scholars, the media, governments, and courts;

(2) a greater number of exposed wrongful convictions;

(3) greater social consensus around the notion that alleged wrongful convictions were real;

(4) greater determination to address the problem;

(5) the existence of a social movement, the "innocence movement" centered around the problem of wrongful convictions *and* other problems with criminal justice systems implied by the problem of wrongful convictions.

Thus, forensic science would seem at first blush to be a *solution* to the wrongful conviction problem. In most of the post-conviction DNA exoneration cases, forensic science provided a seemingly accurate account of the crime that contradicted the false account of the crime provided by conventional investigative tools like eyewitness evidence, interrogations, informants, and so on. What is less known, however, is that Scheck and Neufeld only encountered forensic DNA profiling in the course of defending a client, Marion Coakley, who had suspect forensic evidence being adduced against him (Lynch, Cole, McNally, & Jordan, 2008, p. 258; Scheck, Neufeld, & Dwyer, 2000; Zalman, 2010/2011, p. 1489). Again, what might easily have become a wrongful conviction was averted. Thus, Scheck and Neufeld saw the virtues of forensic science only through seeing its vices; they perceived the role of forensic science in contributing to wrongful convictions even before they saw its role in exposing wrongful convictions. This, in itself, upsets the easy narrative in which forensic science serves only as an exposer and corrector of wrongful convictions.

The narrative might also have been upset by developments around the same time in the United Kingdom, in which forensic science had emerged as a contributor to several high-profile wrongful convictions in Irish Republican Army bombing cases (Edmond, 2002, p. 62; Nobles & Schiff, 2000, p. 117). The narrative was permanently upset by a series of analyses of the post-conviction DNA exoneration cases (Connors, Lundregan, Miller, & McEwen, 1996; Garrett, 2008, 2011; Garrett & Neufeld, 2009; Saks & Koehler, 2005; Scheck et al., 2000). These studies, modeled on earlier studies of wrongful convictions, sought to identify a list of contributions to wrongful convictions. Analyses of the post-conviction DNA exonerations revealed a paradox. Forensic science was not merely the engine for exposing miscarriages of justice; analyses of post-conviction DNA exonerations revealed that forensic science itself was ranked among the most prominent contributors to miscarriages of justice (see Vuille et al., Chapter 8 in this volume). And while most of the false convictions were based on other forms of forensic evidence (most commonly serological testing and microscopic hair comparisons), a few of them were based on errors in pre-conviction DNA testing (Thompson, 2008; Thompson, Taroni, & Aitken, 2003), suggesting that even DNA evidence, by then regarded as the gold standard of forensic evidence, was not immune to error. Based on these analyses, forensic science has earned a place among the canonical list of "causes" of wrongful convictions. Forensic science was not merely an exposer of wrongful convictions; it was also a culprit in them.

Studying Forensic Science Contributions to Wrongful Convictions

As in nearly all areas of scholarship on wrongful convictions, producing knowledge about the contribution of forensic science to wrongful conviction is quite difficult (see Gross, Chapter 3). The exposure of wrongful convictions is incomplete; there is a "dark figure" of unexposed wrongful convictions, but we do not know what proportion of actual wrongful convictions are exposed. The mechanisms that do expose wrongful convictions are almost certainly skewed in ways we don't fully understand; exposed wrongful convictions are almost certainly an unrepresentative sample of actual wrongful convictions. There are definitional differences among scholars over what should be called a "wrongful conviction." And, what it means for forensic science to "contribute" to a wrongful conviction is not an easy matter. Are we interested in whether faulty forensic evidence was used in a case that became a wrongful conviction, or do we need to establish that it was a crucial piece of evidence that led investigators, prosecutors, or fact-finders astray? If so, how do we determine which evidence was the basis for the formation of any of these actors' beliefs? Within these constraints, there have been three main approaches to trying to develop knowledge about the contribution of forensic science to wrongful convictions.

Studies of Wrongful Convictions

The first approach begins with data sets of wrongful convictions and seeks to determine what factors contributed to them. The strength of this approach is that it is able to show a direct contribution by forensic evidence to actual wrongful convictions. The limitation is that wrongful convictions are data sets skewed by their exposure mechanisms. By beginning from exposed wrongful convictions, these approaches will inevitably over-represent certain factors which lend themselves to exposure.

Several researchers have worked with the set of wrongful convictions exposed through post-conviction DNA testing (Connors et al., 1996; Garrett, 2008, 2011; Garrett & Neufeld, 2009; Saks & Koehler, 2005; Scheck et al., 2000). A major strength of this data set is that there is a strong social consensus around the belief that these convictions were indeed wrongful. Its weakness is that it undoubtedly over-represents the kind of convictions that lend themselves to falsification through post-conviction DNA profiling. Generally, these are rape or rape-murder cases for which identity, rather than consent, is the issue and for which showing that the convict is not the source of biological sample provides strong proof of innocence.

Early analyses of these data ranked forensic science second to eyewitness identification as a contributor to wrongful convictions exposed by post-conviction DNA profiling (Saks & Koehler, 2005). Based on the most ambitious analysis of these data to date, Garrett (see Chapter 5) reported that in 185 out of 250 cases (74 percent) forensic evidence was used in the prosecution. This figure also ranked forensic science second to eyewitness identification as a contributor to wrongful convictions exposed through post-conviction DNA profiling (Garrett, 2011, p. 279). Garrett also analyzed trial transcripts for 207 of the 250 cases for which he was able to obtain them. He found that 169 cases had forensic trial testimony. He was able to locate the transcripts for 153 of these 169 trials, and in 61 percent of these 153 trials, "invalid" testimony was given (Garrett, 2011, pp. 89–90). Garrett (2011, p. 7) concluded that "[m]ost . . . forensic analysis at these trials offered invalid and flawed conclusions," and that he "was confronted with a parade of invalid forensics" (p. 9). Garrett found such problems in serology, hair comparison, bite mark comparison, shoe print comparison, and fingerprint comparison (Garrett, 2011, p. 90).

A broader wrongful conviction data set was recently analyzed by Gross and Shaffer (2012). This data set captures wrongful convictions exposed from 1989 through 2012 by any means, rather than solely by post-conviction DNA exoneration, and the criteria for counting a case as a wrongful conviction are more inclusive. The strength of this data set is that it is less skewed than a data set limited to post-conviction DNA exonerations, though it is still certainly skewed. For example, it undoubtedly over-represents serious cases (Gross & Shaffer, 2012, p. 14). The limitation is that some of the claimed wrongful convictions may be more vulnerable to claims by determined innocence skeptics that they are not in fact wrongful convictions.

"False or misleading forensic evidence" contributed to around a quarter of the wrongful convictions in this data set, ranking it fourth among the five "leading" causes of exposed wrongful convictions (Gross & Shaffer, 2012, p. 40). Gross and Shaffer offer little detail as to what specific forensic techniques were used or in what ways the evidence was "false or misleading." But they do add forensic pathology and comparative bullet lead analysis to the list of forensic techniques implicated in wrongful convictions (Gross & Shaffer, 2012, p. 64). Gross and Shaffer also discuss a number of "no-crime" wrongful convictions. Included among these are a number of cases involving arson and medical evidence concerning unexpected infant death (often called "shaken baby syndrome"). These forensic techniques are now suspected of being major contributors to wrongful convictions, so much so that shaken baby syndrome has been called "the next innocence project" (e.g., Cooley, 2004; Cunliffe, 2011; Findley, 2011, p. 1161; Plummer & Syed, 2012; Science and Technology Committee, 2005, p. 74; Tuerkheimer, 2009). However, while some convictions based on these kinds of evidence have been overturned because the scientific evidence implicating the defendant was, in retrospect, deemed very weak, or even discredited, "no-crime" cases involving these kinds of evidence rarely produce the sort of strong consensus around "actual innocence" that is produced by post-conviction DNA testing.

The conclusion that forensic science is the second leading contributor to wrongful conviction has been challenged by proponents of forensic science who claim that forensic science itself has been "wrongly convicted." They argue that forensic error presents "a comparatively small risk to the criminal justice system," estimating that forensic science contributed to 16 percent of wrongful convictions exposed by post-conviction DNA profiling (Collins & Jarvis, 2009, p. 17), rather than 51 percent, as estimated by Garrett (2011, p. 114). To be sure, rankings of forensic science among lists of contributors to wrongful convictions should not be over-interpreted. Such rankings are relatively crude measures, in which a factor was counted as contributing to a wrongful conviction if it was used in the prosecution. It was not a measure of whether that factor *caused* the wrongful conviction or even of how much influence that factor may have had on various criminal justice system actors. Moreover, as discussed above, wrongful conviction data sets are undoubtedly skewed in ways that favor certain factors.

We would argue that ultimately what we might call the "causal" framework is not the most useful way to think about the role of forensic science in wrongful convictions. We suggest that it is less useful to think of forensic science as a "cause" of wrongful convictions than to think of it as a system component with the potential to support or fail to support investigative hypotheses (Cole, 2012; Rudin & Inman, 2011 and figure 7.1). Within this framework, we would ask not to how many exposed wrongful convictions forensic science contributed, but rather how good a job forensic science does at supporting correct investigative hypotheses and failing to support incorrect ones. More generally, we would ask to what extent forensic science lives up to its potential to support the doing of justice and to correct potential injustices.

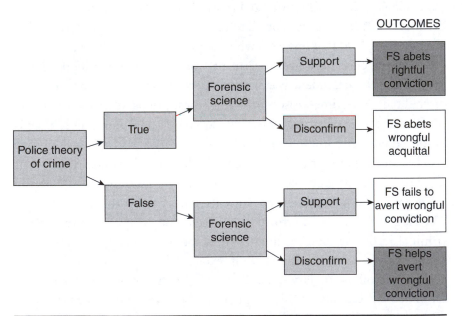

Figure 7.1 Conceptual model of role of forensic science in miscarriages of justice. Negative outcomes are in white boxes; positive outcomes in dark grey.

Studies of Forensic Science

The second major approach begins from an analysis of forensic science and attempts to draw inferences about its potential contribution to wrongful convictions. The strength of this approach is that it does not reason backward from exposed wrongful convictions; it seeks to estimate the potential contribution of forensic science to *actual*, rather than merely exposed, wrongful convictions. The limitation is that it is essentially seeking to make inferences about the "dark figure" of unexposed wrongful convictions. It is able to show direct connections between forensic science and exposed wrongful convictions only anecdotally, and it is unable to produce robust estimates of the contribution of forensic science to wrongful convictions. This approach has documented numerous problems in contemporary forensic science, including incompetent practitioners; lack of certification and accreditation; poor education and training; poor supervision of crime laboratories; poor quality control; pro-prosecution bias; lack of validation and lack of basic research. By showing how these problems have led to exposed errors in casework or on proficiency tests, this research suggests that forensic science undoubtedly has contributed to other, unexposed, errors. While not all such errors would necessarily contribute to wrongful convictions, these studies suggest that forensic science contributes to unexposed wrongful convictions. Some scholars and journalists have focused on the weaknesses of specific forensic techniques (e.g., Beecher-Monas, 2009; Bowers, 2002; Cole, 2005; Edmond, Biber, Kemp, & Porter, 2009; Epstein, 2002; Haber & Haber, 2004; Hsu, 2012a, 2012b; Imwinkelried & Tobin, 2003; Mnookin, 2001; Risinger, Denbeaux, & Saks, 1989; Schwartz, 2005; Stafford Smith & Goodman, 1996; Thompson, 2008, 2012; Thompson & Dioso-Villa, 2008). Others have studied problems with forensic laboratories as institutions (e.g., Cooley, 2004; Giannelli, 2007; Jonakait, 1991). Still others have focused on the weaknesses of forensic science generally (e.g., Berger, 2006; Cooley, 2004; McRoberts, Mills, & Possley, 2004; Moriarty, 2007; Risinger & Saks, 2003; Roach, 2009; Saks, 2000; Saks & Faigman, 2008; Saks & Koehler, 2005; Zerwick, 2005). These findings of weaknesses in forensic science have now been corroborated by a variety of official reports (e.g., Kaufman Commission, 1998; NRC, 2009; Science and Technology Committee, 2005).

Criminal Justice System Actor Estimates

A third approach, modeled on the approach taken by Huff et al. (1996) and Zalman, Smith, & Kiger (2008) for wrongful convictions generally, is to ask criminal justice system actors to estimate the contribution of forensic science to wrongful convictions. Schiffer's (2009) interviews showed that criminal justice system actors agree with the above approaches that forensic science does contribute to wrongful convictions, although they offered little specificity as to the extent of the contribution. Interestingly, the interviewees stressed the recovery of evidence from the crime scene as a crucial point at which error was most likely to be introduced, something mentioned relatively rarely by the other approaches.

As the above review shows, precise knowledge about the forensic contribution to wrongful convictions is difficult to come by. The research described above is sufficient to conclude safely that forensic science does contribute to wrongful convictions, but more precise conclusions about how great the contribution, either in an absolute sense or relative to other causes, would be risky. Despite these limitations, common features emerge from all three approaches. These features, which will be described in the next section, can be taken as roughly indicative of the weaknesses of recent and current forensic practice and the ways in which forensic science may contribute to wrongful convictions.

Features of Forensic Contributions to Wrongful Convictions

Incompetent/Corrupt Analysts

Some contributions to wrongful convictions have involved individuals who appeared to be either incompetent or corrupt or both (Scheck et al., 2000, pp. 107–125). Analysts have engaged in such practices as "dry labbing" (reporting tests that were never actually conducted) and falsification of results (Giannelli, 1997, 2007). Some analysts may have been motivated by vigilantism—seeing their role as assisting investigators who they assumed had identified the correct suspect. Others appear to have been poorly trained, overworked, and overwhelmed and trying to cover up their incompetence (Thompson, 2006).

It is, of course, hardly surprising that forensic science, like any other profession, would include some incompetent or corrupt individuals.

The more important question is why forensic science as an institution did not do a better job at detecting and removing such individuals (Thompson, 2008) (see section on 'Poor Regulation' below).

Overclaiming

Many contributions involved what has been called "overclaiming"—the forensic analyst exaggerates the strength of the evidence. In many cases, this involved stating that the analysis was more discriminating than it actually was. By "discrimination," we mean: how much does a proper analysis using this technique reduce the potential donor pool of a crime scene sample? For example, a properly conducted ABO blood type analysis might reduce the potential donor pool to 1 in 10 members of the general population, but a properly conducted DNA analysis at 13 loci might reduce the pool to 1 in 10 million. Forensic DNA profiling is far more discriminating than ABO blood typing.

Forensic DNA profiling and serology are two techniques for which scientifically defensible estimates of discrimination exist. For many other techniques—fingerprinting, hair comparison, toolmark analysis, bite mark analysis, shoe print analysis—such estimates do not exist. What can and should a forensic analyst report when such estimates do not exist? Strictly speaking, they can say little more than that evidence was consistent with the defendant being the source but also was consistent with an unknown number of other people being the source. Such testimony is rather vague, potentially confusing to the jury, and—if correctly understood—of little help to the prosecution. Many contributions involved analysts going further and stating that the analyses were highly discriminating. In some cases, this involved making up statistics or performing improper statistical analyses (see Vuille et al., Chapter 8 in this volume). In other cases, it involved verbal characterizations of the discrimination of the technique that made the evidence sound extremely strong. Microscopic hair comparison evidence was particularly vulnerable to overclaiming. But overclaiming also occurred for bite marks, shoe prints, fingerprints, and DNA (Garrett, 2011, p. 90). In some disciplines, overclaiming contradicted best practice (hair comparison); in others, it occurred in the absence of data (bite mark analysis); in still others, it conformed with professional rules (fingerprint identification).

Biased Interpretations

Many contributions involved biased interpretations of forensic evidence. By "biased interpretations," we mean that when faced with evidence that is subject to multiple possible interpretations, the analyst, cognizant of the investigators' theory of the crime, chooses an interpretation consistent with that theory. Even more perniciously, when analysts report their results, they fail to account for their elimination of other possible interpretations. A forensic conclusion consistent with the prosecution's theory thus looks more surprising—and more incriminating—than it actually was (Thompson, 2009a). The most common example involved the phenomenon of "masking" in serological analysis (Garrett, 2011, p. 94). However, biased interpretation has also been documented in cases involving other techniques, such as forensic DNA profiling (Thompson, 2008).

These problems arguably arise from the general failure of forensic scientists to use "blinding" or "masking" (not the same use of the term as in the preceding paragraph) procedures when interpreting test results. In order to guard against the well-known human tendency to interpret data in a manner consistent with one's expectations and desires, scientists in most fields require that the person making critical interpretations be "blind" to the expected results, particularly when the interpretations depend on subjective judgment. Yet forensic scientists rarely take steps to shield themselves from extraneous information—i.e., information unnecessary for making a scientific assessment—when making comparisons or interpreting test results (see also Brants, Chapter 9). Indeed, forensic scientists often have access to information about the case that may lead them to expect (and perhaps hope) to reach a particular interpretation (Risinger, Saks, Thompson, & Rosenthal, 2002; Thompson, 2011). Analysts are often in direct contact with the detectives who are investigating the case, and their laboratory notes sometimes include detailed information about possible suspects and about police theories of the case. Even when analysts do not have access to investigative facts, they typically interpret evidentiary samples and reference samples at the same time, creating a risk that knowledge of a reference sample may bias interpretation of evidentiary samples in a confirmatory direction (Thompson, 2009a). In its 2009 report on forensic science, the National Research Council (NRC, 2009, p. 8) declared unequivocally that "forensic science experts are vulnerable to cognitive and contextual bias" and that this bias "renders experts vulnerable to making erroneous identifications."

Lack of Basic Validation Research

While overclaiming is always possible, it was facilitated by the fact that in many areas of forensic science, proper claims are difficult to make because the actual value of the evidence cannot be estimated in any scientifically defensible way. Many disciplines lack the kinds of rarity estimates, like random match probabilities for DNA profiles, that would allow analysts to characterize properly the value of a finding of consistency (see Vuille et al., Chapter 8). This leaves analysts with little choice but to offer verbal characterizations of the rarity of features they found consistent. Since "the sample was consistent with the defendant, and I would also expect it to be consistent with an unknown number of other people" has a pretty weak feel to it, the temptation to say "the sample was consistent, and the features that I found consistent are very, very rare" may be great.

Many disciplines also lack properly conducted validation studies which measure the accuracy of the technique against ground truth. This leaves analysts with little choice but to say "I have never made an error"—a statement that invites the fact-finder to confuse the rate at which analysts are made aware of having made errors with the rate at which analysts do, in fact, make errors—or, in more extreme cases, "the error rate is zero."

Where validation studies have been performed, they often followed the use of evidence in court, rather than preceded it, as one would logically expect. For example, accuracy and frequency studies of fingerprint identification are only beginning to be conducted now, after a century of routine use in criminal prosecutions. Frequency studies of comparative bullet lead analysis were only conducted by individuals concerned about the use of this technique, more than two decades after prosecutors began offering this evidence in court to prosecute defendants (Imwinkelried & Tobin, 2003). Thus, the lack of studies that address the fundamental empirical questions raised by many forensic techniques, especially studies that estimate the frequencies of features and accuracy rates, would seem to have facilitated forensic contributions to wrongful convictions.

Poor Regulation

Much of the above discussion may seem like it is painting with a broad brush, labeling forensic science with the attributes of its worst practitioners and techniques. There is some validity to this complaint, especially with regard to specific techniques: a large portion of the forensic contribution to wrongful convictions can be traced to two particularly weak techniques, serology and microscopic hair comparison. To be sure, as discussed above, the prevalence of these techniques in the post-conviction DNA exoneration data set is to a large extent explained by the amenability of convictions secured with these techniques to reversal through post-conviction DNA testing. But, even taking this skewing effect into account, the contribution of these two techniques is striking.

This complaint suffers somewhat from the retrospective fallacy: these two techniques were not labeled "bad" at the time they were used to convict the exonerees. They have been labeled "bad" *post hoc*, now that—through an extraordinarily lucky and unlikely accident—a more powerful technique has been developed that has exposed their failures. Without this fortuitous development, those exonerees would still be in prison, and serology and hair comparison might still be touted as "good" science. The notion of eliminating "bad techniques" is of little comfort to the justice system if these techniques cannot be eliminated prospectively, rather than retrospectively. From this perspective, the important issue is the broader failure of forensic science as an institution to eliminate problematic techniques and individuals *before* their exposure as such by the fortuitous development of DNA profiling. Seen from this perspective, we can only conclude that forensic science, which historically has been self-regulated, has done a poor job of self-regulation. Suspect techniques, laboratories, and practitioners continued to practice until their errors were exposed by the sorts of extraordinary external events—post-conviction DNA profiling, media investigations, the fortuitous (and illegal) posthumous storage of samples in a notebook—that cannot be relied upon as regular oversight mechanisms.

Courts

One cannot escape the conclusion that all of the above issues passed through the trial and appeal processes with hardly a peep of protest from the courts. Forensic evidence that in hindsight was false or misleading was almost never restricted by courts. Trial and appellate courts can claim very little credit for the exposure of known wrongful conviction cases (Garrett, 2008). Thus the NRC's stinging conclusion, all the more so coming from a committee co-chaired by a judge: "The bottom line is simple: In a number of forensic science disciplines, forensic science professionals have yet to establish either the validity of their approach or the accuracy of their conclusions, and the courts have been utterly ineffective in addressing this problem" (NRC, 2009, p. 53). Likewise forensic contributions to wrongful convictions offer ample evidence to assign blame to attorneys. Prosecutors used false and misleading testimony without protest and often bolstered the value of the evidence in closing statements. Defense attorneys missed numerous opportunities to expose problems with forensic evidence (Garrett, 2011, p. 114).

Policy Recommendations

Based on the above analyses, a wide variety of policy recommendations have been proposed. The most prominent of these are detailed below.

Independent Forensic Laboratories

For historical reasons, most forensic laboratories, especially in the United States, are located in law enforcement agencies or tied to prosecuting authorities. One of the most common criticisms of contemporary forensic science holds that this arrangement inevitably creates a pro-prosecution bias, whether conscious or unconscious (e.g., Cooley, 2004, p. 422). For many reformers, the ideal would be an independent government agency whose identity was tied to science, rather than to public safety. The NRC (2009, p. 24), for example, recommends "removing all public forensic laboratories and facilities from the administrative control of law enforcement agencies or prosecutors' offices." The main criticism of such proposals, aside from political or resource considerations, is that forensic scientists need to be in close contact with law enforcement in order to decide what items to analyze and how, place the evidence in the context of the case, and so on. To be sure, true "independence" may be difficult to achieve. National laboratories, such as in some European countries, are still controlled by the state, which is the prosecuting party in criminal cases, and private laboratories are still heavily reliant on the state as their primary client.

Independent Oversight

Even if all forensic laboratories are not independent, they might be regulated by a body independent of law enforcement. The NRC's (2009, p. 19) leading recommendation was the creation of a new government agency, a National Institute of Forensic Science (NIFS), independent of law enforcement. Such institutes exist in some countries, such as Australia and the Netherlands, and some U.S. states, such as New York and Texas, have created forensic science commissions (Giannelli, 2007, p. 228).

Competition

Economists, led by Roger Koppl, have argued that the issue is less the independence of crime laboratories than the fact that in each case one laboratory has a "monopoly" over the interpretation of the evidence. They advocate a system of competition in which laboratories would naturally compete to provide the best scientific analysis of evidence. Although the main criticism of this proposal is that it is redundant and will, therefore, entail unnecessary costs, Koppl and colleagues have performed cost-benefit analyses that suggest that the added costs would be outweighed by the costs saved by avoiding wrongful convictions (Koppl, 2005, 2010; Koppl & Cowan, 2010; Koppl, Kurzban, & Kobilinsky, 2008; Whitman & Koppl, 2010).

Accreditation, Certification, Quality Assurance, Quality Control

Contrary to proposals for government regulation, forensic science is currently almost entirely self-regulated. For laboratories, this generally means that they may be accredited by a professional organization and that they implement internal quality assurance and quality control measures. For individual analysts, this generally means that they may be certified by a professional organization. Forensic laboratories have made great improvements over the past couple of decades to increase the coverage and rigorousness of these measures. Nonetheless, recent reviews still find these processes lacking on both counts. For example, the NRC (2009, p. 25) recommends that accreditation and certification be mandatory, which they are not in the U.S. Commentators have called for further improvements in the coverage and rigor of accreditation, certification, and quality control (e.g., Garrett, 2011, p. 116), but they have cautioned that these measures are not panaceas. Accreditation, for example, ensures that laboratories have proper documentation of procedures in place, but it is quite limited in the extent to which it measures laboratory adherence to these procedures. Moreover, accreditation processes are highly dependent on self-reporting by laboratories.

Scientific/Research Culture and Basic Research

Many commentators have commented on the apparent lack of scientific reasoning in many forensic disciplines, and the NRC has attributed the ills of forensic science to the lack of a "scientific culture" (e.g., Margot, 2011, p. 90; Mearns, 2010; Moriarty, 2007, p. 8; NRC, 2009, p. 39). While "scientific culture" is a vague term, such criticisms seem to be pointing to an absence of the sort of intellectual curiosity that is supposed to characterize science. Why, for example, were so many forensic techniques— fingerprinting, comparative bullet lead analysis, bite mark analysis—put into regular use in the criminal justice system before basic validation studies were conducted to determine whether they could do what they claimed to be able to do? The implication is that institutional forensic science prioritizes the law enforcement goal of enabling the prosecution of crime over the scientific goal of measuring the capabilities of the technique. The NRC (2009, p. 125) has advocated the adoption of "scientific culture" as a remedy for forensic science, and commentators have called for the establishment of a "research culture" in forensic science (e.g., Mnookin et al., 2011). Commentators have also called for the conduct of more basic research on forensic science (e.g., Cooley, 2004). Such research has fallen between the crime laboratories, whose primary mandate is to provide forensic services, and universities and government laboratories which have tended not to prioritize forensic problems.

Education and Training

Criticisms of the culture of forensic science inevitably raise the issue of education and training. If forensic scientists are not reasoning statistically or if they are not thinking scientifically about how to validate their assumptions, they must not have been trained to do so. Consequently, many commentators call for better scientific education and training for forensic personnel (e.g., Cooley, 2004, pp. 424–428; Margot, 2011, p. 96; Mnookin et al., 2011, p. 764; NRC, 2009, p. 27).

Sequential Unmasking

If biased interpretation arises from the failure of forensic scientists to use blind procedures for interpreting test results (as noted above), an obvious solution might be to require them to use such procedures. One particularly concrete proposal for how this might be done has been put forward by an interdisciplinary group and labeled "sequential unmasking" (Krane et al., 2008). It would require that analysts interpret and record their assessment of evidentiary samples before knowing the characteristics of reference samples in order to reduce the risk that knowledge of a reference sample may bias interpretation of evidentiary samples in a confirmatory direction. Information about the reference samples would be "unmasked" only after the interpretation of the evidence is recorded. Although the Krane et al. (2008) proposal referred to the interpretation of DNA evidence, the group that made the proposal has suggested that similar approaches would be possible for a wide variety of forensic disciplines, such as fingerprinting, DNA profiling, hair comparison, and so on.

Risinger et al. (2002) proposed that courts impose the requirement that forensic scientists use blind procedures for interpretation as a condition for the admissibility of forensic science evidence. While no court has, as yet, followed this suggestion, forensic scientists have, in a few instances, begun to introduce what might be called "blinding" procedures in order to reduce the potential for contextual bias. For example, the 2010 SWGDAM guidelines for forensic DNA testing state: "to the extent possible DNA typing results from evidentiary samples are interpreted before comparison with any known samples, other than those of assumed contributors" (SWGDAM, 2010, §3.6.1). The FBI's latent print unit has reportedly adopted a procedure called "linear ACE-V" that requires examiners to analyze latent prints and record their findings before looking at reference prints (Office of the Inspector General, 2011). While these steps do not go as far as many academic commentators would like (compare the SWGDAM Guidelines with the "sequential unmasking" procedure proposed by Krane et al., 2008), they suggest a growing recognition that the problem of contextual bias is sufficiently serious to justify changes in forensic science procedures.

But many forensic scientists remain unconvinced that such changes are warranted (Budowle et al., 2009; Margot, 2011, p. 92; Ostrum, 2009; Thornton, 2010). They argue that forensic scientists need access to investigative facts in order to decide what samples to collect at a crime scene and how to test them. Proponents of blind procedures, such as sequential unmasking, argue that this need can be accommodated through separation of functions in the laboratory. One forensic scientist could serve as a "case manager" to decide what to test and how to test it and control the flow of information to a second forensic scientist (the analyst) who would make key comparisons or conduct and interpret the tests. The analyst could thus remain blind to investigative facts and other potentially biasing information while the case manager remained fully informed (Thompson, 2011).

Disclosure and Information Sharing

Many commentators contend that the adversarial culture associated with litigation has dampened the spirit of open disclosure and information sharing that is supposed to be associated with science. Better disclosure, both in the context of criminal cases and for research purposes, it is argued, will allow for better adversarial scrutiny of evidence, which, ideally, should be in the interest of all parties (e.g., Krane et al., 2009; Mnookin et al., 2011, p. 773; Risinger & Saks, 2003).

Reporting

Shockingly, the NRC noted that the reporting of forensic conclusions was not standardized in most disciplines. Known cases of wrongful conviction clearly show that vague reporting practices allowed analysts to make evidence with little value seem highly incriminating. The NRC (2009, p. 22) called for the development of standard terminologies for reporting the conclusions of forensic analyses. Such standardization would increase transparency and communication and ease the process of reviewing forensic reports. Some European laboratories and some groups of scholars have attempted to develop more logical and standardized frameworks for reporting forensic conclusions.

Resources

It might be argued that all of the above problems stem from poor funding. Many have commented on the poor funding for forensic science, relative to other areas of government-funded science (e.g., Cooley, 2004, pp. 419–420; Mnookin et al., 2011, p. 762). Indeed, one of the primary motivations behind the convening of the NRC committee on forensic science was to address the issue of inadequate funding. Without better funding, implementation of any of the above proposed reforms will be difficult.

Law Reform

Forensic science exists in an environment in which the courts are its primary, if not only, client. The *telos* of all forensic analyses, whether it is realized or not, is some sort of report to a court. Judges could incentivize forensic science to carry out desired reforms by threatening to preclude or limit forensic evidence that hasn't implemented them. Prosecutors, who may also be conceived as forensic science's primary clients, might have similar leverage. Judges or prosecutors might do this out of a desire to improve forensic science or as a matter of ethics (Garrett, 2011, p. 116; Moriarty, 2007, p. 20, also see Chapter 6, this volume). However, numerous commentators have argued that courts have been remarkably lenient on forensic science, relative to other forms of scientific evidence (e.g., Cooley & Oberfield, 2007; Dwyer, 2007; Risinger, 2007; Rozelle, 2007; Saks, 2007; Sanders, 2010). Therefore, courts have failed to incentivize the panoply of reforms discussed above, and, in some cases, they may have even disincentivized them. It has, therefore, been argued that none of the above reforms are likely to occur unless the courts force them to occur (e.g., Sanders, 2010; Thompson, 2009b). The NRC, notably, takes a more pessimistic view of the courts' willingness to be the agents of reform— hence the proposal for a regulatory agency.

Conclusion

The study of wrongful convictions is beset by a temporal problem. We are seeking to study, and reduce, a problem that will occur in the future and, when it does occur, will, by its very nature, be undetected for a period of time, if not forever. We seek insight into this problem by studying exposed wrongful convictions from the past and extrapolating lessons for the future. But this extrapolation is always somewhat problematic because the criminal justice system changes over time. Moreover, specific problems identified by exposed wrongful convictions can, one hopes, be targeted and fixed. Thus, the wrongful convictions of the future may not have the same proximate causes as those of the past, but they may have the same general causes.

The same general principles apply to forensic contributions to wrongful convictions. For this reason, we think it is crucial to think about exposed wrongful convictions as a "window of opportunity" for insight into criminal justice systems, rather than as indicators of proximate causes of wrongful convictions. This is all the more true in the age of post-conviction DNA exonerations, in which we have been blessed with an especially effective, and temporary, "window."

Although Garrett (2011, p. 114) notes that "in the overwhelming majority of criminal cases, labs still use methods like those used in [the post-conviction DNA] exonerees' trials," one hopes that the problems he found with serology and microscopic hair comparison will recur far less frequently in the future. But the proper conclusion to be drawn is not that problems have been solved, but rather to inquire into the broader structural conditions that allowed these problems to occur in the first place. Why were conclusions skewed toward guilt? Why were validation studies not conducted and incorporated into reporting? Why were practitioners of stronger techniques not harder on the flaws in weaker techniques? And, why did the courts allow all this to occur? Correcting these structural conditions will require a more thorough remaking of forensic science as an institution and enterprise than the mere weeding out of some individual practitioners, laboratories, or disciplines. And this remaking will need to occur while the temporary window of opportunity provided by post-conviction DNA exonerations still lends urgency to the cause.

Note

1 Authors' Note: Some of the material in this chapter also appears in: Cole, S. A. (2012), "Forensic Science and Wrongful Convictions: From Exposer to Contributor to Corrector," *New England Law Review*, 46, 711–736; and in Cole, S. A. (2013), "Forensic Science and Miscarriages of Justice." In G. J. N. Bruinsma & D. L. Weisburd (Eds.), *Encyclopedia of Criminology and Criminal Justice*. New York: Springer.

References

Aronson, J. D., & Cole, S. A. (2009). Science and the Death Penalty: DNA, Innocence, and the Debate over Capital Punishment in the United States. *Law & Social Inquiry, 34*(3), 603–633.

Beecher-Monas, E. (2009). Reality Bites: The Illusion of Science in Bite-Mark Evidence. *Cardozo Law Review, 30*, 1369–1410.

Berger, M. A. (2006). The Impact of DNA Exonerations on the Criminal Justice System. *Journal of Law, Medicine and Ethics, 34*(2), 320–327.

Borchard, E. (1942). *Convicting the Innocent: Errors of Criminal Justice*. Hamden, CT: Archon.

Bowers, C. M. (2002). Identification from Bitemarks: Scientific Issues. In D. L. Faigman, D. H. Kaye, M. J. Saks & J. Sanders (Eds.), *Science in the Law: Forensic Science Issues* (pp. 244–293). St. Paul: West.

Budowle, B., Bottrell, M. C., Bunch, S. G., Fram, R., Harrison, D., Meagher, S., et al. (2009). A Perspective on Errors, Bias, and Interpretation in the Forensic Sciences and Direction for Continuing Advancement. *Journal of Forensic Sciences, 54*(4), 798–809.

Cole, S. A. (2005). More Than Zero: Accounting for Error in Latent Fingerprint Identification. *Journal of Criminal Law and Criminology, 95*, 985–1078.

Cole, S. A. (2012). Forensic Science and Wrongful Convictions: From Exposer to Contributor to Corrector. *New England Law Review, 46*, 711–736.

Collins, J. M., & Jarvis, J. (2009). The Wrongful Conviction of Forensic Science. *Forensic Science Policy and Management, 1*(1), 17–31.

Connors, E., Lundregan, T., Miller, N., & McEwen, T. (1996). *Convicted by Juries, Exonerated by Science: Case Studies in the Use of DNA Evidence to Establish Innocence After Trial* (Research Report NCJ 161258). Washington: National Institute of Justice.

Cooley, C. M. (2004). Reforming the Forensic Science Community to Avert the Ultimate Injustice. *Stanford Law & Policy Review, 15*(2), 381–446.

Cooley, C. M., & Oberfield, G. S. (2007). Increasing Forensic Evidence's Reliability and Minimizing Wrongful Convictions: Applying *Daubert* Isn't the Only Problem. *Tulsa Law Review, 43*(2), 285–380.

Cunliffe, E. (2011). *Murder, Medicine and Motherhood*. Oxford: Hart.

Dwyer, D. (2007). (Why) Are Civil and Criminal Expert Evidence Different? *Tulsa Law Review, 43*(2), 381–396.

Edmond, G. (2002). Constructing Miscarriages of Justice: Misunderstanding Scientific Evidence in High Profile Criminal Appeals. *Oxford Journal of Legal Studies, 22*(1), 53–89.

Edmond, G., Biber, K., Kemp, R., & Porter, G. (2009). Law's Looking Glass: Expert Identification Evidence Derived from Photographic and Video Images. *Current Issues in Criminal Justice, 20*(3), 337–377.

Epstein, R. (2002). Fingerprints Meet *Daubert*: The Myth of Fingerprint "Science" is Revealed. *Southern California Law Review, 75*, 605–657.

Findley, K. A. (2011). Defining Innocence. *Albany Law Review, 74*(3), 1157–1208.

Frank, J., & Frank, B. (1957). *Not Guilty*. Garden City, NY: Doubleday.

Garrett, B. L. (2008). Judging Innocence. *Columbia Law Review, 108*, 55–142.

Garrett, B. L. (2011). *Convicting the Innocent: Where Criminal Prosecutions Go Wrong*. Cambridge: Harvard University Press.

Garrett, B. L., & Neufeld, P. (2009). Invalid Forensic Science Testimony and Wrongful Convictions. *Virginia Law Review, 95*(1), 1–97.

Giannelli, P. (1997). The Abuse of Scientific Evidence in Criminal Cases: The Need for Independent Crime Laboratories. *Virginia Journal of Social Policy & the Law, 4*, 439–478.

Giannelli, P. (2007). Wrongful Convictions and Forensic Science: The Need to Regulate Crime Labs. *North Carolina Law Review, 86*, 163–235.

Gross, S., & Shaffer, M. (2012). *Exonerations in the United States, 1989–2012*: National Registry of Exonerations. Retrieved July 16, 2012, from http://www.law.umich.edu/special/exoneration/Documents/exonerations_us_1989_2012_full_report.pdf.

Haber, L., & Haber, R. N. (2004). Error Rates for Human Fingerprint Examiners. In N. K. Ratha & R. Bolle (Eds.), *Automatic Fingerprint Recognition Systems* (pp. 339–360). New York: Springer-Verlag.

Hsu, S. S. (2012a, Apr. 16). Convicted Defendants Left Uninformed of Forensic Flaws Found by Justice Department. *Washington Post.*

Hsu, S. S. (2012b, July 10). Justice Department to Review Use of Forensic Evidence in Thousands of Cases. *Washington Post.*

Huff, C. R., Rattner, A., & Sagarin, E. (1996). *Convicted But Innocent: Wrongful Conviction and Public Policy*. Thousand Oaks: Sage.

Imwinkelried, E. J., & Tobin, W. A. (2003). Comparative Bullet Lead Analysis (CBLA) Evidence: Valid Inference or Ipse Dixit? *Oklahoma City University Law Review, 28*(1), 43–72.

Jonakait, R. (1991). Forensic Science: The Need for Regulation. *Harvard Journal of Law and Technology, 4*, 109–191.

Kaufman Commission. (1998). *Report on Proceedings involving Guy Paul Morin*: Ontario Ministry of the Attorney General.

Koppl, R. (2005). How to Improve Forensic Science. *European Journal of Law and Economics, 20*, 255–286.

Koppl, R. (2010). Romancing Forensics: Legal Failure in Forensic Science Administration. In E. Lopez (Ed.), *Government Failure in the Legal System: A Public Choice Review of the Law*. Basingstoke: Palgrave.

Koppl, R., & Cowan, E. J. (2010). A Battle of Forensic Experts in Not a Race to the Bottom. *Review of Political Economy, 22*(2), 235–262.

Koppl, R., Kurzban, R., & Kobilinsky, L. (2008). Epistemics for Forensics. *Episteme, 5*(2), 141–159.

Krane, D. E., Bahn, V., Balding, D. J., Barlow, B., Cash, H., Desportes, B., et al. (2009). Time for DNA Disclosure. *Science, 326*(5960), 1631–1632.

Krane, D. E., Ford, S., Gilder, J. R., Inman, K., Jamieson, A., Koppl, R., et al. (2008). Sequential Unmasking: A Means of Minimizing Observer Effects in Forensic DNA Interpretation. *Journal of Forensic Sciences, 53*(4), 1006–007.

Kreimer, S. F. (2005). Truth Machines and Consequences: The Light and Dark Sides of 'Accuracy' in Criminal Justice. *New York University Annual Survey of American Law, 60*, 655–674.

Lynch, M., Cole, S. A., McNally, R., & Jordan, K. (2008). *Truth Machine: The Contentious History of DNA Fingerprinting*. Chicago: University of Chicago Press.

Margot, P. (2011). Forensic Science on Trial—What Is the Law of the Land? *Australian Journal of Forensic Sciences, 43*(2–3), 89–103.

McRoberts, F., Mills, S., & Possley, M. (2004, Oct. 17). Forensics Under the Microscope. *Chicago Tribune*.

Mearns, G. S. (2010). The NAS Report: In Pursuit of Justice. *Fordham Urban Law Journal, 38*(2), 429–434.

Mnookin, J. L. (2001). Fingerprint Evidence In An Age of DNA Profiling. *Brooklyn Law Review, 67*(1), 13–70.

Mnookin, J. L., Cole, S. A., Dror, I. E., Fisher, B., Houck, M. M., Inman, K., et al. (2011). The Need for a Research Culture in the Forensic Sciences. *UCLA Law Review, 58*(3), 725–780.

Moriarty, J. C. (2007). "Misconvictions," Science, and the Ministers of Justice. *Nebraska Law Review, 86*(1), 1–42.

NRC (National Research Council). (2009). *Strengthening Forensic Science in the United States: A Path Forward*. Washington: The National Academies. (National Academies Press).

Nobles, R., & Schiff, D. (2000). *Understanding Miscarriages of Justice: Law, the Media, and the Inevitability of Crisis*. Oxford: Oxford University Press.

Office of the Inspector General. (2011). *A Review of the FBI's Progress in Responding to the Recommendations in the Office of the Inspector General Report on the Fingerprint Misidentification in the Brandon Mayfield Case*: U.S. Department of Justice. From http://www.justice.gov/oig/special/s1105.pdf.

Ostrum, B. (2009). Commentary on: Author's Response. *Journal of Forensic Sciences, 54*(6), 1498–1499.

Plummer, C., & Syed, I. (2012). 'Shifted Science' and Post-Conviction Relief. *Stanford Journal of Civil Rights & Criminal Law, 8*(2), 259–297.

Radelet, M., Bedau, H., & Putnam, C. E. (1992). *In Spite of Innocence: Erroneous Convictions in Capital Cases*. Boston: Northeastern University Press.

Radin, E. D. (1964). *The Innocents*. New York: William Morrow.

Risinger, D. M. (2007). Goodbye to All That, or A Fool's Errand, by One of the Fools: How I Stopped Worrying about Court Responses to Handwriting Identification (and 'Forensic Science' in General) and Learned to Love Misinterpretations of *Kumho Tire v. Carmichael. Tulsa Law Review, 43*(2), 447–475.

Risinger, D. M., Denbeaux, M., & Saks, M. J. (1989). Exorcism of Ignorance as a Proxy for Rational Knowledge: The Lessons of Handwriting Identification 'Expertise'. *University of Pennsylvania Law Review, 137*, 731–788.

Risinger, D. M., & Saks, M. J. (2003). A House with No Foundation. *Issues in Science and Technology, 20*(1), 35–39.

Risinger, D. M., Saks, M. J., Thompson, W. C., & Rosenthal, R. (2002). The *Daubert/Kumho* Implications of Observer Effects in Forensic Science: Hidden Problems of Expectation and Suggestion. *California Law Review, 90*(1), 1–56.

Roach, K. (2009). Forensic Science and Miscarriages of Justice: Some Lessons from Comparative Experience. *Jurimetrics, 50*, 67–92.

Roberts, P., & Willmore, C. (1993). *The Role of Forensic Science Evidence in Criminal Proceedings* (Research Study No. 11). London: The Royal Commission on Criminal Justice. (Her Majesty's Stationery Office).

Rosen, R. A. (2006). Reflections on Innocence. *Wisconsin Law Review, 2006*, 237–289.

Rozelle, S. D. (2007). *Daubert,* Schmaubert: Criminal Defendants and the Short End of the Science Stick. *Tulsa Law Review, 43*(2), 597–607.

Rudin, N., & Inman, K. (2011, Dec. 7). *Turning the Investigation on the Science of Forensics: Written Statement for the Record*, United States Senate.

Saks, M. J. (2000). Banishing *Ipse Dixit:* The Impact of *Kumho Tire* on Forensic Identification Science. *Washington and Lee Law Review, 57*, 879–900.

Saks, M. J. (2007). Protecting Factfinders from Being Overly Misled, While Still Admitting Weakly Supported Forensic Science into Evidence. *Tulsa Law Review, 43*(2), 609–626.

Saks, M. J., & Faigman, D. L. (2008). Failed Forensics: How Forensic Science Lost Its Way and How It Might Yet Find It. *Annual Review of Law and Social Science, 4*, 149–171.

Saks, M. J., & Koehler, J. J. (2005). The Coming Paradigm Shift in Forensic Identification Science. *Science, 309*, 892–895.

Sanders, J. (2010). "Utterly Ineffective": Do Courts Have a Role in Improving the Quality of Forensic Expert Testimony. *Fordham Urban Law Journal, 38*(2), 547–569.

Scheck, B. (2006). Wrongful Convictions. *Drake Law Review, 54*, 597–620.

Scheck, B., Neufeld, P., & Dwyer, J. (2000). *Actual Innocence: Five Days to Execution and Other Dispatches from the Wrongly Convicted* (1st edn.). New York: Doubleday.

Schiffer, B. (2009). *The Relationship between Forensic Science and Judicial Error: A Study Covering Error Sources, Bias, and Remedies.* Unpublished Ph.D. diss., University of Lausanne, Lausanne, Switzerland.

Schiffer, B., & Champod, C. (2008). Judicial Error and Forensic Science. In C. R. Huff & M. Killias (Eds.), *Wrongful Conviction: International Perspectives on Miscarriages of Justice* (pp. 33–55). Philadelphia: Temple University Press.

Schwartz, A. (2005). A Systemic Challenge to the Reliability and Admissibility of Firearms and Toolmark Identification. *Columbia Science and Technology Law Review, 6*, 1–42.

Science and Technology Committee. (2005). *Forensic Science on Trial*. London: House of Commons.

Stafford Smith, C. A., & Goodman, P. D. (1996). Forensic Hair Comparison Analysis: Nineteenth Century Science or Twentieth Century Snake Oil? *Columbia Human Rights Law Review, 27*, 227–291.

SWGDAM. (2010). *Interpretation Guidelines for Autosomal STR Typing by Forensic DNA Testing Laboratories.* Scientific Working Group on DNA Analysis Methods. Retrieved July 17, 2012, from http://www.fbi.gov/about-us/lab/codis/swgdam.pdf.

Thompson, W. C. (2006, Jan./Feb.). Tarnish on the 'Gold Standard': Understanding Recent Problems in Forensic DNA Testing. *The Champion, 30,* 10–16.

Thompson, W. C. (2008). Beyond Bad Apples: Analyzing the Role of Forensic Science in Wrongful Convictions. *Southwestern University Law Review, 37,* 1027–1050.

Thompson, W. C. (2009a). Painting the Target Around the Matching Profile: The Texas Sharpshooter Fallacy in Forensic DNA interpretation. *Law, Probability and Risk, 8*(3), 257–276.

Thompson, W. C. (2009b). The NRC's Plan to Strengthen Forensic Science: Does the Path Ahead Run Through the Courts? *Jurimetrics, 50,* 35.

Thompson, W. C. (2011). What Role Should Investigative Facts Play in the Evaluation of Scientific Evidence? *Australian Journal of Forensic Sciences, 43*(2–3), 123–134.

Thompson, W. C. (2012). Forensic DNA Evidence: The Myth of Infallibility. In S. Krimsky & J. Gruber (Eds.), *Genetic Explanations: Sense and Nonsense* (pp. 227–255). Cambridge: Harvard University Press.

Thompson, W. C., & Dioso-Villa, R. (2008). Turning a Blind Eye to Misleading Scientific Testimony: Failure of Procedural Safeguards in a Capital Case. *Albany Law Journal of Science and Technology, 18,* 151–204.

Thompson, W. C., Taroni, F., & Aitken, C. G. G. (2003). How the Probability of a False Positive Affects the Value of DNA Evidence. *Journal of Forensic Sciences, 48*(1), 47–54.

Thornton, J. I. (2010). Letter to the Editor: A Rejection of "Working Blind" as a Cure for Contextual Bias. *Journal of Forensic Sciences, 55*(6), 1663.

Tuerkheimer, D. (2009). The Next Innocence Project: Shaken Baby Syndrome and the Criminal Courts. *Washington University Law Review, 87,* 1–58.

Wambaugh, J. (1989). *The Blooding.* New York: Bantam.

Whitman, G., & Koppl, R. (2010). Rational Bias in Forensic Science. *Law, Probability and Risk, 9*(1), 69–90.

Zalman, M. (2010/2011). An Integrated Justice Model of Wrongful Convictions. *Albany Law Review, 74*(3), 1465–1524.

Zalman, M., Smith, B., & Kiger, A. (2008). Officials' Estimates of the Incidence of 'Actual Innocence' Convictions. *Justice Quarterly, 25*(1), 72–100.

Zerwick, P. (2005, Aug. 29). Mixed Results: Forensics, Right or Wrong, Often Impresses Jurors. *Winston-Salem Journal.*

8

THE IMPORTANCE OF HAVING A LOGICAL FRAMEWORK FOR EXPERT CONCLUSIONS IN FORENSIC DNA PROFILING

ILLUSTRATIONS FROM THE AMANDA KNOX CASE

Joëlle Vuille, Alex Biedermann, and Franco Taroni

Colin Pitchfork, accused of the murder of two young girls in England in 1986, was the first man ever incriminated by results of modern DNA profiling analyses. After this first success, the forensic use of DNA spread and was quickly acclaimed as a powerful means to fight crime. Soon, however, it became apparent that DNA could also be used for a different purpose: in 1992, Barry Scheck and Peter Neufeld founded the Innocence Project, which relied heavily on DNA to detect wrongful convictions and to analyze their causes. At the time, eyewitnesses and jailhouse informants had long been suspected of unreliability. Surprisingly, though, DNA also exposed scientific expertise as a cause of miscarriages of justice, and sometimes even exposed DNA itself as a cause of justice gone wrong.

Besides conscious malpractice by forensic scientists, which can obviously lead to innocent people being prosecuted for crimes they did not commit, the inappropriate understanding of applied science itself can at times lead investigators in wrong directions, as will be exemplified throughout this chapter. In this regard, the place and role of scientific experts in criminal proceedings is central, as well as the need to frame their conclusions logically. DNA—due to its now widespread use in legal practice—helps illustrate this aspect adequately in varying respects.

Forensic DNA Evidence[1] From a Legal Point of View

The place and role of forensic (DNA) experts in criminal proceedings vary across jurisdictions, especially between inquisitorial and adversarial criminal justice systems. In certain respects, however, problems encountered and their possible remedies are similar.

In adversarial jurisdictions, the parties must establish the facts. Expert witnesses are hired, paid and instructed by them, which can create a (fear of) bias. Generally, litigators and decision-makers are well aware of this, and forensic evidence is usually severely scrutinized. In inquisitorial jurisdictions, on the other hand, the responsibility to establish the facts of the case relies on the investigating magistrate and later the court, and experts are commissioned by the authority. This may be thought to ensure their impartiality,[2] but also raises the issue of trust between them and the mandating authority. In fact, in such a system, it is often thought that the validity of scientific evidence is rarely thoroughly discussed because fact-finders tend to accept expert conclusions as certainties.[3]

In both systems, though, a forensic scientist is commissioned when the decision-makers lack the knowledge needed to establish or assess the meaning of given scientific results. At the same time, actors with often limited scientific training, such as a judge or a jury, remain responsible for assessing the admissibility and/or the probative value of any piece of scientific evidence presented in the case. This paradoxical situation can lead to an assessment of evidence that relies more on the trappings of science and the formal authority of experts that on the real merits of work carried out in the case.

To complicate matters, society in general—and lawyers and juries in particular—holds an idealistic view of science, seeing it as an endeavor devoid of any possibility of error or flawed interpretation, in the sense that science is thought to establish objective truths. But there are at least two problems with this assertion. First, there are so-called "scientific methods" which are based on questionable science.[4] Second, science may be said to be 'objective' where it involves, for example, agreed ways of proceeding or a provisional consensus on foundational or theoretical issues; but this is not always the case. Besides, forensic examinations cannot be dissociated from the reality of human capacities that are limited and prone to errors. This may be a result of insufficient education or, at times, bias, and cannot generally be remedied by the simple fact that laboratories run sophisticated and impressive machinery. Scientific evidence can thus, potentially, lead[5] to wrongful convictions because of the uncertainty that characterizes both scientists' and legal actors' relationships with scientific disciplines.

DNA Profile Analyses in Criminal Proceedings

A simplified, but illustrative, description of DNA is one that compares it to a long necklace entangled in each of our cells[6] and composed of pearls of different sizes (called *alleles*) inherited from our parents. At each given location (called *locus*, plural: *loci*), each of us has two pearls, one passed along by our mother, the other inherited from our father, and designated by numbers.[7] The size of the different pearls varies widely among individuals, so much so that each DNA in its entirety is thought to be unique.[8]

Currently, forensic DNA profiling seeks to measure the size of the pearls that are present at 10 or 15 precise locations on the DNA molecule. The specific combination of alleles across these locations is the so-called DNA profile. It is this profile that is retained when comparing analytical results for distinct items, such as an item of unknown source recovered on a crime scene and a sample from a known individual (e.g., a suspect). To obtain a DNA profile, a reagent will first break down the necklace in order to isolate each pearl. The pearls will then be sent through a very fine tube (called a capillary), to measure the speed at which they move through it. Typically, larger pearls will move more slowly than their lighter counterparts. The machine used for this purpose will be able to detect and register the size of each pearl by comparing its speed to internal standards. By expressing the size in terms of numbers, the machine thus produces a profile expressed as a sequence of numbers.

When two profiles have pearls of the same size (i.e., the same number) at the same loci, the two profiles are said to "match" at these loci. The term "match" is improper, however, because the correspondence between two "necklaces" is only a relative conclusion that depends on the level of observation. In particular, it should be noted that the series of numbers that characterizes a DNA profile in fact summarizes a complex process that encompasses biological, physical and chemical dimensions.[9] At best, two profiles may thus be said to be 'reported as indistinguishable'[10] in view of the particular measuring system chosen in the case at hand. Thus, a reported correspondence is an observation that involves a personal judgment on the part of the observer[11] and entails an unavoidable aspect of uncertainty, as will be illustrated below. As such, a "match" relies on an inference, whose validity is only as good as the logic underlying each step of the reasoning process.

More importantly, a reported "match" does not, in itself, express the probative value of the observed correspondence between an item and a reference sample. This requires further considerations that embrace uncertainty in a more formal approach, notably in terms of probability,[12] that can lead to computationally demanding developments depending on the type of trace, the suspect population considered, or the competing propositions put forward in the case at hand.

Conventional forensic DNA profiling analyses can be performed in a satisfactory and reliable manner only if certain conditions are met, notably in terms of the amount and quality of the available DNA template. Several factors and circumstances can render analyses more complicated or can induce variations in the results. Examples include contamination, multiple contributors, transfer, and persistence. Their occurrence can make it more difficult to establish accurately the types and quantity of alleles that are present, sometimes to a point where it is impossible to draw any meaningful conclusions from the profiling results.

To illustrate the wide range of considerations and elements that can have a bearing on the coherent interpretation and evaluation of results from DNA profiling analyses, we will rely on a real case that has recently attracted much attention on both sides of the Atlantic: the Amanda Knox case.[13]

DNA Profiling Analyses in the Amanda Knox Case: Preliminaries

The Facts of the Case

Meredith Kercher was a British student on an exchange program who was murdered in Perugia, Italy, on the night of November 1, 2007, after allegedly having been sexually assaulted. One of her roommates, Amanda Knox, and Amanda's boyfriend, Raffaele Sollecito, as well as an acquaintance of the victim, Rudy Guede, were prosecuted for the crime, convicted, and sentenced, respectively, to 26, 25, and 30 years in prison. Knox and Sollecito were acquitted on appeal in October 2011, whereas Guede saw his 30-year conviction affirmed.

The victim was found in her room in the late morning of November 2. The scientific police arrived on the scene of the crime on November 2 in the afternoon and worked until November 5. They came back on December 18 to complete their crime scene work.

Sources

The authors of this chapter have relied on documents that are publicly accessible on the internet, including:

- The first instance judgment, rendered by the criminal court of Perugia on December 4 and 5, 2009 (Sentenza della Corte di Assise di Perugia 4–5/12/2009; referred to hereafter as the "Massei Judgment").
- The report by the forensic laboratory on the DNA analysis conducted in the case, signed by Dr Patrizia Stefanoni (Servizio Polizia Scientifica, Relazione tecnica indagini di genetica forense, Rome, June 12, 2008; referred to hereafter as the "Laboratory DNA Report").
- The report of the two experts appointed by the presiding appeal judge, Claudio Pratillo Hellmann, to review the DNA evidence in the case (referred to hereafter as the "Conti & Vecchiotti Report").
- The appeal brief filed by Knox's lawyers (Luciano Ghirga and Carlo Dalla Vedova, Atto di Appello, April 16, 2010; referred to hereafter as the "Appeal Brief").
- The report on shoemarks and footmarks drawn by the Italian police (Lorenzo Rinaldi and Pietro Boemia, Relazione di consulenza tecnica, Rome, May 30, 2008; referred to hereafter as the "Rinaldi & Boemia Report").

Seized Items Submitted for DNA Profiling Analyses and Subsequent Review

With respect to results of forensic DNA profiling analyses in the case against Knox and Sollecito,[14] discussions mainly gravitated around two items:

- a clasp of Kercher's bra (item 165b), on which the prosecution claimed to have found the victim's and Sollecito's DNA;

- a knife found at Sollecito's apartment (item 36), which, the prosecution claimed, had Knox's DNA on the handle, and the victim's DNA on the blade.

DNA Profiling Analyses in the Amanda Knox Case: Case Study and Discussion

Analysis of Low Quantities of DNA (Low-Template DNA, or LT-DNA)

Regarding DNA, one of the complexities of the case derives from the fact that, on both the bra clasp and the knife, only minute amounts of DNA were reported to be present. Genetic material present only in low amounts does not render analyses impossible in principle, but it may make them more difficult to conduct practically, and results may show more variation than is typically found in regular quality or conventional traces.

This is typically the case for so-called low-template (LT) DNA specimens.[15] Even though such items may contain small amounts of DNA, it can be copied. Yet, difficulties can arise which might broadly be compared to photocopying: if the original document is of good quality and the machine itself is functioning correctly, chances are that the copies will be a fair reproduction of it, even though they will contain blemishes inherent to the process of Xeroxing. However, if the original document is of poor quality, the copies might well be illegible when one adds the blemishes that are inevitable in the process. In the context of DNA analyses involving low quantities of genetic material, such drawbacks are called stochastic effects.[16] To minimize the occurrence and intensity of such stochastic effects, analysts generally avoid analyses with less than 100 picograms (pg) of genetic material, but such threshold levels are not universally agreed upon; their very existence and usefulness are explicitly doubted (e.g., Gill & Buckleton, 2010).

In the Knox case, the DNA on the bra clasp was scarce. The expert who conducted the analysis confirmed that, due to the limited quantities of DNA, stochastic effects might have occurred. But she did not replicate the analysis, because, in her own words, she had "no reason to do so."[17] Yet, if it can be done, a replication may be useful in clarifying interpretative issues of the first analysis (Petricevic et al., 2010).

It seems that the practice of the Italian police was inconsistent when it came to determining the quantity of DNA necessary to allow for amplification of the DNA. They sometimes proceeded with the analysis when the machine informed them that the quantity of DNA was too low to be analyzed, and sometimes not.[18] Such a variable proceeding allowed the defense experts to argue that the police were not following a well-settled protocol, and worse, that they may have been biased against the suspect, and may have changed the rules by which they were operating in order to implicate the accused.[19] It should be noted, though, that the analyst appeared to have proceeded with the analysis, in spite of a warning by the machine that the level of DNA was too low with respect to the knife. In fact, on several other occasions, she did not proceed when the machine informed her that the quantity of DNA was too low to be analyzed.[20] Furthermore, it is disturbing to note that she did not inform the court of this practice when she testified. The information surfaced only when she was compelled by the judge to give the defense the raw data of the analyses.[21]

The question remains unanswered as to whether, in the case at hand, DNA profiling results were generated for which, subsequently, no robust and defensible assessment could be made. Although the Conti & Vecchiotti report concludes that claims of categorical source attributions cannot be maintained under the circumstances under which the items were analyzed, it does not offer any indication of what, instead, the recipient of the expert information in that case should have done with the reported DNA profiling results.

Contamination

Contamination occurs when a trace is mixed with some other genetic material, resulting in the appearance of additional signals (i.e., "allele peaks") in the profiling results. It can occur before, during, or after the commission of the crime, during the collection of the stains and items, or during analyses in the laboratory. Contamination is becoming an increasingly challenging aspect because, with time, DNA profiling technologies have become increasingly sensitive, allowing one to obtain profiling results from more remote quantities that, otherwise, would have gone undetected. It follows from this that contaminations must be avoided at all costs, lest the results report the presence of a DNA that is in fact irrelevant and could implicate an innocent person.

Contamination implies the contribution of material from a real contributor. In this respect, it must be distinguished from another phenomenon known as "drop-in." Allele drop-in refers to the appearance of additional signals in the profile (typically one or two) that do not stem from a true contributor, but originate from independent sources (like single alleles that could come from fragmented or degraded DNA) and can randomly affect tubes in which a genetic material is processed.[22]

Due to the limited amount of DNA recovered on some items seized in the Knox case, LT-DNA analyses were performed, which, as noted above, require stringent measures to guard against possible contaminations. The Italian police may have taken such measures, but these were not clearly documented, which allowed the defense to argue that contaminations might indeed have occurred. According to the Massei judgment, some of the police officers admitted that they were wearing gloves when at the scene of the crime, but they did not change their gloves after touching each object.[23] Another official testified that she did not remember how often or when she changed her gloves when she was collecting blood traces in one of the bathrooms.[24] Another expert stated that she told her colleagues to change their gloves every time they touched an object that was soaked in blood, or every time that the gloves were dirty.[25] Further, one expert declared that there were a dozen people in the victim's room (i.e., the main crime scene) during the first visit of the scientific police on November 2, and that some of them might have gone from one room to another without changing their shoe protections.[26] Such circumstances, and the level of crime scene management, shed a doubtful light on the conditions under which LT-DNA analyses were conducted.

Another element that raises concern is that the clasp of the bra that the victim was apparently wearing around the time she got murdered was not found during the initial processing of the crime scene that took place the day after the murder, but only six weeks later. One expert witness reported that the bra itself had been seen during the first visit of the scientific police, and that it was observed at that time that a part of it was missing. The clasp appeared on some pictures and video recordings made at the scene of the crime, which showed it to be under the pillow on which the victim's body had been lying.[27] The police did not list it, however, and later discounted the omission by explaining that the bra itself had already been put on record, that the clasp was only a part of it, and thus, that it did not require a record for itself.[28]

Six weeks later, when the police returned to the scene of the crime, the clasp of the bra was spotted one meter away from where it had originally been photographed, and the forensic expert who was questioned about it said she could not explain how it could have moved.[29] Once (re)discovered, the clasp was moved and put on the floor of the room to be photographed, which, according to her, was not a problem since the floor was dry when the clasp was put on it. In such circumstances, she affirmed, no transfer of DNA from the floor to the clasp was possible.[30] Later, DNA recovered from the clasp was reported to match with Sollecito's DNA profile, and the clasp became a crucial item of the prosecution case. Yet, it is troubling to think that the prosecution would rely on a piece of evidence that was not properly recorded when it was first discovered, completely forgotten during six weeks, and then appeared to have moved by its own volition from one place to another. Without a record, who can vouch for the chain of custody? These elements reinforce the concerns expressed previously about the reliability of the operations conducted by the Italian police at the scene of the crime.

Regarding a possible contamination in the laboratory where the analyses of the various objects and traces collected at the scene of the crime were conducted, one expert witness said that she had no knowledge of any data relating to the matter, and that her laboratory followed all usual recommendations. Even if it is true that, at present, systematic and empirical accounts on contamination are rather scarce, it would be incorrect to argue that there are no reports and discussions on this topic in specialized literature,[31] and it is generally not contested that contaminations do occur, once in a while.[32]

The preceding considerations leave the reader with a breach of argument, however. Neither excluding the possibility of a contamination entirely nor saying that contaminations are always possible is very useful. The fact is that environmental contamination is common when one deals with DNA, and it can be serious when it risks implicating an innocent suspect, but it does not automatically render the evidence useless. From an interpretational point of view, the interesting question is to determine how contamination affects probative value when it occurs, and how to express this possible effect to the recipient of expert information, in order for him to make sensible use of it. None of the expert witnesses and discussants in this case addressed such questions, however.

Stains Versus Profiles

The discussion about contamination in the Knox case reveals a further misconception about low-template DNA, in that it equates the absence of a clearly visible stain with the possibility of contamination.[33]

This outset is confusing because it is now widely recognized that—given the sensitivity of current analytical techniques—it is not necessarily the case that a particular profiling result derives from a stain that was actually visible. Stated otherwise, it is possible to obtain DNA profiling results from a location where no particular biological material is recognizable. And, to complicate matters, even if there is visible staining, it may be that it is degraded but bears invisible material from another source that is in better condition, and from which the profiling results actually stem.

Although it is generally desirable and useful that scientists point out whether or not particular DNA profiling results might be related to a visible staining, and it is important that the inability to do so should have an impact on considerations of probative value, invoking the possibility of contamination in such cases in order to discard the evidence entirely does not serve the purpose of justice adequately.

Instead, the absence of visible staining to which DNA profiling results could be related should, first of all, lead to a shift in the definition of the competing propositions under which the profiling results are evaluated. That is, instead of a traditional pair of propositions of the kind, "the crime stain comes from the suspect (respectively, from some unknown person)"—a context known as "source level" propositions (Cook et al., 1998)[34]—it may be more appropriate to consider propositions at a "sub-source" level, defined as follows: "The DNA is that of the suspect (respectively, of some unknown person)" (Evett et al., 2002).

Considerations of DNA profiling results at a sub-source level leads to a paradoxical outset. While courts are typically interested in questions such as "how did this DNA get here?" rather than "whose DNA is this?" (Evett et al., 2002), propositions at a sub-source level precisely embrace the latter category of questions so that, in a strict sense, the scientist's reporting is not tailored to the requests of the mandating authority. As a consequence of this, it is left to the courts to move to higher propositional levels that better suit their needs, even though this requires taking into account phenomena such as transfer, persistence, recovery, and contamination, all of which are rather technical in nature. It is questionable, then, if the courts can be expected to meet this challenge, because the proper understanding of such factors demands solid empirical knowledge. At present, most scientists refrain from such evaluations because empirical data on these matters are scarce. Current forensic practice thus demonstrates a considerable gap between the information offered by scientists and the actual needs of the judiciary.

Stuttering

The word "stutter" designates the production of a signal (i.e., peaks indicative of alleles) that does not reflect the presence of an actual allele, and at positions that do not correspond to that which would be expected for the allele considered.[35] This profile morphology characteristic becomes an issue of interest particularly in the context of presumed mixed stains, when analysts need to decide whether a peak signal is due to a stutter associated with a neighboring peak, or if it represents a genuine allele peak due to DNA from another source. In practice, analysts rely on rules that instruct them to compare the size of a suspected stutter with the associated principal allele signal, elaborated either through internal validation procedures or by following the recommendations of analysis kit manufacturers.

In the Knox case, one of the expert witnesses gave a rather optimistic definition of stutters. Although she acknowledged that the software does not differentiate between real alleles and other peaks such as stutters, the expert witness alleged that stutters could be quantified and predicted, as described by the manufacturer of the analysis kit. Further, she added that stutters are recognizable by the analyst.[36] However, the scientific police made a couple of incoherent decisions in the course of determining which peak was or was not representing a real allele. The following instances of discussion about results obtained from the bra clasp illustrate this point:

- One expert had previously explained that, on a given locus, when one peak is smaller than 15 percent of the other peak to which it presumably relates, it should be discarded as a stutter; otherwise, it should be considered as a genuine and distinct allele. However, she discounted as a stutter a peak that was 94 RFU[37] in relation to another peak of a height of 603 RFU. This is higher than the limit she had said she used for allele designation.[38] As it turned out, her decision to discard that peak implicated one of the suspects.

- Regarding locus D21S11, the police declared three alleles. Two of these, alleles 30 and 33.2, agree with the victim's genotype. A third allele, 32.2, was thought to come from an unknown source. It was attributed to Sollecito, who has genotype 32.2 and 33.2 on that locus. A fourth allele was discarded, at position 29, even though it was higher than the 15 percent threshold. It did not correspond to Sollecito's genotype, though.

- In some other instance, two alleles (11 and 12) were declared for locus D5S818, but a third peak was discarded as a stutter although it actually had a height of 108 RFU. Yet, the expert witness earlier explained that above 50 RFU, a peak should be considered an allele and not a stutter, and had done so with a peak of 65 RFU.[39] Thus, again, the practice of the analyst was clearly inconsistent.

Bias, Scientific Standards, and Accreditation

As noted in the previous paragraphs, it may be of interest in a case review to inspect the conditions under which examinations were carried out. The process of allele designation in profiles from evidentiary items holds an important position in this context essentially because it may later serve as a basis for comparison with profiles of potential donors. Obviously, the correctness of reported matches found from such comparative examinations depends on the stringency with which the allelic designation has been performed for the evidentiary profiles in the first place. For example, the risk of falsely declaring an allele when in fact the signal is only spurious is increased when the analyst knows the profile of a suspect. In the case studied here, the analyst actually said that she had such knowledge at the time she was interpreting[40] the DNA profiling results. When asked about bias, she answered that she was well aware of the risk of bias, but that she had been careful to be objective.[41] These declarations are rather discomforting, however, because research on this topic has shown that awareness, education and intelligence are not a safeguard against bias. Most importantly, bias happens even when one is aware of it, so that the expert's affirmation to the contrary cannot be reassuring.[42]

Some of the experts' allegations are also troubling in another aspect: their general (mis)understanding of standards in scientific practice.

At some point, one expert witness apparently told the court that all the material used and the protocols that were followed were validated at the international level (implying that it would be a safeguard against errors).[43] But this is like arguing that the authors of this contribution could successfully land a 747-400 jetliner simply because there are international protocols that tell the pilots how to proceed. The expert's view on this topic is all the more troublesome because the same expert witness said that the scientific laboratory in Rome was not accredited by ISO 9001 and 17025 standards, but that they expected to be so in the near future.[44] This is not to argue that accreditation guarantees correct results in any given case, nor that correct work could not also be conducted without accreditation. The argument is actually irrelevant either way. What really matters is whether scientists are able to do what they claim to do. Arguably, it would be more relevant to inquire about their performance in trials under controlled conditions, such as in proven records of proficiency testing. But such an issue was apparently never raised in the case.

Discussion

Evaluation Versus Interpretation

The careful reader might have noted that, up to this point, the whole discussion about DNA profiling results in the Knox case essentially focused on the degree to which particular signals in raw data are indicative of the true donor's allelic constitution. Although this is a crucial step in the use of forensic DNA in criminal proceedings, it is far removed from the questions of interest to the court. The court is not interested in allele designation, but requires from the experts the assignment of a "degree of proof" once the profiles have been obtained. But what is such a degree of proof and why did the scientists working the case fail to address this request adequately?[45] The fundamental question when evaluating the probative value of results of forensic examinations is: "What is the capacity of these results to distinguish between the competing propositions put forward at trial?" Any discourse on the probative value of scientific findings thus requires starting with the definition of the competing propositions of interest. As such, scientific results do not have an intrinsic value that scientists who conduct examinations on material and seized items could derive in isolation from the framework of a case (Robertson & Vignaux, 1995). The value of findings can only be specified in a given context.

A seminal paper by Cook and co-authors (1998) suggests the framing of propositions in a hierarchical way—depending on the circumstances of a case at hand. That hierarchy is not rigid, but seeks to offer a flexible template to help position propositions with respect to the issues that concern the court. The ultimate propositional level is called "crime level" and can be exemplified with propositions of the kind, "the suspect (some unknown person) is the offender." Often, however, scientific findings cannot readily be considered in the light of such an advanced level of propositions, essentially because this requires a broad knowledge about circumstantial information that lies beyond the scope of the expert's area of competence (notably, intent to commit the crime). It is for this reason that the hierarchy of propositions also covers lower levels, such as the "activity level" (i.e., propositions referring to a human activity or event) or "source level" (i.e., propositions about the source of physical matter).

A given level of propositions cannot by default be extended to another level of propositions. The failure to recognize this by either scientists or other members of the judiciary is also known as a violation of the hierarchy of propositions. Observing a correspondence between analytical characteristics of the trace and comparison material from the suspect (source level) does not mean that the suspect has actually left the crime stain at hand (activity level). The former question only requires consideration of the rarity of the corresponding characteristics, whereas the latter necessitates taking into account other phenomena, such as transfer, persistence, and background.

In the Knox case, this inferential perspective of evaluation with respect to selected propositions was missing. In fact, lengthy discussions about source attribution were paired with other topics, such as contamination and transfer. This thematic amalgam is, however, pointless from an argumentative point of view. If the question of interest is that of inferring the source of DNA, then the rarity of the compared characteristics in a relevant population is the main influencing factor.[46] Issues such as contamination and transfer are relevant—to inquire about the time and manner in which the biological material came to be there where it was found—independent of the question of who was the source of that material. Contamination and transfer become relevant in the case against the corresponding suspect only when the target propositions are formulated on the activity level and stipulate, for example, that the suspect conducted the incriminated activity (e.g., assaulted the victim). In the Knox case, the court obviously wanted to know how the DNA had landed on the bra clasp and knife, but this was never properly discussed in the written reports or at the hearings.

The Probability of the Findings

Specifying a pair of competing propositions is a necessary requirement for a balanced assessment of DNA profiling results and has, for this reason, been designated as one of three key principles of forensic evaluation (Evett & Weir, 1998). However, expert witnesses cannot state a direct conclusion about an issue, such as whether a particular suspect is at the source of a crime stain of interest, on the sole basis of the scientific results. Such conclusions must be drawn by the judiciary because they require the consideration of the case as a whole. Scientists thus cannot determine the probability of a proposition given the scientific findings. Instead—and this is a second key principle of forensic evaluation— scientists should focus on the probability of the findings given each of the competing propositions. This is a comparative exercise in which scientists consider whether their findings are more probable for one proposition rather than the stated alternative; the extent to which this can be affirmed expresses probative strength.

For an evaluation at a source level, for example, scientists would thus need to answer the following questions:

1. What is the probability of obtaining a scientific finding (e.g., a correspondence between DNA profiles) if the suspect is the source of the crime stain and given what is known about the case?
2. What is the probability of observing a scientific finding if an unknown person[47] is the source of the crime stain, and given what is known about the case?
3. Under which proposition is a scientific finding more probable?

Whenever, in reply to question 3, the scientist can be more affirmative for one probability than for the other, a scientific result supports the respective proposition by a factor that is given by the relative magnitude of the two probabilities assessed under questions 1 and 2.[48] It is important to emphasize that this is not an expression of a probability for that proposition, but an indication of the degree of support that is independent of the probability that a legal actor holds about that proposition prior to considering the scientist's report.[49]

Confusions about, on the one hand, the probability of scientific findings given a proposition and, on the other hand, the probability of a proposition given the findings, have a long history in both the theory and practice of law and forensic science (Taroni, Champod & Margot, 1998), and have been described repeatedly in scientific literature.

The Knox case, too, provides an instance in which an expert witness did not seem to be aware of this logical nuance. She is reported as saying that "it is possible, with DNA analyses, to determine whether the suspect is or is not the owner of a given trace."[50] Clearly, this is a categorical statement about a proposition.[51] Besides the fact that scientists are procedurally prohibited from expressing an opinion that is outside their area of competence, the statement is essentially unsubstantiated because it is not clear what the alternative proposition is and why that alternative ought to be considered appropriate in the case.

More generally, the definition of alternative propositions holds a crucial position in discourses about probative value essentially because they can have a bearing on an assessment's output (Buckleton, Walsh & Evett, 1991). This is illustrated by the fact that, given the assumptions made about the unknown person (if we assume that the suspect is not the source of the crime stain), such as ethnicity or degree of relatedness with the suspect, the probative value of the scientific findings may change. In turn, which assumptions can legitimately be made in a case at hand depends on the contents of the framework of circumstances (e.g., information about the true offender; how the crime was committed). As a third principle of forensic evaluation, scientists should thus include in their reports what circumstantial information they had at the time of their evaluations (Evett & Weir, 1998). In view of these three general principles of forensic inference, scientists cannot legitimately "jump" from the observation of a correspondence in analytical characteristics to the conclusion that a suspect is the source of the crime stain.

A further instance in the Knox case where this precept was violated, using inappropriate wording, occurred when the scientists who initially analyzed the trace on the bra clasp reported on the results of the Y-chromosomal analyses (i.e., one of the sex-determining chromosomes).[52]

They were quoted as follows: "The analysis of the Y chromosome has permitted the determination of the Y haplotype [. . .] relative to the DNA extracted from trace B. This result also confirms the presence of DNA belonging to Raffaele SOLLECITO in the analyzed trace, since the Y haplotype obtained is equal to that belonging to Raffaele SOLLECITO [. . .]."[53] Although one might argue that the word 'confirms' expresses a degree of support, the sentence clearly suggests that the DNA is that of Sollecito. There is no clearly stated alternative, nor are the scientists expressing themselves in terms of the probability of the evidence. Doing so would have been crucial, however, to specify the degree to which the observed correspondence supports the proposition, according to which the detected DNA comes from Sollecito. Therefore, a relevant question to which scientists should have replied is: "What is the probability of the observed haplotype if an unknown person, different from Sollecito, is the source of the detected DNA?" It is not possible to answer this question at this juncture because we cannot speculate about who that unknown person is (e.g., related or unrelated to the suspect, ethnic background, etc.). What can be said, however, is that this probability is not zero, essentially because the discussion at this point relates to Y haplotypes that are paternally transmitted to offspring. That is, unless some special circumstance such as mutation has happened, Y haplotypes can be expected to be the same in all males in the same paternal lines of heritage. If we judge that, even for conventional DNA profiles, it is reasonable for us to reserve some probability (different from zero) for the event of observing a correspondence, given that an unknown person is the source of the crime stain (Balding, 1999), we must do so all the more for Y haplotypes simply because of their population genetic characteristics (i.e., paternal inheritance). Consequently, the less surprising it would be to see this haplotype under the stated alternative, the less confirmatory strength this reported correspondence would have.[54]

Conclusions

Today's technologies allow forensic scientists to analyze the genetic constitution of even very remote quantities of biological material. Legal practitioners—in particular recipients of expert information—should remember, however, that this does not imply that all biological traces that contain DNA will actually be characterized accurately every time such examinations are conducted. Indeed, experience shows that it is important to distinguish between performance characteristics of analytical techniques in general and their actual application in casework. The reason for this is that there may be case-related aspects and circumstances that greatly affect the probative value of profiling results. In order to place DNA profiling results in an appropriate context, all judicial actors should inquire about the credentials of DNA profiling results in the case of interest.

As the Knox case clearly illustrates, readers of expert reports should carefully check whether a laboratory's conclusions are appropriately supported by the actual observations that were made, because the same results may be given different readings according to one's point of view. And then, whatever the outcome of such a comparative examination, it should only be considered as an intermediate step in the evaluative process, not the end of the matter. The next crucial step is to inquire about the inferences that can be legitimately drawn from it. This refers to principles of reasoning that are not in the sole province of the expert, but, as argued by Robertson & Vignaux (1995, p. 219) "[. . .] can and should be understood by everybody involved in the legal process."

As we have seen, inferences based on forensic findings are not pre-determined, because they depend on the competing propositions put forward at trial. Whether they operate in an adversarial or an inquisitorial setting, scientists need to consider their findings in the light of both the version of events as told by the prosecution and the version of events as reported by the defense, and they have to do so in a way that is recognizable by all participants in the proceedings.[55] It is not only fair from a legal point of view; it is also necessary to reason logically.

Addressing this precept correctly must lead scientists to an expression of the degree to which their findings allow one to distinguish between the competing versions of the events, while reserving the expression of an opinion about the events themselves to the recipients of expert information. The scientist must help the decision-maker revise his beliefs about the competing stories in a case in light of the scientific results, but must not make the decision for him, because it does not logically follow from a correspondence between trace and suspect profile that the suspect is the source of the trace. This deterministic view of acceptance and rejection of particular propositions conflicts with the logically correct way of reasoning, according to which, scientific findings can only have a gradual discriminative capacity for distinguishing between propositions, even if a reported "match" is in fact a true "match" (Redmayne et al., 2011). The initial formulation of the mission given to the experts by the court in the Knox case did not appear far from this precept, as it requested "a degree of proof." Unfortunately, the experts did not succeed in meeting this demand.

Finally, the courts should bear in mind that, even though scientific evidence can be powerful, the results of the analyses carried out don't mean anything out of the context in which they were produced and will be applied. Expert witnesses can, and do often, provide valuable information, but it is always the decision-maker's responsibility to tailor that information to the case at hand, and thus ensure that science does not lead justice down the wrong path.

Notes

1　The term 'evidence' is used here in a generic sense. In a strict perspective, evidence denotes outcomes of forensic examinations that, at a later point, may be retained and used by legal decision-makers in a court of law to reach a reasoned belief on a *probandum*.

2　It is worth mentioning, however, that many experts working in an inquisitorial setting work in police or state laboratories. Their longstanding work relationships with the prosecution can thus raise legitimate questions as to their actual impartiality.

3　See, for example, the discussion presented in Champod & Vuille (2010).

4　Bullet lead analysis or hair comparisons provide some examples in this respect. This should not be taken to mean, however, that scientific approaches could not provide relevant means for studying the underlying physical matter (i.e., bullet lead or hairs) as such. The issue, instead, is whether results of *comparative* examinations of such trace matter can be meaningfully assessed so as to help answer questions of legal interest.

5　Generally, the causal relationship between two events is very difficult to establish, and in most cases where a wrongful conviction has been ascertained, its causes were numerous. In this contribution, we will use the verb "lead" to underline the fact that evidence that was exculpatory in a given case failed to exonerate an innocent suspect.

6　Except red blood cells in mammals.

7　The number refers to the size of the allele. At any given locus, one individual can thus be described with the two numbers referring to the alleles he possesses. More generally, the allele size (or number) represents the number of times a particular combination of more basic molecules are repeated. Notice further that if the two alleles are described by the same number, the individual is said to be homozygous. If the two alleles are different, then the individual is said to be heterozygous.

8　Except in the case of identical twins. Note that it is the whole molecule of DNA, which is composed of thousands of pearls, that is considered to be unique. It does not follow from this, though, that the combination of 10 or 15 locations analyzed during standard forensic examinations will be different in each individual who is considered.

9　See also further discussion in Evett & Weir (1998).

10　See Thompson, Taroni & Aitken (2003) for further details on the distinction between a true correspondence (i.e., an unobserved state of nature) and a reported correspondence (as it is given, for instance, in a written report).

11 For example, detected signals may be of varying intensity (due to the quality and amount of the analyzed DNA) so that analysts must decide, for each locus considered, which alleles make up the profile at hand. Ultimately, such decisions rely on the analyst's personal judgment, but may be informed by guidelines.

12 E.g., Evett & Weir (1998), Buckleton et al. (2004).

13 The authors of this chapter do not have an opinion as to whether the people involved in this case were in fact guilty or innocent of the crime for which they were prosecuted. The purpose of the discussion in this chapter is to point out certain aspects of the way in which biological traces were handled and processed in that case—according to publically accessible reports as quoted hereafter—that raise legitimate concerns.

14 The case against Rudy Guede, including DNA traces used in that context, is beyond the scope of this chapter.

15 It is worth emphasizing that the term LT-DNA qualifies a DNA stain in terms of its quantity, whereas *low-copy number* (LCN) DNA—another frequently encountered term in this context—refers to a particular technique for analyzing DNA traces (e.g., with an elevated cycle number or increased injection time).

16 Very generally speaking, stochastic effects are phenomena that are now widely recognized as factors that influence profile morphology. For example, they may lead to the appearance of additional signals or the non-detection of alleles that are actually present in the sample.

17 "*Non aveva ripetuto l'analisi perchè 'in questo caso l'altezza dei picchi della frazione minore del DNA presente nell'elettroferogramma non mi dava motivo di pensare che ci potesse essere da qualche parte un effeto drop out*'" (Stefanoni, Massei Judgment, p. 238).

18 For example, from the three DNA traces lifted from the knife, A, B, and C, A and B were declared to be positive at quantification, whereas specimen C was discarded for being 'too low.' Yet, specimens B and C both got the reading 'too low' at quantification (see deposition of Tagliabracci, Massei Judgment, p. 265). There might have been a legitimate reason for this discrepant practice, but none appeared in the various reports and depositions made by the Italian police officers.

19 We are not implying that such was the case, but the fact is that their practice allowed the defense attorneys to argue that making such an assumption was reasonable.

20 Such was the case, for instance, for items 67 through 80; see Laboratory DNA Report, pp. 119–124. See also Appeal Brief, p. 61.

21 Appeal Brief, p. 55.

22 This means that an event of drop-in could affect a given tube but not a parallel negative control, while the reverse observation may also hold. When contamination occurs, on the other hand, it is expected to affect a stain profile across several loci.

23 Profazio, Massei Judgment, pp. 92 ss; Napoleoni, Massei Judgment, pp. 95 ss.

24 Brocci, Massei Judgment, pp. 100 ss.

25 "*Precisava che i guanti nel corso del sopralluogo venivano cambiati ogni qualvolta fosse stato toccato un oggetto particolarmente intriso di sangue o con delle evidenze che fanno ritenere che i guanti si sporcano*" (Stefanoni, Massei Judgment, pp. 211–212).

26 Apparently, the shoe protections were changed only when one would exit the house, but not when one went from the corridor to the rooms, from one room to the other, etc. See Stefanoni, Massei Judgment, pp. 208–209.

27 Stefanoni, Massei Judgment, p. 208.

28 Stefanoni, Massei Judgment, p. 208.

29 Stefanoni, Massei Judgment, p. 208.

30 Stefanoni, Massei Judgment, p. 213.

31 The analyst could have had knowledge of several relevant publications that she could have readily found in general reference books when she was processing the case, such as Buckleton

et al. (2004). As more recently reiterated by Gill & Buckleton (2010), a particular example is the paper by Gill & Kirkham (2004) that discusses the mechanisms in detail and covers an evaluative approach that is also known in the field from training workshops held at an international level.

32   Stefanoni, Massei Judgment, p. 230.

33   In fact, on both the knife and the bra clasp, the scientists were unable to characterize the nature of the biological material that gave rise to the profiling results.

34   Further discussion on the hierarchy of propositions is pursued later in this chapter.

35   Most often, a stutter lies one unit below the actual size, although sizes of minus two units or plus one unit are also occasionally observed (Balding & Buckleton, 2009).

36   Stefanoni, Massei Judgment, pp. 215–216.

37   RFU is an abbreviation for 'relative fluorescence unit,' a unit used to measure signal intensity.

38   Stefanoni, Massei Judgment, p. 218.

39   Massei Judgment, p. 257.

40   At this point, the term 'interpretation' refers to the study of the raw data, that is, the examination of the signals of the instrument's output in order to decide which signals are representative of genuine alleles.

41   Stefanoni, Massei Judgment, p. 217.

42   See the chapter by William Thompson and Simon Cole in the present volume. The court was of another opinion, and stated that the argument of bias had no foundation in logic: "*Non ritiene questa Corte condivisibile tale censura. La stessa, oltreché priva di fondamento logico, appare smentita dalle emergenze acquisite*" (Massei Judgment, p. 277).

43   Stefanoni, Massei Judgment, p. 194.

44   Massei Judgment, p. 206.

45   Note that the reviewers of the DNA evidence (Conti and Vecchiotti) also failed to address that question. Their report has received both positive and skeptical comments by recognized specialists in the field. For example, in a talk held at the International Conference, "The hidden side of DNA profiles. Artefacts, errors and uncertain evidence" (Rome, Italy, Università Cattolica del Sacro Cuore, 27 to 28 April, 2012), Prof. Balding expressed the opinion that the reporting of Profs. Conti and Vecchiotti was excellent in many respects. However, he also mentioned that it has had unfortunate impacts by reinforcing the idea that profiling results from low quantity DNA traces are inherently dangerous. Moreover, this report did not consider any quantification of the probative value of DNA profiling results.

46   The probability of a false positive (Thompson, Taroni & Aitken, 2003) or, more generally, the probability of error (Robertson & Vignaux, 1995; Buckleton et al., 2004) may also be considered at this juncture.

47   Notice that, at this point, the "unknown person" proposition is used as a generic illustration. More generally, the defense could argue for other propositions (e.g., a close relative, such as a brother).

48   In more technical accounts on the topic, this factor is also known as the likelihood ratio (Aitken & Taroni, 2004; Aitken et al., 2010). It allows scientists to specify by how much the odds in favor of a proposition (as compared to the stated alternative) are reinforced by the scientific findings, whatever the odds for this proposition were prior to considering the findings. The likelihood ratio is a generic result in probability theory and prescribes—on a normative basis—how to revise beliefs coherently in the light of new information.

49   These precepts can also be developed and stated in a more formal way using probability theory, which allows one to demonstrate that these considerations are requirements that assure logical coherence (e.g., Aitken & Taroni, 2004). This level of presentation is beyond the scope of this contribution.

50   *"E' possibile confrontare tale DNA e quello rinvenuto in una traccia con le medesime metodologie, con i medesimi mezzi analitici e dire se il sospettato sia o no il proprietario della traccia"* (Stefanoni, Massei Judgment, pp. 182–183).

51   Similarly biased sentences have also been expressed in the Rinaldi & Boemia Report.

52   The result of such an analysis is called a haplotype, a notion that designates the genetic constitution of an individual for a genetic trait that is only present as one exemplar.

53   Conti & Vecchiotti Report, p. 130.

54   As a side-note it is interesting to add that, actually, the Conti & Vecchiotti Report questioned the reported correspondence in the first place. According to their reading of the raw data, they argue that the detected DNA should be more properly considered as a mixture, rather than a single donor stain. Generally, inference of source is weakened for mixed DNA stains compared to single donor stains.

55   The European Court of Human Rights derives from the right to a fair trial the concept of equality of arms, according to which no party in the proceedings should be put at a disadvantage compared to the other parties. In our view, this entails the obligation for any expert witness commissioned in the course of the case to assess his or her findings in light of the hypotheses put forward by each side, and to do so explicitly (Champod & Vuille, 2010).

References

Aitken, C. G. G., Roberts, P., & Jackson, G. (2010). *Fundamentals of probability and statistical evidence in criminal proceedings, Guidance for judges, lawyers, forensic scientists and expert witnesses.* Royal Statistical Society's Working Group on Statistics and the Law.

Aitken, C. G. G., & Taroni, F. (2004). *Statistics and the evaluation of evidence for forensic scientists.* Chichester: John Wiley & Sons.

Balding, D. J. (1999). When can a DNA profile be regarded as unique? *Science & Justice*, 39, 257–260.

Balding D. J., & Buckleton J. (2009). Interpreting low template profiles. *Forensic Science International: Genetics*, 4, 1–10.

Buckleton, J., Triggs, C. M., & Walsh, S. J. (2004). *Forensic DNA evidence interpretation.* Boca Raton: CRC Press, 2004.

Buckleton, J., Walsh, & K. A. J., Evett, I. W. (1991). Who is "random man"? *Journal of the Forensic Science Society*, 31, 463–468.

Champod, C., & Vuille, J. (2010). *Scientific evidence in Europe—Admissibility, appraisal and equality of arms.* Strasbourg: Council of Europe, European Committee on Crime Problems.

Cook, R., Evett, I. W., Jackson, G., Jones, P. J., & Lambert, J. A. (1998). A hierarchy of propositions: deciding which level to address in casework. *Science & Justice*, 38(4), 231–239.

Evett, I. W., Gill, P., Jackson, G., Whitaker, J., & Champod, C. (2002). Interpeting small quantities of DNA: the hierarchy of propositions and the use of Bayesian networks. *Journal of Forensic Sci*ences, 47(3), 520–530.

Evett, I. W. & Weir, B. S. (1998). Interpreting DNA evidence: statistical genetics for forensic scientists. Sunderland, MA: Sinauer.

Gill, P., & Buckleton J. (2010). A universal strategy to interpret DNA profiles that does not require a definition of low-copy number. *Forensic Science International: Genetics*, 4, 221–227.

Gill, P., & Kirkham, A. (2004). Development of a simulation model to assess the impact of contamination in casework using STRs. *Journal of Forensic Sciences*, 49, 485–491.

Petricevic, S., Whitaker, J., Buckleton, J., Vintiner, S., Patel, J., Simon, P., Ferraby, H., Hermiz, W., & Russell, A. (2010). Validation and development of interpretation guidelines for low copy number (LCN) DNA profiling in New Zealand using the AmpF1STR® SGM PlusTM multiplex. *Forensic Science International: Genetics* 4, 305–310.

Redmayne, M., Roberts, P., Aitken, C. G. G., & Jackson, G. (2011). Forensic science evidence in question. *Criminal Law Review*, 5, 347–356.

Robertson, B., & Vignaux, G. A. (1995). *Interpreting evidence, evaluating forensic science in the courtroom*. Chichester: John Wiley & Sons.

Taroni, F., Champod, C., & Margot, P. (1998). Forerunners of Bayesianism in early forensic science. *Jurimetrics*, 38, 183–200.

Thompson, W. C., Taroni, F., & Aitken C. G. G. (2003). How the probability of a false positive affects the value of DNA evidence. *Journal of Forensic Sciences*, 48, 47–54.

9

TUNNEL VISION, BELIEF PERSEVERANCE AND BIAS CONFIRMATION

ONLY HUMAN?

Chrisje Brants

Over the past years, four major cases of wrongful conviction have shocked the Netherlands. There are probably others and there are certainly cases in the public domain that are dubious, although those convicted have not (yet?) been exonerated. The miscarriages of justice represented by these four cases—that did, eventually, end in exonerations—were not all directly due to the same type or combination of mistakes. There was police incompetence and police misconduct; unethical behavior on the part of prosecutors and expert witnesses; failure to disclose; misunderstandings about expert evidence; false confessions; and courts believing improbable theories. In one case there was no mistake at all in a legal or procedural sense—except that the defendant went to jail for a crime that never took place.[1]

What these cases do have in common is that, despite what seems blindingly obvious to us all in hindsight, policemen, prosecutors and courts genuinely believed they had convicted a guilty person. Indeed, the investigation, prosecution and trial progressed relentlessly toward the guilty verdict. Not because the evidence of guilt against the different defendants was overwhelming but because, from the beginning, the criminal justice authorities believed they were guilty and sought throughout the criminal process to confirm that belief. What caused the Dutch miscarriages was a combination of tunnel vision, belief perseverance, and bias confirmation—related, but not identical phenomena that occur in both adversary and inquisitorial systems of criminal justice and throughout the criminal process—from pre-trial investigation to trial, appeals, and post-conviction exoneration procedures (Findley and Scott, 2006: 295). They are very human, cognitive errors that are made by all concerned—police, prosecutors, judges, even defense attorneys.

Adversarial and inquisitorial criminal justice systems are vulnerable in different ways and at different points in time to tunnel vision, belief perseverance, and bias confirmation, although each has safeguards against precisely this type of error. The inquisitorial system has monitoring and control of the police by a non-partisan prosecutor and of the prosecution by investigating magistrates and active trial judges. The adversary system relies on equality of parties, and autonomous defense rights to unmask weaknesses in the prosecution evidence and present in full the case for the defense. This chapter is not concerned with the direct causes of wrongful convictions but with the question of why they are not noticed, intercepted and rectified during pre-trial investigation and at trial. Why do the inbuilt safeguards not prevent police, prosecutors, and courts from ignoring exonerating facts, overlooking discrepancies in evidence, knitting together unlikely theories of guilt and, in the final outcome, sinning in concert against one of the most important maxims of criminal justice: *in dubio pro reo* (or, in adversarial terms, guilt must be proved beyond reasonable doubt)?

The first part of this chapter deals with tunnel vision, belief perseverance, and confirmation bias and their potential effects on criminal justice. This is followed by a short overview of the most important characteristics of Dutch criminal procedure in relation to the procedural safeguards that should prevent wrongful convictions, and a factual description of the four Dutch cases. These will then form examples in a discussion of how tunnel vision, belief perseverance and confirmation bias have affected the Dutch inquisitorial system and which measures have been adopted to try and prevent such mistakes from happening again. Although the emphasis is very much on the Dutch system, it is discussed in terms of the characteristics of inquisitorial criminal justice in general and against the background of comparable issues in adversarial systems. I shall argue that, although the inquisitorial system would seem to have by far the better chance of catching and rectifying misjudgments caused by cognitive errors, the difference with the adversary system is not as great as it would seem at first sight.

Tunnel Vision, Belief Perseverance and Confirmation Bias

In its strict (medical) sense, tunnel vision means that a person can no longer see to the side, so that the field of vision becomes circular and tunnel-like. Derived from this physical impairment is a broader, psychological meaning in which tunnel vision means cognitive bias, or rather "the product of a variety of cognitive distortions that impede accuracy in what we perceive and how we interpret it" (Findley and Scott, 2006: 307). In the criminal justice process, this can lead authorities at all stages of the procedure to become fixated on a certain person while ignoring clear indications—at least, they would be clear if they were not out of the range of vision—that the suspect or defendant could be innocent. Definitions of tunnel vision abound and usually include not only the concept itself, but also a number of interrelated cognitive phenomena. Although these have been recognized as major contributors to wrongful convictions for many years (e.g., MacFarlane (2010: 20–31) refers to the work of Borchard (1932) and Frank (1957)), the most extensive study to date of the causes and effects of tunnel vision in criminal process has been that of Findley and Scott (2006) who, in turn, cite Dianne Martin (2002) and Myrna Raeder (2003) in their definition:

> By tunnel vision, we mean that "compendium of common heuristics and logical fallacies," to which we are all susceptible, that lead actors in the criminal justice system to "focus on a suspect, select and filter the evidence that will 'build a case' for conviction, while ignoring or suppressing evidence that points away from guilt" [citing Martin—cb]. This process leads investigators, prosecutors, judges, and defense lawyers alike to focus on a particular conclusion and then filter all evidence in a case through the lens provided by that conclusion [citing Raeder—cb]. Through that filter, all information supporting the adopted conclusion is elevated in significance, viewed as consistent with the other evidence, and deemed relevant

and probative. Evidence inconsistent with the chosen theory is easily overlooked or dismissed as irrelevant, incredible, or unreliable.

(Findley and Scott, 2002: 292–293)

This definition describes a process in which tunnel vision is both the
consequence of fixation on a certain suspect (bias) and the reason why this
leads to a one-sided search for more incriminating evidence or to
interpretations of evidence as incriminating (bias confirmation), even in
the face of facts that point in the opposite direction (belief perseverance).
Other types of bias also play a role in promoting and sustaining tunnel
vision. Hindsight bias ("I-told-you-so") results from the inclination to
believe, in hindsight, that the outcome was inevitable because it confirms
the original bias, leading investigators to overestimate the degree to which
the suspect always appeared guilty and to emphasize evidence that seems
to confirm this (Findley and Scott, 2006: 317; MacFarlane, 2010: 40).
And, finally, outcome bias, although related to hindsight bias, refers not to
"the effect of outcome information on the judged probability of an
outcome, but to its effect on the evaluations of decision quality" (Baron
and Hershey, 1988: 570; Findley and Scott, 2006: 319–320). Was the
decision—in hindsight—good or bad? The effects of belief perseverance,
hindsight bias and outcome bias occur not only during criminal
investigations and/or trials, but can also stymie post-conviction attempts
to have a case reopened.

Such misjudgments are the result of how people normally deal with the
informational environment—seeking, sifting, accepting and accommodat-
ing presumed facts and excluding and rejecting others. "People collect
information until it satisfies a previously determined goal" (Van Koppen,
2011: 145) and "if [they] have taken a certain stance or believe a certain
theory for whatever reason, they do not deal symmetrically with information that reaches them later. Rather, they actively seek information that
supports their original belief …" (Crombag, 1997: 567). This is not
always, even usually not, a conscious process of deliberately ignoring
information that does not fit preconceived ideas, and it is not, per
definition, a bad thing. "Cognitive biases are a byproduct of our need to
process efficiently the flood of sensory information coming from the outside world. Without some system of categories or 'schemata' to organize
that information, it would remain, in the imagery of noted psychologist

and philosopher William James, a 'blooming, buzzing confusion'"(Findley and Scott, 2006: 309).

Tunnel vision, then, is the result of the natural, human way of making sense of the permanent overload of information with which people have to deal. The problems occur when it affects the type of professional decision-making that requires that all information be taken into account, perhaps especially information that seems contradictory to any preliminary conclusion. Few doctors would wilfully ignore signals that their first diagnosis was wrong, yet in the medical world tunnel vision is responsible for many a misdiagnosed condition. Likewise, few policemen or prosecutors would intentionally "pin guilt" on an innocent suspect and probably even fewer judges (or juries) would deliberately convict an innocent person. But tunnel vision prevents us from seeing anything other than what is within our restricted range and, more importantly, leads us to believe there is nothing beyond what we can see and, as a result, assume to be obvious. Tunnel vision is a *process of interrelated and mutually reinforcing, cognitive biases* that occurs in individual information-processing, but can also be passed along the chain of decision-making that leads to a verdict in a criminal case. It is an inevitable element of human fallibility in criminal justice.

MacFarlane (2010: 44) emphasizes the importance of recognizing "tendencies that are quite natural [but] can distort normal decision-making processes." This seems a somewhat contradictory statement insofar as, given that it is inherently human, it is normal for tunnel vision to occur in decision-making. What is more important—and perhaps this is what MacFarlane means with "natural" and "normal"—is that decision-making in the criminal justice process should take place within a normative structure of rules and professional ethics, with safeguards designed to prevent tunnel vision from perverting individual, professional decisions in the first place and, should it nevertheless occur, to intercept and nullify the effects as the process progresses. Such rules, ethical prescriptions and safeguards are about making sure that all avenues of investigation are explored and all doubts that there could be another explanation of events examined and removed before a finding of guilt is pronounced—the exact opposite of tunnel vision.

Yet, cognitive biases play a major role in most wrongful convictions, even if the latter appear to be the result of other, more obvious factors, such as mistaken eyewitness identification, false confessions, snitch testimony, incorrect or misunderstood expert evidence, even intentional bullying or distortion of the evidence by police or prosecutors. All of these factors can be both the cause and the result of tunnel vision. To give but one example: Convinced of a suspect's guilt (because it seems "obvious"), police may over-pressurize the interrogation, which may lead to a false confession, which in turn confirms the original bias, which may lead to ignoring (and not informing the prosecutor of) discrepancies in that confession or the existence of exculpating information, which may in turn lead the prosecutor to introduce the confession as evidence—and so it goes on.

The Dutch Criminal Justice Process[2]

In many ways, the Dutch criminal justice process is one of the most typical of all inquisitorial systems, and it takes some fundamental inquisitorial notions to the extreme. Those notions derive from a belief that codified criminal procedures will ensure that the state guarantees both truth-finding and fair trial, with the overarching aim of discovering the substantive truth. That requires a criminal investigation and presentation of evidence at trial that are as complete as possible but also non-partisan and it puts the concept of a non-partisan, impartial prosecutor at the heart of the inquisitorial process—which is all the more important because investigation and prosecution are not separate functions as in an adversary process. The prosecutor is in control of pre-trial investigation activities by the police and compiles the trial "dossier," which in turn sets the agenda for the trial (Brants and Ringnalda 2011: 17–26). While pre-trial investigation in adversarial systems also influences what happens at trial, the defining truth-finding moment is still verbal presentation and contestation of the prosecution and defense cases before a passive tribunal of fact. Strictly speaking, in inquisitorial systems there is no such thing as a case for the defense. There is simply a case, with all incriminating and exculpating evidence contained in the dossier, including transcripts of witness statements. Therefore, although the trial judge has an active investigative function, it is not theoretically necessary to physically produce all evidence or witnesses in court. It is not verbal contestation of evidence from and by both parties that guarantees a reliable verdict on guilt or innocence; rather, the integrity of state officials and their commitment to non-partisan truth-finding is relied upon to produce a just result.

The Actors

In the Netherlands, pre-trial investigation and truth-finding at trial are exclusively entrusted to state professionals. Unlike the adversarial attorney, Dutch defense lawyers do not investigate, introduce evidence or call witnesses and do not cross-examine. There is no lay-involvement at trial and cases are adjudicated by professional judges. Bringing a criminal investigation and trial to a successful—*i.e.*, truthful—conclusion is seen as requiring the considered and distanced judgment of state-employed legal professionals, acting in accordance with written rules of criminal procedure and professional ethics and policy.

Pre-trial investigation is conducted by the police, who take instructions from and are answerable to the Prosecution Service. While they are not literally required by law to investigate all aspects of the case impartially, this is a professional and ethical criterion deriving from the assumption of non-partisan prosecution which includes the police–prosecutor relationship and the inseparability of investigation and prosecution. Constitutionally, the Public Prosecutor is both a member of the career judiciary and a government employee. Prosecutors are expected to play a quasi-judicial role—that is, they must weigh all interests, including those of the suspect in controlling and monitoring police investigations, deciding whether or not to prosecute, compiling a trial dossier, and presenting the case at trial. But they are also bound to policy rules issued by the heads of the Service, the Council of Procurators-General, who in turn answer to the politically accountable Minister of Justice. After law school, prosecutors train in the same way as judges and thus have no training in advocacy. Many prosecutorial functions once belonged to the investigating magistrate (who still exists in many other inquisitorial jurisdictions). In the Netherlands, his main task now is to authorize pre-trial detention, telephone taps and bugs requested by the prosecution, and to interview witnesses who will not be called in court.

Dutch trial judges sit alone in minor cases, in panels of three in more serious cases, and in panels of five in the appeal courts. Judges are fully acquainted with the dossier before trial, but are expected (and trained) to keep an open mind as to guilt or innocence. Impartiality and a commitment to an active investigative role are the mainstays of the professional ethic. A court case must begin before the suspect has spent more than 100 days in pre-trial custody, but can be adjourned immediately if the prosecutor needs more time. Consequently, suspects may spend many months in custody, during which they may be questioned by the police in the context of the prosecution investigation. While every defendant in a criminal case has the right to a lawyer and will be assigned one if indigent, only minors have a right to have their lawyer present during interrogation.

Pre-trial, defense lawyers monitor the compilation of the dossier. In court they attempt to weaken the prosecution case and prompt the judge toward evidence favorable to the defendant. They cannot subpoena witnesses or experts and must request the prosecutor to do so, although they can bring a witness physically to the courtroom. The court has the final say on whether a witness will be heard. Experts are appointed to the court and are not witnesses for the defense or the prosecution. They produce written reports but may be called to elucidate their findings. Although most work for forensic laboratories or psychiatric assessment centers that are part of the criminal justice system, they too are expected to be impartial and non-partisan.

Paper Trials

Compared to adversary procedures, a Dutch trial is short, document-based, and with limited debate in court. With no requirement that all evidence be produced in open court, the use of hearsay testimony is widespread. Threatened and/or vulnerable witnesses are usually heard under oath by the investigating magistrate in chambers, who then provides a report of his findings, which are regarded as evidence given to the trial court. The defense may challenge the accuracy of the prosecution case and request additions to the dossier or the hearing of new witnesses at trial. Here too, the court has the final decision on whether new witnesses are heard; whether the dossier is complete and relevant or whether documents should be added to it or may be left out; and whether expert opinion may be challenged by the introduction of other experts—in short, on whether it considers itself in possession of all relevant facts. The court also questions the witnesses first, followed by the prosecution and the defense. The trial ends with the prosecutor summing up the evidence of guilt and demanding a certain penalty (although he may conclude that the defendant should be acquitted), and the defense pleading the defendant's case and emphasizing weaknesses in the evidence and/or mitigating factors.

Safeguards Against Wrongful Convictions

In essence, the Dutch criminal justice process relies on the integrity of the system, its ability to police itself and the power of the law to keep it on track (Jörg et al., 1995). Pre-trial, legislation grants (and limits) police, prosecutorial and judicial powers to arrest, detain, interrogate, and investigate. While suspects have pre-trial rights (access to the dossier, assistance of a lawyer, lawyer–client contact and confidentiality), these are not regarded as the most essential guarantees of an accurate outcome of the trial. If substantive truth-finding by the state is considered endangered by defense rights, most can be curtailed "in the interests of the investigation" and, for the same reason, there is no right for adults to have a lawyer present during police questioning. It has always been thought sufficient that the police are forbidden by law to use undue pressure against the suspect and that he must be told of his right to remain silent. Even this is relatively recent (Brants, 2011b). The greatest safeguards against pre-trial error are the requirements of non-partisan investigation, control by the quasi-judicial prosecutor, and the possibility that mistakes, irregularities, or illegalities will emerge in court because they will have left a paper trail in the dossier and can (if not already corrected by the prosecutor) be discovered and corrected by the court.

At trial, the guiding principle is not open contestation during which alternative scenarios may be put forward by the defense, but "internal transparency": all participants must be acquainted with the information in the dossier. This allows the court actively to investigate and verify the prosecution case, and if necessary to ask (on its own initiative or at the prompting of the defense) that more information be provided. Internal transparency is a guarantee that the verdict will not be based on incomplete evidence and will indeed reflect the substantive truth. It rules out charge bargaining, because the prosecutor and the defense cannot agree to leave things unsaid, and it requires a full trial even if the defendant has admitted guilt, which is also why the prosecutor cannot stop the prosecution once started, even if he believes there is no case to answer. It also means there can be no conviction on evidence not known to the defense. But again, the defense is secondary, since the right to access the complete dossier only becomes absolute ten days before trial.

The rules of evidence are also designed to lead the court to an accurate outcome. They determine how evidence may be used to construe guilt, the weight that attaches to different sorts of evidence, and the relationship between evidence and guilty verdict. Only the judges' own observations during trial, statements/confessions by the defendant, witness statements, other statements or written documents (such as reports by experts), and official written statements by investigating officers may be used as evidence. With the exception of the latter (insofar as they do not amount to the—hearsay—testimony of a single witness or the defendant), all evidence requires corroboration. Moreover, the court may not convict without sufficient evidence even if it is convinced of guilt, and it may also not convict if there is sufficient evidence but it is not convinced (a negative system of proof). The standard is "beyond reasonable doubt." As an extra guarantee, the court must give a reasoned verdict. Both the defendant and the prosecutor have the right to appeal.

Appeal is an important safeguard against wrongful convictions, since it involves a full retrial (according to more or less the same rules as apply in the first instance). Many verdicts by lower courts are overturned in this way and miscarriages avoided. The appeal court's decision on the facts is final. Appeal to the Supreme Court (cassation) is possible on points of law only. A convicted person or the prosecutor at the Supreme Court can also ask that court to review the case, order it reopened and, if necessary, retried. This will only succeed if new evidence casts doubt on the original decision, for the review procedure is designed to prevent the Supreme Court from becoming a court of third (factual) instance. It must first establish the existence of new evidence not known to the tribunal of fact, and then that such evidence, had it been known at the time, would have led to an acquittal in the final, factual decision. The case is then referred to another appeal court for retrial.

Four Dutch Cases of Wrongful Conviction

Compared to adversarial systems, the most obvious difference in the safeguards against wrongful conviction and the occurrence of tunnel vision in the Dutch criminal justice process is the lack of independent, external control to allow a challenge to the prosecution case through the presentation of evidence supporting an alternative scenario. But it is an entirely coherent procedural system, and if the safeguards work as intended,[3] it needs no external guarantees such as autonomous defense rights based on equality with the prosecution. Indeed, until the 1980s, wrongful conviction was a non-issue and only two major cases had ever come to light. A study of 35 "dubious cases" (Crombag et al., 1992), showed how entrenched was the view that "such things do not happen here". Although there are undoubt-edly some wrongful convictions among these 35 (and one has since been overturned), the research was dismissed out of hand by almost the whole legal community. After the four cases outlined below, which all led to exonerations within a few years—sometimes a few months—of each other, it can no longer be denied that Dutch criminal justice too is prone to tun-nel vision and its effects.

The Putten Murder Case[4]

In 1994, a woman was raped and strangled at her home in the village of Putten. A month later, four men were arrested following eyewitness testimony that their car had been seen parked near the house. They themselves gave conflicting statements on their whereabouts at the time of the murder. During police interrogations, two of them said they had seen the others go to the house, and, through the window, had seen them sexually assault and strangle the victim. These other two confessed after lengthy questioning. The confessions were introduced as evidence, although both (and one of the incriminating statements) were retracted at trial. There were also other, contradictory, eyewitness statements and (uncertain) reports from the forensic laboratory: DNA from a hair on the victim's clothing and from semen on her thigh did not match that of the defendant's; a pubic hair found at the scene was first said not to be from one of the suspects, then "not ruled out"; fibers on one of the defendant's trousers "probably matched" a rug at the crime scene. An independent expert testified that the semen, explained by intercourse with a person unknown prior to the murder, was most likely "dragged out" by one of the defendants during the rape. The two defendants were convicted on the accumulation of this evidence, at trial and later on appeal.

The case was reinvestigated in depth by a television journalist and a retired chief of police. They concluded that the crime could not have taken place within the time frame, or in the manner, claimed by the prosecution and that the evidence was seriously flawed. The police had used undue pressure and tricks during the interrogations. All four men had then given false statements. The two witnesses (one of whom was of subnormal intelligence) who said they saw the murder committed, admitted on camera they had lied. The expert who presented the "dragged-out-semen" theory now said that crucial information had been withheld from him and declared his findings spurious. New, improved DNA testing showed that the semen and both hairs came from the same unknown person. The Supreme Court refused to admit these findings as "new evidence" and denied several requests to have the case reopened. Finally, the expert wrote a new report retracting his original findings about the semen. The Supreme Court accepted this, referring the case for retrial. The men were exonerated. In 2009, a third person was convicted of the crime.

The Schiedam Park Murder[5]

In June 2000, two children were sexually assaulted by a man in a park in Schiedam, near Rotterdam. The girl was strangled, the boy seriously injured. A passer-by called the police, and they soon focused on this man as the suspect: he was in the park and was a known pedophile, although the boy's description of the attacker did not fit and other witness statements were contradictory (although all mentioned a bicycle). He confessed under protracted police interrogation but retracted the confession two days later. DNA from the crime scene did not match the suspect's, who also had an alibi and practically no time to commit the crime. He was convicted at trial and again on appeal. The convictions were based primarily on the (retracted) confession and circumstantial evidence such as the fact that the defendant was in the park at the time, with a bicycle. Neither court nor defense were told that unidentified DNA found on the body had also been on the murder weapon, nor that scientists at the forensic laboratory had expressed serious doubts to the prosecution about the defendant's guilt. In 2003, the Supreme Court refused a petition for cassation.

While he was in prison, his case was investigated by the innocence project at Maastricht University.[6] This cast serious doubt on the conviction (Van Koppen, 2003). The report was sent to the head of the Prosecution Service in 2002; he never answered. In September 2004, the Supreme Court dismissed a request for review, because nothing pointed to there being "new evidence." Journalists then discovered that in August 2004, someone had been arrested for another crime and had confessed spontaneously to the Schiedam murder. Had this been known, it would certainly have constituted new evidence at the review hearing a month later. Gradually it also emerged there was a match with the new suspect's

DNA, and that he had no alibi and had committed several other violent sexual offenses against children. The Prosecution Service continued to deny any mistakes. After a prolonged media campaign, the convicted man was released and then exonerated after the Supreme Court referred the case for retrial in January 2005. As a result of this case, a temporary innocence commission (CEAS) was instigated with powers to investigate suspected wrongful convictions.

Lucia de Berk[7]

Lucia de Berk was a nurse at a children's hospital. Between 2000 and 2001, her colleagues began to spread rumors that she was suspiciously often present when a child died. The hospital director consulted a medical expert (who found it unlikely that these deaths were all due to natural causes) and then engaged in some amateur statistics, alleging that Lucia was always either the one responsible for the children's medication or the last person present before they died. Deciding this couldn't be coincidence, he held a press conference about the deaths, named the nurse as a possible suspect and informed the police. The police gathered information about the hospital unit concerned and about sudden, inexplicable deaths at other hospitals where De Berk had worked, tapped her telephone and consulted a statistician whose findings they took as proof that the suspicions were well-founded. Lucia de Berk never confessed and there was no direct evidence against her, but in 2003 she was convicted and sentenced to life imprisonment for four murders and three attempted murders; in 2004 the sentence was upheld on appeal, but now she was convicted of seven murders and three attempted murders. The court of first instance convicted on the basis of statistical probability posited by an expert, a professor in statistics, in combination with corroborating medical evidence of unnatural death. On appeal, the statistical evidence was rejected (it had come in for much criticism in the media), but once on the stand, a new medical expert (requested by the defense) testified that he "was now of the opinion" that the first child had been killed. The appeal court found corroboration for this "proof of murder" in Lucia's diary where she had written of "her secret" and having to "stop this compulsive behavior." The final verdict rested on these two pieces of evidence and on what became known as "repeating proof": given that there was proof she had murdered the first child and that the deaths of the other six were inexplicable, there could be no other explanation than that Lucia had murdered them too.

Some, including her lawyer, were convinced that Lucia de Berk was innocent. A few worried citizens started websites or blogs to get her case reopened.[8] Statisticians and doctors appeared on television disputing the findings of the experts at trial. A professor specializing in the philosophy of science published a book outlining the mistakes that had been made in the case, citing the world's leading expert in this type of death in sick children (Derksen, 2006). He approached the CEAS commission. It reinvestigated and advised the Prosecution Service to push for review. Although in doubt as to whether the disputations of other scientists could be regarded as "new evidence," the prosecutor at the Supreme Court requested review because, in his opinion, the children had died of natural causes and there had therefore been no crime. The Supreme Court referred the case for review, the new evidence being "progressive scientific insight." Lucia de Berk was exonerated in April 2010.

The Ina Post Case[9]

The case of Ina Post is the most recent exoneration but the oldest case, only reopened because of the existence of the CEAS Commission. In August 1986, an old lady was strangled in an apartment block for the elderly. Checks were stolen and later cashed, presumably by the murderer. The police used these checks for a graphology test of the handwriting of the victim's caretakers, one of whom was Ina Post. She immediately became the chief suspect. Her signature resembled that of the presumed murderer and the police thought that she was "nervous" when asked to produce a sample of her handwriting and signature. During police questioning, she confessed twice, but later retracted the confessions. She was found guilty in the first instance and again on appeal. The evidence consisted of the (retracted) confessions, her "nervous behavior," and the graphologist's opinion that the signature on the checks was not the victim's and "could not be ruled out" as the defendant's.

The Supreme Court refused four requests for review. These were based on new graphology tests; expert testimony that Ina Post was highly suggestible; information contained in interviews with police officers who had participated in the investigation and reported serious incompetence; expert reports on new developments in graphology; and reports questioning the authenticity of the confessions (Israëls, 2004). The Supreme Court regarded none of this as "new evidence." The conviction of Ina Post attracted a great deal of media attention and in later years (the conviction took place long before the general accessibility of the Internet), blogs and websites were created on her behalf. The innocence project at Maastricht University also examined this case and found it to be flawed. They later referred it to the CEAS Commission, which recommended that it be reopened. In 2009 the Supreme Court granted Post's fifth request for review. She was exonerated after a retrial in October 2010.

The Inevitability of Tunnel Vision in Dutch Criminal Justice

The central role of the prosecutor in the Netherlands and the emphasis on pre-trial procedure as the focus of substantive truth-finding imply risks of wrongful conviction, of which the legislature was well aware when the Code of Criminal Procedure was enacted. It explicitly states that its aim is "to impose the criminal law on those who are guilty and to prevent both conviction of the innocent and their subjection to prosecution."[10] It compensates for the paucity of defense rights by providing stages in the criminal justice process at which the prosecutor, investigating judge, trial court and appeal court are meant to scrutinize the conduct and results of the previous phase. At the junction of the interrelationship between procedure and legal culture sit the principles of non-partisan prosecution and active investigation at trial, bolstered by the training and professional ethics that permeate the Prosecution Service and the judiciary and, strange as it may sound to adversary ears, even the police. Criminal justice professionals in the Netherlands know that they bear the main responsibility for making sure that all avenues of investigation are explored, including those that could point to innocence rather than guilt. Yet, as these four cases make abundantly clear even at first sight, those same professionals are as prone to tunnel vision as professionals anywhere else.

After all, Dutch prosecutors and judges are as human as American DAs and jury members, and just as likely to want to persevere in believing what they have come to think is the right conclusion. If it were not so serious, it would be comical to note the exact same form that belief perseverance can take. Findley and Scott (2006: 316) cite Professor James Liebman: "prosecutors have become . . . sophisticated about hypothesizing the existence of 'unindicted co-ejaculators' (to borrow Peter Neufeld's phrase) to explain how the defendant can still be guilty, though another man's semen is found on the rape-murder victim." This is a variation on the "dragged-out-semen-theory" that allowed prosecutors and courts to explain away exculpating evidence in the Putten case. In general, closer examination of the Dutch cases brings to light the same factors that have been put forward to explain tunnel vision in adversary systems.[11]

Systemic Flaws

One explanation is that the proces itself is systemically flawed and contains elements that, far from preventing tunnel vision, actually encourage it. Leopold (2005: 1124) maintains that the adversary pre-trial process in the United States can, "even when it is working properly [. . .] distort the gathering and presentation of exculpatory evidence." He notes that while the process should ensure that evidence supporting both prosecution and defense versions of events are presented to a jury, many of its pre-trial features (rules of evidence, criteria for bail, quality of public defenders, venue rules) undermine the ability of the defense to gather exculpatory evidence and, therefore, increase the likelihood of wrongful conviction. Inquisitorial systems that rely on the prosecutor rather than the defense to gather and inform the court of exculpatory evidence obviously do not suffer from this failing. But other, equally problematic and systemic features play an important role in wrongful convictions, in both the pre-trial and the trial phase.

In the Netherlands, the predominance of the search for the substantive truth has always stood in the way of any external control on how police interrogations are conducted. Instead, the system relies on a non-partisan attitude on the part of the police (which implies that police investigations will be conducted with an open mind), on the legal provisions forbidding undue pressure and requiring that the suspect be cautioned, and on hierarchical control by the prosecutor to prevent or correct over-persuasive and/or abusive interrogation and its potential result: a false confession. The system itself, however, only allows the police to interrogate if they have reason to believe that the suspect is guilty, so interrogation is always skewed toward gathering evidence to support that suspicion. It is hard to see how the police can be expected to have an open mind, especially if there is no lawyer to sow doubt. Then, undue pressure is a relative concept in the light of the foregoing, for the Dutch police, while certainly not brutal, use the same sort of persuasive interrogation techniques that are common in adversary systems and again, there is no lawyer to protect the suspect.

In the four wrongful convictions, the police concluded from the beginning that the suspect was guilty: because of mistaken eyewitness testimony (Putten); because she acted nervously (Ina Post); because he was a known pedophile (Schiedam); and because colleagues and her boss slandered her as peculiar and suspect (Lucia de Berk). All of these represent well-documented causes of tunnel vision at the front of the decision-making process (see, e.g., MacFarlane, 2010: 52), especially if backed up by circumstantial evidence: the seemingly unshakable—but mistaken—eyewitness; the unpopular outsider; the suspect with a background of similar crimes. Three of the four cases involved false confessions. They were made in the Putten case during a highly stressful, though by no means illegal, interrogation situation that lasted two months during which the suspects had no contact with the outside world or with their lawyers ("in the interests of the investigation"). In the Schiedam Park murder, the police not only pressured the suspect to confess but also, as confirmation bias set in, exerted what the official report described as inadmissible and intolerable pressure on the boy witness to make him admit the description of his attacker was a fabrication (which he never did). In the case of Ina Post, suggestive, forceful questioning led her to confess twice to both theft and murder. Only external controls such as the presence of a lawyer, or audio-visual recording of the interrogations could have prevented this or brought it to light.

Recording of interrogations has been suggested as an improvement in adversarial jurisdictions and indeed made obligatory in the UK 1984 Police and Criminal Evidence Act after a number of high-profile miscarriages of justice. But it is particularly important in the Dutch system. MacFarlane (2010: 53) suggests that because of separation of investigation and prosecution, prosecutors generally base their case on one-dimensional, guilt-confirming police evidence and do not see other information generated by the investigation. For this reason, Findley and Scott (2006: 385) advocate a standard police practice of keeping "a complete log of all evidence gathered in the investigation—physical and testimonial evidence, both confirmatory and exculpatory" and submitting it to the prosecutor. That is already not only standard practice in the Netherlands; it is a legal requirement. The problem is that there is no way of knowing what exactly was said during an interrogation, whether it was skewed to produce confirmation of a suspicion, or whether a confession was tainted by coercion. Written police reports are not verbatim, do not contain the questions and are written in the form of a continuous statement by the suspect. It is up to the prosecutor to recognize and correct police bias, but he rarely attends police interrogations. The non-separation of investigation and prosecution, although intended as a safeguard, in fact makes the prosecutor and the police interchangeable in the investigation phase and serves to bolster the prosecutor's belief that he can rely on police results.

Confirmation bias, which occurred in all four of the Dutch cases, then becomes a particular problem. The police in the Putten case, for example, focused exclusively on the two suspects, attempted to find evidence to "fit" existing suspicions, and failed to follow up on apparently contradictory eyewitness testimony or to check whether events could have taken place as alleged. The investigation of Ina Post focused exclusively on proof of her guilt. Her alibi was not verified; information that the murder could be linked to another death in the same apartment block with roughly the same modus operandi—in which Post could not possibly have been involved—was not followed up; and neither were other indications that this was the wrong suspect. The day-to-day reliance of the prosecutor on the very organization he is supposed to be supervising makes it highly probable that such belief perseverance and confirmation bias is passed on. Moreover, the prosecutor has his own incentive to continue to believe the suspect is guilty and not to want to question police evidence too closely.

While the adversary system may be construed as a contest and fosters an attitude of wanting to win, the adversary prosecutor is nonetheless ethically obliged to prosecute only those whom he believes are guilty. And so, as Findley and Scott note (2006: 329), it is in "those most committed to the ideal of doing justice [that] the prosecutorial role inevitably fosters tunnel vision." MacFarlane adds that, in Canada, an honest belief in guilt on the part of the prosecutor is a legal requirement. For the Dutch prosecutor, the specific and legal responsibility for a non-partisan police investigation and for the impartiality of the decisions he bases on it, means even greater pressure. The resulting belief perseverance may not take the form of deliberate attempts to doctor the evidence presented to the court, if only by omitting discrepencies and contradictions, but some elements of our four cases point to just that. The official report on the Ina Post case, although laying most of the blame on incompetent policing, also found that the dossier had been incomplete, evidence destroyed, and expert reports presented as decisive proof of guilt although they were either ambiguous or based on deliberately incomplete information.

In its exonerating judgment on the Putten case, the referral court severely criticized the prosecutor who appeared before it for misrepresenting and failing to acknowledge exculpating new (DNA) evidence that pointed to innocence, as did most of the witness statements and the fact that the victim could not have been strangled as alleged by the defendants in their false confessions. Even after the exoneration, many prosecutors and judges—in particular those at the appeal court that had handed down the final verdict—continued to maintain the defendants were guilty. This is belief perseverance taken into the retrial and beyond, although there is no suggestion it was deliberate. The Schiedam case however probably caused by far the greatest outrage, precisely because of the lack of integrity on the part of the prosecution that it demonstrated.

Here, the prosecutor in the first instance ignored anything that pointed to the suspect's innocence. Although scientists at the state forensic laboratory told the prosecutor before the trial that they doubted the defendant was guilty, nothing of this found its way into the final version of their report or the dossier. The prosecutor at the appeal court also had doubts but left them unsaid in court. It is unclear what persuaded the scientists to leave *their* doubts out of the report except that the district prosecutor told them to make sure "the defense can't run away with this DNA-business." As well as deliberately witholding this information and the crucial DNA findings from the courts and the defense, the prosecution also misled the Supreme Court when it considered the request for review, by not making it known that another person had confessed to the murder. They may not have been informed by the police (unlikely), or they may have been prompted by belief perseverance, but the prosecution continued to assert that no mistakes had been made well after exculpating information had become public knowledge. That may also be the result of that other very human failing – the dread of losing face.

This case highlights another systemic problem: the independence of forensic experts who work within the system. That forensic evidence can be, indeed often is, partisan in adversary trials is acknowledged as problematic and as a contributing factor in tunnel vision. Experts who identify with one of the parties may come to see their task as promoting that party's cause, rather than providing impartial scientific evidence

(MacFarlane, 2010.) This was specifically identified by the English Court of Appeal as one of the causes of the wrongful conviction of Judith Ward, jailed for IRA terrorism offenses in 1974, which noted that "the adversarial character of the proceedings tends to promote this process."[12] In the Netherlands, experts are appointed to the court but, given the nature of the inquisitorial process, they are nevertheless "working for the prosecution," although most would deny this. However, the very fact that their appointment makes them beholden only to the court, as is it is intended to do, reinforces their and the court's perception of expert findings as totally non-partisan, impartial science. While not a direct cause of tunnel vision, this can certainly reinforce it if they become embroiled in prosecution strategies of confirmation bias or belief perseverance.

Trial procedure, rules of evidence and judicial decision-making processes can also promote wrongful convictions by allowing judges to indulge in tunnel vision. In the three Dutch cases in which the defendants confessed falsely to the crime, those confessions were quickly retracted but nevertheless figured prominently in the court's reasoning of the evidence. The other evidence was either circumstantial, ambiguous, or highly debatable. The rules should ensure that judges adopt a neutral and impartial attitude in weighing each type and piece of evidence on its own merits, after which they should come to a decision on the basis of that evidence. In practice these rules, although designed to do the opposite, allow courts to scrape together a conviction without really questioning the prosecution case. It is also difficult to avoid the conclusion that evidence is used, and verdicts so reasoned, as to confirm what the court thinks in the first place.

Crombag (1997: 565–569) attributes this to the predominance of the dossier in Dutch trial procedure. Courts see the dossier and therefore have already formed some idea of the case; a one-sided idea, given that the dossier has been compiled by the prosecution. At trial, it is the task of counsel to undermine that idea but, as we have seen, that is not facilitated by the structure of the process. Perhaps that is why judges, according to Crombag, rarely talk about the defense when deliberating the verdict (nor about what the prosecution has said in summation). Their preliminary judgment, based on the dossier, seems to carry considerable weight. With a reference to German research,[13] Crombag (at 569) not only concludes that belief perseverance also affects judges, but that "the usual procedural order of things in the Netherlands and in most other continental European countries . . . seems especially designed to incite to this particular type of faulty thinking." It is compounded by the fact that, in their written reasoning, the court need not discuss all the evidence and any doubts they may have had; it merely has to enumerate the legally permissible evidence upon which the decision is based, although they must give a reasoned response to some defenses and specific arguments.

The procedural order of things and the decision-making process itself are factors in promoting confirmation bias and belief perseverance among judges, and such cognitive errors are exacerbated by legal requirements. Dutch courts must "speak with one voice" in order to promote legal certainty and the legitimacy of the particular decision. There are no dissenting opinions, or if there are, they never become public (judges are bound to keep secret whatever is discussed in chambers). The logical consequence is that a panel of judges will attempt to reach, if at all possible, a unanimous decision (although that is not a legal requirement; a majority suffices). According to Van Koppen (1997: 557), this leads to groupthink and the suppression of minority opinions. And because judges are professional and there is a professional way of doing things, deciding, and concurring, young judges will be most likely to dissent, discovering very quickly that this is not the way to be accepted by one's peers. That this socialization process among judges has very real effects on judicial decisions is borne out by research (De Keijser et al., 2004).

The court that convicted the Putten defendants on appeal unquestioningly accepted controversial and dubious evidence, relying on two retracted confessions, convenient eyewitness statements and ambiguous expert reports, and disregarding evidence that pointed to an alternative explanation. Likewise in the Schiedam Park murder, the court went blithely along with the prosecution, dismissing the boy victim's evidence as not credible, accepting the prosecution's improbable time frame that explained away the alibi, and the assertion that the fact that the defendant's DNA was *not* found at the crime scene was proof of guilt and deviousness rather than innocence: "He had been careful not to leave evidence behind."

But while in all four cases the courts continued in confirming the prosecution bias, the case of Lucia de Berk is perhaps the most distressing example. Lucia did not confess. After the statistical evidence that had served to convict her at first instance had been discredited, the only legal proof at appeal was the (unexpected) opinion of one medical expert that one of the children had not died a natural death. All the rest was circumstantial, and based on malignant gossip, but it was interpreted by the appeal court as corroboration of murder. Lucia had indeed overseen the medication of many children and had been present at many deaths. It did not occur to the judges that it would have been strange had it been otherwise, given that she was a staff nurse. Her diary entries (referring to her "secret" and "compulsive behavior") were taken as references to killing children, although this was repudiated by the forensic psychiatrist who examined the diary, and she herself said she was writing about an addiction to laying the tarot in the presence of dying patients, which she felt was inappropriate behavior for a nurse. The construction of "repeating proof" is particularly alarming for it is literally a way of legalizing belief perseverance. The appeal court put the worst possible interpretation on the evidence and then resorted to some very tortured logic to prove its own point.

Finally, all of the convicted defendants had great trouble in getting their cases reopened and were refused review by the Supreme Court, some on several occasions. It is difficult to judge to what extent the review procedure itself exacerbates the consequences of tunnel vision. In all juridisctions, criminal cases must come to an end. Not allowing a retrial serves to protect society, the legitimacy of the criminal justice system, and the authority of the judiciary from the effects of the uncertain justice of reopening cases simply because somebody disagrees with the verdict. For that reason, only new evidence that was not known to the court at the time and could have influenced the verdict, will suffice. It is also legitimate that the Supreme Court, which is not a tribunal of fact, is careful not to become a third instance; in the constitutional order of things, that is not its job. However, it cannot be denied that the definition of new evidence is exceedingly narrow and that in this sense the review procedure hardly protects wrongfully convicted defendants from the effects of tunnel vision.

There are a number of systemic reasons why the new evidence criterion is a problem, one of the most important being that Dutch defense lawyers are neither trained nor have the authority to conduct in-depth investigations and therefore have difficulty in uncovering new evidence. Given that expert evidence carries a great deal of weight with the legal professionals who judge Dutch cases (and the four miscarriages were no exception), one of the most easily available sources of new evidence is an independent expert. However, unlike, for example, the adversary system in the U.K., Dutch defendants and "their" experts (an anomaly—an expert who testifies in favor of the defendant is still an expert to the court) do not have the right to access physical evidence held by the police or the forensic state laboratory, and need permission from the prosecutor at the Supreme Court to examine it in connection with review. If this is already a barrier, for many years it has been standing case law that new or revised expert opinion, or the possibilty of more sophisticated scientific tests, does not constitute new evidence. In our four cases, an exception was made for the Putten defendants, the Supreme Court referring explicitly to "exceptional circumstances." Ina Post had no such luck. Whether the Supreme Court also fell prey to belief perseverance in these cases is a moot question. What is certainly true is that external pressure from the media, academics, and the general public was instrumental in getting them reopened.

Institutional Pressures and Predisposing Circumstances

Criminal process does not operate in a vacuum, and even procedures such as the Dutch process that are careful to exclude the influence of the lay public, are affected by extraneous factors. Studies of tunnel vision group such factors under "institutional pressures" (Findley and Scott, 2006: 322–333) and "predisposing circumstances" (MacFarlane, 2010: 4–6). There is much overlap in these categorizations. MacFarlane's predisposing circumstances, for example, include some of the institutional pressures which constitute separate factors for Findley and Scott. Both studies take some legal features to be extraneous (the role pressures associated with adversary prosecution, for example) that are described above as internal and systemic. More important, however, is that external pressures and internal characteristics of the system interact and are mutually reinforcing.

Where the previous section delves extensively into the influence of inquisitorial process itself on tunnel vision, the external factors need less explication. Here there is little difference from the situation in most other Western democracies, and they have been extensively documented in almost all of the studies that deal not only with tunnel vision but with wrongful conviction in general. They can be summarized as the pressures of public opinion and the media in a harshening criminal justice climate, in which increasing demands are made on the state to protect society from crime and criminals. Such pressures may cause police, prosecutors, and

judges to feel that speed in bringing the case to a successful conclusion—
that is, a conviction—is the overarching objective and that procedural
rules are a secondary consideration, to "blind themselves to their own
inappropriate conduct and to perceive that conduct as legitimate in the
belief that they are pursuing an important public interest" (MacFarlane,
2010: 6). This is particularly the case if the public is especially outraged
by horrendous or very frightening crimes involving, for example, child
victims or terrorism. While all this in itself is conducive to tunnel vision,
the likelihood increases greatly if, in reaction to public and political
pressure, new legislation, caselaw or policy measures reduce the guarantees
of due process that guard against wrongful conviction, because they are
seen as standing in the way of convictions—in which case external pressure
results in systemic problems, or exacerbates existing flaws.

One point does require a little more explanation, and that is why
wrongful convictions have shifted from being a non-issue to an issue of
major public interest in the Netherlands and how the system itself has
reacted. For a long time, that country was regarded as a paragon of
enlightened criminal justice (Downes, 1988), a reputation based in a reality
that lasted perhaps 20 years (Van Swaaningen, 1995). Part of this reputation
derived from the fact that the Dutch criminal justice authorities and the
media existed in an arrangement of peaceful coexistence that allowed
the system to operate relatively uncriticized at a time when crime and
incarceration rates were low and the prevailing paradigm held that criminal
justice should be the very last resort in solving social problems.[14] This was,
perhaps, less benevolent than at first sight and, in any event, the past 20 to
30 years have revealed an iron fist in the ideological velvet glove.

By the end of the 20th century, crime and fear of crime had become
politicized issues and professionalized and commercialized media were
translating general feelings of insecurity into criticism of the criminal
justice authorities, in particular the Prosecution Service. Public and
political demands for more and better crime control and speedier
procedures that offered more protection to society and less to criminals,
undermined the legitimacy of criminal justice. The Dutch system is built
on the exclusion of public participation and public opinion because these
are regarded as irrational and emotional and thus an unwarranted
interference in a process of rational, professional justice. It now became
highly sensitive to critical media coverage and public demands for results.

The response was new legislation to increase the efficiency of pre-trial investigation and court procedure, and the number of trials that end in convictions. As a result, the powers of the prosecutor were enhanced, those of the investigating magistrate (intended as an extra non-partisan safeguard in criminal investigation) reduced and defense rights curtailed, most especially with regard to disclosure of the dossier before the ten day limit, the right to have witnesses called and the right to full retrial. The latter is meant to guard against tunnel vision by providing for a fresh investigation of the case, unhindered by conclusions about the evidence. Now, for reasons of efficiency, appeal courts may, and do, rely on the transcript in the first instance trial concerning evidence and witness statements without re-examination, so that any bias from the original court investigation is simply incorporated into the next. It has also become more difficult for the defense to suggest alternative interpretations of the evidence as case law increasingly requires that reasons be shown why the court should doubt the accuracy of the dossier, or the legality or reliability of the evidence. The politicization of crime has brought not only procedural change but politicization of the Prosecution Service itself, with the emphasis shifting from the role of the prosecutor as a quasi-judicial official with individual responsibility for non-partisan investigation and prosecution to one who is executing government criminal justice policy.

All of these factors played a part in the four wrongful convictions, not least public opinion, and all of the cases were reported widely in the media. In the case of Lucia de Berk—a prime example of MacFarlane's first predisposing circumstance: public and media pressure—the police, prosecution, and courts (and experts) were swept along on the vicious preconception of guilt that informed public opinion. Like Lindy Chamberlain in Australia, whose case MacFarlane highlights (2010: 17–20),[15] Lucia was the typical outsider, disliked and viewed as peculiar by both her colleagues and the investigators and regularly depicted as a witch—sometimes literally—by the media. But what these cases also show is that it takes external pressure to break through established tunnel vision. The reopening of all four was the result of moral crusading by journalists or outsiders using the media. Moreover, what came to light about the unprofessional behavior of the prosecutors in the Schiedam murder case forced the Prosecution Service to conduct an internal inquiry, while the court of first instance was so shocked by its own decision that it too conducted an internal review into how these things had occurred. And there have been lasting consequences. Courts are now significantly more inclined to acquit in cases of homicide (Van Koppen, 2011: 289), "a program of improvements" has been implemented by the Prosecution Service and legislation is pending to amend the review procedure.

Policy and Legislation to Improve the System

Changes to the system that followed recommendations by the internal inquiry commission after the Schiedam Park murder are contained in an extensive report by the police, the Prosecution Service and the state forensic institute (Versterking opsporing, 2005). Throughout, the report seeks to strengthen the role of the non-partisan, quasi-judicial prosecutor in finding a balance between truth-finding and fair trial. In many ways, this mirrors recommendations by Findley and Scott who advocate "layer[ing] some features of a more neutral, inquisitorial system within the adversarial framework" (2006: 37), in particular with regard to policing and prosecution, and they propose precisely the measures now in force or coming into force in the Netherlands in the near future. The Dutch authorities are specifically concerned with guarding against tunnel vision and exhort police and prosecution to look further than sufficient evidence to convict. Organized evaluation of all aspects of the case, including any possibly exculpating evidence, is mandatory, first internally by the police and then by the prosecution. New policy rules also prescribe that prosecutors reflect with colleagues on a regular basis on the aspects of the cases they are handling. If there is any doubt, prosecutors should have a third party, such as an academic, review the case (Versterking opsporing, 2005: 18–22).

Measures such as organized evaluation and third-party review are intended to prevent tunnel vision and confirmation bias being passed along the chain from the police investigation onwards. Others specifically aim to prevent the false confessions that can be both the effect and the cause of tunnel vision. The police have introduced a new manual and improved training on interrogation techniques and the danger of false confessions. The Prosecution Service has produced binding guidelines on situations in which audiovisual recording of police questioning of suspects and witnesses is mandatory (Aanwijzing, 2010). They specify exactly how it should take place and how data should be stored, but, in accordance with standing case law, expressly rule out the defense's or the suspect's receiving copies of the recording. The defense does have a right to know it has taken place and to request that (parts of) it be filed as evidence in the dossier, a right that may be limited in the interests of the investigation or (vulnerable) witnesses until ten days before trial.

The one right that an adversarial lawyer would fight to retain, however dissatisfied with the "polarizing pressures" of the adversary system and enamored of inquisitorial pre-trial process (Findley and Scott, 2006: 372), is the right to the presence of a lawyer during police questioning. It has remained an absolute no-no in the Netherlands, despite the recognition of the real dangers of false confessions. This centuries old aversion among most jurists—in criminal justice and academia—to the idea of lawyer-assisted suspects during police interrogations, "because then they will refuse to say anything", has brought the Dutch system into conflict with recent case law from the European Court of Human Rights that suggests this is a fundamental element of a fair trial.[16] The impact of these European decisions was even greater since they coincided with the public debate on wrongful convictions. In a mission of damage control primarily concerned with minimizing the effect, the Dutch courts and criminal justice authorities have interpreted the ECHR judgments to mean that only minors have a right to have a lawyer present; adults have no more than the right to consult a lawyer prior to or during interrogation. This is regulated in a set of binding instructions from the Procurators General (Aanwijzing rechtsbijstand, 2010), although legislation is to be expected. What it will bring is uncertain. Political pressure and ongoing developments in European cases led the Minister of Justice and Security reluctantly to concede that "it can by no means be ruled out that in future" there will be a right to have a lawyer present during police interrogations (Letter to the Second Chamber, 2010).

Legislation is already in the process of being enacted concerning two related matters: a commission of investigation to review criminal cases, and the review procedure.[17] Again, the former is a reform advocated by Findley and Scott (2006: 396), but it does not resemble the U.K.'s Criminal Cases Review Commission and neither is it independent. The convicted person may petition the Procurator General at the Supreme Court to investigate his case,[18] who can then seek the advice of a commission (mandatory if the sentence exceeds ten years) as to the necessity of further investigation. If it takes place, the assistance of an investigation team of

police officers, prosecutors and, if necessary, external experts may be called
in, or the judge of instruction ordered to open an investigation. The
Supreme Court will still have the last word on whether a case is to be
reopened but will in the future be bound to interpret "new evidence" as
including new forensic insights.

Conclusions

Adversary process is based on the myth that adversarial debate between
equal parties will produce the "truth" so long as procedural rules are
followed. The myth of the Dutch inquisitorial process is that law-governed,
state-controlled state investigation and professional integrity are sufficient
to guard against inaccurate outcomes. But even if, in real life, parties were
equal, procedural rules always followed, and the integrity of professionals
always beyond doubt, as we have seen, neither type of procedure is
sufficiently equipped to prevent or correct the cognitive biases of tunnel
vision. In some cases, both actually encourage them.

In the Dutch case, the accumulation of hierarchical and judicial
controls, the rules of evidence and the possibilities of retrial and review, are
designed to make it possible to catch and correct bias at every stage in the
procedure—for bias is anathema to a process based on non-partisan
investigation and prosecution. Adversary systems are based essentially on
partisan contest, and pre-trial process must run its course before biased
policing and prosecution can be exposed at trial. To say that adversary pre-
trial process, even if the rules are followed, encourages tunnel vision—or at
least the impossibility of correcting it—comes down to an argument that
party inequality makes correction through the presentation of an alternative
defense case impossible and encourages plea bargains that are based on
tunnel vision. On these grounds, it looks as if the Dutch inquisitorial
process has by far the better pedigree. But at the same time, its reliance on
non-partisan professionals and cumulative controls to find the substantive
truth are precisely what may allow errors to accumulate in a chain reaction
of misguided actions and decisions.

While a full retrial by a higher court perhaps means that the mistakes
that inquisitorial systems make are less irredeemable than those made by
adversary ones where the defendant has only one chance, the very existence
of a chain of guarantees that is meant to intercept and eradicate mistakes
also facilitates passing them on. Tunnel vision invariably starts at the front

end of the chain, with the police, followed by the prosecution. Paradoxically, it can be exacerbated by the very foundation of inquisitorial logic: that the state can be trusted to carry out a non-partisan investigation at the heart of which is a prosecutor in control of the police. Again, although yet more internal control makes the courts the most important monitors of police and prosecution activities, judges are greatly influenced by the way prosecutors build the dossier (De Keijser et al., 2004) so that they become susceptible to tunnel vision on the basis of their prior knowledge of the prosecution case. Van Koppen and Schalken (2004) even maintain that, despite the ideological commitment to the substantive truth, Dutch trial procedure is not about whether the evidence points beyond reasonable doubt to the defendant's guilt but about whether the available evidence does not contradict the prosecutor's assertion that he is indeed guilty. It is hard to think of a better recipe for belief perseverance and confirmation bias.

So no, the Dutch system does not have a better pedigree. It has a different family tree, but it remains as prone to tunnel vision as the adversary system, albeit in a different way. One of the reasons is that the same external factors, institutional pressures and predisposing circumstances magnify the systemic flaws that were so dramtically exposed in the four cases discussed here. Now that they have led to the shocked awareness that Dutch criminal justice is, after all, only a human endeavor, the question is whether the proposed solutions will have the desired effect. The way in which they have been, and will be, implemented perhaps contains a lesson for those who would introduce inquisitorial elements into adversary (pre-trial) process. With regard to proposals for American criminal review commissions on the lines of CCRC in the U.K., which is indeed an inquisitorial institution in an adversarial system, it has been said these would be no more than "state strategic selection mechanisms," designed to take the sting out of public criticism and unrest and to prevent further reaching demands for reform (Schehr, 2005). To my mind, that is too simplistic and cynical an explanation that also smacks too much of conspiracy theory.

It is, however, true that the legal culture that underlies criminal justice systems produces a tunnel vision of its own and makes it well-nigh impossible to contemplate reform that is not based on their fundamental characteristics. This has been the case in England, where the enhanced power of the Crown Prosecution Service and notions of non-partisan investigation and prosecution have been translated into elaborate disclosure rules that have further undermined party equality by making the defense even more dependent on the prosecution. In Scotland, the same developments have led to reductions in legal aid because, if prosecutors are non-partisan and disclosure is mandatory, why should the defense need money to conduct their own investigation? (Brants and Ringnalda, 2011). The same mechanism is apparent in the Dutch measures of improvements that are all based on the presumption that the system can ensure its own coherence and integrity—can police itself. They provide internal monitoring and do not allow for real defense participation or external controls; those that have that potential (audiovisual recording, lawyers attending police interrogations, a review commission) have all been modified to fit the inquisitorial model. They may help counter the specific forms of tunnel vision with which that model struggles. Perhaps, but they may also encourage it, restricting our range of vision and therefore making it more difficult to spot.

Notes

1 Only two of these four cases are wrongful convictions in the sense that other suspects have been identified and convicted. However, one case involves a crime that took place almost 25 years ago and now falls under the statute of limitations. In the other, a court eventually found that no crime had occurred. Given that under these circumstances the investigations will never be reopened and no other perpetrator will ever be found, it is inappropriate to argue, as some continue to do, that these cases cannot be regarded as miscarriages of justice because the "real" murderer was never identified.
2 For a more detailed account, see Brants, 2008: 157–182.
3 On the relationship between truth-finding and fair trial in all criminal justice processes and the different ways in which this relationship is expressed in the safeguards of adversarial and inquisitorial procedure, see Brants (2011a).
4 Based on the final exonerating decision by Appeal Court Leeuwarden, April 24, 2002, LJN: AE1877.
5 The facts are taken from the official report commissioned in January 2005 by the Prosecution Service after it became apparent that someone else was most probably the perpetrator. The full report is available on www.rijksoverheid.nl.
6 This project, "*Gerede Twijfel*", is the only private innocence project in the Netherlands.
7 Based on review judgment, HR October 7, 2008, LJN: BD4153 and exonerating judgment Hof Arnhem April 14, 2010, LJN: BM0876, on J. De Ridder et al. (2008, Chapter 6), and on the official report on the case, available on www.om.nl.
8 See, for example, the website www.luciadeb.nl, and the blog http://pietg.wordpress.com [accessed April 27, 2012].
9 Based on the exonerating judgment of June 6, 2010, LJN BN94444 and the reconstruction by the CEAS Commission (CEAS 2006/0018), on www.om.nl.
10 *Kamerstukken II* (Parliamentary Documents second chamber) 1913/14, 286, 3, 55.
11 See notes 5, 6, 8, and 10 *supra* for the sources of information about the four cases.

12 R. v. Ward [1993] 2 All E.R. 577 (C.A.) per Glidewell J.

13 German court procedure is very much like the Dutch process insofar as judges are acquainted with the (prosecution) file beforehand, although in the German case the effects are perhaps mitigated by the fact that German judges sit with lay assessors and all evidence must be presented in open court.

14 On the political, social and legal-cultural background of this period in Dutch history, see Brants, 2010.

15 She was jailed in 1980 for the murder of her baby daughter. In 2012, the coroner finally established that the most likely scenario, as Lindy herself had always maintained, was that the child had been killed by a dingo.

16 ECtHR, April 26, 2007, appl. no. 36391/02 (Salduz v. Turkey); also: ECtHR, September 24, 2009, appl. no. 7025/04 (Pishchalnikov v. Russia), ECtHR, October 14, 2011, appl. no. 1466/07 (Brusco v France).

17 Wijziging van het Wetboek van Strafvordering in verband met een hervorming van de regeling betreffende herziening ten voordele van de gewezen verdachte (Wet hervorming herziening ten voordele, TK 2010/2011, 32 045.

18 The PG at the Supreme Court is not a member of the Prosecution Service and is regarded as independent. His appointment is for life and his main function is to advise the Supreme Court as to the applicable law and the interests of justice in the specific cases that come before it.

References

Aanwijzing auditief en audiovisueel registreren van verhoren van aangevers, getuigen en verdachten (2010). *Stc.* no. 11885.

Aanwijzing rechtsbijstand politieverhoor (2010). *Stc.* no. 4003.

Baron, Jonathan and John C. Hershey (1988). Outcome Bias in Decision Evaluation, *Personality & Soc. Psychol.* 54, 569–579.

Brants, Chrisje (2008).The Vulnerability of Dutch Criminal Procedure to Wrongful Conviction, in: *Wrongful Conviction. International Perspectives on Miscarriages of Justice* (eds. C. Ronald Huff & Martin Killias), Philadelphia: Temple University Press, 157–182.

Brants, C.H. (2010). Legal Culture and Legal Transplants. In *Netherlands Reports to the Eighteenth International Congress of Comparative Law, Washington 2010* (eds. J.H.M. van Erp & L.P.W. van Vliet), Antwerp: Intersentia, 1–92.

Brants, Chrisje (2011a). Comparing Criminal Process as Part of Legal Culture. In *Comparative Criminal Justice and Globalisation* (ed. D. Nelken), Ashgate, 49–68.

Brants, Chrisje (2011b). The Reluctant Dutch Response to Salduz, *Edinburgh Law Review* 15, 298–305.

Brants, C.H. & A. Ringnalda (2011). *Issues of Convergence: Inquisitorial Prosecution in England and Wales*, Nijmegen: Wolf Legal Publishers.

Crombag, H.F.M. (1997). Ook Rechters Maken Menselijke Fouten. In *Het Hart van de Zaak. Psychologie van het Recht* (eds. P.J. van Koppen, D.J. Hessing & H.F.M. Crombag), Deventer: Gouda Quint, 561–577.

Crombag, H.F.M., P.J. Koppen & E.W. Wagenaar (1992). *Dubieuze zaken. De psychologie van strafrechtelijk bewijs*, Amsterdam: Uitgeverij Contact.

De Keijser, J.W, H.G. van de Bunt & H. Elffers (2004). Strafrechters over maatschappelijke druk, responsiviteit en de kloof tussen rechter en samenleving. In *Het maatschappelijk oordeel van de strafrechter. De wisselwerking tussen rechter en samenleving* (eds. J.W. de Keijser & H. Elffers), Den Haag: Boom Juridische uitgevers, 21–52.

De Ridder, J. et al. (2008). *De CEAS aan het werk (Rapport WODC)*, Den Haag: Stu.

Derksen, Ton (2006). *Lucia de B. Reconstructie van een gerechtelijke dwaling*, Diemen: Veen Magazines.

Downes, David (1988). *Contrasts in Tolerance: Post-war Penal Policy in The Netherlands and England and Wales*, Oxford: OUP.

Field, S.A. (2009). Fair Trial and Procedural Tradition in Europe, *Oxford Journal of Legal Studies* 29, 365.

Findley, Keith A. (date unknown), The Problem of Tunnel Vision in Criminal Justice, at www. innocenceproject.org [accessed June 12, 2012].

Findley, Keith A. and Michael S. Scott (2006). The Multiple Dimensions of Tunnel Vision in Criminal Cases, *Wis. L. Rev.* 291.

Israëls, Han (2004). *De bekentenissen van Ina Post*, Alphen aan den Rijn: Kluwer.

Jörg, Nico, Stewart Field & Chrisje Brants (1995). Are Inquisitorial and Adversarial Systems Converging? In *Criminal Justice in Europe. A Comparative Study* (eds. Phil Fennell, Christopher Harding, Nico Jörg and Bert Swart), Oxford: Clarendon Press.

Leipold, Andrew D. (2005), How the Pretrial Process Contributes to Wrongful Convictions. *Am. Crim. L. Rev.* 42, 1123.

Letter to the Second Chamber of Parliament from the Minister of Security and Justice, 16 November 2010 (DDS5673300), www.rijksoverheid.nl/bestanden/documenten. . ./brief-raadsman [accessed May 26, 2012].

MacFarlane, Bruce A. (2010). Wrongful Convictions: The Effect of Tunnel Vision and Predisposing Circumstances in the Criminal Justice System, at www.attorneygeneral.jus.gov. on.ca [accessed May 26, 2012].

Martin, Dianne L. (2002). Lessons About Justice from the "Laboratory" of Wrongful Convictions: Tunnel Vision, the Construction of Guilt and Informer Evidence, 70 *UMKC L. Rev.*, 847.

Raeder, Myrna (2003). What Does Innocence Have to Do With It?: A Commentary on Wrongful Convictions and Rationality, *Mich. St. L. Rev.*, 1315.

Schehr, Robert Carl (2005). The Criminal Cases Review Commission as a State Strategic Selection Mechanism, *Am. Crim. L. Rev.* 42, 1289.

Van Koppen, P.J. (1997). Beslissende Rechters. In: *Het Hart van de Zaak. Psychologie van het Recht* (eds. P.J. van Koppen, D.J. Hessing & H.F.M. Crombag), Deventer: Gouda Quint, 552–560.

Van Koppen, P.J. (2003). *De Schiedammer Parkmoord: een rechtspsychologische constructie*, Nijmegen: Ars Aequi Libri.

Van Koppen, P.J. (2011). *Overtuigend bewijs. Indammen van rechterlijke dwalingen*, Amsterdam: Nieuw Amsterdam Uitgevers.

Van Koppen, P.J. & T.M. Schalken (2004). Rechterlijke denkpatronen als valkuilen: over zes grote zaken en derzelver bewijs. In: *Het maatschappelijk oordeel van de strafrechter. De wisselwerking tussen rechter en samenleving* (eds. J.W. de Keijser & H. Elffers), Den Haag: Boom Juridische uitgevers, 5–132.

Van Swaaningen, R. van (1995). *European critical criminologies*, Rotterdam: EUR.

Versterking opsporing en vervolging: naar aanleiding van het evaluatierapport van de Schiedammer parkmoord—Openbaar Ministerie, Politie NFI, November 4, 2005.

10

"Voluntary" False Confessions as a Source of Wrongful Convictions

The Case of Spain

Marcelo F. Aebi and Claudia Campistol

The vast majority of the scientific literature on wrongful convictions focuses on innocents convicted against their will. In this article, on the contrary, we will concentrate on persons who are wrongfully convicted by their own will. This sort of "voluntary wrongful conviction" is usually based on a false confession. False confessions have been studied mainly as the result of coercion exerted on suspects during interrogation. In that case, the suspects are confessing the offense in order to escape police pressure. They have also been studied in the context of guilty pleas, in which suspects plead guilty in order to obtain a milder punishment than the one they would get by pleading not guilty. Researchers have also analyzed cases in which individuals make false confessions voluntarily, either because they are seeking attention or because they suffer from delusions or are mentally disturbed. However, there are cases in which innocent people take responsibility for an offense without having been subjected to any pressure, without any psychological cause, and without obtaining a tangible personal benefit, such as a milder punishment or some attention from the public. These cases of "voluntary false confessions" have not received much

193

attention from researchers. They will be the subject of this chapter, which focuses on cases of *voluntary false confessions motivated by the perception of an intangible benefit* that can be identified in Spain.

We shall first discuss the way in which false confessions fit the definition of wrongful convictions. In that context, the available typologies of false confessions are reviewed and combined. Focusing later on voluntary false confessions, a proposal is made to classify their causes into two types: those motivated by the perception of a tangible benefit and those motivated by the perception of an intangible benefit. Next, we review the empirical research available on this type of confession, followed by a methodological section that describes the way in which data were collected for this study. A final section presents the results of this research, organized according to the different typologies of voluntary false confessions that are motivated by the perception of intangible benefits observed in Spain. Finally, the results and their implications are discussed in the conclusion.

Voluntary False Convictions: Definition and Causes

In *Convicted but Innocent: Wrongful Conviction and Public Policy*, Huff, Rattner & Sagarin (1996: 10) defined convicted innocents as "people who have been arrested on criminal charges, although not necessarily armed robbery, rape, or murder; who have either pleaded guilty to the charge or have been tried and found guilty; and who, notwithstanding plea or verdict, are in fact innocent." Most of the research available on the topic of wrongful conviction is based on similar definitions (see, for example, Pizzi, 1999; Walker & Starmer, 1999).

Persons convicted following false confessions fit this definition because they are factually innocent. Nevertheless, this constellation has received far less attention from researchers than have other causes of wrongful conviction. This is probably due to the fact that voluntary false confessions are rare. For example, in their review of 205 wrongful convictions, Huff, Rattner & Sagarin (1996: 64) found that 8.4 percent were due to coerced confessions, but they did not find any case of voluntary false confessions.

A false confession takes place when an individual admits to a crime that he/she has not committed. False confessions were initially classified by Kassin & Wrightsman (1985) into three types: voluntary, coerced-compliant, and coerced-internalized. This classification was later modified and enlarged by Ofshe & Leo (1997), who identified five types of false confessions: voluntary; stress-compliant; coerced-compliant; coerced-persuaded; and non-coerced-persuaded.[1] McCann (1998) has also modified the classification of Kassin & Wrightsman (1985) adding the category of *coerced-reactive false confessions*. A combination of these classifications leads to six types of false confessions: stress-compliant; coerced-compliant; coerced-persuaded; coerced-reactive; non-coerced-persuaded; and voluntary.

Stress-compliant confessions "are elicited by the excessive use of psychological, and sometimes physical, stressors that, at a lower level of intensity, are ubiquitous in accusatorial interrogation ... A *coerced-compliant confession* is defined as a statement elicited by the use of classically coercive interrogation techniques, and is given knowingly in order to receive leniency or escape the harshest possible punishment ... [A] *non-coerced-persuaded confession* is elicited in response to the influence tactics and techniques of modern, psychologically sophisticated accusatorial interrogation, and given by a suspect who has temporarily come to believe that it is more likely than not that he committed the offense despite no memory of having done so ... *Coerced-persuaded confessions* ... are elicited ... in response to ... an interrogation that ... incorporates threat, promise or other classically coercive interrogation techniques" (Ofshe & Leo: 1997, 211–219, emphasis added).

According to Kassin (1997: 225, emphasis added): "a *voluntary false confession* is a self-incriminating statement that is offered without external pressure from the police".[2] This definition has been criticized by McCann (1998) because the external coercion can be exerted not only by the police but also by other persons in the suspect's psychosocial environment. McCann (1998) thus suggests a distinction between voluntary false confessions and *coerced-reactive false confessions*. The latter are defined as "confessions obtained through the coercive acts of others (such as threats to harm one's self or loved one), intimidation, and so forth" (McCann, 1998: 448). We can thus redefine a *voluntary false confession* as a self-incriminating statement that is offered without any external pressure. The main component of such a confession is the fact that it is made deliberately.

What are the reasons that lead innocent persons to accept criminal responsibility for offenses they did not commit? Recent research (see, especially, Kassin & Wrightsman, 1985; Kassin, 2008; Leo, 2009;

Sigurdsson & Gudjonsson, 1996a) has suggested a series of causes that we classify into two groups[3]:

- Voluntary false confessions produced by anomalous psychological processes.
- Voluntary false confessions produced by rational psychological processes.

Voluntary false confessions produced by anomalous psychological processes include statements motivated by a pathological need for attention, notoriety, or self-punishment, the need to expiate guilt over imagined or real acts, mental illness, or delusions. These false confessions belong to the fields of psychology and psychiatry and will not be covered by this article, which follows a criminological approach. The examples usually quoted by researchers include the 200 people that "confessed" to the kidnapping of Charles Augustus Lindbergh, Jr. in 1932 (Kassin & Wrightsman, 1985), the more than 50 persons that confessed to the murder of Elizabeth Short—the *Black Dahlia*—in 1947 (Offshe & Leo, 1997), or the case of Henry Lee Lucas who, in the 1980s, falsely confessed to hundreds of unsolved murders (Kassin et al., 2010).

Voluntary false confessions produced by rational psychological processes include confessions elicited by the perception of a tangible or an intangible benefit.[4] They can be explained through rational choice theory (Cornish & Clarke, 1986; Clarke & Cornish, 2000) although this theory has not yet been applied in this context.

Voluntary false confessions motivated by the perception of a tangible benefit include cases in which someone pleads guilty to avoid a harsher punishment. This is particularly the case in some states of the United States, where a guilty plea may allow the defendant to avoid capital punishment. In continental Europe, as well as in most other countries of the American continent, a guilty plea by an innocent person accused of a serious offense such as homicide or rape is difficult to imagine because it can have little influence on the verdict. In fact, according to the vast majority of laws on procedure in Europe and on the American continent, a person found guilty will receive the punishment specified in the criminal code regardless of whether or not he or she pleads guilty. The case could be slightly different when minor offenses are included, due to the recent development of limited forms of plea bargaining in continental Europe, usually under a different name, such as *comparution sur reconnaissance préalable de culpabilité* in France; *Strafbefehl* in Germany; *pattegiamento* in Italy; *voluntary submission to penalty* in Poland; *acordos sobre a sentença no processo penal* in Portugal; *juicio de conformidad* in Spain; or *procédure simplifiée* in Switzerland. These limited forms of plea bargaining—whose development seems related to an important increase in the number of criminal proceedings in many European countries (Dongois, 2006: 99)—may induce some offenders to plead guilty to a different offense than that which they committed, or some innocent defendants to accept responsibility for an offense they did not commit. However, in continental Europe, the negotiations between the prosecutor and the defendant are limited in order to protect the fundamental rights in criminal procedure. The main limitation is that the agreement reached between the prosecutor and the defendant has to be approved by the judge, who can also refuse such deals (Dongois, 2006: 98).

Finally, voluntary false confessions motivated by the perception of an intangible benefit—which are the focus of this article—refer to cases in which the defendant does not seek material benefits, but subscribes to a particular moral code that leads him/her to protect the real offender.

Research on Voluntary False Confessions

Research on voluntary false confessions motivated by the perception of an intangible benefit is scarce. On the basis of a study with 17 adolescents, Beyer (2000) identifies some juveniles who consider it inappropriate to testify against a friend, even if that would mean a harsher punishment for the person who refuses to testify. Krzewinski (2002) quotes the case of Latasha, a thirteen-year-old charged with first degree murder, who falsely confessed having given to her boyfriend the cord he used to commit the murder because she thought she was protecting him by assuming some of the responsibility for the crime. According to Beyer (2000), juveniles some-times act according to a moral code that regards loyalty as one of its highest values. Beyer (2000) attributes this logic to the immature moral reasoning of adolescents. However, loyalty is also an important value for adults, espe-cially, as we will see later, among specific groups of the population. In an unpublished M.Sc. dissertation, Richardson (1991, quoted by Sigurdsson & Gudjonsson, 1996a: 322), also found cases of voluntary false confessions among adolescents who confessed in order to protect their peers.

Sigurdsson & Gudjonsson (1996a) conducted a study with 509 adult inmates and 108 juvenile offenders in Iceland. Sixty-two (12 percent) of the adults admitted having made a false confession during a police interview. However, and contrary to what has been found by Richardson (1991), none of the juveniles admitted such a confession. The three most common reasons for having made a false confession were police pressure (51 percent); protecting somebody else (48 percent); and avoidance of police detention (40 percent). There was also some overlap among these three reasons. Among the 30 inmates that indicated having made a false confession to protect somebody else, the person that was being protected was usually a friend (60 percent, 18 cases), followed by a relative (20 percent), a fiancé or spouse (10 percent), and some other persons (10 percent). According to different psychological tests, the false confessors were significantly more antisocial, compliant, emotionally labile, and had lower self-deception and other-deception scores than the rest of the inmates.

In a more detailed analysis of the 62 false confessors, Sigurdsson & Gudjonsson (1996b) placed this group into the typology of Kassin & Wrightsman (1985) and considered that this typology did not describe adequately the persons that made a false confession in order to protect someone else. According to Sigurdsson & Gudjonsson (1996b) such a confession may be typically voluntary, but it may sometimes be related to the coerced-compliant type. As we have seen, this weakness of the classification led McCann (1998) to create the category of coerced-reactive false confessions. Sigurdsson & Gudjonsson (1996b) found significant differences between the inmates who claimed to have confessed falsely in order to protect somebody else and the rest of the other self-claimed false confessors. The former scored significantly lower on the external pressure factor of the Gudjonsson Confession Questionnaire (GCQ), suggesting that they experienced less police pressure during the interrogations; they were also less inhibited about confessing to the police and reported less regret for having made the claimed false confession. Finally, they also scored high on the drug intoxication factor of the GCQ that measures drug intoxication at the time of offending and during the interrogations. In that context, Sigurdsson & Gudjonsson (1996b) do not deny that being under the influence of drugs, or feeling bad because of withdrawal symptoms, could have made them confused and unrealistic in their reactions to the police accusations and could partly explain their motivation to falsely incriminate themselves.

Voluntary false confessions are also related to offenses committed by organized bands, such as mafias and juvenile gangs, in which the feelings of solidarity and a non-written rule demanding a conspiracy of silence (*omertà*) would command such behavior. Research has often showed that loyalty is one of the main components of the subculture of mafias, juvenile gangs (Klein, 1995), and terrorists (Silke, 2008). However, specific cases of persons having assumed responsibility for offenses committed by other members of such groups are not easy to find.

Methodology

Our review of the available scientific literature, based on *Criminal Justice Abstracts*, the abstracts included in the National Criminal Justice Reference Service, Google Scholar, and the main criminological Spanish reviews, shows that apparently no research on voluntary false confessions motivated by the perception of an intangible benefit has been conducted in Spain.

As a consequence, in order to identify examples of this kind of confession, the online archives of three Spanish newspapers were consulted: *El País*, *El Mundo*, and *ABC*. These archives are currently available since the founding of each of the three journals. This means that for *ABC* they are available since 1903; for *El Mundo*, since 1989; and for *El País*, since 1976. The online archives of the News Agency *Europa Press*, available since 1996, were also consulted.

Different keywords were used for the search. The most appropriate turned out to be "auto-inculpation" (*autoinculpación*). Using this keyword in July 2012 we found 1087 matches (i.e., articles) on the website of *El País*; 144 from *El Mundo*; and 293 from *ABC*. However, an analysis of these articles and those obtained using other keywords showed that most of them were inappropriate and some were redundant, in that they referred to the same event in different articles. The remaining articles were classified according to the logic described in the following section.

Results

Our analysis of the cases found in the Spanish press allows a classification of them into two main types: (1) voluntary false confessions intended to promote a change in the criminal code; and (2) voluntary false confessions intended to protect a person or a group of persons.

Voluntary false confessions intended to promote a change in the criminal code are made in order to put pressure on legislators, judges, and politicians. In Spain, the two cases identified correspond to confessions made by persons wanting to change the laws on abortion and euthanasia. To our knowledge, this type of confession has never received any attention until now.

Among the voluntary false confessions intended to protect a person or a group of persons, we were able to identify confessions made by juveniles, members of the Roma ethnic minority and, possibly, some made by terrorists. In the following subsections, we present the results of our research according to this classification.

Voluntary False Confessions Intended to Promote a Change in the Criminal Code

Abortion

Leaving aside a short period of time during the Spanish Second Republic (1931–1939), abortion was considered a criminal offense in the Spanish Criminal Code until 1985. At that time, it became legal in three specific situations. The adoption of the law on abortion in 1985 was preceded and followed by an important debate which required the intervention of the Constitutional Court. In order to protect the right to abortion and in defense of women and clinics practicing abortion against legal actions by opponents of the law, some women started a campaign of self-incrimination where they admitted to having obtained or having performed an abortion. The number of voluntary false confessions received was so important that in December 1986, the State General Attorney (*Fiscal General del Estado*) issued an internal order to all the State Attorneys of the country to drop these statements, which risked paralyzing the court system. The Attorney ordered that the cases should be filed and the persons who falsely confessed should not be punished for the crime of "offense simulation," which was included in article 338 of the former Spanish Criminal Code and was punishable by imprisonment and a fine (El Pais, 06.12.1986).[5] In 2008, a similar campaign took place with the goal of decriminalizing additional circumstances for legal abortion. In February 2008 alone, 8,000 voluntary false confessions—sometimes presented by men and even by the leaders of a political party—were presented to the courts (El Periódico de Aragón, 29.02.2008).[6] The conditions authorizing abortion were enlarged through a new law approved in 2010.

Euthanasia

In 1998, Ramón Sampedro, a former fisherman who had become quadriplegic in 1968, at the age of 25—and had since then been asking the courts without success for the right to assisted suicide—convinced a series of friends to help him commit suicide. He divided the work of preparing the poison and administrating it to him into small tasks performed by different persons, with the hope that none of them would be accused of assisted suicide. He left an open letter explaining his actions and videotaped his last words and the moment in which he drank the poison. The assisted death of Sampedro—whose life inspired the film *Mar Adentro/The Sea Inside*, directed by Alejandro Amenábar, which won an Academy Award in 2004—forced the judges to open a criminal proceeding for assisted suicide. One of his friends was arrested. At the same time, the Association for the Right to Die with Dignity (*Derecho a Morir Dignamente*) started a campaign and managed to obtain more than 2,000 signatures of people who confessed to having assisted Sampedro to die (El Pais, 27.02.1998).[7] Finally, no one was punished for this death because of lack of evidence. The Spanish Senate created a commission on euthanasia, but no related law has yet been approved.

Voluntary False Confessions Intended to Protect a Person or a Group of Persons

Juveniles

Among juveniles who make voluntary false confessions, two main patterns can be observed. One corresponds to juveniles who lie to protect their friends, and the other to those who lie to protect adults. Both types can be combined when the person whom the juvenile is protecting is, for example, an adult from his group of friends. Since the number of juveniles involved in serious offenses is relatively low, these cases are seldom found in the press.

For example, in 2002, a 15-year-old boy confessed to having acted alone in killing his grandmother in order to protect his mother who was, presumably, involved in the homicide as well. The juvenile was sentenced to two years' imprisonment in an institution for juveniles. However, in 2008, his mother was accused by the District Attorney, who asked for a sentence of 25 years' imprisonment. The trial judge dissolved the jury and acquitted the mother. The District Attorney made an appeal but, in 2010, the Supreme Regional Court rejected it, invoking constitutional rights and the need to avoid never-ending proceedings (ABC, 04.03.2008; 11.03.2010).[8]

In the case of juvenile gangs, some apparently voluntary false confessions could in fact be coerced-reactive false confessions. For example, in February 2006 a member of the "Forty-Two," a Spanish Latin Gang composed of Dominican immigrants, confessed to having killed another juvenile but later retracted his confession, arguing that he made it under pressure from the leaders of the gang, who had threatened to attack his family. He justified his disavowal by saying that the leaders of the gang were under arrest at that time. However, the Court sentenced him to 13 years of imprisonment for murder (El Mundo, 01.10.2007; 25.10.2007).[9]

Terrorists

During a conference given at the University of Seville in May 2001 by members of the Andalusian Association of Terrorism Victims (AAVT, 2001), it was suggested that members of the terrorist group ETA (*Euskadi Ta Askatasuna* or "Basque Homeland and Freedom") could have been making voluntary false confessions. In order to protect the organization, one terrorist accused of a crime could confess other crimes or indicate that he/she had committed the crime alone while in fact, he/she was helped by other terrorists.

This hypothesis could have been generated by a case that took place in 1988. During that year, an alleged ETA member was exonerated by the National High Court (*Audiencia Nacional*) for having put a bomb in the private car of a Civil Guard (one of the Spanish Police Forces) that, when it exploded, killed both the owner of the car and another Civil Guard. The only proof against him was his confession, which took place in front of a judge but while the suspect was hospitalized, suffering from a diabetic coma. The Court determined that the judge who took the deposition did not respect the requirements of the law, and that the suspect could have been temporarily mentally disturbed because of the diabetic coma (El País, 25.02.1998).[10] There was also a case in which a member of ETA retracted his voluntary confession thirteen years later, claiming that it was a coerced confession. However, the Court finally ruled that he was the real perpetrator of the murder of which he was accused (El País, 07.10.2000).[11]

Thus, the available empirical evidence does not support the idea that members of the ETA have falsely confessed to crimes committed by other ETA terrorists. The main Spanish scientific expert on terrorism, who has conducted many interviews with former ETA members, informed the authors that he has no evidence of such a strategy (Reinares, personal communication, July 2, 2012).

The Roma Ethnic Minority

In 2010, females represented 8 percent of the prison population under the authority of the Spanish Prison Administration and 7.3 percent in prisons under the authority of the Catalan Prison Administration (Aebi & Delgrande, 2012). These are the highest percentages of females in European countries with at least one million inhabitants, and they have been stable during the last twenty years (see, for example, Tournier, 1992).

According to Hernández et al. (2001), at the turn of the 21st century, 20 percent of the Spanish female prison population was composed of foreign prisoners. Among those with Spanish citizenship, 25 percent were Roma women. Taking into account that the Roma population represents 1.4 percent of the general Spanish population, this means that Roma women are over-represented by a factor of 20 in the Spanish female prison population. One of the reasons often invoked to explain this over-representation of Roma women is that they accept responsibility for offenses committed by other members of their family; i.e., they make voluntary false confessions. Nevertheless, until now, this hypothesis has not been systematically studied.

On the basis of her long experience as director of female prisons, Yagüe (2002) points out that she has spoken with women who admitted that they were in jail because they took responsibility for offenses committed by their partners or sons thinking that their absence would be less harmful for the survival of the family than would the absence of the partner or the son. However, there is no indication of the percentage of cases that they may represent among the total population and, in particular, of the percentage of Roma females among them.

On the basis of a questionnaire completed by a sample of 292 imprisoned Roma women and 24 semi-structured interviews with different representatives of the Roma community (including six imprisoned females), Hernández et al. (2001) reported mixed results. Although some cases do exist, the idea that Roma women are imprisoned for offenses committed by their partners does not fit the general picture. Even if such cases exist, the question remains whether false confessions were actually voluntary or coerced-reactive (i.e., forced by other family members).

Considering the available information published in the press, some cases look doubtful. For example, on June 28, 2011, a Court of Valladolid sentenced the 43-year-old wife of a multi-recidivist drug trafficker of the Roma community known as *El Bule* to four years of imprisonment on the basis of her auto-inculpation. Her daughter-in-law, aged 21, was also sentenced to three years of imprisonment for a drug related offense. The two women had been arrested in 2008 together with El Bule, one of his sons, one of his daughters (16 years old) and two other men. The police believed that El Bule was the head of a network of traffickers but, finally, only the women were sentenced. El Bule even declared that his wife acted with such discretion that he, a drug-addict for 25 years, was unaware that such an amount of merchandise was available in his own home (Europa Press, 21.06.2011).[12]

Other cases involving members of the Roma community do not concern women allegedly protecting men, but instead involve members of the community protecting each other. Thus, in 2003, the 15-year-old brother of the famous Flamenco dancer *Farruquito* admitted having been the driver of the car that hit and killed a man. However, it was discovered during the proceedings that the driver was indeed Farruquito, who in 2006 was sentenced to three years' imprisonment (El País, 10.09.2006).[13]

On April 23, 2008, a popular jury in Barcelona acquitted a 67-year-old Roma man—considered as the patriarch of a clan—who had confessed to killing a young man (age 18) from a rival clan in 2005. The auto-inculpation of this man led the District Attorney to withdraw the charges against his 27-year-old son. However, the popular jury considered that the patriarch of the family could have been protecting his son, taking into account that the witnesses could not identify him as the one who fired the lethal shot. As a consequence, he was acquitted (Europa Press, 23.04.2008).[14]

Conclusions

This chapter has focused on the issue of voluntary false confessions motivated by an intangible benefit that occurred in Spain. Such confessions are usually motivated by the desire to protect the real offender. When voluntary false confessions are not discovered by judges, they constitute a sort of "perfect crime." First, they lead to a wrongful conviction (an innocent is sentenced). Second, the real offenses committed by the person sentenced are obstruction of justice and perjury, and they are not discovered or punished by the criminal justice system. Third, the real offender is not punished.

The cases that are known are those in which the voluntary false confession was retracted or discovered during the criminal proceedings, or those revealed through self-reported studies. Indeed, empirical research on the topic of false confessions is rare and has been conducted mainly in the United States and in a few European nations. These works focus on the issue of false confessions in general, which sometimes include cases of voluntary false confessions motivated by an intangible benefit.

No empirical research has been conducted in Spain on this issue. Thus, our research was based on a review of press articles on that topic. This review showed that voluntary false confessions were motivated either by the wish to change some sections of the criminal code or by loyalty to a person or a group of persons. Among the cases of voluntary false confessions intended to promote a change in the criminal code, two main cases were identified: the fight for the right to abortion and the one for the right to euthanasia. Thus in 1986 and 2008, hundreds of persons confessed abortion in order to force changes in the law regarding abortion, and in 1998, following the assisted suicide of a quadriplegic man, hundreds of persons falsely confessed having been the ones who assisted him in committing suicide. The 1985 law on abortion was finally modified in 2010, while a law on euthanasia has not yet been approved. The main message here is that voluntary false confessions can be used to exert pressure on law-makers for further decriminalization.

Concerning those cases of voluntary false confessions motivated by loyalty to a person or a group of persons, three main cases were analyzed: terrorists, members of the Roma ethnic minority, and juveniles. In the case of terrorists belonging to ETA, no empirical evidence of an organized strategy encouraging false confessions was found. In the case of juveniles and in the case of persons belonging to the Roma ethnic minority, some cases of voluntary false confessions have been discovered.

Finally, this topic deservers further research. The best research strategy could be to conduct interviews with particular groups, such as former terrorists and members of the Roma ethnic minority, and self-report studies among prisoners. The validity of self-report studies among prisoners may be fairly high, as long as anonymity can be guaranteed.[15] Face-to-face interviews could be conducted once the offenses involved fall under the statutes of limitation.

Notes

1   Gudjonsson (2003; see also Gudjonsson et al., 2004) also proposed a revised version of the classification of Kassin & Wrightsman (1985) in which he replaces the term "coerced" by "pressured," and proposes a bivariate classification system that distinguishes the three types of false confessions (i.e., voluntary, compliant, and internalized) and categorizes the source of pressure (i.e., internal, custodial, non-custodial).

2   More recently, Kassin (2008) proposed a slightly different wording for the definition but kept the emphasis on the absence of police pressure: "Voluntary false confessions are those in which people claim responsibility for crimes they did not commit without prompting from police" (Kassin, 2008: 249).

3   It must be mentioned, however, that some of these causes were already identified, for example, by Guttmacher & Weihofen (1952) and in the unsigned note "Voluntary False Confessions" (1953).

4   The desire to avoid "police pressure" (see, for example, Sigurdsson & Gudjonsson, 1996a) has been excluded as one of the causes of voluntary false confessions because the pressure exerted by the police acts as an external factor which places the case under the heading of coerced-reactive false confessions, as proposed by McCann (1998).

5   http://elpais.com/diario/1986/12/06/sociedad/534207606_850215.html.

6   http://www.elperiodicodearagon.com/noticias/sociedad/8-000-autoinculpaciones-por-aborto-irrumpen-en-debate-electoral_390989.html.

7   http://elpais.com/diario/1998/02/27/sociedad/888534002_850215.html.

8   http://www.abc.es/hemeroteca/historico-11-03-2010/abc/Galicia/el-tsxg-desestima-celebrar-un-nuevo-juicio-por-el-crimen-de-neda_11491176475.html;http://www.abc.es/hemeroteca/historico-04-03-2008/abc/Galicia/una-mujer-se-enfrenta-a-25-años-por-matar-a-su-suegra-y-arrojarle-acido_1641694677588.html.

9   http://www.elmundo.es/elmundo/2007/10/01/madrid/1191249951.html;http://www.elmundo.es/elmundo/2007/10/25/madrid/1193328329.html.

10   http://elpais.com/diario/1988/02/25/espana/572742013_850215.html.

11   http://elpais.com/diario/2000/10/07/espana/970869613_850215.html.

12   http://www.europapress.es/castilla-y-leon/noticia-mujer-bule-asume-culpa-excluye-marido-otros-cuatro-procesados-trafico-drogas-20110621130437.html.

13   http://elpais.com/diario/2006/09/10/espana/1157839215_850215.html.

14   http://www.europapress.es/nacional/noticia-absuelven-hombre-autoinculpo-matar-escopeta-joven-mollet-valles-barcelona-20080423154522.html.

15   See the review of Aebi (2009, with references).

References

AAVT (Asociación Andaluza de Víctimas del Terrorismo) (Mai 2001). Conference given at the Andalusian Institute of Criminology of the University of Seville, Spain.

Aebi, M. F. (2009). *Self-reported Delinquency Surveys in Europe/Enquêtes de délinquance autoreportée en Europe*. Guyancourt: CRIMPREV.

Aebi, M. F. & Delgrande, N. (2012). *Council of Europe Annual Penal Statistics SPACE I: Survey 2010*. Strasbourg: Council of Europe.

Anonymous (1953). Voluntary False Confessions: A Neglected Area in Criminal Administration, *Indiana Law Journal* (Unsigned Note), 28, 374–392.

Beyer, M. (2000). Immaturity, Culpability & Competency in Juveniles: A Study of 17 Cases. *Criminal Justice Magazine, 15*(2): 26–37.

Clarke, R. V. & Cornish, D. B. (2000). Rational Choice. *In* Paternoster, R. & Bachman, R. (Eds.). *Explaining Crime and Criminals: Essays in Contemporary Criminological Theory* (pp. 23–42). Los Angeles: Roxbury.

Cornish, D. B. & Clarke, R. V. (1986). Introduction. *In* Cornish, D. & Clarke, R. V. (Eds.). *The Reasoning Criminal* (pp. 1–16). New York: Springer Verlag.

Dongois, N. (2006). Les formes de bargain en Europe consacrent-elles une américanisation des droits continentaux? *In* Dongois, N. & Killias, M. (Eds.). *L'américanisation des droits suisse et continentaux* (pp. 81–100). Genève: Schulthess.

Gudjonsson, G. H. (2003). *The Psychology of Interrogations and Confessions: A Handbook*. Chichester: Wiley.

Gudjonsson, G. H., Sigurdsson, J. F., Bragason, O. O., Einarsson, E. & Valdimarsdottir, E. B. (2004). Confessions and Denials and the Relationship with Personality. *Legal and Criminological Psychology, 9*(1): 121–133.

Guttmacher, M., & Weihofen, H. (1952). *Psychiatry and the Law*. New York: W. W. Norton.

Hernández, G., Imaz, E., Martín, M., Naredo, M., Pernas, B., Tandogan, A. & Wagman, D. (2001). *Proyecto Barañí: Criminalización y reclusión de mujeres gitanas*. Madrid: Caray. Available on http://web.jet.es/gea21/indice.htm.

Huff, C. R., Rattner, A. & Sagarin, E. (1996). *Convicted but Innocent: Wrongful Conviction and Public Policy*. Thousand Oaks, California: Sage.

Kassin, S. M. (1997). The Psychology of Confession Evidence. *American Psychologist, 52*(3): 221–233.

Kassin, S. M. (2008). False Confessions: Causes, Consequences and Implications for Reform. *Current Directions in Psychological Science, 17*(4), 249–253.

Kassin, S. M., Drizin, S. A., Grisso, T., Gudjonsson, G. H., Leo, R. A. & Redlich, A. D. (2010). Police-Induced Confessions: Risk Factors and Recommendations. *Law and Human Behavior, 34*: 3.38.

Kassin, S. M. & Wrightsman, L. S. (1985). Confession Evidence. *In* Kassin, S. M. & Wrightsman, L. S. (Eds.), *The Psychology of Evidence and Trial Procedure* (pp. 67–94). Beverly Hills: Sage.

Klein, M. (1995). *The American Street Gang: Its Nature, Prevalence, and Control*. New York/Oxford: Oxford University Press.

Krzewinski, L. M. (2002). But I Didn't Do It: Protecting the Rights of Juveniles During Interrogation, *Boston College Third World Law Journal, 22*(2): 355–388.

Leo, R. A. (2009). False Confessions: Causes, Consequences and Implications. *Journal of the American Academy of Psychiatry and the Law, 37*(3): 332–343.

McCann, J. T. (1998). A Conceptual Framework for Identifying Various Types of Confessions. *Behavioral Sciences and the Law, 16*, 441–453.

Ofshe, R. J. & Leo, R. A. (1997). The Social Psychology of Police Interrogation: The Theory and Classification of True and False Confessions. *Studies in Law, Politics, and Society, 16*: 189–251.

Pizzi, W. T. (1999). *Trials without Truth: Why our System of Criminal Trials has Become an Expensive Failure and What we Need to do to Rebuild it*. New York: New York University Press.

Richardson, G. (1991). *A Study of Interrogative Suggestibility in an Adolescent Forensic Population*. M.Sc. Dissertation. Newcastle: University of Newcastle upon Tyne.

Sigurdsson, J. F. & Gudjonsson, G. H. (1996a). The Psychological Characteristics of 'False Confessors'. A Study Among Icelandic Prison Inmates and Juvenile Offenders. *Personality and Individual Differences, 20* (3), 321–329.

Sigurdsson, J. F. & Gudjonsson, G. H. (1996b). The Relationship Between Types of Claimed False Confession Made and the Reasons Why Suspects Confess to the Police According to the Gudjonsson Confession Questionnaire (GCQ). *Legal and Criminological Psychology, 1*, 259–269.

Silke, A. (2008). Holy Warriors: Exploring the Psychological Processes of Jihadi Radicalization. *European Journal of Criminology, 5*(1): 99–123.

Tournier, P. V. (1992). Statistiques sur les populations carcérales dans les Etats membres du Conseil de l'Europe (Enquêtes de 1990). Bulletin d'information pénitentiaire/Penological Information Bulletin, *16*: 28–35.

Walker, C. & Starmer, K. (1999). *Miscarriages of Justice: A Review of Justice in Error*. Oxford: Oxford University Press.

Yagüe, C. (2002). Mujer: delito y prisión, un enfoque diferencial sobre la Delincuencia Femenina. *Revista de Estudios Penitenciarios, 249*: 135–170.

11

THE CHANGING FACE OF MISCARRIAGES OF JUSTICE

PREVENTIVE DETENTION STRATEGIES IN CANADA AND THE UNITED STATES

Kathryn M. Campbell[1]

The subject of miscarriages of justice usually brings to mind the picture of an innocent person who has been convicted of a crime he/she did not commit, through a criminal prosecution, by virtue of an unfair process. This image has often been repeated in the media, and in some more fortunate cases accompanied by triumphant release from years of wrongful imprisonment. The previous three decades have evinced a large body of innocence scholarship reflecting research into the myriad factors contributing to wrongful conviction, as well as proffering policy and practical means of prevention. However, largely ignored in this process are a host of victims of wrongful accusations, and at times wrongful convictions, as a result of the post 9/11 "war on terror." The difficulties encountered through the use of preventive detention measures can be understood as contributing to miscarriages of justice. Roach and Trotter (2005) have examined the concept of miscarriages of justice within the broader context of the "war on terror" and they underline the importance of maintaining legal standards of fair treatment and protecting civil liberties. Similar to Walker's (1999) earlier arguments about the unjust application of laws against Irish terrorist suspects in the U.K. in the 1970s and 1980s, measures taken since September 11, 2001, to address the threat of terrorism in North America and parts of Europe have resulted in miscarriages of justice for those designated as enemy combatants.[2] A by-product of excessive and forceful governmental reactions to real and alleged terrorist activity has resulted in insufficient recognition and treatment of the rights of many individuals to whom they are applied. The emergent discourse regarding miscarriages of justice within the context of terrorism illustrates the dangers involved when governments circumvent the fetters of criminal prosecutions and use immigration and military law to detain and deport individuals suspected of terrorist activities. In the decade since the horrific terrorist attacks of 9/11, nation states have enacted a number of measures, both legally and extra-legally,[3] in an attempt to quash further terrorism. At the same time, to a large degree this has occurred at the expense of civil liberties of accused persons, both citizens and non-citizens of nation states. The purpose of this chapter is to underline how two democracies, Canada and the United States, have used executive and legislative powers in the wake of 9/11 to stem the tide of terrorism and have inadvertently also created new cases of miscarriages of justice.

Many of the "canonical list of factors" (Gross, 2008) that are known as the hallmarks of a wrongful conviction can also be found in the pursuit of terrorist suspects: reliance on false confessions (often obtained through torture), reliance on unreliable and unsubstantiated evidence (often secret) and the high profile nature of terrorism (more generally) have resulted in an expeditious response to gather evidence and pursue or charge a suspect. Moreover, following an accusation of terrorist complicity, the stigma of that label is especially difficult to overcome and in many cases a suspect's rights are further eroded through indeterminate detention without charge or trial, deportation (which simply exports terrorism) and in some cases, even torture. It would seem that the presumption of innocence, a right afforded individuals in any democracy, has been transformed into a presumption of guilt for terrorist suspects. The extent to which the following list of rights is respected in cases of suspected terrorism is also questionable: full disclosure of all relevant evidence; prosecutorial burden of proof beyond a reasonable doubt; the right to make full answer and defense; the right to silence; the right against self-incrimination; the right against unlawful search and seizure; the right against arbitrary detention; the right to be informed of the reasons for detention; the right to trial within a reasonable time; and the overall right to exclude incriminating evidence (Sherrin, 2008). It could be argued that the devastatingly tragic loss of life and injury that resulted from the terrorists' attacks on 9/11 served to overwhelm rights considerations of terrorist suspects. The enormity of that tragedy, particularly in the first months and years following the attacks, also served to rationalize the erosion of suspects' rights, to justify an unjust war in Iraq and further to create a whole host of security restrictions on international travel that remain today. Ironically, such rationalizations do very little to promote national security.

As any wrongful conviction scholar would note, when a wrongful conviction does occur in many cases the "rightful" offender goes free and is free to commit further offenses. The same axiom remains true for terrorism cases: in a rush to "punish" those responsible for reprehensible acts of terrorism, the result may be a form of tunnel vision – where the wrong suspect is initially targeted and exculpatory evidence ignored, resulting in a wrongful conviction. The enormity of loss and devastation created by acts of terrorism demands a response that strives for accuracy, whether through targeting or charging suspects. At the same time, the reach of some anti-terrorism statutes is so all encompassing that it raises a further fundamental question as to whether targeted persons are guilty of anything at all. However, a large part of the "war on terror" involves the prevention of future terrorist acts, stopping terrorism before it can occur. In this manner pursuing terrorist suspects is akin to the designation of "dangerousness" by Canadian criminal courts. The dangerousness provisions, set out in Part XXIV of the Canadian *Criminal Code* (ss. 753(2)), apply to those offenders who are considered to be at risk of reoffending, but who have already been convicted of a serious sexual or violent offense. The objective of this designation allows for the indefinite incarceration of these individuals, as long as they continue to pose a risk to society (Valiquet, 2008). How this differs from the pursuit of terrorist suspects is that individuals subject to a dangerous or long-term offender designation are normally Canadian citizens, have already been found guilty in a Canadian criminal court with its evidentiary safeguards, and presumably have had all of their legal rights respected in the process. The process and procedures that follow the pursuit of a terrorist suspect may also result in indefinite detention, but do not carry the same procedural safeguards.

It would seem that the heart of the dilemma remains, how do nation states define terrorist acts? Are they considered acts of war or criminal infractions? At the same time, how far can the criminal law model be pushed into future anticipatory crimes? How these questions are answered further directs the response: Should suspects be processed through a war model or a crime model? Is terrorism ultimately the purview of a military commission or should it be treated as a crime, subject to prosecution? In most democracies, law-breaking behavior normally garners a response through criminal law and criminal prosecution. Such a system, while clearly flawed, as the many cases of "domestic" wrongful convictions illustrate, adheres to an adversarial model with procedural and evidentiary rules, requiring proof beyond a reasonable doubt prior to a conviction, often decided by a jury of one's peers. However, the criminal law model in the immediate aftermath of 9/11 was rejected in both Canada and the United States as a means of responding to the terrorist attacks and the threat of future terrorism in favor of administrative law, immigration law, military law, executive orders and national security policy. The consequence has been that numerous individuals have been unjustly detained, in some cases for years, or even deported based on secret information.

This chapter will attempt to illustrate how individual liberty interests have now taken a back seat to national security interests by examining aspects of both the Canadian and the American responses to terrorism suspects. The first part of the chapter will examine the Canadian reliance on immigration law as anti-terrorism law and the difficulties inherent in that response. To illustrate, the use of security certificates to export non-citizens and deportation to torture are examples of the consequences of relying on intelligence as evidence. Next, the American response, while incredibly complex and multifarious, underscores the complications inherent in balancing individual rights while at the same time ensuring national security concerns. The Bush administration's initial heavy-handed response to 9/11 illustrates how that government was able to circumvent due process in the name of security, while continuing today to hold terrorist suspects without trial at Guantánamo Bay detention camp.

Canada's Response to 9/11

Canada's initial reaction to the terrorist attacks of 9/11, and partially in response to the United Nations Security Council Resolution 1373,[4] was the enactment of the *Anti-terrorism Act* (S.C. 2001, c. 41). This law contained a two-fold definition of terrorism. The first incorporates a series of offenses enacted to implement international agreements against terrorism and the second describes terrorist activity as an act or omission undertaken "in whole or in part for a political, religious, or ideological purpose, objective or cause" that is intended to intimidate the public or compel a person, government or organization to do or refrain from doing any act, if the act or omission intentionally causes a specified serious harm (*Criminal Code,* 83.01(1)(a–b)). It further defined sweeping police powers (including the use of electronic surveillance); allowed for detention without charge for up to three days; allowed for preventive arrest; allowed judges to compel witnesses to give evidence during an investigation; and allowed the designation of a group as a terrorist organization. In particular, the preventive arrest provisions were followed by a judge's requirement that an individual enter into a recognizance or peace bond for up to one year, the breach of which was punishable by up to 2 years of imprisonment. Refusal to enter into a bond was punishable by one year of imprisonment (*Criminal Code,* sec. 83.3). Moreover, it did not make membership in a terrorist organization a crime, nor did it criminalize speech associated with terrorism or criminalize association itself, in part due to the fact that it would be inconsistent with Canada's bill of rights, the *Charter.*[5]

Furthermore, UN Resolution 1373 also emphasized the importance of preventing the movement of terrorists or their groups by effective border controls. The resultant effect on immigration law was both over-inclusive, by hindering the movement of legitimate immigrants, and under-inclusive, since it was ineffective in addressing domestically based terrorist acts (Roach, 2011, p. 40). As a consequence, immigration law could be used as anti-terrorism law and Canada has long had statutory provisions that can be used to curtail the rights of foreign nationals[6] or permanent residents[7]. However, the effect of 9/11 allowed for greater ease in detaining and expelling those individuals who were considered threats to national security.

Immigration Law as Anti-Terrorism Law: A means to expel "undesirables"

> "Can you do indirectly through immigration what you are not able
> to do, for various reasons, through criminal law?"
>   (Binnie, J., in Schmitz, 2005)

Canada is a nation of immigrants. Its cultural mix, ethnic make-up and linguistic diversity are the result, to a large degree, of the influx of immigrants, both pre- and post-Confederation from all corners of the world. In the past, Canada's immigration policy and practice, however, has been replete with examples of exclusion, questionable discretion and blatant racism. The internment of Japanese-Canadians during World War II and the Chinese Head Tax[8] are two historical examples, while the current climate of fear toward those from Islamic countries is a contemporary illustration. While Canadian immigration policy has been described as going through a period of "liberalization" since the end of World War II, the "shifting norms pertaining to race, ethnicity, and human rights cast longstanding discriminatory policies in Canada and the United States in a highly critical light" (Triadafilopoulos, 2010, p. 169). There are far too many examples in the past of the treatment of non-citizens as "others," who are not viewed as deserving the same protections as citizens, whose rights can be overlooked or withdrawn; "today, the 'others' are Muslim men" (Kassam, 2010; Waldman, 2009, p. 155). It could be argued that the blatantly racist restrictions on immigration policies of the past have evolved to more covert, subversive limitations today. Likewise, a security agenda has now begun to dominate immigration policy in many nations in the post 9/11 period, reflecting a greater concern for national security, to the detriment of civil liberties and human rights.

Security Certificates

Immigration law has allowed Canadian officials to use investigative detention; to use secret evidence obtained from Canada and its allies not disclosed to the accused; to require a lowered standard of proof and wider liability rules than those seen under the *Anti-terrorism Act* (Roach, 2011, p. 396). Furthermore, a security-based agenda, as evinced through the issuance of security certificates, has racist undertones. Security certificates have been part of Canadian immigration law since 1978 and they allow

Ministers of Citizenship and Immigration and Public Safety to declare a permanent resident or foreign national to be inadmissible to Canada on security grounds, including engaging in terrorism or "being a member of an organization that there are reasonable grounds to believe engages, has engaged, or will engage" in acts of terrorism (*Immigration and Refugee Protection Act*, [IRPA] S.C. (2001), C. 27, sec. 34). Razack argues that the five detainees in 2007, all Arab Muslim men, were more than simply victims of racial profiling; rather, their backgrounds and histories "mark them as individuals likely to commit terrorists acts, people whose propensity for violence is indicated by their origins" (2007, p. 3). She outlines how it was Hassan Almrei's "profile" that marked him as a possible terrorist – a profile of an Arab man who spent time as a youth in Afghanistan fighting the Soviet Union in the 1980s–1990s, who knew other Arab men with similar histories – and that was sufficient for Canadian Security and Intelligence Service[9] and the Federal Court to believe he could be an actual terrorist. Many of these men were refugee applicants, emerging from repressive Arab states where, through resistance and flight, their strategies for survival become labeled as terrorism.

Canadian immigration law functions to provide a means of controlling the threat posed by non-citizens through a hierarchy of sanctions. The provisions of inadmissibility and issuance of security certificates on security grounds apply only to foreign nationals or permanent residents and not to Canadian citizens. Once deemed inadmissible, a report is filed (sec. 44) and an admissibility hearing takes place either by way of the immigration division or through a security certificate, which is then referred to the federal court (Norris, 2008, p. 12). The issuance of security certificates is based on information, which is comprised of security or criminal intelligence information obtained in confidence from a domestic or foreign source. The information obtained and compiled into the security intelligence report prepared by Canadian Security Intelligence Service is submitted to both the Minster of Citizenship and Immigration and the Minister of Public Safety. Prior to the recent amendments to the IRPA, the judge of the federal court would then determine the reasonableness of the security certificate by examining it in private within seven days (sec. 78(d)).

Given that this is an administrative review, the safeguards surrounding the protection of liberty interests are not engaged, in spite of the fact that the potential outcome of the issuance of a security certificate may involve a deportation order. Moreover, sec. 78(j) of the IRPA allows the judge to base his/her decision on anything he or she believes to be appropriate, regardless of whether such information would be inadmissible in a court of law. Nor can the information that forms the basis for the security certificate be shared with the applicant; due to security reasons "evidence might be undisclosed in order to protect the identity and therefore the life of an informant, to keep investigative techniques confidential, or to protect the confidentiality of information provided by a foreign government" (Becklumb, 2008, p. 3). The secret evidence that forms part of security certificates is heard in the absence of the named person and their counsel if a judge is of the opinion that disclosure of it would be injurious to national security or the safety of any person (IRPA, sec. 83).

Security certificates under the IRPA since the amendments of 2002 are now issued in cases where a foreign national or permanent resident is considered inadmissible "on grounds of security, violating human or international rights, serious criminality or organized criminality" (IRPA, sec. 77(1)). The certificate allows the government to detain non-citizens and if found to be reasonable, it becomes proof the individual is inadmissible and becomes a removal order (IRPA, sec. 82.5, sec. 80). However, the named person may apply to the Minister of Citizenship and Immigration, during the reasonableness review, to be considered a refugee or a person in need of protection (IRPA, sec. 112(1)). The government may issue a "danger opinion" following this, but nonetheless may also deport the individual to face possible persecution or even torture.[10]

What is of particular interest about this procedure is that it is in fact preventive and prescriptive; it involves judgments made about the *possibility* of future illegal or terrorist behavior. As a consequence, the nature of these proceedings, their justification and the suspension of liberties that follow "rest on the notion that it is necessary to strike at the enemy before he strikes at us" (Razack, 2007, p. 10). When individuals are labeled as holding the ideology of Islamic extremism, in fact as "Jihadists,"[11] and perceived as having a propensity for violence, this should raise important questions about the nature of these engrained stereotypes. The good Muslim/bad Muslim dichotomy, a part of modern day terrorism scholarship, occurs within an ahistorical context and polarizes these groups, with the former thought to be able to adapt to the modern West and the latter, inherently violent and destructive (Mamdani, 2004).

Many aspects of the process surrounding the issuance of security certificates are problematic. First of all, the procedure itself is designed to be "informal" and "expeditious." In terms of the admissibility of evidence, there are few restrictions and evidence is allowed that would be inadmissible in a court of law. Prior to the amendments to the law evidence was heard in the absence of the named person and their counsel and was maintained in secret as long as considered necessary, with only a summary given to the named person. Moreover, while these procedures are administrative in nature, they have the potential to detain and deport non-citizens and are procedurally lacking in protections normally afforded to those detained under criminal law. Equally problematic is the intelligence that forms the basis of security certificates, as it is often obtained from foreign sources, where the standards and practices of policing and evidence gathering are not necessarily those that are followed in Canada. Thus, it is possible that this evidence may have been obtained through torture or other intrusive intelligence techniques not permitted in many Western democracies.

While security certificates have been described as "Canada's prime counter-terrorism instrument" in the immediate aftermath of 9/11 (Roach, 2011, p. 396), they have been used very infrequently. Since 1991, only 28 have been issued (six since 9/11) of which three have been found to be unreasonable (one of which was subsequently re-issued), with 19 resulting in removals from Canada (Becklumb, 2008, p. 4). Three individuals are currently subject to a form of control order and remain under house arrest, with strict conditions, while the security certificates of Hassan Almrei and Adil Charkaoui were quashed in federal court in 2009. Early legal challenges to the security certificate regime were found to be without merit. In the case of *Ahani v. Canada*,[12] the court disregarded the argument that the principles of fundamental justice under sec. 7 of the *Charter* were violated, as it was thought that criminal law principles were not applicable to immigration law hearings. However, the court has since reconsidered that position in *Charkaoui I*.

Adil Charkaoui, originally from Morocco, was a permanent resident of Canada when he was named in a security certificate in May 2003 based on allegations that he had been involved in an anti-Soviet training camp in Afghanistan in the 1990s. He was subsequently detained until February 2005. In *Charkaoui I*, the court decided that, in fact, security certificate proceedings impact on the life, liberty, and security of named persons, and protections afforded in criminal court proceedings should also apply. The court ruled that individuals subject to security certificates are entitled to a fair hearing, as well as the ability to know the case and to meet and challenge the evidence against them (para. 35). What is interesting about this case is that it is based on faith in the power of adversarial challenge, or rather on the idea that the courts will eventually get it right. While the outcome in *Charkaoui I* was fortunate for him, unfortunately there are a number of high profile Canadian wrongful conviction cases where adversarial challenge did not prevent a miscarriage of justice. David Milgaard spent 22 years in prison for a sexual assault and murder he did not commit. He had repeatedly challenged his wrongful conviction on numerous grounds, without success. His conviction occurred in 1970 when he was 18 years old. The Saskatchewan Court of Appeal and the Supreme Court of Canada rejected his appeal in 1971. Early in 1991, despite mounting evidence of his innocence, the Minister of Justice refused to review his case. Due in part to growing public pressure, later that year the minister ordered the Supreme Court to review his conviction. While Milgaard was finally released in 1992, he was not formally acquitted until 1997 when DNA proved his innocence. He received $10 million in compensation and the government ordered a commission of inquiry to examine the errors in his case in 2004.

In *Charkaoui II*, the court considered questions regarding intelligence acquisition and distribution, specifically referring to the disclosure of the information forming the basis of the security certificate to the named person. Counsel for Charkaoui had argued that the security certificate should be quashed and Charkaoui conditionally released based on the fact that the certificate was issued on incomplete information and its reasonableness could not be tested. The court ruled that in fact CSIS must disclose such information to reviewing judges and court-appointed special advocates. The court found that a judge could disclose the information to the named person, unless it would endanger Canada's security. Consequently Charkaoui's security certificate was quashed on October 14, 2009. Due to the refusal to reveal key evidence, the case against Charkaoui folded and he was released unconditionally.

Refusing to disclose relevant evidence to the defendant has been a consistent theme in many miscarriages of justice in Canada. Romeo Phillion, who had suffered from psychiatric troubles, falsely confessed to murdering a local fireman in Ottawa in 1967. Crucial evidence that revealed Phillion was two hours away from the crime scene at the time of the murder surfaced only after he had served 31 years in prison; it was never disclosed to his defense attorney. He was released in 2003 and the Ontario Court of Appeal re-examined his case in 2008. In 2009, his conviction was struck down and a new trial ordered. In 2010, the Crown Attorney finally dropped the charges against him.

It was a lack of disclosure in the murder case against Donald Marshall Jr., his subsequent conviction and exoneration that brought about changes to evidence disclosure rules in Canada. In 1971, Marshall was convicted of stabbing his friend when he was 17 years old. Juvenile witnesses were coerced by the police into giving statements that were consistent with the police version of events. Shortly after his conviction, another witness came forward to the police with solid evidence regarding the real killer and this was never disclosed to the defense or the prosecution. Marshall served 11 years in prison before he was released. In 1989, a Royal Commission examining the errors that occurred in this case also brought about sweeping changes to the administration of justice in Nova Scotia. Later, in 1991, the Supreme Court of Canada ruled that the prosecution must disclose all relevant evidence to the defendant in *R. v. Stinchcombe*;[13] thus, wrongful convictions due to lack of disclosure may now be less likely to occur in criminal prosecutions. At the same time, the state secrets doctrine will continue to allow for the withholding of evidence in immigration law cases, arguably creating new forms of miscarriage of justice.

The Role of Special Advocates

Following *Charkaoui II*, the sections of the IRPA dealing with procedures related to security certificates were of no force and effect and Parliament had one year to amend the law. The subsequent amendments represented, *inter alia*, a number of changes to the security certificate process. Specifically, it provides for the appointment of a special advocate to protect the interests of the permanent resident or foreign national, particularly when "information or other evidence is not disclosed to him or her" (Becklumb, 2008, p. 15). This person is given a copy of all of the secret information once appointed and, while acting on the named person's behalf, is responsible for challenging reasons for not disclosing information or evidence and the relevance, reliability and sufficiency of the information (IRPA, sec. 85.1(2)). The special advocate is not a party to the proceedings, per se (sec. 85.1(3)), nor is the relationship between the special advocate and the named person one of solicitor–client. Nonetheless, their communications are protected and the special advocate is not a compellable witness in any proceedings (sec. 85.1(4)). He or she has the power to make oral/written submission regarding the information, participate and cross-examine witnesses, and exercise powers to protect the interests of the permanent resident or foreign national (sec. 85.2). The special advocate's use of the secret evidence is greatly circumscribed, as are the communications of other persons who may be privy to the secret evidence. The most troubling criticism of the role of the special advocate is that once the secret evidence has been received, he/she cannot communicate with the named person, absent special authorization.

The special advocate regime, adopted by a number of common law jurisdictions, including Canada, the U.K., New Zealand, and Australia in recent years has been described as inherently flawed and "raises fundamental questions about the development of the law in response to new challenges and the extent to which individual rights can be abrogated in the name of national security" (Inverarity, 2009, p. 471). Code and Roach provide a compelling example of the problems that may arise with so-called "secret" information:

> A vital piece of security intelligence in a security intelligence case might be that person x reports that the detainee was in Pakistan and attended a terrorist training camp at a certain time. Such intelligence, and in particular the name and nature of the source, might legitimately be covered by claims of national security confidentiality. At the same time, however, it might be crucially important for a detainee in a security certificate case to know both the precise time that person x reported on that person's presence in a terrorist camp and perhaps the identity of person x in order to challenge the case. For example, it is possible that the detainee will be able to establish that he was not present in Pakistan at the relevant time or that person x did not know him or alternatively that person x has a reason to lie about him. With respect to the latter, the detainee might also need to know the conditions under which person x made the statement that is being offered in evidence.
>
> (2006, p. 100)

A special advocate, who would likely have knowledge of some of the intelligence behind the above accusations, would also be unable to share any information classified as secret that could prove to be an essential part in defending against these allegations. Many legal scholars have pronounced on the troublesome aspects of this disregard for the protections normally afforded under criminal law in immigration law proceedings "since the harms the security certificate process targets have little to do with immigration and might be better dealt with under other legislation such as the anti-terrorism sections of the *Criminal Code*, where fair hearing provisions and other procedural protections would be afforded" (Davies, 2006, p. 28).

Detention and Removal to Torture

A number of Canadian citizens have been subjected to extraordinary rendition to countries that tortured them, and in most cases the information upon which their detention was based was false. What these cases represent is a further example of the over-inclusiveness of the war against terrorism and how miscarriages of justice can occur when information is unsubstantiated and not held up to the scrutiny of criminal courts. Maher Arar was wrongly suspected of terrorism and subject to torture upon deportation to Syria. He has dual Canadian and Syrian citizenship and immigrated to Canada at age 17. In 2002, while flying home from a family vacation, Arar was laid over in New York City and held for questioning. The U.S. government suspected him of being a member of al Qaeda, based on inaccurate information provided in part by Canadian officials. He was held in solitary confinement for two weeks before being deported to Syria, where he was detained and tortured for a year prior to being released back to Canada. Arar's ordeal was the subject of a commission of inquiry, where he was completely exonerated of any links to terrorism. He subsequently received an apology from Prime Minister Harper and $10.5 million in compensation; however, he remains on the U.S. No-Fly List. The inquiry revealed the "dangers of torture, mistreatment, false confessions, and inaccurate intelligence when Canada cooperates with countries with poor human rights records" (Roach, 2011, p. 413). Also subject to an inquiry were the cases of three other foreign-born Canadians, who were rendered back to Syria based on false information. Muayyed Nureddin, Abdullah Almalki, and Ahmad El Maati were all detained and tortured in Syria, based on unfounded information that the three men were extremists, information that Canadian officials shared with foreign governments. The inquiry found that the actions of Canadian officials contributed indirectly to their torture. Most recently, the U.N. Committee Against Torture called for Canada to apologize to Almalki, El Maati and Nureddin and to compensate the men, who are suing the federal government for its role in their detention abroad (Blanchfield, 2012a).

Also highly controversial is the case of Omar Khadr, a Canadian citizen detained at Guantánamo Bay detention camp since 2002. Khadr comes from a self-described "al Qaeda family," whose father was an associate of bin Laden. As a child soldier, aged 15, Khadr participated in an attack on U.S. soldiers in Afghanistan. In 2010, he pled guilty to five offenses under the U.S. Military Commissions Act, including murder, attempted murder, conspiracy, spying, and material support of terrorism and received an eight-year sentence (Blanchfield, 2012b). However, this was only after many decisions taken by varying courts regarding violations of Khadr's rights under international law and the Canadian *Charter*. The Canadian government has reluctantly agreed to accept Khadr back to Canada, and only did so in September of 2012. This case raises a number of important questions about transnational linkages in terrorism investigations, the balancing of diplomacy with human rights issues, the complicity of child soldiers, and the Canadian position on international human rights.

America's Response to 9/11

The "sheer volume" of what has occurred in the United States in response to terrorism since 2001 precludes a thorough overview of all strategies, including *inter alia* executive orders, legislation, detentions, extraordinary renditions, targeted killings, and national security policies.[14] However, for comparison purposes the focus of this section of the chapter will be on examining varying forms of preventive detention that occurred in the wake of 9/11, and continue today to a certain extent. The forceful American response to 9/11 is understandable to a degree, given the American targets of the attacks and the politically expedient and now long-standing position that America was at war. As a consequence, a large part of anti-terrorism efforts fit into an executive and war-based model, accompanied by an approach that has frequently been executive, rather than legislative. Consistent with the need for pragmatism and immediate action in times of war, the executive of a government can justify decision-making that circumvents the rather lengthy and circuitous process of legislative change.

A first and almost immediate response to 9/11 was the enactment of the *U.S.A. Patriot Act* 2001 on October 26, 2001, which stands for "Uniting and Strengthening America by Providing Appropriate Tools Required to Intercept and Obstruct Terrorism" Act of 2001. The act itself was aimed at deterring and punishing terrorist acts. It defined terrorism more narrowly than in the past by including domestic terrorism as "acts dangerous to human life that are in violation of the criminal laws of the US or any state; appear intended to intimidate or coerce a civilian population; to influence the policy of a government by intimidation or coercion; to affect the conduct of a government by mass destruction, assassination, or kidnapping; and occur primarily within the territorial jurisdiction of the United States" (sec. 802). It allowed for the expansion of surveillance and search powers, and it also enhanced measures to prevent, detect, and prosecute international money laundering and financing of terrorism. At the same time, it did not criminalize membership in a terrorist group nor did it suspend habeas corpus.

While the Patriot Act caused many commentators to be concerned that it would ultimately invade their privacy rights, far more nefarious events occurred through extra-legal actions on the part of the executive that were outside the reach of the Patriot Act or any other legal authority. There is no American statute that explicitly authorizes preventive detention of suspected terrorists without charge (Cole, 2009). At the same time, many existing laws and statutes[15] have been invoked in an emergency to effectuate preventive detention, including pre-existing immigration and criminal law; the use of material witness warrants; civil commitment; the power to detain fighting "enemy combatants" and foreign nationals from enemy countries during wartime; Section 412 of the U.S.A. Patriot Act, which allows for the detention of foreign nationals suspected of terrorist ties; and the suspension clause of the writ of habeas corpus.[16] What becomes obvious is that, despite the fact that no statute exists that authorizes preventive detention, there are other means available to detain suspected terrorists that have been subject to abuse and "afford the government too much unchecked power to detain" (Cole, 2009, p. 706).

Post 9/11 Immigration Round-Up

A common form of preventive detention for those formally accused of violating criminal or immigration law is through the *Bail Reform Act*,[17] which allows a judge to deny bail and keep a defendant jailed pending trial or resolution of the proceedings if he/she poses a flight risk or danger to others (Cole, 2009, p. 700). While there are limits imposed on this form of detention, as they only apply to those who have violated existing laws, the burden of proof is on the government to justify the detention. Moreover, the *Enemy Alien Act*[18] allows for the detention of anyone who is a national of a country engaged in war with the United States, without requiring a determination that the person is likely to engage in espionage or sabotage, or is hostile toward the U.S. Also, sec. 412 of the U.S.A. Patriot Act allows for the detention of foreign nationals suspected of terrorist ties without a hearing or without showing they pose a danger or flight risk. While this section of the law allows persons to be detained for seven days without charge and held indefinitely in some circumstances, it has never been invoked or tested. Within weeks of 9/11, the Attorney General of the United States rounded up over 1,000 mainly Arab and Muslim men for preventive detention, none of whom were ever charged, despite the fact that most judges who reviewed the policy found it unlawful (Cole, 2005, p. 30). In fact, by 2003, over 5,000 people were preventively detained, none of whom has been charged with terrorist activity. Many were further detained by delaying bond hearings, keeping them in detention after ordered release and in custody on immigration pretexts (Cole, 2009, p. 704). Moreover, a special registration program by the Immigration and Naturalization Service (I.N.S.) required 80,000 male non-citizens from 25 predominantly Arab and Muslim countries to submit to detailed questioning and fingerprinting. A further 8,000 young men of Arab and Muslim descent were sought for FBI interviews – none of which resulted in any terrorist arrests (Roach, 2011, p. 188).

De Facto Preventive and Investigative Detention Under Material Witness Warrants

An additional form of preventive detention is authorized through the material witness statute,[19] which allows witnesses to be held pending criminal trial or grand jury to ensure their testimony. In essence, this statute permits detention without probable cause and following 9/11, the Bush administration used material witness warrants to detain suspects for investigation without probable cause (Human Rights Watch, 2005) and in many cases, never called them to testify. The Department of Justice refuses to release the number of individuals it detained in connection with its post 9/11 investigations, however Human Rights Watch has determined that at least 70 individuals were held. Of the individuals detained, all were men and all but one was Muslim; one-third were detained for two months and came from the same towns as the 9/11 hijackers and presumably had interacted with them in some capacity (2005, p. 16). Moreover, of that number, only seven were charged with terrorism offenses, 24 were deported, and two were designated as enemy combatants. What seemed to be lacking in most of these cases was sufficient evidence to issue a criminal arrest warrant, so essentially the government was able to use material witness warrants to detain suspects (not witnesses) counter to the purpose of the statute. What becomes clear is that by manipulating procedure and abusing its authority to use detention to carry out deportations, the Justice Department held "special interest" detainees until clearing them of ties to terrorism (Human Rights Watch, 2002). One example of abuses under material witness warrants is the experience of Dr. Albader al-Hazmi, a San Antonio physician with no prior criminal record. He was arrested as a material witness in September 2001 based on the fact that the government believed he was involved in the 9/11 attacks, since he shared the last name of one of the hijackers and had been in phone contact with someone at the Saudi Arabian Embassy with the last name "bin Laden," despite the fact that it is a common Arabic name. He was arrested, with guns drawn, by five FBI agents in front of his wife and children, held for two weeks, beaten, and searched while naked on a daily basis. He was never called to testify (Human Rights Watch, 2011).

Indeterminate Military Detention/Suspension of the Writ of Habeas Corpus

The Bush administration used its own executive power and the Authorization for Use of Military Force against Terrorists (AUMF, 2001) to detain anyone it claimed was an "enemy combatant," captured either at home or abroad in the immediate aftermath of 9/11. The AUMF enacted in the days following 9/11 allowed the Armed Forces to use all "necessary and appropriate force" against those who the President determined had "planned, authorized, committed or aided" in the September 11 attacks.

This power was used to hold enemy combatants incommunicado, deny them hearings, and subject them to cruel and inhumane coercive interrogation, including torture (Sands, 2008).

Many enemy combatants (who are non-citizens) have been held in indeterminate military detention at Guantánamo Bay detention camp without trial. Given its remote location and its unique legal status as an American "possession," it exists in a type of legal vacuum, where the United States exercises complete jurisdiction and control over the base, but Cuba retains ultimate sovereignty (Ip, 2007, p. 777). While initially many innocent people were detained there, it is no longer the legal "black hole" it once was. A great deal of international human rights opinion derided the United States' position regarding the designation and treatment of prisoners held at Guantánamo Bay as enemy combatants and accused the U.S. government of betraying its own highest principles (McNamara, 2005). Initially opened in 2002, it was intended to detain prisoners from Iraq and Afghanistan for detention and interrogation purposes. Government officials have also admitted that torture has been used in interrogations. The Bush administration attempted to suspend the rights allowed detainees under the Geneva Convention, essentially justifying its own harsh interrogation practices, and argued that it need not provide hearings to determine if the detainees were enemy combatants or allow for judicial review. While the writ of habeas corpus, a long held principle in common law, requires that a government justify the detention of individuals, this writ was suspended following 9/11. The Suspension Clause of the U.S. Constitution allows for suspension of this writ only in very limited circumstances. In most cases judicial review of detention is required but in "times of Rebellion or Invasion," where required by public safety, Congress may suspend the writ.[20]

Several attempts have been made to establish what legal jurisdiction applies at Guantánamo Bay, whether it is U.S. domestic law, international law, or international human rights law, and the U.S. Supreme Court has established a number of precedents with respect to the rights of detainees. It established, in *Rasul v. Bush* and *Boumediene v. Bush*, that detainees were entitled to habeas corpus review of their detention. In *Hamdan v. Rumsfeld*, it ruled that Common Article 3 of the Geneva Convention did in fact apply, and in *Hamdi v. Rumsfeld*, it held that a U.S. citizen detained as an enemy combatant was constitutionally entitled to a fair hearing regarding his status (Cole, 2009, p. 727). Regardless, controversy surrounds the continued detention of detainees and while President Obama promised to close Guantánamo through an executive order in 2009, he has failed to do so and it remains a troubling example of U.S. extra-legalism.

Roach notes that the saga at Guantánamo "illustrates a willingness by both the Bush and Obama administration as well as Congress to use indeterminate detention without trial and trial by military commission as alternatives to criminal prosecutions" (2011, p. 198). At the same time, a number of enemy combatants are also being held at Bagram Air Force Base in Afghanistan. In 2008 there were 630, more than twice the 275 held at Guantánamo (Golden, 2008). Some of these individuals are indeed terrorists or members of al Qaeda or the Taliban, whereas a number are merely accused of being associated in some way with these groups (Cole, 2009, p. 726). However, in 2011 President Obama issued an executive order in an attempt to regularize detention without trial at Guantánamo. It allowed for the right to seek habeas corpus in federal court and provided for periodic review of detention. However, the review process could be based on secret evidence not disclosed to the detainee in order to protect security interests. Habeas corpus relief is not necessarily a panacea, and while it has worked for a minority of the Guantánamo Bay detainees, Roach notes (see Chapter 14, this volume) that although the U.S. Supreme Court extraordinarily granted habeas corpus relief to convicted murderer Troy Davis (*Re Troy Davis* 130 S Ct.1) to allow him to establish actual innocence, he ultimately failed and was executed.

Use of Military Commissions

Congress passed the Military Commissions Act in 2006, partly in response to the decision of *Hamden v. Rumsfeld* that established that military commission trials taking place at Guantánamo Bay were not consistent with the rights protected under the Geneva Convention. Essentially, the Act made the military trial process fairer by prohibiting the use of secret evidence and excluding evidence obtained through torture, but it also expanded the range of crimes tried under the laws of war to include terrorism, material support for terrorism, and conspiracy to commit any of the listed crimes (Roach, 2011, p. 210–11). Unlawful enemy combatants who are subjected to military commissions have fewer civil rights protections than they would be afforded in a regular trial. Mainly, this applies to members of the Taliban and al Qaeda who are not citizens of the United States.

Following much legal wrangling, the alleged conspirators behind 9/11 will be tried by military commission. In particular, Khalid Sheikh Mohammed (KSM), the self-described Kuwaiti-born mastermind behind the 9/11 attacks, will be tried with four other men for war crimes, including mass murder, a trial that is expected to take years. KSM has been held at Guantánamo Bay for over five years; prior to that he was held in a secret prison run by the CIA since his capture in 2002. The government has confirmed that while in custody, KSM was tortured through waterboarding—or simulated drowning—183 times in 2003, before this interrogation technique[21] was banned (BBC, 2012). In a 2008 hearing KSM admitted to being responsible for 9/11 "from A to Z," as well as for a number of other terrorist attacks—some successful, others foiled. That same year, the Attorney General had recommended that KSM and four others be criminally charged and tried in New York in federal court. However, following much public outcry the Obama administration withdrew criminal charges in 2011 and returned KSM and the others to face the military commission. While pleas have yet to be entered, KSM has said in the past that he will plead guilty and welcomes the death penalty, believing that a fair trial where the judge and jury are employed by the U.S. military is not possible. At initial hearings in May 2012, the defendants refused to answer questions and disrupted the process (Savage, 2012).

Extraordinary Rendition

The extraordinary rendition program has a history in the United States that pre-dates 9/11. It has been used to remove terrorists to be tried in their home countries, despite reputations for torture, by President Reagan in the 1980s and by President Clinton in the 1990s. Regardless, it functions "on the edges of legality" and has been described as tapping into "a deep American tradition of resorting to extralegal measures in times of emergency" (Roach, 2011, p. 168). In spite of a campaign promise to end rendition, shortly after his election President Obama announced that he would continue the practice of sending terrorist suspects back to third world countries for detention and interrogation, but pledged to monitor their treatment to ensure they will not be tortured (Johnston, 2009).

However, assurances from questionable governments should hardly foster confidence that such individuals will be treated fairly. The experiences of Gulet Mohamed illustrate how meaningless they can be. While travelling and studying in the Middle East Mohamed, a 19-year-old Somali-American, was detained in Kuwait for one week. He was questioned by Kuwaiti and U.S. government officials about known terrorists and claims to have been beaten with sticks on the soles of his feet, forced to stand for hours, threatened with electric shock, and warned that his mother would be imprisoned if he did not respond truthfully regarding his travels to Yemen (Mazzetti, 2011). He was then placed on the "no-fly list" due to his previous travels to Yemen and Somalia and refused re-entry to the United States for a number of weeks. Some have described the Obama form of extraordinary rendition as an equally abusive "proxy detention program" (Evitar, 2011).

Conclusions

In this modern era, how nation states define terrorism ultimately dictates their response. Clearly, the initial response of the American and Canadian regimes indicated that 9/11 constituted an act of war and, consequently, both abandoned criminal prosecution as a means of dealing with terrorist activity early on in the conflict. This is consistent with the uniquely American view that terrorism is really a foreign policy issue that requires a military response. Terrorists were viewed as soldiers and not citizens, but enjoyed the rights of neither soldiers nor citizens. Moreover, the war model is awkward, as terrorists are "non-state" actors and do not necessarily represent one nation, nor one particularly clear conflict or issue. Criminal law seemed ill-suited as a forum for trying terrorist cases, as the criminal law standard of proof beyond a reasonable doubt for a conviction was considered too high a bar, and the use of secret intelligence evidence could not be disclosed under state secrets doctrines. However, the abandonment of criminal law in favor of a war model has evolved, particularly in the United States, to a new system that follows neither the laws of crime nor the laws of war (Roach, 2011, p. 438). Moreover, Roach further notes that while the Canadian government initially abandoned criminal prosecutions in favor of immigration law proceedings, the courts' negative reaction to detention without trial and the use of secret evidence has forced a re-examination of and greater reliance on criminal law today (2011,

p. 439). In fact, the argument that the danger with criminal prosecutions is that secret intelligence evidence will be jeopardized cannot be upheld as certainly in Canada. Criminal trial judges have been able to protect unused intelligence from disclosure while also being vigilant in ensuring that criminal trials are fair and do not result in miscarriages of justice (Roach, 2011).

Preventive detention, whether through the issuance of security certificates in Canada or material witness warrants in the United States, is a highly problematic means of dealing with the threat of terrorism on a number of levels. Primarily, it rests on the prediction of future behavior and, like the prediction of dangerousness, it is a very inexact science. Second, governments run the risks of false positives in detaining innocent people and subsequently creating new forms of miscarriages of justice, since decision-makers are more likely to err on the side of caution. Finally, preventive detention is inconsistent with basic notions of human autonomy and free will, while issues of guilt or innocence regarding suspicion or charge are impossible to prove (Cole, 2009, p. 696). More importantly, the use of preventive detention as a means of holding terrorist suspects accountable has not been a particularly effective strategy. At best, it has served simply to incapacitate terrorist suspects for a period of time; at worst, it is a blatant violation of human rights and serves to denigrate the reputations of nation states. In fact, Cole argues that preventive detention should only be used as a last resort when a situation cannot be adequately addressed through the criminal justice system (2009, p. 698). He supports the notion that terrorism should remain a matter of criminal prosecution and preventive detention authorized only during wartime. Terrorists should be detained if they engage in armed conflict and not because they are terrorists, per se.

Canada's approach toward terrorism has evolved since 2004 to include a greater emphasis on criminal prosecutions, as seen with the prosecution of those involved in the homegrown terrorist attempt of the "Toronto 18"[22], and courts are not averse to imposing long sentences (see *R. v. Amara*). And while many of the extra-legalisms that occurred immediately following 9/11 have since been constrained through policy and legislation, there are no guarantees that in the face of future terrorist activity, governments will not once again resort to the abrogation of rights in the name of national security. Moreover, the illegal practices undertaken on behalf of the U.S. government in response to terrorism or the threat of terrorism have been sheltered from legal challenge through resources within the legal system, including political questions doctrine, narrow standing rules, and expansive state secrets doctrine (Roach, 2011, p. 436). Certainly the Obama administration has attempted to right some of the wrongs of the Bush administration with respect to addressing terrorism and the prosecution of terrorists. However, targeted killings, extraordinary renditions, indeterminate detention without trial, and military commissions still occur, with all of their attendant human rights violations.

Perhaps it has been the absence of formal, statutory powers of preventive detention that has encouraged the extra-legal conduct so rampant in the years following 9/11 in the United States (Roach, 2011, p. 391). The "war on terror" is not over, nor is an end in sight. As a result, nation states will continue to require powers to pursue, charge, and even expel those who represent a threat to national security. At the same time, these powers also necessitate concomitant responsibilities for governments to respect and acknowledge the rights of citizens and non-citizens alike. It is only through such recognition that further miscarriages of justice can ultimately be prevented.

Notes

1 I would like to thank Professor Kent Roach and Professor Evan Fox-Decent for comments on an earlier draft of this paper.
2 Roach and Trotter (2005) have a narrower focus on factual innocence which includes those who are detained without just cause, whereas for Walker (1999) the concept of a miscarriage of justice is rather multi-faceted, individualistic and rights-based, occurring whenever individuals are treated by the state in breach of their rights due to deficient process, through the law itself or the manner in which it was applied. My own position is more in line with Walker's.
3 Extra-legalism has been described by Roach as "illegal conduct that was nevertheless supported by dubious claims of legality and the apparent paradox of the American response to 9/11 being dominated by lawyers yet so often resulting in illegal acts such as rendition, torture and warrantless spying" (2011, p. 164).
4 http://www.un.org/News/Press/docs/2001/sc7158.doc.htm. This resolution passed on September 28, 2001 and required member states to enact legislation against terrorism financing and report to its Counter-Terrorism Committee within 90 days.
5 *Canadian Charter of Rights and Freedoms*, Part I of the Constitution Act, 1982, being Schedule B to the Canada Act 1982 (U.K.), 1982, c. 11 [*Charter*]
6 A "foreign national" is a person who is not a Canadian citizen or a permanent resident, and includes a stateless person (*Immigration and Refugee Protection Act*, sec. 2(1)).
7 A "permanent resident" is a person who has acquired permanent resident status and has not subsequently lost that status under section 46 (*Immigration and Refugee Protection Act*, sec. 2(1)).

8 Japanese-Canadians were interned in camps in the province of British Columbia during
   WWII, following the attack on Pearl Harbour, while their property and assets were seized
   and sold. In 1988 a formal inquiry by the Canadian government resulted in an apology and
   compensation. Early on, during the 1880s a large number of Chinese immigrants were
   brought to Canada to build the national railway system. To deter long-term immigration a
   fee was charged, for a period of 38 years, on each Chinese person entering Canada. In 2006
   the affected Chinese community was offered an apology and compensation by the
   government.

9 The Canadian Security and Intelligence Service, or CSIS, was created in 1984 by an act of
   Parliament and is Canada's civilian security intelligence service. It does not have law
   enforcement powers, which are the purview of the Royal Canadian Mounted Police
   (RCMP) and provincial and municipal police forces. There is also a Security Intelligence
   Review Committee (SIRC) and the Inspector General (IG) for CSIS to review the activities
   of CSIS and report to Parliament. There is no functionally equivalent group in the United
   States.

10 IRPA, s.115 (2)(b). However, the decision in *Suresh v. Canada*, 1 S.C.R. 3 (2002) indicated
   that deportation to torture was acceptable only in "exceptional circumstances." The
   government has relied on this to justify the continued immigration detention of suspected
   terrorists from countries such as Syria, where the use of torture against terrorist suspects is
   notorious, at the same time recognizing that this would be in violation of international
   obligations (Roach, 2011, p. 402–403).

11 The term "jihad" has multiple meanings. While the concept of Jihad in Islam means an
   intimate struggle to purify one's soul of evil influences or of sin, since the "war on terror" it
   has also been used as a synonym for Holy War or a use of violence in defense of Islam
   (retrieved from: http://www.religioustolerance.org/isl_jihad.htm).

12 *Ahani v. Canada*, [1995] 3 FC 669, 694 and 696 (FCC).

13 [1991] 3 S.C.R. 326.

14 For an excellent and concise review of U.S. anti-terrorism policy and practice see *The 9/11
   Effect: Comparative Counter-terrorism* (Roach, 2011). See also, Goldsmith (2007) and Wittes
   (2009).

15 Other laws that justify these actions include immigration law, the material witness statute,
   broad criminal statutes penalizing material support of terrorist groups and the Authorization
   for Use of Military Force (AUMF) against al Qaeda (Cole, 2009, p.698).

16 Given that immigration laws could be used pre-textually to detain individuals, suspension
   of the writ was never used. However, the fact that the writ can be suspended underlines the
   limits of the factual innocence model; while some individuals caught up in the post 9/11
   round-up were factually innocent of being terrorists, some were not factually innocent of
   being in the U.S. illegally.

17 18 U.S.C. § 3142 (d)(2) (2006).

18 50 U.S.C. § 21 (2000).

19 18 U.S.C. § 3144.

20 U.S. Constitution, art. I, § 9, cl. 2.

21 The most unlawful aspect of the Bush administration's national security policy was the issue
   of torture and the executive authorization of harsh interrogation practices. The torture
   memos of 2002 and the legal machinations around their justification and subsequent
   repudiation represent the extreme lengths this administration went to in rationalizing its
   own brutality in the name of the "war on terror."

22 In 2006 police arrested a number of young men, 14 adults and four youths, for a plot to blow
   up the Toronto Stock Exchange and other buildings and for conspiring to create an al
   Qaeda-type cell in Toronto. They were charged with a number of offenses, including
   participating in a terrorist group, intending to cause an explosion, importing firearms, etc;

11 were convicted. Their sentences ranged from six and one-half years to life imprisonment (for the main organizer).

References

Anti-terrorism Act, S.C. 2001, c. 41.

Authorization for Use of Military Force against Terrorists, (AUMF) (2001). Retrieved June 24, 2012, from http://www.gpo.gov/fdsys/pkg/PLAW-107publ40/pdf/PLAW-107publ40.pdf [Public Law No: 107–40]

Bail Reform Act of 1984, 18 U.S.C. § 3142 (d)(2) (2006).

BBC World News, (May 5, 2012). *Profile: Khalid Sheikh Mohammed*. Retrieved June 25, 2012 from http://www.bbc.co.uk/news/world-vs-canada-17966362.

Becklumb, P. (2008). *Bill C-3: An Act to Amend the Immigration and Refugee Protection Act (Certificate and Special Advocate) and to make a consequential amendment to another act— legislative summary*. Ottawa: Library of Parliament, Parliamentary Information and Research Service.

Blanchfield, M. (June 7, 2012). Federal lawyers dismiss UN criticism of Canada on torture, rights violations. *The Canadian Press*. Retrieved June 29, 2012, from ca.news.yahoo.com/federal-lawyers-dismiss-un-criticism-canada-tort

Blanchfield, M. (June 21, 2012). Omar Khadr's lawyers appeal to Ottawa for Gitmo transfer. *The Globe and Mail*. Retrieved June 29, 2012 from www.theglobeandmail.com/news/.../omar-khadrs.../article4359960/

Canadian Charter of Rights and Freedoms, Part I of the Constitution Act, 1982, being Schedule B to the Canada Act 1982 (U.K.), 1982, c. 11 [*Charter*].

Canadian Security Intelligence Service Act, RSC 1985 c C-23, s 38.

Code, M. & Roach, K. (2006). The role of the independent lawyer and security certificates. *Criminal Law Quarterly, 52*, 85–111.

Cole, D. (2005). *Enemy aliens: Double standards and constitutional freedoms in the war on terrorism*. New York: The New Press.

Cole, D. (2009). Out of the shadows: Preventive detention, suspected terrorists, and war. *California Law Review, 97*, 693–750.

Commission of Inquiry into the Actions of Canadian Officials in Relation to Maher Arar (2006). *Report of the Events Relating to Maher Arar: Analysis and Recommendations*. Ottawa: Public Works.

Criminal Code, R.S.C. 1985, c. C-466.

Davies, M. (2006). Unequal protection under the law: Re. Charkaoui and the security certificate process under the Immigration and Refugee Protection Act. *Saskatchewan Law Review, 69*, 375–400.

Enemy Alien Act, part of Alien and Sedition Acts, 50 U.S.C. § 21 (2000).

Evitar, D. (January 7, 2011). Is proxy detention the Obama administration's extraordinary rendition-lite? *Human Rights First*. Retrieved online June 25, 2012 at www.humanrights first.org

Golden, T. (Jan. 7, 2008). Foiling U.S. plan, prison expands in Afghanistan. *New York Times*, p.A1.

Goldsmith, J. (2007). *The terror presidency*. New York: W.W. Norton.

Gross, S. (2008). Convicting the Innocent. *Annual Review of Law and Social Science, 4*, 173–192.

Human Rights Watch. (August 2002). *Presumption of guilt: Human rights abuses of post-September 11 detainees*. Retrieved June 25, 2012, from http://www.hrw.org/reports/2002/us911/USA0802.pdf

Human Rights Watch. (June 2005). *Witness to abuse: Human rights abuses under the material witness law since September 11*. Retrieved June 24, 2012, from http://www.aclu.org/Files PDFs/materialwitnessreport.pdf

Human Rights Watch. (January 2011). *US: Misuse of the material witness statute*. Retrieved June 25, 2012 from www.hrw.org/news/2011/01/28/us-misuse-material-witness-statute

Immigration and Refugee Protection Act, S.C. 2001, c. 27.

Inverarity, L. (2009). Immigration Bill 2007: Special advocates and the right to be heard. *Victoria University of Wellington Law Review, 40(2)*, 471–506.

Ip, J. (2007). Comparative perspectives on the detention of terrorist suspects. *Transnational Law & Contemporary Problems, 16(3)*, 775–876.

Johnston, D. (August 29, 2009). US says rendition to continue but with more oversight. *The New York Times.*

Kassam, K. (2010). The terrorist "other": The fundamentalist and the Islamist. In K. S. Kassam (Ed.), *Understanding terror: Perspectives for Canadians.* (pp. 153–162).

Mamdani, M. (2004). *Good Muslim, bad Muslim: America, the cold war, and the roots of terror.* New York: Doubleday.

Mazzetti, M. (January 5, 2011). Detained American says he was beaten in Kuwait. *The New York Times.*

McNamara, K. (2005). Lawfulness of detentions by the United States in Guantánamo Bay. In Council of Europe, *Guantánamo: Violation of human rights and international law?* (pp. 7–30). Strasbourg: Council of Europe Publishing.

Military Commissions Act 2006 Pub. L. No. 109–366, 120 Stat. 2600 (Oct. 17, 2006), enacting Chapter 47A of title 10 of the United States Code (as well as amending section 2241 of title 28).

Norris, J. (2008). Security certificates come under fire. *For the Defence, 29(2)*, 18.

Razack, S. (2007). 'Your client has a profile': Face and national security in Canada after 9/11. *Studies in Law, Politics and Society, 40*, 3–40.

Roach, K. (2005). Must we trade rights for security? The choice between smart, harsh or proportionate security strategies in Canada and Britain. *Cardozo Law Review, 27*, 2151–2221.

Roach, K. (2011). *The 9/11 effect: Comparative counter-terrorism.* New York: Cambridge University Press.

Roach, K., More Procedure and Concern About Innocence But Less Justice? Remedies for Wrongful Convictions in the United States and Canada (see Chapter 14).

Roach, K. & Trotter, G. (2005). Miscarriages of justice in the war against terror. *Pennsylvania State Law Review, 109(4)*, 967–1041.

Sands, P. (2008). *Torture team: Rumsfeld's memo and the betrayal of American Values.* New York: Palgrave MacMillan.

Savage, C. (May 6, 2012). Five defendants in 9/11 attacks disrupt tribunal. *The New York Times.* Retrieved June 25, 2012 from www.bostonglobe.com/. . ./five-defendants-attacks-disrupt-tribunal

Schmitz, C. (8 April 2005). SCC Justice Binnie: Due Process Tested by Anti-terrorism Cases. *The Lawyers Weekly, 24*, 1–17.

Sherrin, C. (2008). The Charter and protection against wrongful conviction: Good, bad or irrelevant? *Supreme Court Law Review, 40*, 377–414.

Triadafilopoulos, T. (2010). Global norms, domestic institutions and the transformation of immigration policy in Canada and the US. *Review of International Studies, 36*, 169–194.

United States Constitution, art. I, §9, cl. 2.

USA Patriot Act, 8 U.S.C. § 1226a(a) (2006) Pub. L. No. 107–52.

Valiquet, D. (2008). *The dangerous offender and long-term offender regime.* Parliamentary Information and Research Service. Ottawa: Library of Parliament.

Waldman, L. (2009). No one above the law: Reflections of an immigration lawyer on the importance of the rule of law, *Law Review Lecture. Saskatchewan Law Review, 72*, 143–156.

Walker, C. (1999). Miscarriages of justice in principle and practice. In C. Walker & K. Starmer (Eds.), *Miscarriages of justice: A review of justice in error* (pp. 31–63). London: Blackstone Press Ltd.

Wittes, B. (2009). *Legislating the war on terror: An agenda for reform.* Washington, DC: Brookings Institution Press.

Cases

Ahani v. Canada, [1995] 3 FC 669, 694 and 696 (FCC).

Boumediene v. Bush, 128 S. Ct. 2229 (2008).

Charkaoui v. Canada (Citizenship and Immigration), 2007 SCC 9, [2007] 1 S.C.R. 326 [*Charkaoui I*].

Charkaoui v. Canada (Citizenship and Immigration), 2008 SCC 38, [2008] 2 S.C.R. 350 [*Charkaoui II*].

Hamdi v. Rumsfeld, 542 U.S. 507 (2004).

Hamdan v. Rumsfeld, 548 U.S. 557 (2006).

Rasul v. Bush, 542 U.S. 466; 124 S. Ct. 2686 (2004).

Re. Troy Anthony Davis, 130 S. Ct. 1 (2009).

R. v. Amara, [2010] O.J. No. 181.

R. v. Stinchcombe, [1991] 3 S.C.R. 326.

Suresh v. Canada, 1 S.C.R. 3 (2002).

12

THE RISKS OF SUMMARY PROCEEDINGS, PLEA BARGAINS, AND PENAL ORDERS IN PRODUCING WRONGFUL CONVICTIONS IN THE U.S. AND EUROPE

Gwladys Gilliéron

Trials have traditionally been the normative procedure for determining criminal charges. Today, the overwhelming majority of convictions occur by way of summary proceedings. The difference between ordinary proceedings and alternative proceedings is that the latter are not surrounded by the same degree of safeguards that are present at trial. A trial serves as a check on governmental excesses and intends to assure the accuracy of the verdict. Simplification of proceeding usually goes along with restrictions on a criminal defendant's rights and thus may reinforce the risk of wrongful convictions. So far, most of the attention has been devoted to wrongful convictions in which innocent people have been convicted after trial. Since most cases are handled through summary proceedings, such as plea bargaining in the U.S. and statements of guilt under continental law, the problem of wrongful convictions in these kinds of proceedings deserves much more attention. This chapter addresses this problem by discussing key issues related to summary assessments of "truth" in continental, inquisitorial systems in Europe and in the U.S. adversarial system of justice.

After a brief overview of the different types of criminal justice systems, I will describe the alternative and summary proceedings available in inquisitorial criminal justice systems and identify the factors that contribute to wrongful convictions. In the next part I will center my discussion on how the U.S. practice of plea bargaining may enhance the risk of wrongful convictions and what measures can be taken to limit coercion in this process.

Models of Criminal Justice Systems

Traditionally, a distinction can be drawn between inquisitorial and adversarial criminal justice systems. While the adversarial system is prevalent in common law countries, the inquisitorial system of justice is employed in many continental European jurisdictions. Both criminal justice systems have a number of safeguards designed to ensure that wrongful convictions are avoided. In an inquisitorial system the court plays an active role in collecting the evidence and in determining the guilt. In order to uncover the truth of the case, judges read the investigative file of the prosecution. The examination hearings are conducted through the court. There is no cross-examination. The judge determines the verdict and the sentence. A full jury is uncommon in continental systems. In an adversarial system, the parties, acting independently, are responsible for investigating the case and presenting their evidence before a passive and neutral judge or jury that will decide on guilt. The responsibility in seeking the truth of the case relies on the defense and the public prosecutor, while the duty of the judge is to ensure the fair play of due process. If the parties decide not to present all the evidence, the judge will not intervene. In this system, the truth is supposed to emerge as a result of the contest between the two parties. Rationalization of criminal justice systems in recent years gave rise to mixed systems combining inquisitorial and accusatorial elements (Piquerez, Macaluso, & Piquerez, 2011; Steiner, 2010). By introducing the possibility of informal negotiations between the prosecution and the defense, several continental European jurisdictions have adopted adversarial elements.

The distinction between adversarial and inquisitorial criminal justice systems has become less important since, in all criminal justice systems, criminal trials have become relatively infrequent. Today, the vast majority of criminal matters are resolved by alternative proceedings, where the prosecutor plays a determinant role. In the U.S. criminal justice system, a great majority of criminal charges are resolved by pleas of guilty. In 2010, more than 97 percent of the cases in the federal system were settled by guilty or *nolo contendere* pleas (Maguire, 2010). At the state level, the situation is similar. In the nation's 75 largest counties in 2006, 98.2 percent of felony charges were resolved through a guilty plea. Only murder charges produced frequent trials (48 percent of the cases). For misdemeanor charges, guilty pleas accounted for 91 percent of the convictions (Maguire, 2006). In continental European criminal justice systems, penal order proceedings play a predominant role. This is particularly true for the Swiss legal system where approximately 90 percent of the convictions are based upon a penal order, a decision issued by a public prosecutor (Hutzler, 2010). In addition, in response to the pressure for greater efficiency in criminal justice systems, a number of inquisitorial criminal justice systems have implemented proceedings similar to the U.S. plea bargaining.

In sum, criminal justice today is less judicial. In reality, a shift from the judiciary to the prosecution has taken place over the last few decades (Walther, 2004). The prosecutor combines executive and judicial powers. He is a public official with decision-making powers that are, to a large extent, adjudicatory. The prosecutor, in making his decision, faces extremely limited oversight; thus, wrongful convictions are a risk that must be given serious consideration.

Alternative and Summary Proceedings in Inquisitorial Criminal Justice Systems and Their Risk of Wrongful Convictions

Penal Order Proceedings

The penal order allows prosecution by written instrument. It is a simplified procedure that allows conviction without a trial. This procedure is used when the judicial police inquiry has verified the matters of which the defendant is accused. Depending on the jurisdiction, this summary proceeding may be limited to either petty offenses or misdemeanors or may even include felonies. In the latter version, its scope of application is then limited by the length of the prison sentence that can be imposed. Penal order proceedings are usually applied in cases of traffic offenses, minor thefts, and possession of drugs.

In some criminal justice systems the court may be involved in the final stage to impose a sanction; in others, the prosecutor has sole responsibility for imposing a sanction. In the French and German criminal justice systems, the prosecutor may make a written application to the judge, using a standard form. In the application, the prosecutor requests the imposition of a specific sanction. In the French penal order, only a fine may be imposed (article 495-1 and article 525 F-CCP), while in the German penal order a prison sentence of up to one year combined with probation may be pronounced (§407 D-CCP). In case the judge is considering granting the prosecutor's application to issue a penal order with the imposition of a suspended sentence of imprisonment, he has to appoint a defense counsel (§408b D-CCP). The court rarely refuses to follow the prosecutor's advice. Hence, in reality, the penal order is a decision issued by the prosecution which is checked and usually approved by the court (Jehle, 2006). In the Swiss criminal justice system, the court is not involved. The prosecutor has broad power since he has the authority to impose a prison sentence of up to six months (article 352 para 1 CH-CCP).

Despite these differences, all penal order proceedings have in common that the decision is issued without a hearing of the defendant. This decision may then be appealed by the defendant within a certain deadline. In that case the defendant is given a public hearing. If no objection is made, the penal order becomes final and has the same effect as a judgment following a main hearing. This has the consequence that this written procedure may result in a judgment without the parties being heard.

At first sight, the penal order proceeding violates the right to a fair trial laid down in article 6 ECHR. Among others, this provision guarantees the right to a public hearing in the determination of any criminal charge by an independent and impartial court. When issuing the penal order, the prosecutor enjoys neither judicial independence nor impartiality. However, according to established Strasbourg case law, this does not in itself mean that the Convention is breached. In such instances, the Court requires that domestic law provides for the possibility of having all aspects of the decision reviewed by a judicial institution, which does fully comply with the requirements of article 6 ECHR (ECHR, 29 April 1988, *Belilos – Switzerland* (Series A-132), §§69 et seq.). Criminal justice systems having a penal order proceeding give the defendant the opportunity to raise an objection and ask for a full trial, so that the right to be heard, as well as all other procedural rights guaranteed by the ECHR, are subsequently respected. In renouncing his right to make opposition, it is assumed that the accused person waives the procedural guarantees of the ECHR. Such a waiver is effective provided that it is clear and unequivocal and that the accused makes his decision with the full knowledge of the legal and factual situation of the case (ECHR, 27 February 1980, *Deweer – Belgium* (Series A-35), §49). However, this may not always be the case since a non-negligible percentage of the population has some difficulties in understanding a text of some complexities (see below).

The penal order is commonly referred to as the continental form of plea bargaining (Langbein, 1974; Trechsel & Killias, 2004). However, various aspects differ between those two proceedings. In the penal order proceedings, a superordinate and subordinate relationship between the prosecution and the accused still exists. In case of a penal order, the evaluation of the criminal matter is exclusively made by the prosecutor. Since a hearing of the defendant is not compulsory, the defendant usually does not participate in the preliminary proceedings. The defendant may only accept or refuse the order by raising an objection. A "bargain" between the prosecution and the defendant does not take place. Contrary to the U.S. plea bargaining, a defendant who objects to a penal order and insists on a full trial does not run the risk of having a harsher sentence imposed by the court (Killias, 2008; Trechsel & Killias, 2004). This is mostly due to the fact that a penal order can only be issued if the facts are sufficiently clear and the culpability is not dubious, so that a reduction of the original charges is unlikely to occur. Therefore, the risk of false confession (that is, accepting the penal order), does not exist to the same extent in continental law as in the U.S. system.

Risk of Wrongful Convictions in Penal Order Proceedings

Different factors inherent in penal order proceedings may increase the risk of wrongful convictions (for a detailed discussion of these risks, see Gilliéron, 2010). Basically, five causes can be identified: careless investigation, prosecution, the requirement for a written form and imposition of an inadequate time limit to contest the charges, and the defendant's behavior.

In the vast majority of cases, the prosecutor makes his decision based solely on the police accounts. Those, however, may be inaccurate or incomplete and since the prosecutor has no duty to hear the accused prior to his decision (even when he intends to recommend a prison sentence), this incompleteness remains undiscovered. Hence, the prosecutor's investigation is often not conducted with the required diligence. Furthermore, the prosecutor may expect the defendant to make the case for his innocence.

In the Swiss criminal justice system, the prosecutor alone is responsible for issuing the penal order. As a consequence, the decision is only subject to judicial control if the defendant makes opposition. The prosecutor, acting as an inquisitor, may contribute to the increased risk of wrongful convictions. In criminal justice systems where the prosecutor does all the preparatory work and formulates a written recommendation to the judge, the court refuses to follow the prosecutor's advice only rarely, so it may be assumed that the court is not really an efficient safeguard against wrongful convictions (Riklin, 2007). Thus, the check of the prosecutor's recommendation is of a purely formal nature.

Defendants have a legal right to make opposition within a certain deadline if they do not agree with the prosecutor's decision. This deadline varies by jurisdiction. It may range from ten days in Switzerland (article 354 CH-CCP) to 30 (petty offenses; article 527 F-CCP) or 45 days (misdemeanors; article 495-3 F-CCP) in France. In addition, depending on the jurisdiction, the defendant has to file an opposition in written form. This is the case in the Swiss criminal justice system (article 354 CH-CCP). In Germany, the defendant may lodge an objection either in writing or orally within two weeks to be recorded by the registry (§410 D-CCP). France has a similar provision. The Swiss criminal justice system cumulates all disadvantages to make opposition: the short time span of ten days and the required written form may hinder the defendant's exercise of his right.

A number of reasons can explain why defendants miss the deadline to make opposition or renounce the exercise of this right. It is possible that due to functional illiteracy, the defendant is unable to understand the instructions about legal remedies. This assumption has some support in light of the fact that according to the Adult Literacy and Lifeskills Survey (ALL) of 2003, which provides information on the skills and attitudes of adults aged 16 to 65, about 16 percent of the Swiss population is unable to understand a text of some complexity (Notter, Arnold, von Erlach, & Hertig, 2006). The Pisa survey (2009), which tested students at age 15, shows similar results. Literacy competencies across Europe are situated on the same level as in Switzerland (Nidegger et al., 2010). Further reasons for not contesting the penal order include indifference, ignorance of the law, and fear of unfavorable outcome, such as costs of the procedure.

A Swiss research study on wrongful convictions supports the higher susceptibility to error of the penal order proceedings. The research was supported by the Swiss National Science Foundation (SNSF) and has analyzed all mistaken convictions (successful petitions of revision) in Switzerland between 1995 and 2004 (Killias, Gilliéron, & Dongois, 2007). Over the considered time period, a total of 237 petitions of revision have been admitted. The majority concerned penal orders, with 159 successful petitions of revision. However, this outcome is not out of proportion when considering that over 500,000 penal orders were issued between 1995 and 2004 (Killias, 2008). But it is very likely that in this field, there are many more mistaken convictions than those discovered by the study. It is highly probable that the majority of those convicted waive their right to challenge the decision and agree to pay a fine (Gilliéron, 2010; Killias, 2008).

The results of the research show that wrongful convictions of factually innocent persons after a trial play a minor role. In most cases, the sentence imposed by the court was too high, since some mental problem of the convicted had not been recognized by the court and therefore had not been taken into account. In fact, the ignorance by the court of some mental problems of the convicted, affecting his criminal responsibility, was a factor in 46.4 percent of admitted petitions of revision based on new evidence. Factually innocent persons have been convicted in about one-third of the cases, mostly due to perjury by victims of crimes against sexual integrity or, in other cases, because of eyewitness misidentification or false confession by the defendant that he later recanted. The research did not identify exonerations due to DNA evidence (Killias, Gilliéron, & Dongois, 2007), which might be the consequence of not storing items of physical evidence over a long period of time.

In contrast, the study revealed that wrongful convictions by penal order mainly concerned factually innocent defendants. The granting of the petition of revision led in 21 cases to a reduced sentence, in one case to a harsher sentence, and in 109 cases to the acquittal of the convicted. Wrongful identification (e.g., confusion of names) and investigation not conducted with the required diligence by the police and the prosecution were the leading factors contributing to wrongful convictions (Killias, Gilliéron & Dongois, 2007).

"Plea Bargaining" in Inquisitorial Criminal Justice Systems

In response to the pressure for greater efficiency in criminal justice systems, elements of plea bargaining emerged in the last few decades. However, no other system is identical to the U.S. with respect to plea bargaining. Rather, when plea bargaining has been considered and incorporated in new legal systems, they have each adapted the practice to their own needs and values (Turner, 2009). The most important element in this kind of proceeding is consent and/or confession. While plea bargaining has become increasingly common around the world, many scholars believe that this practice conflicts with several fundamental principles of the inquisitorial tradition. In particular, they argue that plea bargaining affects the principle of legality[1] and the principle of instruction. Those principles require the prosecutor to search for the truth *ex officio* and bring a charge whenever there are sufficient grounds to suspect a person of having committed an offense. On the contrary, in plea bargains, all facts of the case need not be entirely clarified, since the facts are based on a "deal" between the defendant and the prosecution. Thus, the factual truth is replaced by a formal truth. The right to a public trial, the principle of orality, the presumption of innocence, and the right against self-incrimination are also undermined. However, as long as the accused person waives his rights in a clear and unequivocal manner, this alternative procedure does not breach the ECHR (ECHR, 27 February 1980, *Deweer − Belgium* (Series A-35), §§48 et seq.).

In the following section, the adoption of "plea bargaining" in Switzerland and Germany is illustrated. In this way, differences from the U.S. will be highlighted and potential benefits and weaknesses identified. Common advantages and disadvantages of the Swiss and German models of plea bargaining will be discussed in a separate section.

Plea Bargaining in Switzerland: The Abridged Proceedings

The Swiss Code of Criminal Procedure, which became law on January 1, 2011, and replaced the 26 cantonal criminal procedure codes, has introduced the possibility of ending a case by way of abridged proceedings (*abgekürztes Verfahren*).

This alternative allows the prosecutor to make a deal with the defendant. Sentence bargaining is possible as well as charge bargaining. According to the current practice of the Federal Supreme Court, a confession may lead to a reduction of one-fifth to one-third of the foreseen penalty (BGE 121 IV 202, 205 et seq.). In the abridged proceedings, a further reduction is possible when additional reasons to mitigate responsibility and reduce a sentence exist, such as sincere repentance and confession of other crimes. Unlike the U.S., fact bargaining is prohibited.

The accused person may submit an application to the prosecution for the case to be conducted by way of abridged proceedings, provided that he accepts liability for those circumstances essential to the legal evaluation of the case and that he accepts, at least in principle, the civil claims (article 358 para 1 CH-CCP). The requirement that only the accused person can submit an application aims to protect him from coercion by the prosecutor. However, the prosecutor is allowed to inform the accused person of this alternative. The application can be made at any time prior to the bringing of charges. An abridged proceeding is only possible if the prosecutor requests the imposition of a prison sentence not exceeding 5 years (article 358 para 2 CH-CCP). The public prosecutor evaluates the application and decides whether the case is to be conducted by way of abridged proceedings or not (article 359 para 1 CH-CCP). The accused has no legal recourse against the prosecutor's decision. The prosecutor has entire discretion in making his decision. The prosecutor has no duty to state the reasons for his decision, so his discretion remains uncontrolled. A rejection does not preclude the possibility of resubmitting an application at a later stage in the preliminary proceedings. If the case is heard by way of abridged proceedings, the defendant must be represented by defense counsel (article 130 (e) CH-CCP). The mandatory assistance of defense counsel is intended to protect the accused during the informal negotiations with the prosecution.

Informal negotiations are closed by an indictment, which the prosecution conveys to the parties (i.e., the accused and the private claimant). They have ten days to accept or reject the indictment (article 360 para 2 CH-CCP). While the accused has to accept the indictment formally, a tacit acceptance by the private claimant suffices. In addition to the points usually found in an indictment, this document contains the sentence, the regulation of the civil law claims of the private claimant and the warning to the parties that by accepting the indictment they waive the right to ordinary proceedings and to initiate legal remedies (article 360 para 1 CH-CCP). The consequence of this last point is that the convicted can file a petition for revision only on limited grounds. Since the court in an abridged proceeding does not conduct an evidentiary hearing—this in contrast to the ordinary proceedings—it is not possible to file a petition for revision based on new evidence. However, the use of this legal remedy should remain possible to eliminate decisions that are unacceptable from a constitutional point of view (e.g., exercise of coercive power by the prosecution or abuse of public office). Some scholars argue that in case of false confession of the convicted, the possibility to file a petition of revision should still be open in order to correct a wrongful conviction (Jeanneret, 2010; Kuhn, 2009). If the parties reject the indictment, the prosecution will conduct ordinary proceedings (article 30 para 5 CH-CCP). In that case, declarations provided by the parties with respect to the abridged proceedings cannot be used in ordinary proceedings.

On the other hand, if the indictment is accepted, the prosecution transmits the indictment, together with the files, to the Court of First Instance (article 360 para 4 CH-CCP). Instead of conducting an evidentiary proceeding at the principal hearing, the court questions the accused person in order to establish whether he accepts the circumstances of the case on which the charge is based, and whether this assertion corresponds to the position as set out in the files (article 361 CH-CCP). The examination is limited to ascertaining that the rights conferred to the parties have been respected and that the confession of the accused is credible. Following the principal hearing, the court retires and conducts its deliberation in private. The court has to determine whether the carrying out of abridged proceedings is lawful and appropriate, whether the charge corresponds to the conclusions of the principal hearing and to the files, and whether the sanctions requested are reasonable (article 362 para 1 CH-CCP). Hence, the court does not determine whether the conviction of the accused person is lawful, but whether it is lawful to convict him by way of abridged proceedings (Bommer, 2010).

Since legal criteria for the evaluation of appropriateness are missing, it will be up to the courts to develop such criteria. Legal equality considerations may, for instance, be considered. A judgment that would significantly deviate from judgments pronounced in similar cases in ordinary proceedings should be deemed inappropriate. However, the prosecutor enjoys vast discretion regarding the sanction requested and thus, the court should only intervene in cases of manifest abuse (Jeanneret, 2010).

If the court comes to the conclusion that the requirements for a judgment by way of abridged proceedings are met, it converts the criminal offenses, sentence and civil claim of the indictment into a judgment (article 362 para 2 CH-CCP). Against such a judgment, a party may only appeal on the basis that it did not accept the indictment or that the judgment does not correspond to the indictment (article 362 para 5 CH-CCP). On the other hand, if the court determines that the requirements are not met, it sends the files back to the prosecution in order to proceed by way of ordinary proceedings (article 362 para 3 CH-CCP). The court's decision cannot be challenged. Declarations, such as confessions, provided by the parties with respect to the abridged proceedings cannot be used in ordinary proceedings (article 362 para 4 CH-CCP). A matter of debate concerns whether the same or another prosecutor than the one having conducted the abridged proceedings should be entrusted with the continuation of the investigation. However, when a defendant withdraws his confession, the case must be assigned to a different prosecutor (for a systematic change of prosecutor when the abridged proceedings have failed, see Pieth, 2009).

In sum, in abridged proceedings the court does not evaluate the legal circumstances of the case. In these alternative proceedings, the assessment of the defendant's responsibility is made within the executive branch (the prosecutor's office) so the prosecutor acts a quasi-judicial decision-maker. However, the point of view of the prosecutor is different from the court. The prosecutor does not sit as a neutral fact finder but will focus on the incriminating circumstances. Despite the obligation to objectivity, the prosecutor is not a judge. The prosecutor's submission to the court remains only an indictment, even if it is converted into a judgment.

Plea Bargaining in Germany: Agreements

In the 1980s a discussion emerged around the phenomenon of informal agreements (*Absprachen*). Although the practice of negotiating for justice did not have a basis in law, this type of agreement soon played an important role in achieving out-of-court settlements of criminal cases (Weigend, 2008). During the 1990s, a number of decisions of the Supreme Court and of the Federal Constitutional Court held that negotiations between the court and the parties before or during the trial are, in principle, allowed if certain conditions are observed (for an overview and discussion of these decisions, see Peters, 2011). However, in 2005 the Supreme Court, in a landmark decision, appealed to the legislature to take action (BGHSt 50, 40-64). Thus, the parliament drafted a law regulating informal agreements, which went into force in mid-2009.

The law specifies that discussions about the status of the proceedings are allowed at every stage of the proceedings (§§160b, 202a, 212, 257b D-CCP). The central provision of this reform is displayed in §257c D-CCP. According to this new rule, the court may, in suitable cases, reach an agreement with the participants in the main trial on the further course and outcome of the proceedings. The subject of such an agreement may only include the legal consequences that may be imposed in a judgment, other procedural measures related to trial proceedings, and procedure-related acts of the parties. A confession should be an integral part of any negotiated agreement. The verdict of guilt, as well as sentences of rehabilitation and security, may not be part of the negotiated agreement. With the defendant's consent, the court can indicate the minimum and maximum sentence that it will impose. If none of the parties objects, the provisional proposal becomes binding upon the court. But the court is not bound by a negotiated agreement if legal or factually important incidents have been overlooked or have arisen after the agreement was concluded and if the court is of the opinion that under such new circumstances, the prospective sentencing range is not appropriate to the gravity of the offense or the degree of guilt. In addition, an agreement is not binding if the further conduct of the defendant at trial does not match the facts which were assumed by the court to have occurred. In such cases, the defendant's confession may not be admitted as evidence. In negotiated agreements, the parties retain the right to lodge an appeal regarding a petition of revision. In the event that a negotiated agreement preceded the judgment, a waiver of the right to file an appellate remedy is excluded.

As in the United States, negotiations may concern the charges, the sentence, or both. Fact bargaining, on the contrary, seems to occur rarely, if at all (Turner, 2006). In contrast with the United States and Switzerland, plea bargaining in Germany usually involves not only the defendant and the prosecution, but also the judge. One of the main reasons for involving the judge in negotiations is that he has very broad discretion in the area of sentencing, so the prosecutor cannot certify that the court will accept a particular sentence bargain (Turner, 2009).

Risk of Wrongful Convictions in the Swiss and German Plea Bargaining Models

The benefit of plea bargaining is that it significantly shortens the trial. In this kind of proceeding, however, the court will not verify the factual basis for the defendant's admission of guilt to the same extent as it would in an ordinary proceeding. A plea bargain may produce a worse outcome for the defendant than a full trial if the defense attorney and the prosecution make an inaccurate assessment of the facts uncovered early in the proceedings.

The Swiss model of plea bargaining faces many of the same concerns as U.S. plea bargaining. Scholars argue that there might be a risk of increased wrongful convictions. In fact, the accused might admit guilt to avoid the uncertainties of trial outcomes (Bommer, 2009; Kuhn, 2009). Furthermore, the prosecutor, to be in a better position, might accuse the defendant of a more serious crime or of an additional crime of which he is clearly innocent in order to induce a plea to the proper charge. Since abridged proceedings have been introduced only recently, empirical data that would prove these assumptions are missing. Another concern is that this alternative might disadvantage socially weaker defendants since they are often not defended with the same diligence (Greiner, 2009).

The German model of plea bargaining also raises some concerns. Critics argue, for instance, that judges do not supervise the plea carefully enough and that a dominant judge might coerce a defendant into entering a guilty plea. During informal negotiations, a judge (who has vast discretion in determining the sentence after a contested trial) might tell a defendant that the sentence that would be imposed after a trial would be much higher than the sentence likely in the case of a confession, in order to make sentence bargaining more attractive (Turner, 2006). Confronted with the potential risk of disproportionate negotiated sentences with regard to the defendant's culpability, the Federal Supreme Court has held that sentences must neither be too lenient as a result of plea bargaining, nor too harsh where plea negotiations have failed (Turner, 2009). Furthermore, in order to minimize this risk of coercion, the Federal Supreme Court has held that the defendant cannot be pressured to enter a plea bargain through threats of a higher sentence or through unlawful promises (Turner, 2006). In addition, on the procedural side, the president of the court is obliged to announce in public whether talks about agreements have taken place and, if an agreement has been concluded, what its content is, so that in theory, transparency in negotiated agreements is guaranteed (§243 (4) D-CCP). Nevertheless, despite this rule and the principle of a public trial, the essence of agreements will still remain hidden. In open court, potentially unlawful promises or threats that might influence the defendant to accept the bargain will certainly not be presented. Thus, this rule is neither a guarantee of protection nor an efficient safeguard against judicial coercion (Turner, 2006). However, in the German system, the defendant may raise the question of judicial coercion on appeal. Thus, the availability of appellate remedies is a safeguard against judicial coercion. Empirical research concerning the question of whether wrongful convictions have occurred as a result of plea bargaining still remains to be done.

Advantages of the Swiss and German Models of Plea Bargaining as Compared to U.S. Plea Bargaining

The Swiss and German models of plea bargaining reject the idea of defendants pleading guilty while at the same time contesting their innocence. Thus, judges in inquisitorial criminal justice systems are still oriented toward truth-seeking.

In contrast to the U.S. criminal justice system, as a consequence of the right to be heard, the prosecution is required to disclose its evidence fully to the defendant. In this way, a person accused of a crime will be aware of the strengths and weaknesses of the case. If the accused then decides to confess to a criminal offense, he will act with full knowledge of the prosecutor's file. In addition, defense lawyers can better evaluate the fairness and accuracy of a proposed plea bargain.

In inquisitorial criminal justice systems, the prosecutor is obliged to investigate in an objective way, meaning that he has to investigate both exculpatory and inculpatory evidence with equal care. Fuller investigation of the facts has the consequence that prosecutors will be less likely to charge innocent persons and that they will be less likely to give enormous sentence reductions to accused who have committed serious crimes.

Overall, the Swiss and German criminal justice systems are less coercive than the U.S. justice system. While in the U.S. federal courts, a guilty plea may lead to a reduction of two-thirds of the sentence expected, in Germany, a confession is commonly rewarded with a one-quarter to one-third reduction in the expected sentence. In Switzerland, an admission of guilt is commonly rewarded with a one-fifth to one-third reduction in the foreseen penalty.

Plea Bargaining in the U.S. Criminal Justice System and the Risk of Wrongful Convictions

A plea bargain is an agreement in a criminal case between the defendant and the prosecutor. In this agreement, the defendant agrees to plead guilty without trial. In return, the prosecutor agrees to dismiss certain charges or to reduce the charge to something less serious than that which is supported by the evidence (*charge bargaining*). Or the prosecutor can make a specific sentence recommendation or refrain from making certain recommendations (*sentence bargaining*). A relatively new and less common type of bargaining is *fact bargaining*. This kind of negotiation occurs when prosecutors and defendants bargain over what circumstances of an event should be stipulated as true by the parties and presented to the court. It may also happen that the plea is the result of *implicit plea bargaining*. This means that the defendant pleads guilty without prior negotiation or any promise from the prosecutor, because he expects to be treated more leniently than he would be if he exercised the right to trial. The negotiated plea is subject to court approval. Usually, plea bargaining occurs prior to trial, but in some jurisdictions, it may occur at any time before a verdict is reached. Under many victims' rights statutes, victims have the right to have input in the plea bargaining process (see Tobolowsky, 2010). A guilty plea implies that the defendant waives the constitutional right to a jury trial, and the concomitant rights to cross-examination and confrontation, as well as the requirement that the government meet the burden of proving guilt beyond a reasonable doubt. Most state and federal courts have concluded that a defendant may explicitly waive his right to appeal as part of the agreement (Miller & Wright, 2007).

The practice of plea bargaining, though controversial in the U.S. criminal justice system, benefits everyone through the criminal process. The defendant avoids the uncertainties of a trial and gains a speedy disposition of the case. For the prosecutor, the negotiated plea saves time and other resources in order to concentrate on higher priority cases, and it has the advantage of increasing the conviction rate. The court is able to dispose of a case quickly and will therefore conserve scarce resources. On the other hand, one major concern of plea bargaining is that innocent persons might plead guilty. This question has preoccupied many scholars and today the controversy over the "innocence problem" plays a leading role in the plea bargaining debate (Gazal-Ayal, 2006).

Critics of the plea bargaining system argue that the practice is dangerous for innocent defendants. There might be a serious risk that a defendant pleads guilty not because he is guilty but because the prosecutor offers some concessions in return. Thus, an innocent person might prefer a lenient sentence rather than running the risk of a much harsher sentence resulting from a wrongful conviction at trial. This argument has led some scholars to argue in favor of abolishing this practice (Alschuler, 1983; Langbein, 1979; Schulhofer, 1992). Following this approach, it is argued, would mean that wrongful convictions after a full trial occur less frequently than after a plea bargain.

Empirical research hardly exists concerning the question of whether a full trial or a plea bargain better protects the innocent. In *Exonerations in the United States, 1989 Through 2003*, Professor Gross and his colleagues found that in 6 percent of the cases in their database, innocent persons had pleaded guilty and had been convicted. Fifteen innocent murder defendants and four innocent rape defendants pleaded guilty to avoid the risk of life imprisonment or the death penalty (Gross et al., 2005). Not included in this total are exonerees whose wrongful convictions were the result of large-scale patterns of police perjury and corruption, including 31 of the 39 defendants who pled guilty to drug charges in Tulia, Texas, and the majority of the 100 or more exonerated defendants in the Rampart scandal in Los Angeles who pleaded guilty to offenses they did not commit (Gross et al., 2005). This research seems to indicate that innocent defendants tend to elect trials over pleas. Does this outcome really reflect the reality? Are wrongful convictions more prevalent in ordinary proceedings than after a plea bargain? The 2005 database of wrongful convictions compiled by the team of researchers led by Samuel Gross was limited to serious cases since all exonerees were sentenced to a long term of imprisonment or to death. This represents a highly atypical group, since the majority of defendants are convicted of misdemeanors and those who are convicted of a felony are mostly sentenced to probation or to lesser terms of incarceration in jail. Moreover, the pathway to exoneration is extremely time consuming. On average, the whole process from conviction to exoneration lasts 11 years (Gross et al., 2005). Thus, it is primarily those wrongfully convicted defendants with long sentences who will have an interest in proving their innocence, while others prefer to accept their convictions. Therefore, it can be assumed that wrongful convictions after a plea bargain occur much more frequently than the database would suggest.

The prosecutor's enormous power in the plea bargaining process creates a potential risk for abuses and the limited oversight of his decisions by the judge is not sufficient to reduce this risk. After the prosecutor and the defendant have reached an agreement, the court must give its approval. In general, a judge will accept a plea agreement if he is convinced that the defendant makes a voluntary and knowing waiver of his trial rights. Furthermore, he must ascertain that there is a factual basis to support the charges to which the defendant pleads guilty (Miller & Wright, 2007). A guilty plea is involuntary if it is induced by false promises, fraud, mistake, or misapprehension of the conditions. Furthermore, prosecutors are not allowed to use meaningless or illusory promises to induce a plea. A prosecutor's failure to disclose exculpatory evidence may result in vacating the guilty plea for the reason that such information is crucial to enable the defendant to decide whether to plead guilty. The use of threats and promises intended to deprive the defendant of his freedom of choice constitutes a denial of procedural fairness (Gershman, 2007–2008). However, it is not an easy task to define under which circumstances promises and threats are considered as coercive. In *Bordenkircher v. Hayes* (1978), the Supreme Court addressed the applicability of prosecutorial vindictiveness to the practice of plea bargaining. It held that the threat to seek more serious charges if the defendant did not plead guilty to the initial indictment but insisted on a jury trial was constitutionally acceptable in the context of plea bargaining. The Supreme Court stated that "in the 'give-and-take' of plea bargaining, there is no such element of punishment or retaliation as long as the accused is free to accept or reject the prosecution's offer" (*Bordenkircher v. Hayes*, 1978: 363). Thus, the threat of additional charges made during plea negotiations is not a denial of due process but is legitimate to induce a plea. In contrast to the aforementioned behaviors, the prosecutor's offer of a more lenient sentence does not constitute coercion. In fact, a guilty plea is often obtained by the prosecutor through the offer of a plea to a lesser charge, the dismissal of other charges, or the recommendation of a specific sentence (*Brady v. U.S.*, 1970). Courts normally consider the plea of a defendant as non-coerced if he pleads guilty to avoid a possible death sentence after a trial (see e.g., *Brady v. U.S.*, 1970; *Parker v. North Carolina*, 1970; *North Carolina v. Alford*, 1970).

Forty-seven states, Washington D.C., and the federal jurisdiction permit *Alford* pleas (Bibas, 2003). The *Alford* plea allows defendants to plead guilty while actively professing innocence (*North Carolina v. Alford*, 1970). The defendant agrees to plead guilty because the evidence of guilt is overwhelming and thus the defendant realizes that an acquittal is very unlikely. This plea differs slightly from the *nolo contendere* plea in which the defendant agrees to be sentenced for the crime, but refuses to admit guilt. The federal jurisdiction, as well as thirty-eight states and Washington D.C., allow *nolo contendere* pleas (Bibas, 2003). In 2004, an estimated 76,000 inmates in state prison claimed to have entered *Alford* pleas, which accounted for about 8.5 percent of all guilty pleas (*Alford* pleas, *nolo contendere* pleas, and guilty pleas). An estimated 131,100 state inmates entered *nolo contendere* pleas, which accounted for slightly more than 14.5 percent of all pleas (Redlich & Özdoğru, 2009). There are currently no reliable estimates concerning the number of innocent defendants who have entered *Alford* pleas. Since a non-negligible percentage of defendants enter such pleas, further research on wrongful convictions with respect to *Alford* pleas is needed.

From the aforesaid, it follows that the actual doctrine of the Supreme Court provides little protection for defendants. Whether the court is an efficient safeguard against wrongful confession is therefore more than questionable. It is not surprising that the court only rarely refuses to reject a guilty plea. The reason invoked for accepting guilty plea proposals is that the prosecutor knows all details of the criminal matter, while the judge has less background information on the alleged crime and the defendant. In addition, if the court started to call the prosecutors' decisions into question, the caseload would become overwhelming. Judicial inquiry is limited to ascertaining that the defendant is of sound mind and understands the consequences of his actions rather than examining the accuracy of the facts to which he is attesting. The court is only required to assure that the conduct to which the defendant confesses constitutes an offense under the statutory provision under which he is pleading guilty. In reality, the assessment of the defendant's responsibility is made within the executive branch, namely in the prosecutor's office, and does not occur in court (Lynch, 1998). The prosecutor, in deciding whether to punish the defendant, is an "inquisitor seeking the 'correct' outcome" (Lynch, 1998, p. 2135). U.S. plea bargaining may be defined as an "informal, administrative, inquisitorial process of adjudication, internal to the prosecutor's office—in absolute distinction from a model of adversarial determination of fact and law before a neutral judicial decision maker" (Lynch, 2003, p. 1404). The risk in plea bargaining practice is best described by Barkow. According to her, plea bargaining "causes a systematic imbalance of power by allowing prosecutors to bypass the check of the judicial process" (Barkow, 2006, p. 1050). As explained above, the prosecutor faces extremely limited oversight over his decision so that abuse of his position is not excluded. This, of course, increases the risk of wrongful convictions.

Possible Measures to Reduce the Risk of Wrongful Convictions in Plea Bargaining in the U.S. Criminal Justice System

Coercion is a major problem in the practice of plea bargaining. Since other criminal justice systems have adopted similar procedures, it would be possible to take certain practices from these jurisdictions and try them in the United States. Coercion may be reduced in different ways. The sentencing discount for confessing to a crime is lower in inquisitorial criminal justice systems than in the United States. In addition, the defendant has access to the prosecutor's files and thus he can better evaluate the strengths and weaknesses of the case. Another way to reduce the coerciveness of plea bargaining is to limit the practice to less serious crimes (see also Turner, 2009).

Conclusion

Every criminal justice system has adopted alternative and summary proceedings to reduce the court's caseload. This had the inevitable consequence of strengthening the prosecutor's power and weakening the defendant's procedural rights. The prosecutor, by making important decisions in alternative proceedings, combines both executive and judicial powers. In fact, his decisions are to a large extent adjudicatory. A major problem is that the prosecutor faces extremely limited oversight over his decisions. This is particularly true for the Swiss penal order proceedings, where the prosecutor is allowed to impose a prison sentence of up to six months without judicial control. Alternative proceedings, such as the abridged proceedings under the Swiss legal system and the U.S. plea bargaining system, still require a decision by the court, but the main hearing in these procedures provides restriction on prosecutorial power of a much lesser degree than in the ordinary proceedings. If the aim of the criminal justice system is bureaucratic efficiency, alternative proceedings certainly make sense, but if the aim of the justice system is the protection of individual rights, alternative proceedings are harder to justify.

So far, many studies have focused their attention on wrongful convictions in which innocent people have been convicted after trial. In this context, the question of whether an inquisitorial or an adversarial criminal justice system is better able to protect the innocents has been widely discussed (see e.g., Thomas, 2008; Walpin, 2003). Alternative proceedings merit much more attention as potential sources of wrongful convictions. The quality of judicial systems can only be improved by a better understanding of the risks of wrongful convictions in alternative and summary proceedings.

Note

1 This criticism does not apply to criminal justice systems adhering to the principle of opportunity such as that of France.

References

Alschuler, A. W. (1983). Implementing the Criminal Defendant's Right to Trial: Alternatives to Plea Bargaining System. *University of Chicago Law Review, 50*, 931–1050.

Barkow, R. E. (2006). Separation of Powers and the Criminal Law. *Stanford Law Review, 58*, 989–1054.

Bibas, S. (2003). Harmonizing Substantive Criminal Law Values and Criminal Procedure: The Case of Alford and Nolo Contendere Pleas. *Cornell Law Review, 88*, 1361–1411.

Bommer, F. (2009). Abgekürztes Verfahren und Plea Bargaining im Vergleich. *Zeitschrift für Schweizerisches Recht, 128*, 5–124.

Bommer, F. (2010). Kurzer Prozess mit dem abgekürzten Verfahren? In M. Heer (Ed.), *Schweizerische Strafprozessordnung und schweizerische Jugendstrafprozessordnung* (pp. 149–172). Bern: Stämpfli.

Gazal-Ayal, O. (2006). Partial Ban on Plea Bargains. *Cardozo Law Review, 27*(5), 2295–2351.

Gershman, B. L. (2007–2008). *Prosecutorial misconduct* (2nd edn.). Eagan, MN: Thomson/West.

Gilliéron, G. (2010). *Strafbefehlsverfahren und plea bargaining als Quelle von Fehlurteilen*. Zürich: Schulthess.

Greiner, G. (2009). Schuld ohne Sühne? Am Beispiel des "plea bargaining" nach neuer StPO. *forumpoenale*, 234–243.

Gross, S. R., Jacoby, K., Matheson, D. J., Montgomery, N., & Patil, S. (2005). Exonerations in the United States 1989 through 2003. *The Journal of Criminal Law and Criminology, 95*(2), 523–560.

Hutzler, D. (2010). *Ausgleich struktureller Garantiedefizite im Strafbefehlsverfahren: Eine Analyse der zürcherischen, schweizerischen und deutschen Regelungen, unter besonderer Berücksichtigung der Geständnisfunktion*. Baden-Baden: Nomos.

Jeanneret, Y. (2010). Les procédures spéciales dans le Code de procédure pénale suisse. In R. Pfister-Liechti (Ed.), *La procédure pénale fédérale* (pp. 137–195). Berne: Stämpfli.

Jehle, J.-M. (2006). The Function of Public Prosecution within the Criminal Justice System. Aim, Approach and Outcome of a European Comparative Study. In J.-M. Jehle & M. Wade (Eds.), *Coping with overloaded criminal justice systems. The rise of prosecutorial power across Europe* (pp. 3–25). Berlin [etc.]: Springer.

Killias, M. (2008). Wrongful Conviction in Switzerland: The Experience of a Continental Law Country. In C. R. Huff & M. Killias (Eds.), *Wrongful conviction. International perspectives on miscarriages of justice* (pp. 139–155). Philadelphia: Temple University Press.

Killias, M., Gilliéron, G., & Dongois, N. (2007). *Erreurs judiciaires en Suisse de 1995 à 2004. Report to the Swiss National Science Foundation.* University of Lausanne and University of Zurich, Lausanne and Zurich.

Kuhn, A. (2009). La procédure pénale suisse selon le CPP unifié. *Zeitschrift für Schweizerisches Recht, 128*, 125–184.

Langbein, J. H. (1974). Controlling Prosecutorial Discretion in Germany. *The University of Chicago Law Review, 41*, 439–457.

Langbein, J. H. (1979). Land Without Plea Bargaining: How the Germans Do It. *Michigan Law Review, 78*(2), 204–225.

Lynch, G. E. (1998). Our Administrative System of Criminal Justice. *Fordham Law Review, 66*, 2117–2151.

Lynch, G. E. (2003). Screening Versus Plea Bargaining: Exactly What Are We Trading Off? *Stanford Law Review, 55*, 1399–1408.

Maguire, Kathleen, (Ed.). Sourcebook of Criminal Justice Statistics [Online], Bureau of Justice Statistics, (table 5.57.2006). Available: http://www.albany.edu/sourcebook/pdf/t5572006.pdf [4/9/2012].

Maguire, Kathleen, (Ed.). Sourcebook of Criminal Justice Statistics [Online], Bureau of Justice Statistics, (table 5.22.2010). Available: http://www.albany.edu/sourcebook/pdf/t5222010.pdf [4/9/2012].

Miller, M., & Wright, R. F. (2007). *Criminal Procedures: Prosecution and adjudication: cases, statutes, and executive materials* (3rd edn.). Austin: Wolters Kluwer Law & Business/Aspen Publishers.

Nidegger, C., Moser, U., Angelone, D., Brühwiler, C., Buccheri, G., Abt, N., Mariotta, M., & Roos, E. (2010). *PISA 2009—Schülerinnen und Schüler der Schweiz im internationalen Vergleich: Erste Ergebnisse.*: Neuchâtel Konsortium PISA.ch.

Notter, P., Arnold, C., von Erlach, E., & Hertig, P. (2006). *Lesen und Rechnen im Alltag: Grundkompetenzen von Erwachsenen in der Schweiz.* Neuchâtel: Office fédéral de la statistique (OFS).

Peters, J. (2011). *Urteilsabsprachen im Strafprozess: Die deutsche Regelung im Vergleich mit Entwicklungen in England und Wales, Frankreich und Polen.* Göttingen: Univ.-Verl. Göttingen.

Pieth, M. (2009). *Schweizerisches Strafprozessrecht: Grundriss für Studium und Praxis.* Basel: Helbing Lichtenhahn.

Piquerez, G., Macaluso, A., & Piquerez, L. (2011). *Procédure pénale suisse* (3rd edn.). Genève: Schulthess.

Redlich, A. D., & Özdoğru, A. A. (2009). Alford Pleas in the Age of Innocence. *Behavioral Sciences & the Law, 27*(3), 467–488.

Riklin, F. (2007). Der Strafbefehl im deutschen und schweizerischen Strafprozessrecht—eine rechtsvergleichende Betrachtung. In H. Müller-Dietz, E. Müller, K.-L. Kunz, H. Radtke, G. Britz, C. Momsen, & H. Koriath (Eds.), *Festschrift für Heike Jung. Zum 65. Geburtstag am 23. April 2007* (1st edn., pp. 761–779). Baden-Baden: Nomos.

Schulhofer, S. J. (1992). Plea Bargaining as Disaster. *The Yale Law Journal, 101*(8), 1979–2009.

Steiner, E. (2010). *French law: A comparative approach.* New York, Toronto: Oxford University Press.

Thomas, G. C. (2008). *The Supreme Court on trial: How the American justice system sacrifices innocent defendants.* Ann Arbor: University of Michigan Press.

Tobolowsky, P. M. (2010). *Crime Victim Rights and Remedies* (2nd edn.). Durham, NC: Carolina Academic Press.

Trechsel, S., & Killias, M. (2004). Law of Criminal Procedure. In F. Dessemontet & T. Ansay (Eds.), *Introduction to Swiss law* (3rd edn., pp. 269–286). The Hague, Frederick, MD: Kluwer Law International; Sold and distributed in North, Central and South America by Aspen Publishers.

Turner, J. I. (2006). Judicial Participation in Plea Negotiations: A Comparative View. *American Journal of Comparative Law, 54*, 199–268.

Turner, J. I. (2009). *Plea Bargaining across Borders: Criminal Procedure.* New York: Aspen Publishers.

Walpin, G. (2003). America's Adversarial and Jury Systems: More Likely to do Justice. *Harvard Journal of Law and Public Policy, 26*, 175–186.

Walther, S. (2004). Communication over Confrontation: Modern Criminal Procedure in Transformation. In A. Eser & C. Rabenstein (Eds.), *Strafjustiz im Spannungsfeld von Effizienz und Fairness. Konvergente und divergente Entwicklungen im Strafprozessrecht; Internationales Kolloquium 8.–11. Mai 2002 auf Schloss Ringberg (Criminal justice between crime control and due process)* (pp. 367–379). Berlin: Duncker und Humblot.

Weigend, T. (2008). The Decay of the Inquisitorial Ideal: Plea Bargaining Invades German Criminal Procedure. In J. Jackson, M. Langer, & P. Tillers (Eds.), *Crime, Procedure and Evidence in a Comparative and International Context. Essays in Honour of Professor Mirjan Damaska* (pp. 39–64). Oxford: Hart Publishing.

Cases

Bordenkircher v. Hayes, 434 U.S. 357 (1978).
Brady v. U.S., 397 U.S. 742 (1970).
North Carolina v. Alford, 400 U.S. 25 (1970).
Parker v. North Carolina, 397 U.S. 790 (1970).

PART II
WRONGFUL CONVICTIONS AND MISCARRIAGES OF JUSTICE
CONSEQUENCES AND REMEDIES

13

LIFE AFTER EXONERATION

EXAMINING THE AFTERMATH OF A WRONGFUL CAPITAL CONVICTION

Saundra D. Westervelt and Kimberly J. Cook[1]

They have been fighting for this moment for years, often decades—the moment they walk out of prison a free person. They were wrongly convicted of horrific crimes. They have been incarcerated and labeled as among America's most dangerous—robbers, rapists, murderers, monsters. They have told countless others—family, friends, coworkers, police, prosecutors, defense attorneys, juries, judges, inmates—that they did not commit these heinous crimes. No one listened. On this day, finally, someone listened. They emerge into the fresh air no longer convicted felons but exonerees: innocent individuals wrongly convicted and exonerated. They leave prison filled with joy and hope, relief and anticipation. They walk out . . . and then what?

Until recently, little was known about what happens when exonerees resume their lives after release. Instead, criminal justice officials, advocates, and educators have focused on how wrongful convictions are created and how to correct those mistakes. Success has been defined as exoneration day when the newly minted exoneree is set free. Yet, is that truly the ultimate success story? What if that exoneree returns to her community only to be shunned and stigmatized, preventing her from getting a job and feeling welcome at her place of worship? What if that exoneree becomes homeless because he has no money for food or housing, having sacrificed all of his assets to fight his wrongful conviction? What if that exoneree is reincarcerated because he now has no marketable skills, a felony record that has not been expunged, and no employment prospects? Exonerees may be "free," but many remain trapped in conditions of social and economic exclusion after their release. Their re-entry is not "free" from the stigma, trauma, and social consequences of wrongful incarceration and condemnation. While the "success" of exoneration day is considerable, the challenges following exoneration day must be acknowledged and understood. What is life like in the days and weeks after their release from prison? What struggles do they encounter? What affects their ability to successfully reintegrate into their communities? How do they fit in?

Personal narratives and journalistic accounts of life after exoneration reveal that aftermath for exonerees is, more often than not, quite difficult (e.g., Cook, 2008; Grisham, 2006; Locke, 2011; Roberts and Stanton, 2007; Vollen and Eggers, 2005; see also, Illinois Criminal Justice Information Authority, 2002; Innocence Project, 2009). Health and mental health concerns, ruptured relationships, stigma, financial and employment struggles are among the many obstacles exonerees commonly encounter. Early studies of Canadian exonerees confirm these accounts (Campbell and Denov, 2004; Grounds, 2004), while systematic analysis of the post-exoneration experiences of American exonerees remains underdeveloped. Our examination of the post-release experiences of death row exonerees in the U.S. emerged as an effort to explore and explain how they cope with these struggles (see Westervelt and Cook, 2008, 2010, 2012 [June]).[2]

Based on in-depth personal interviews with 18 death row exonerees, we find they encounter obstacles to reintegration ranging from the very practical—finding a home and a job, relearning how to drive, shop, and sleep—to the deeply personal and emotional—managing their grief and anger, relearning how to trust, battling stigma (see Table 13.1 for biographical information about the 18 participants in our study).[3] While they report some differences specific to their experiences, taken together they reveal a common search for acceptance and recognition. Having been forcibly removed from their families, their work, and their communities, they return to find so much has changed and that, in many ways, they have lost their place. They struggle to discover, or remake, a place where they fit

Table 13.1 Biographical Details of Participants*

Name	Sex	Race	Age at Conviction	State Where Tried	Yrs in Prison[i]	Yrs on Death Row[ii]	Yr of Exoneration	DNA?	Actual Offender[s] Identified?[iii]	Compensation Received?[iv]
Beeman	M	W	23	OH	3	2.5	1979	No	Yes	No
Bloodsworth	M	W	24	MD	8	1.5	1993	Yes	Yes	Yes
Brown	M	B	24	FL	13	13	1987	No	No	No
Butler	F	B	19	MS	5.5	2.5	1995	No	No	Yes
Cobb	M	B	37	IL	7	4	1987	No	Yes	Yes
Fain	M	W	35	ID	18	17.5	2001	Yes	No	No
Gauger	M	W	41	IL	3	0	1996	No	Yes	No
Gell	M	W	23	NC	6	4.5	2004	No	Yes	Yes
Howard	M	B	23	OH	26	1	2003	No	No	Yes
James	M	B	23	OH	26	1	2003	No	No	Yes
Keaton	M	B	19	FL	2	1	1973	No	Yes	No
Krone	M	W	35	AZ	9.5	2.5	2002	Yes	Yes	Yes
McMillian	M	B	47	AL	5	5	1993	No	No	Yes
Melendez	M	L	33	FL	17.5	17.5	2002	No	Yes	No
Rivera	M	L	25	NC	2	1.5	1999	No	Yes	No
Taylor**	M	B	29	IL	13	10	2003	No	No	Yes
Tibbs	M	B	35	FL	2	1.5	1982	No	No	No
Wilhoit	M	W	32	OK	4	4	1993	No	No	No

*   This table is reprinted with permission from Westervelt and Cook's *Life after Death Row: Exonerees' Search for Community and Identity*, Rutgers University Press (2012).

**   This exoneree prefers to remain anonymous. We have assigned this pseudonym to him.

i   This category includes only the years in prison for this wrongful conviction and does not include any prior years of incarceration on other charges. In addition, several participants were not released from prison immediately after exoneration as they completed sentences on other, unrelated charges. That time is not included here. This category also does not include time they spent in jail or prison awaiting trial, which in some instances was two to three additional years. Numbers (for years in prison and years on death row) are not exact and may have been rounded slightly up or down by 1–3 months.

ii   The number of years spent on death row may not equal the years spent in prison. Several exonerees received retrials after appellate review, were reconvicted on the same charges, but were sentenced to life in prison rather than death. At that point, they were moved from death row into the general population of prison until their eventual exonerations.

iii This category includes cases in which the actual perpetrator of the crime for which the exoneree was wrongfully convicted either has been tried and convicted for that crime or has been publicly acknowledged in some way as the actual offender, even if not convicted.

iv   Of those receiving compensation, only three—Bloodsworth, Butler (17 years after exoneration), and Cobb (14 years after exoneration)—were provided compensation via state statutes. The others were compensated as a result of litigation pursued against local, county, and/or state officials and agencies.

in, where they are accepted and where the injustice they suffered is acknowledged and addressed. They must cope with and manage myriad obstacles as they seek a new place in the world. All of this, as one can imagine, is no easy task.[4]

The Aftermath of a Wrongful Capital Conviction

The 18 participants in our study reveal a complex array of consequences resulting from their wrongful capital convictions after exoneration and release from prison. While we cannot generalize to all death row exonerees, or to non-capital exonerees, we find that many obstacles to reintegration noted by our participants have been discussed by other exonerees in a variety of contexts (e.g., Grounds, 2004; Illinois Criminal Justice Information Authority, 2002; Innocence Project, 2009; Roberts and Stanton, 2007; Vollen and Eggers, 2005; Weigand, 2009; Wildeman et al., 2011). The aftermath of their wrongful capital convictions is evidenced in their daily lives, their relationships, their emotional well-being, and their degree of acceptance within their communities.

The Problems of Everyday Life

Exonerees face both short- and long-term challenges when confronted with the daunting transition to daily life. Basic activities, such as grocery shopping, using a computer, pumping gas, and sleeping, can be intimidating and confusing to exonerees whose life skills have eroded during their period of incarceration. In our sample of 18 exonerees, six had been in prison for over ten years and eight for over eight years. With jail time included, half of our participants spent ten or more years incarcerated. They often discuss how much had changed in that amount of time: the explosion in choices at their local grocery store; clothing styles; dating rituals and expectations; and the overwhelming pace of technological innovation. The world they have come back to is quite different from the one they left. They discuss having to relearn how to eat with utensils and digest complex foods, how to walk without fear of being shot, and how to sleep in a dark, quiet bedroom or with an intimate partner.

One immediate problem many exonerees face is where to live upon release. Unlike parolees who typically know when to anticipate release, exonerees frequently have no advance notification that their exoneration and release is imminent. Gary James learned of his release the night before on the evening news, and Charles Fain was informed of his release when a prison guard slipped him a note under his cell door just a few hours before he walked through the prison gates a free man. Juan Melendez discovered he was to be released early one afternoon after being taken from his cell for what he thought was a call from his attorney. He walked out of prison only a few hours later. Gary Gauger sums it up with, "I didn't know I was going to be released until the day I walked out the door."[5]

This pattern of unanticipated release leaves exonerees with no time to plan for life after prison. They cannot investigate housing or employment options or locate post-release services that may be available to them. The immediate days after release are jolting as exonerees scramble to determine where they will go and who will take them in. In most cases, the state provides no assistance and simply "cuts them loose" to find their own way. Ronald Keine's (2012, pp. 1503–1504) experience reflects this pattern. Keine is a death row exoneree, though not one of our participants. He writes:

> One day, the guards arrived at our cells and announced we had a court date that day. The winter wind blew right through the orange jumpsuit I wore. Underwear would have at least helped a little, but the guard on death row guffawed at the idea of letting us wear any. Underwear was not allowed because the authorities believed we could rip the cloth into strips to make a rope to hang ourselves . . . To us, this was just another court hearing to reject our latest plea to let us show our innocence—there had been many. It was no more to us than a chance to get out of the death row drudgery for a day, to actually experience what most people take for granted— fresh air, trees, landscapes, and new people to talk to . . . It was a total shock, then, when the judge freed us at the hearing that day. We were totally unprepared for it. I can remember standing on those courthouse steps contemplating my next move. I first had to take stock of my situation. I was a twenty-nine-year-old and had nothing. Every asset I owned was sold to raise money for a lawyer who abandoned us after our arraignment, forcing the court to furnish us with a young, inexperienced lawyer. The rumor that the prison would give us clothes and bus fare home was not a reality for we, exonerated men. That was only for parolees and guilty offenders who had maxed out. When someone is exonerated, they are no longer the ward of the court. The penal system has nothing more to do with them. They are done with you.

Exonerees also confront several long-term problems after release: finding employment, securing medical care, and negotiating space. They struggle to find employment because, although they are exonerated, their criminal convictions are not automatically expunged. A simple background check by a potential employer may reveal their felony conviction. Exonerees struggle to provide an accurate response to the question—"Have you ever been convicted of a felony?"—and few employers listen to explanations about their exonerations. Furthermore, their marketable skills have deteriorated, and they lack proficiency in the latest technology, with a long gap in their employment history that is difficult to explain. Many want employment that has flexibility for time off to participate in speaking engagements that offer some financial compensation. But few employers are willing to provide that flexibility. Stigma reduces their employment opportunities as they are recognizable figures in their communities, and people often believe they simply "beat the system." And mental health issues and substance use may hamper their ability to maintain stable employment.

Without employment, exonerees struggle to find housing, improve their job skills through education or training, and put food on the table. Their financial constraints also diminish their access to health, mental health, and dental care, all of which they need (though rarely receive) after release. They emerge from prison with health problems—arthritis, asthma, diabetes, hepatitis, tooth decay, depression, and addiction—problems they believe are caused by the poor food, poor conditions, and stress related to their wrongful convictions and incarcerations. Without employment (and access to health insurance), these needs go unmet and deteriorate even further.

Another long-term problem exonerees face is their struggle to negotiate space and their discomfort in confining and restrictive spaces. After long periods of close confinement, they get lost easily and dislike being closed in or cornered. They may find employment only to struggle with the close quarters of their workspace or return to communities of their childhood only to get lost on a daily basis. This frustration compounds the already disheartening array of obstacles they confront after release, making the most basic activities of everyday life challenging and obstructing their capacity to reintegrate into society.

Ruptured Relationships

As is true of the experience of incarceration in general (Austin and Hardyman, 2004; Ferraro, Johnson, Jorgensen, and Bolton, 1983; Fullerton and Ursano, 1997; Travis and Waul, 2003; Vandiver, 1989), wrongful incarceration is disruptive to relationships with family, intimates, and support networks (see also, Grounds, 2004; Sharp, 2005). Family members in particular are greatly impacted by the wrongful conviction and incarceration of their loved ones, leaving the family to fight for their freedom while also building a life without them. In all cases, this strains family relationships. In some cases, that strain creates distance and disruption that cannot be repaired, even after their loved one's exoneration and release.

Exonerees report losing relationships with those who chose to believe in their guilt, even after exoneration. In some cases, exonerees were abandoned by family and friends during incarceration. Scott Taylor's anger over this is palpable:

> I'm angry . . . Where were these people when I was pleading these things? Where were you? Where were you? Sixteen years. Where were you? Now everybody wants to be my friend . . . I don't need your support and concern now. I needed it when I was being falsely accused and I was in this hellhole and these people are intending on killing me.

Even if not fully lost, these relationships are difficult to remake after such significant gaps in time and shared experiences. Alan Gell's experience with his younger sister is emblematic of this struggle:

> My youngest sister, she was nine whenever I went away, and she was at the elementary school. I remember a lot from nine back, but I don't have no memories of nine forward until I got out . . . Going in with her nine and coming out with her seventeen fixing to graduate high school was like, what in the world? We can't talk about the same things we used to talk about. And this is odd to suddenly realize that she was a stranger, and I didn't know who in the hell she was. And we had to build the relationship from scratch.

It is important to remember that family members have been traumatized by the wrongful conviction and must adjust to the exonerees' return. As Greg Wilhoit says of those early attempts to remake relationships with his family, "our anguish was overlapping."

Many exonerees discuss difficulty in reestablishing intimate relationships with spouses or partners. The relationships they had going into their wrongful convictions ended while they were in prison or soon after release. Dating and social interaction styles appropriate prior to their incarceration often have changed by the time of their release, leaving them in an anomic condition regarding the current rules of the dating game. Their significant problems with trust only compound this confusion. And after many years in prison where sexual activity is openly associated with violence and coercion, establishing a level of comfort with intimacy can be frustrating.

Although difficult, some exonerees report stronger relationships with family and friends than they had before their wrongful convictions (see also, Vollertsen, 2012). They recognize the enormous sacrifices that parents, siblings, children, and other supporters have made, financially and emotionally, to fuel their fight for freedom. They feel a responsibility to recognize and repay them in some way for their unwavering support, and they reveal a deep level of appreciation for the relationships they now have.

The Emotional Toll

As if their wrongful convictions and incarcerations have not already exacted a significant emotional cost, the emotional trauma continues to accrue after release. In many cases, the emotional aftermath is overwhelming and debilitating (see also, Simon, 1993; Wildeman et al., 2011). Just because they are free does not mean that their pain and suffering ends. They must mourn the many losses they have suffered as a result of their wrongful convictions—losses of loved ones and relationships, time and missed opportunities, and feelings of security. Exonerees struggle to rebuild trust in those around them and in the institutions that failed them so miserably. They search for ways to manage their anger, depression, and survivor guilt. The emotional terrain of aftermath is rugged.

Four of our participants were convicted of killing close family members, and five others lost family members while they were incarcerated. Many watched as fellow death row inmates, people they had befriended, were taken to their executions. Grief over these losses is common among exonerees; however, they cannot fully embrace and process that grief while incarcerated. At the time of these losses, they were fighting for their own lives or managing the trauma of incarceration and wrongful conviction. Their grief under these conditions is postponed or frozen in time (Boss, 1999; Sharp, 2005), and comes rushing in with full force after release when they first visit the gravesites of loved ones or first embrace those who shared in their losses. These are difficult emotions to process in the best of circumstances. Gary Gauger eloquently describes this grief when he says, "I feel like I'm a plastic barrier holding back the ocean . . . not much substance and a lot of weight."

Exonerees also grieve the time and opportunities lost to their wrongful convictions and incarcerations. Our participants averaged nine and a half years of wrongful incarceration after their convictions, in addition to months and years spent in jail awaiting trial. They missed the births of children and grandchildren, birthdays and anniversaries and holidays; they missed the opportunity to marry and have their own children and opportunities to parent the children they already had. As Juan Melendez says of the nearly 18 years he spent on death row in Florida, "I became an old man in there." Exonerees also grieve the feeling of security they enjoyed prior to their wrongful convictions. Few free citizens worry about random encounters they may have with law enforcement or are concerned over how their daily activities might be perceived by others. But exonerees know how random encounters with police can become ten years behind bars for a crime they did not commit or how every word they utter, no matter how insignificant, can be turned against them. They often take great pains to ensure someone can attest to their whereabouts at all times.

In addition to grief, exonerees manage a range of other emotions that cause them significant distress. They struggle to repair trust that was destroyed by their wrongful convictions, trust in the criminal justice system and its representatives, and trust in people in general. Several of our mostly male participants reveal particular difficulties in trusting women as they seek to establish new intimate relationships. They are concerned about people's motives in befriending them, especially if they have compensation claims pending. Exonerees also experience a significant amount of guilt after release, survivor guilt in particular (see Lifton, 1967). They question why they were saved from execution while others were not. They feel guilt and sadness over those they know who remain on death row, as Scott Taylor admits about the day of his release, "I could look right back to where I was for all those years. And it really made me sad, even though [getting out] was a joyful time in my life. And it's still sad to this day that these guys are still in those cages like animals. I don't even like going to the zoo now." Not surprisingly, they discuss the anger they still feel about their convictions and toward those responsible for their plight, including anger over the failure of the state to take responsibility for the injustice done to them or to offer reparation of any kind. Finally, many describe a constellation of emotions—depression, disorientation, and detachment—often associated with post-traumatic stress disorder (DSM-IV-TR, 2000). They struggle with feelings of emptiness and are frustrated over their inability fully to express or access their emotions. They describe feelings of flatness and numbness as well as some fear over what might happen if they actually were to tap into the depth of pain and anger they try so hard to control. As Gary Gauger again so articulately explains, "once in a while, I'll have a glimpse of a feeling, and I tend to shut them down. I feel if I ever started crying, I wouldn't be able to stop."

Lack of Acceptance

The impact of their wrongful capital conviction also is felt when they return to their communities, which, all too often, may not welcome them. While half of our participants report feeling accepted back into their communities after release, about one-third of our participants discuss how the stigma of their convictions negatively impacted their treatment by community members when they returned home (see also, Ricciardelli and Clow, 2012; Westervelt and Cook, 2012). In these cases, people in the community believed that the exonerees were guilty of the crimes for which they were convicted but got out of prison "on a technicality," rather than because of factual innocence. Often, these beliefs were fueled by statements made by public officials after an exoneree's release, reaffirming their belief in the exoneree's guilt. This was most common when the actual perpetrator had not yet been identified. Thus, some of our participants returned to communities where their actual innocence had been downplayed, proclamations of their guilt had been broadcast widely, and the actual offenders had not been identified, leaving the public with little to dissuade them as to the exoneree's factual guilt.

Several of our participants report incidents where they were "called out" in public, such as when a woman in a grocery store in Kirk Bloodsworth's hometown in Maryland ran from the store after calling him a "child killer." Bloodsworth recalls many times when prior acquaintances shunned him in public or crossed the street to avoid him, when he found "child killer" written in the dirt on his truck, or when strangers left abusive and accusatory voice messages on his answering machine. Sabrina Butler similarly reports being publicly humiliated: she was forced to leave her church after being called to account for her (wrongful) conviction in the death of her nine-month-old son, and her children were bullied because their mother "killed their brother." Gary Gauger angrily describes a day when his wife came home from a shopping trip and tearfully told of a community member who confronted her, claiming that Gauger was guilty. While emotionally damaging in their own right, these incidents also increase the isolation exonerees feel and decrease the available support networks on which they can draw for assistance. Stigma interferes with their ability to find stable work, since employers back away from hiring "notorious" employees. The stigma, and the ensuing isolation it creates, exacerbates the heavy burden exonerees already carry as they confront the task of rebuilding their lives.

At the heart of these many challenges that characterize the aftermath of a wrongful capital conviction is the shared experience of being dislocated, dislodged, and uprooted from their place in the world. When they return to their families and communities, they must find ways to reconnect with themselves and others and to remake a place where they fit in. They search for meaningful employment, good health, and relationships that they value; they seek understanding of their new selves and acceptance from their communities. As we have said elsewhere:

> . . . from the mundane everyday tasks of pumping gas and grocery shopping to the emotionally draining difficulties of managing loss, guilt, and depression, they confront new battles around every turn. Sent into the fray with no preparation and little to no assistance, they struggle to build a new life and find a new home.
>
> (Westervelt and Cook, 2012, p. 104)

Greg Wilhoit sums it up quite accurately when he says, simply, "assimilating is a mother fucker!"

Coping with the Aftermath

The wrongful conviction and incarceration of an innocent person is a "sustained catastrophe." It is a threat to life and self that extends over a period of time, where the traumatizing event itself continues day in and day out, with no end in sight (Lifton, 2001, p. 213). As with trauma survivors of other life-threatening catastrophes, such as floods, earthquakes, disease, and war, being wrongly convicted of a capital crime, or any crime, and incarcerated in prison or on death row is a profoundly traumatizing experience. We, thus, rely on the literature on coping and trauma management to analyze the aftermath of a wrongful capital conviction. As one survivor of the Buffalo Creek mining accident and flood in the Appalachians of West Virginia writes, "I feel as I'm sure a prisoner must feel who has been sentenced to prison for a crime he didn't commit" (Erikson, 1976, p. 13). That catastrophe ripped people from their homes, displaced them from their communities, separated them from family and loved ones, and uprooted them from all that they knew; such is the experience of a death row exoneree. And like other survivors of life-threatening events, exonerees must find ways to confront and negotiate this trauma after release.

An examination of the powerful first-hand accounts of our 18 participants reveals that they use multiple coping strategies, or management techniques, to negotiate the difficulties of life after exoneration. We group these strategies together into two broader styles of coping that characterize their approaches to life after release. We call these the "incorporation approach" and the "avoidance approach." These "approaches are determined by the degree to which survivors confront and integrate the traumatic experience into their reconstructed lives" (Westervelt and Cook, 2012, p. 135). The incorporation approach reflects death row survivors' efforts to engage their new identity as an "exoneree," create resolutions to problems they confront, and move toward positive outcomes in their new lives (for use of similar concepts, see Oyserman and Swim, 2001; Shih, 2004; Siegel, Lune, and Meyer, 1998). Alternatively, the avoidance approach focuses less on confronting the after-effects of trauma and more on reducing or escaping from those after-effects (again, for use of similar concepts, see Oyserman and Swim, 2001; Shih, 2004; Siegel et al., 1998). More succinctly, Florida death row exoneree Shabaka Brown explains, "if you are offered a challenge, you have two choices, either to accept or to reject."

These two approaches serve as ideal types of the strategies exonerees choose as they contend with the aftermath of their wrongful capital convictions. But it is important to remember that coping is a dynamic process, not a stagnant condition (Miller, 2003; Richardson, 2002). Exonerated death row survivors use both approaches and may vacillate between approaches over time. Incorporation and avoidance are not mutually exclusive, nor are the various strategies that characterize each approach. Emblematic of the fluid nature of coping techniques used by exonerees is the experience of Kirk Bloodsworth. He describes his own struggles to cope in the ten years following his exoneration as a process, a transition from one style of coping to another: "I'm not running [from it] no more. I'm running to it now." While he first relied primarily on avoidance strategies by "running [from it]," he transitioned to incorporation strategies by "running to it." In most cases, our participants adopt strategies from both approaches over time and in different contexts to engage the most effective coping mechanisms in shifting circumstances.

We identify specific coping strategies or techniques within each of these broader approaches. Strategies associated with the incorporation approach include telling their trauma story both in private relationships and to public audiences, connecting to other exonerees, creating meaning out of their trauma, and turning that meaning into a "survivor mission" (for discussions of these techniques in the trauma literature, see e.g., Bonanno, 2004; Davis, 2001; Fearday and Cape, 2004; Henry, 2004; Herman, 1997; Neimeyer, 2001; Williams, Davey, and Klock-Powell, 2003). Scott Taylor says that telling his story "was actually like therapy for me, because I wanted everybody to know this is what happened to me." Exonerees explain that they get positive feelings of validation and acceptance from the public speaking they do. As Greg Wilhoit explains, "When I give one of my little talks, for me anyway, it validates my whole experience, personally. And it's really helped me out." The incorporation strategy of connecting with other exonerated death row survivors also creates feelings of validation and acceptance. Many exonerees participate in the same abolitionist organizations or get together at conferences or speaking events. In their shared experiences of trauma, they find comfort and understanding, as noted by Alan Gell: "It was really, really great to be surrounded by people that have the same things in common as me. And it was like weren't nobody looking at me as a poor guy or this and that. We could tell prison stories and just totally relate to each other."

Two additional strategies of incorporation entail exonerees' ability to create meaning from their traumatic experience, and, for some, to use that meaning to raise awareness about wrongful convictions and/or death penalty issues. Finding meaning in their injustice assuages powerlessness and emotional dissonance they often feel, and provides a positive purpose for their experiences. About half of our participants believe that their wrongful conviction and survival of death row happened for a reason, whether to give them new direction in life, to pull them away from negative activities, or to serve as an example to others of the failures of the justice system. Attributing such purpose offers a new and positive frame to evaluate their experience and motivates them toward new opportunities, rather than focusing solely on their losses. About one-third of our participants embrace a "survivor mission" and use their personal experiences to promote social and political change (Herman, 1997). In doing so, they construct positive meaning from their wrongful convictions and use that meaning as a basis to raise awareness about the death penalty, the criminal justice system, and criminal justice policy. Several of our participants are active in the abolitionist movement. They work with organizations such as Witness to Innocence and Death Penalty Focus to bring attention to problems with the death penalty in the United States,[6] and they speak around the country to raise awareness about the mistakes and abuses that lead to wrongful convictions. They use their experiences as a platform from which to advocate, educate, and promote change. Delbert Tibbs, a death row survivor from Florida, sums up his survivor mission when he says, "I believe that [the Great Spirit] took me to death row so that I could be a witness and a voice against it."

These strategies of incorporation are vehicles for exonerees to connect with other survivors and with those in their communities and to proclaim purpose as they move forward after exoneration. They situate their past within their journey, and are better able to combat some of their dislocation to recreate a sense of community.

Exonerees also use strategies of avoidance to manage the trauma they confront after exoneration. These techniques allow exonerees to escape the pain and frustration they experience during re-entry. We caution against viewing avoidance strategies as negative, maladaptive, or ineffective, especially in contrast to strategies of incorporation. The helpfulness of any particular coping strategy depends on the context in which it is used. For example, while avoidance through drug or alcohol use may appear to be problematic, it is likely less problematic than managing one's pain and anger through outbursts of violence. Thus, it is important to evaluate the use of all of these strategies in context and avoid judging exonerees based on their choice of a particular approach.

The two strategies of avoidance most often used by death row exonerees are withdrawal and numbing (for discussions of these techniques in the trauma literature, see e.g., Bonanno, 2004; Erikson, 1976; Herman, 1997; Phillips and Lindsay, 2010; Zamble and Porporino, 1988). Exonerees may withdraw from situations that dredge up strong emotions or memories of their trials or incarceration. They may avoid other exonerees or decline requests to discuss their experiences because such events can overwhelm their capacity to control their emotions. Gary Gauger, for example, explains that he occasionally speaks in public about his wrongful conviction because he believes his witness is valuable and educational, despite the emotional price he pays. He often becomes profoundly depressed after such events and is overcome by anger, frustration, and helplessness. He prefers, instead, to retreat to his farm, working himself to the bone to avoid having to think about his ordeal.

A second strategy of avoidance is numbing the emotional aftermath of the wrongful conviction through substance use. As Herman (1997) explains, numbing provides a way to dissociate from the anguish trauma survivors feel and suppress thoughts about the painful past. About half of our participants report significant struggles with drugs and/or alcohol since their exonerations. They view numbing as a technique to manage their rage over their wrongful convictions and time lost to incarceration, as well as their survivor guilt. Thus, numbing is another form of withdrawal. As Florida death row survivor Dave Keaton says about his drug and alcohol use, "I [would] drink to get drunk to forget." Kirk Bloodsworth concurs when he says, "The only thing I wanted to do [in the early years after my release], and I hate to admit to a misdemeanor, but is get high and drink, and I mean get butthole drunk. You know, just fall down and sloppy because I wanted to forget . . . I wanted to feel nothing."

Whereas the strategies of incorporation often draw exonerees into the community and help alleviate some of the distance and disruption created by their wrongful convictions, the use of strategies of avoidance often do the opposite, exacerbating their disconnection after release, drawing them further away from family and other support networks. While both approaches are useful in varying circumstances, strategies of incorporation can provide community support and combat loneliness and anger with opportunities for acceptance and validation. However, if met with stigma, fear, and lack of acceptance after release, and continued insinuations of guilt by public officials and media, exonerees are likely to find avoidance, rather than incorporation, strategies more useful.

Providing for Reintegration and Restoration

Creating opportunities for connection, community building, and support is vital to exonerees' efforts to remake their lives successfully after exoneration. Unfortunately, the tools they need to support this process typically are not available after release because their needs remain invisible to the very system that created their injustice (Westervelt and Cook, 2010). Since state officials seldom recognize any responsibility to assist exonerees in rebuilding a life, that intransigence becomes yet another obstacle to their reintegration and restoration.

The aftermath experiences of exonerated death row survivors reveal complex needs that mostly remain unmet after exoneration. Their basic needs coalesce around three primary categories—health care needs, financial needs, and legal needs. Their health care needs include medical and dental care, mental health services, and time and place to relearn, resocialize, and decompress before the full weight of personal independence sets in. Financially, they leave prison with very little, having invested their resources in fighting their wrongful convictions. They emerge from prison with no savings, few job skills, and, in some cases, little financial support from family and friends. Yet, they must find a place to live, provide for their own subsistence, buy new clothing, and locate reliable transportation. They need immediate transitional funds and long-term assistance to find employment or pursue education and/or training. Finally, when they emerge from prison, some may erroneously believe that their legal needs have been resolved. Rather, a new set of legal battles that require financial support include expunging their record, applying for a pardon and/or compensation, suing for compensation if not provided in their state, and negotiating child support claims, to name a few (see also, Innocence Project, 2009).

In addition to these basic needs, exonerees want recognition of their situation by the state and restoration of their reputations and identity as innocent people through an apology by state officials. Exonerees:

firmly believe the state should be held accountable for their wrongful convictions and that an essential element of that accountability is voluntarily-offered reparation ... They believe that such good faith offers of support would not only aid them with transition and reintegration but also, possibly more importantly, decrease their feelings of and experiences with rejection and stigmatization.

(Westervelt and Cook, 2012, p. 206)

Furthermore, a public and forthright apology by state officials responsible for their wrongful convictions would help reduce public suspicion and fear and would encourage acceptance into their communities. Ohio death row exoneree Tim Howard articulates this invisibility after twenty-six years in prison for a robbery-homicide he did not commit, saying, "I feel that the state owes me. There's no doubt in my mind ... But, they don't reach out to you. I know that much. As soon as you get out, you have to make it on your own." Exonerees are perplexed by the lack of accountability the state has for their situations and recognize the apparent paradox of responsibility. Charles Fain queries, "if I go to court, I gotta ... admit it, so why shouldn't they?"

Despite these complex needs and the myth that exonerees receive ample compensation, exonerees, more often, receive nothing from the state after release. Sabrina Butler makes this emphatically clear: "No money. No nothing. They didn't give me jack! They just took the handcuffs off me and sent me out the door." Access to compensation depends on several factors beyond their control: if the state they are in has a compensation statute for wrongful incarceration; the availability of legal representation to advocate for them; and restrictive statutory requirements in their state (for more in-depth discussions of the complexity of the compensation issue, see, e.g., Bernhard, 1999, 2004, 2009; Innocence Project, 2009; Kahn, 2010; Norris, 2012).[7] Few states offer reintegration services aside from compensation (Innocence Project, 2009; Norris, 2012). Some non-profit organizations attempt to fill this gap by providing reintegration services for exonerees. While these organizations do their best with limited resources, only ten such organizations currently exist in the United States, and they have limited geographical reach.[8] Consequently, many exonerees cannot access these services and are left to their own devices in facing life after exoneration, turning to family, friends, attorneys, and advocates within their closest networks of support.

Providing for reintegration and restoration for death row survivors requires resources. They need tools to help them provide for themselves and their families—legal and financial mechanisms to overcome the barriers they encounter after release. But reintegration and restoration require more than financial resources. Helping exonerees to rebuild a life requires recognition and acknowledgment of the damage done to them and their families and meaningful attempts to restore their reputations and communities of support. This acknowledgement must include state officials making amends. Rebuilding requires reconnecting to family and community, finding inclusion rather than exclusion, acceptance rather than rejection. Reintegration and restoration will be achieved when exonerees, their injustice and their needs, are no longer invisible to those who created them. To the extent that current policies and provisions fall short of this goal, they are in need of revision and re-evaluation, until justice for exonerees is fully realized.[9]

With 142 exonerated death row survivors identified by the Death Penalty Information Center,[10] over 300 DNA exonerees identified by the Innocence Project,[11] and over 1000 exonerations identified in the National Registry of Exonerations,[12] it is imperative now more than ever that states develop effective strategies for assisting exonerees after their release. These are the tip of the iceberg. As the lists of exonerees continue to grow, the needs exonerees face upon release will remain significant for decades to come.

Notes

1 We gratefully acknowledge the funding sources that made this project possible: the External Proposal Development Incentive Program, Office of the Associate Provost of Research, The University of North Carolina at Greensboro; and the American Sociological Association's Fund for Advancement of the Discipline Award supported by the American Sociological Association and the National Science Foundation.

2 New research focusing on life after exoneration is beginning to emerge. Take, for example, work being done in Canada regarding attitudes toward wrongly convicted individuals (Clow and Leach, 2009; Ricciardelli and Clow, 2012); for an overview, see also Clow, Leach, and Ricciardelli, 2012. Wildeman, Costelloe, and Schehr (2011) use interview-based surveys with 55 exonerees, completed by the Life After Exoneration Program (http://www.exonerated.org), to examine the psychological aftermath of a wrongful conviction. The June edition of *The Albany Law Review* (vol. 75, no. 3, 2012), guest edited by Westervelt and Cook, brings together new social scientific and legal research on a variety of issues related to life after exoneration.

3 For more detailed discussions of the methods used in this study, see Westervelt and Cook, 2007, 2012.

4 A more complete discussion of reintegration difficulties faced by exonerees and coping strategies they use to manage reintegration can be found in Westervelt and Cook's *Life after Death Row: Exonerees' Search for Community and Identity* (2012).

5 Unless otherwise noted, direct quotes from exonerees are taken from our interviews with them.

6 For more information about Witness to Innocence, see http://www.witnesstoinnocence.org; for more information about Death Penalty Focus, see http://www.deathpenalty.org.

7 As is evident from Table 1, nine of our participants received no compensation. Three received compensation via the legislative statutes in their states. Another six participants successfully sued their states for compensation. They waited on average four years for the money, and, thus, these funds were not available to assist them during the critical period immediately after release.

8 Through personal networks and internet research, we were able to identify ten organizations whose mission, at least in part, is to provide reintegration services to exonerees. These include: the Darryl Hunt Project for Freedom and Justice (North Carolina), the Exoneree Project (Texas), FocuzUp (California), the Life After Exoneration Program (California), Life After Innocence (Illinois), Life Intervention for Exonerees Foundation (California), Proving Innocence (Michigan), Resurrection After Exoneration (Louisiana), Wisconsin Exoneree Network (Wisconsin), and Witness to Innocence (Pennsylvania). It also should be noted that the Innocence Project (New York) employs two social workers to assist their DNA exonerees with re-entry needs.

9 For a fuller exploration of policy implications, see Chapter 12 in Westervelt and Cook (2012).

10 The Death Penalty Information Center: http://www.deathpenaltyinfo.org.

11 The Innocence Project: http://www.innocenceproject.org.

12 The National Registry of Exonerations: http://www.law.umich.edu/special/exoneration/Pages/about.aspx.

References

Austin, J. & Hardyman, P. (2004). The Risks and Needs of the Returning Prisoner Population. *Review of Policy Research, 21*, 13–29.

Bernhard, A. (1999). When Justice Fails: Indemnification for Unjust Convictions. *University of Chicago Law School Roundtable, 6*, 73–112.

Bernhard, A. (2004). Justice Still Fails: A Review of Recent Efforts to Compensate Individuals Who Have Been Unjustly Convicted and Later Exonerated. *Drake Law Review, 52*, 703–738.

Bernhard, A. (2009). A Short Overview of the Statutory Remedies for the Wrongly Convicted: What Works, What Doesn't, and Why. *Public Interest Law Journal, 18*, 403–425.

Bonanno, G. (2004). Loss, Trauma, and Human Resilience: Have We Underestimated the Human Capacity to Thrive After Extremely Aversive Events? *American Psychologist, 59*, 20–28.

Boss, P. (1999). *Ambiguous Loss*. Cambridge: Harvard University Press.

Campbell, K. & Denov, M. (2004). The Burden of Innocence: Coping with a Wrongful Imprisonment. *Canadian Journal of Criminology and Criminal Justice, 46*, 139–163.

Clow, K.A. & Leach, A.M. (2009, March). After Innocence: Perceptions of the Wrongfully Convicted. In B.L. Cutler (Chair), *Conviction of the Innocent: Psychological Perspectives and Research*. Symposium conducted at the meeting of the American Psychology-Law Society, San Antonio, Texas.

Clow, K.A., Leach, A.M. & Ricciardelli, R. (2012). Life after Wrongful Conviction. In B. Cutler (Ed.), *Conviction of the Innocent: Lessons from Psychological Research* (pp. 327–341). Washington, D.C.: American Psychological Association.

Cook, K.M. (2008). *Chasing Justice*. New York: Harper.

Davis, C. (2001). The Tormented and the Transformed: Understanding Responses to Loss and Trauma. In R. Neimeyer (Ed.), *Meaning Reconstruction and the Experience of Loss* (pp. 137–155). Washington, D.C.: American Psychological Association.

DSM-IV-TR *(Diagnostic and Statistical Manual of Mental Disorders)*. (2000). 4th edn. Text revised. Washington, D.C.: American Psychiatric Association.

Erikson, K. (1976). *Everything in Its Path*. New York: Simon & Schuster.

Fearday, F. & Cape, A. (2004). A Voice for Traumatized Women: Inclusion and Mutual Support. *Psychiatric Rehabilitation Journal, 27*, 258–265.

Ferraro, K., Johnson, J., Jorgensen, S. & Bolton, F.G. (1983). Problems of Prisoners' Families: The Hidden Costs of Imprisonment. *Journal of Family Issues, 4*, 575–591.

Fullerton, C. & Ursano, R. (Eds.). (1997). *Posttraumatic Stress Disorder, Acute and Long-Term Response to Trauma and Disaster*. Washington, D.C.: American Psychiatric Press.

Grisham, J. (2006). *The Innocent Man*. New York: Bantam Dell.

Grounds, A. (2004). Psychological Consequences of Wrongful Conviction and Imprisonment. *Canadian Journal of Criminology and Criminal Justice, 46*, 165–182.

Henry, V. (2004). *Death Work*. New York: Oxford University Press.

Herman, J.L. (1997). *Trauma and Recovery*. New York: Basic Books.

Illinois Criminal Justice Information Authority. (2002, March 15). The Needs of the Wrongfully Convicted: A Report on a Panel Discussion. *Report to the Governor's Commission on Capital Punishment*.

Innocence Project. (2009). Making Up for Lost Time: What the Wrongfully Convicted Endure and How to Provide Fair Compensation. *An Innocence Project Report*. Benjamin N. Cardozo School of Law: Yeshiva University.

Kahn, D. (2010). Presumed Guilty Until Proven Innocent: The Burden of Proof in Wrongful Conviction Claims Under State Compensation Statutes. *University of Michigan Journal of Law Reform, 44*, 123–168.

Keine, R. (2012, June). When Justice Fails: Collateral Damage. *Albany Law Review, 75*(3), 1501–1508.

Lifton, R.J. (1967). *Death in Life*. New York: Random House.

Lifton, R.J. (2001). History of Trauma. In J. Lindy & R.J. Lifton (Eds.), *Beyond Invisible Walls* (pp. 213–223). New York: Brunner-Routledge.

Locke, M. (2011, September 4). Freedom is sweet, but new problems set in. *The News & Observer*.

Miller, E. (2003). Reconceptualizing the Role of Resiliency in Coping and Therapy. *Journal of Loss and Trauma, 8*, 239–246.

Neimeyer, R. (Ed.). (2001). *Meaning Reconstruction and the Experience of Loss*. Washington, D.C.: American Psychological Association.

Norris, R. (2012). Assessing Compensation Statutes for the Wrongly Convicted. *Criminal Justice Policy Review, 23*(3), 352–374.

Oyserman, D. & Swim, J. (2001). Stigma: An Insider's View. *Journal of Social Issues, 57*, 1–14.

Phillips, L. & Lindsay, M. (2010). Prison to Society: A Mixed Methods Analysis of Coping with Reentry. *International Journal of Offender Therapy and Comparative Criminology, 20*, 1–19.

Ricciardelli, R. & Clow, K.A. (2012). The Impact of an Exoneree's Guest Lecture on Students' Attitudes Toward Wrongly Convicted Persons. *Journal of Criminal Justice Education, 23*(2), 127–147.

Richardson, G. (2002). The Metatheory of Resilience and Resiliency. *Journal of Clinical Psychology, 58*, 307–321.

Roberts, J. & Stanton, E. (2007, November 25). A long road back after exoneration, and Justice is slow to make amends. *New York Times*, p. 38.

Sharp, S. (2005). *Hidden Victims*. New Jersey: Rutgers University Press.

Shih, M. (2004). Positive Stigma: Examining Resilience and Empowerment in Overcoming Stigma. *The Annals of the American Academy of Political and Social Sciences, 591*, 175–185.

Siegel, K., Lune, H. & Meyer, I. (1998). Stigma Management among Gay/Bisexual Men with HIV/AIDS. *Qualitative Sociology, 21,* 3–24.

Simon, R. (1993). The Psychological and Legal Aftermath of False Arrest and Imprisonment. *Bulletin of the American Academy of Psychiatry and the Law, 21,* 523–528.

Travis, J. & Waul, M. (Eds.). (2003). *Prisoners Once Removed.* Washington, D.C.: Urban Institute Press.

Vandiver, M. (1989). Coping with Death: Families of the Terminally Ill, Homicide Victims, and Condemned Prisoners. In M. Radelet (Ed.), *Facing the Death Penalty* (pp. 123–138). Philadelphia: Temple University Press.

Vollen, L. & Eggers, D. (2005). *Surviving Justice.* San Francisco: Voice of Witness.

Vollertsen, N. (2012, June). Wrongful Conviction: How a Family Survives. *Albany Law Review, 75*(3),1509–1528.

Weigand, H. (2009). Rebuilding a Life: The Wrongfully Convicted and Exonerated. *Public Interest Law Journal, 18,* 427–437.

Westervelt, S. & Cook, K.J. (2007). Feminist Research Methods in Theory and Action: Learning from Death Row Exonerees. In S. Miller (Ed.), *Criminal Justice Research and Practice* (pp. 21–38). Boston: University Press of New England.

Westervelt, S. & Cook, K.J. (2008). Coping with Innocence. *Contexts, 7,* 32–37.

Westervelt, S. & Cook, K.J. (2010). Framing Innocents: The Wrongly Convicted as Victims of State Harm. *Crime, Law, and Social Change, 53,* 259–275.

Westervelt, S. & Cook, K.J. (2012). *Life after Death Row: Exonerees' Search for Community and Identity.* New Jersey: Rutgers University Press.

Westervelt, S. & Cook., K.J. (Guest Eds.). (2012, June). *Albany Law Review: Revealing the Impact & Aftermath of Miscarriages of Justice, 75*(3), 1223–1630.

Wildeman, J., Costelloe, M. & Schehr, R. (2011). Experiencing Wrongful and Unlawful Conviction. *Journal of Offender Rehabilitation, 50*(7), 411–432.

Williams, N., Davey, M. & Klock-Powell, K. (2003). Rising from the Ashes: Stories of Recovery, Adaptation and Resiliency in Burn Survivors. *Social Work and Health Care, 36,* 53–77.

Zamble, E. & Porporino, F. (1988). *Coping, Behavior, and Adaptation in Prison Inmates.* New York: Springer-Verlag.

Websites

Death Penalty Focus, http://www.deathpenalty.org.

Death Penalty Information Center, http://www.deathpenaltyinfo.org.

Innocence Project, http://www.innocenceproject.org.

Life After Exoneration Program, http://www.exonerated.org.

National Registry of Exonerations, http://www.law.umich.edu/special/exoneration/Pages/about.aspx.

Witness to Innocence, http://www.witnesstoinnocence.org.

14

More Procedure and Concern About Innocence but Less Justice?

Remedies for Wrongful Convictions in the United States and Canada

Kent Roach

The United States and Canada are similar and neighboring democracies. They both have a wrongful conviction problem. The available evidence suggests that the causes of identified wrongful convictions in both countries are quite similar. Wrongful convictions have been caused in both countries by mistaken eyewitness identification; lying witnesses, including jailhouse informants; false confessions; and faulty forensic evidence (Garrett, 2011; Roach, 2012). The similarity of these causes reveals what Mark Tushnet has identified as universal and functional strains in the study of comparative law (Tushnet, 2008: 10). Although some of these factors are influenced by context, such as the more decentralized delivery of many forensic services in the United States compared to Canada (Roach, 2009), the basic causes of wrongful convictions are likely quite similar in both countries and perhaps in most countries.

The focus in this chapter will not be on the common causes of wrongful convictions, but on the different ways that Canada and the United States remedy wrongful convictions. Such remedies inevitably reflect differences between the American and Canadian criminal justice systems. As such, they relate to what Professor Tushnet has identified as contextual and expressive elements in the study of comparative law. These elements focus not so much on abstract norms, such as the undesirability of convicting the innocent, or on best practices in preventing wrongful convictions that could potentially be borrowed from other nations. Rather, they focus on the influence and constraints that each country's legal system and culture places on its approach to wrongful convictions (Tushnet, 2008: 10–15).

The thesis of this chapter will be that while Canada gives the wrongfully convicted far fewer formal legal remedies than the United States, in practice the Canadian system has been more flexible and generous in providing relief to the wrongfully convicted. I will argue that the Canadian system has been more concerned with evaluating new evidence on its merits and less concerned with the finality of convictions or imposing demanding actual innocence requirements for relief than the American system. The difficulties of obtaining remedies on the merits will be related to the particularly adversarial and legalistic nature of American law (Kagan, 2001; Roach, 2011). It will also be suggested that actual innocence requirements are the flip side of a crime control culture that focuses on factual guilt, imprisons an extraordinary amount of people, and has diminishing support for due process (Garland, 2001). If this thesis can be sustained, it will affirm the importance of context, including legal and political culture, in providing remedies for the wrongfully convicted. It will also suggest that more procedure based on an actual innocence paradigm may not always produce effective remedies for the wrongfully convicted. Finally, it will also reveal the benefits of studying wrongful convictions in the broader context of the law, and politics of criminal justice.

Drawing on Professor Lissa Griffin's path-breaking work comparing American and British approaches to wrongful convictions (Griffin, 2001, 2009), I will suggest that the Canadian system, like the British system, places less emphasis on deference to, and the finality of, jury verdicts than the United States and has a more generous approach to the admission of fresh evidence and appeals out of time. Such findings are perhaps even more striking because Canada has resisted calls to create an independent commission like the Criminal Cases Review Commission with the power to refer cases back to the court (Walker and Campbell, 2010).

I will also argue that it remains more difficult to overturn convictions in the United States than in Canada in spite of the increased sensitivity in the United States to actual innocence. The American attraction to actual innocence is demonstrated by statutes providing for post-conviction access to DNA, the acceptance of innocence verdicts in a number of states including Illinois, Utah, and North Carolina (Finlay, 2011: 1199; Roach, 2012) and the Supreme Court's extraordinary decision in 2009 to grant Troy Davis original habeas corpus relief to allow him an opportunity to establish actual innocence (*Re Davis* 130 S Ct.1). Increased concern with actual innocence in American law and politics has benefited the exonerated and reflects the political success of the Innocence movement, spearheaded by Innocence Projects. Nevertheless, it has also imposed very high burdens on those such as Troy Davis seeking to have wrongful convictions overturned (Finlay, 2011).

After a brief examination of some of the contextual differences between the American and Canadian criminal justice systems, I will compare the performance of American courts in the Troy Davis case to the performance of Canadian courts in a recent series of wrongful convictions stemming from the testimony of a discredited pathologist in child death cases. These Canadian cases are significant because they involved wrongful convictions that resulted from guilty pleas and discredited shaken baby syndrome. Exonerations in such cases in the United States remain quite rare. Only 8 percent of 873 exonerations recorded in the United States from 1989 to 2012 arose from guilty pleas (Gross and Shaffer, 2012: 8). Remarkably, the new registry of wrongful convictions in the United States contains only five exonerations (out of 873) from discredited shaken baby syndrome evidence (ibid., 70–72). The Canadian cases examined in this chapter, as well as comparable cases from the United Kingdom (Sangha, Roach, and Moles, 2010: 285–298), exceed the five recorded shaken baby exonerations in the new American registry even though the United States has a much greater population and even greater prison populations than the United Kingdom and, especially, Canada. These cases suggest that Canadian and British courts have been much more willing to allow new evidence to be introduced in baby death cases than American courts.

The Canadian cases also suggest a willingness of Canadian prosecutors to facilitate review of wrongful convictions; of Canadian appellate courts to allow appeals that would otherwise be time barred and hear new evidence; and even of the Canadian Minister of Justice to grant a new appeal in the face of compelling evidence. The American case study demonstrates that a person claiming to be wrongfully convicted has a vast array of state and federal procedures, but that these procedures often place high and frequently unattainable burdens on that person to demonstrate his or her actual innocence. American prosecutors often aggressively oppose relief and seek convictions even in cases where prisoners have satisfied demanding actual innocence standards (Finlay, 2011; Barry, 2012). In short, there may be less procedure in Canada, but there seems to be a bit more justice for the wrongly convicted.

A Brief Comparison of the American and Canadian Criminal Justice Systems

The differences between the American and Canadian criminal justice systems are staggering for two countries that are, in other respects, so similar. In the United States, criminal justice is a state, and frequently local, matter with many judges and prosecutors being elected and the jury being widely used in those cases that go to trial. In Canada, criminal law and procedure is exclusively federal. The accused is most often tried by an appointed judge sitting alone with juries generally only being used in murder cases. All Canadian judges and prosecutors are appointed. The most striking difference between the two systems is one that is often neglected in the growing scholarship on comparative wrongful convictions. The United States is exceptional for a democracy in its extensive use of prosecutions and imprisonment. The United States imprisons 760 people per 100,000 population whereas Canada imprisons 117 per 100,000 population (Statistics Canada, 2009).

Most criminal cases in the United States are prosecuted under state law, whereas criminal law and procedure is a matter of exclusive federal jurisdiction in Canada. This means that all accused in Canada are tried under a federal Criminal Code which provides common appeal and post-conviction remedies. The accused in Canada is tried in a de facto unitary court system. The vast majority of criminal cases are decided in provincial courts before judges who are appointed by the province and serve with guaranteed tenure until retirement age. Although the accused has a constitutional right to trial by jury if he or she faces five years' imprisonment, and even broader statutory rights to a jury trial, the vast majority of trials in Canada are conducted by a judge alone, with the accused often electing this option (Friedland and Roach, 1997). Murder cases are, however, presumptively tried before a jury. Most discovered wrongful convictions in Canada, as in the United States, have involved jury trials in murder/ sexual assault cases (Roach, in press; Gross et al., 2005; Gross and Shaffer, 2012). In both countries, there may be many more undiscovered wrongful convictions in less serious cases.

Capital Punishment and Wrongful Convictions

In 2001, the Supreme Court of Canada recognized that enough wrongful convictions had been revealed over the last decade to require it to reconsider a 1991 decision that allowed the extradition of a serial killer to face the death penalty in the United States. The Canadian court ruled that the experience of wrongful convictions in both Canada and the United States, as well as in the United Kingdom, meant that it was no longer safe or constitutionally permissible under the due process clause of the Canadian Charter of Rights and Freedoms to extradite fugitives to any country without assurances that the death penalty would not be applied (*United States of America v. Burns and Rafay*, [2001] 1 S.C.R. 283). The Supreme Court of Canada warned that while DNA had helped reveal many wrongful convictions, it would not be available in most cases and that the Canadian experience with DNA exonerations had demonstrated that it was possible to convict the innocent even after a fair trial. A year later, District Court Judge Rakoff employed very similar reasoning to hold that the federal death penalty in the United States was unconstitutional (*United States v. Quinones* 205 F. Supp 2d. 256 (SDNY 2002)). This decision was quickly reversed on appeal, with the 2nd Circuit relying on both prior U.S. Supreme Court and Congressional decisions upholding the death penalty in face of warnings that it could result in wrongful convictions (*United States v. Quinones* 313 F. 3d. 49 (2d. Cir. 2002)).

Appeal and Post-Conviction Relief

The Canadian System

The accused in Canada can launch one appeal with the appeal court having broad rights to admit fresh evidence (Criminal Code s. 683), to allow extensions of time to appeal (ibid., s. 678) and to appoint counsel for the appeal (Criminal Code s. 684). Although new evidence must be credible, potentially decisive and not have been obtainable at trial with due diligence, the Supreme Court of Canada has consistently ruled that the due diligence requirement must yield where a miscarriage of justice would result (*R. v. G.(B)* [2000] 1 S.C.R. 520 at para 37; *R. v. A.J.* 2011 SCC 17 at para 14).

Unlike in the United States, where the Innocence Protection Act and laws in most states specifically address and place conditions on post-conviction access to DNA evidence, there is no specific provision for access to such evidence in Canada. At the same time, the Court of Appeal's powers to admit fresh evidence include the power to order the production of things and witnesses (Criminal Code s.683). In practice, prosecutors in Canada have often (but not always) consented to providing DNA material. The absence of a specific statutory regime means that an accused in Canada, unlike in many American jurisdictions, does not have to claim actual innocence and face possible perjury prosecutions for false claims of actual innocence, as is the case under the American federal act and state acts based on it (18 U.S.C. s. 3600).

Appeal courts can overturn convictions not only on the basis of errors of law that are not harmless, but on the basis that the verdict is unreasonable or cannot be supported by the evidence or on any ground that there is a miscarriage of justice. Although Canadian courts have stopped short of overturning appeals on the basis of a lurking doubt, as is sometimes done in England, they have otherwise emphasized similar concerns about the safety of verdicts. They have also stressed that their power to overturn convictions on the basis of a miscarriage of justice "can reach virtually any kind of error that renders a trial unfair in a procedural or substantive way." Convictions can be overturned even if:

> there was no unfairness at trial, but evidence was admitted on appeal that placed the reliability of the conviction in serious doubt. In these cases, the miscarriage of justice lies not in the conduct of the trial or even the conviction entered at trial, but rather in maintaining the conviction in the face of new evidence that renders the conviction factually unreliable.
>
> (*Re Truscott* 2007 ONCA 575 at para 110)

The Canadian concern with miscarriages of justice includes but is broader than growing American concerns with actual or factual innocence.

Once appeals are exhausted, a convicted person may petition the federal Minister of Justice, who is elected and sits in the federal Parliament and Cabinet. The origins of this power is found in the royal prerogative of mercy, but under 2002 reforms it is subject to a statutory structure that requires the Minister to order a new trial or appeal as an extraordinary remedy if "satisfied that there is a reasonable basis to conclude that a miscarriage of justice likely occurred" (Criminal Code s. 696.3(3)(a)). This standard seems higher than the standard of a real possibility that a conviction will not be upheld on a new appeal used by the CCRC in England (Griffin, 2001, 2009). There has been much criticism of the decision of successive Canadian federal governments not to follow the recommendations of six different Canadian commissions of inquiry and establish an independent commission, modeled after the CCRC, to exercise the Minister of Justice's referral powers (Walker and Campbell, 2010; Roach, 2010). The Canadian Minister both receives and grants far fewer applications on a per capita basis than the CCRC. The Minister is risk adverse in the sense that in almost all cases where he or she orders a new trial or appeal, the conviction is subsequently overturned either by a decision of an appeal court or a decision of a prosecutor not to proceed with a new trial (Roach, 2012).

The American System

It is difficult to describe the American criminal justice system precisely because it is so decentralized with at least 51 different systems. In general, the accused in the United States is entitled to one appeal as of right with state funded counsel. In addition, the accused can often seek a new trial on the basis of new evidence. Although this appears more generous than the Canadian law, which does not have similar procedures, such applications must generally be made within a short limitation period and before the original trial judge, with deferential standards of appellate review (Medwed, 2005; Griffin, 2009: 134). Limitation periods were adopted by many states in the 1970s (Garrett, 2008: 1671) just as rates of imprisonment were increasing in the United States. Limitation periods on re-opening a trial verdict with new evidence (which do not exist in Canada) are an attempt to preserve the finality of verdicts in the high volume American criminal justice system. Judges can deny motions without a full evidentiary hearing and without written decisions. Indeed in only two-thirds of the first 250

DNA exonerations were there any written decisions on appeal even though these were serious rape/murder cases (Garrett, 2011: 184). In general, the approach of American courts to the finality of verdicts should be related to fears of opening the floodgates in a high volume criminal justice system.

Direct appeals of state convictions can go to both state intermediate and supreme courts but these appeals are typically denied "summarily and without writing an opinion" (Garrett, 2011: 194). In many cases, the judges on state appellate courts are elected in some form. After direct appeals are exhausted, post-conviction remedies or collateral attacks may be sought in both state and federal courts. Collateral attacks on convictions, whether by state habeas corpus or the writ of coram nobis or statutory equivalents again start with the original trial judge, raising issues of possible institutional bias in maintaining the verdict (Medwed, 2005: 659–660; Griffin, 2009: 134). Such collateral attacks proceed up through intermediate and state supreme courts with an application of certiorari to the U.S. Supreme Court. This appears to provide a generous system of relief, but most prisoners at this point are not represented by counsel and most petitions are summarily dismissed on technical grounds (Garrett, 2011: 195). To the extent that innocence claims are made in these proceedings, courts typically evaluate them only indirectly and focus on other issues, such as the amount of time that has passed, whether there is a constitutional violation, whether the accused and his lawyer acted with due diligence and whether the accused pled guilty (Garrett, 2008: 1633). A prisoner who satisfies an actual innocence requirement as a gateway to habeas corpus relief will not necessarily have the conviction quashed or be released. In one famous case, a prisoner who satisfied an actual innocence standard was re-prosecuted for the murder and eventually pled guilty to the murder in order to avoid having the death penalty applied (*Schlup v. Delo* 513 U.S. 298; O'Brien, 2009).

Once state collateral attacks on convictions are exhausted, the prisoner can seek habeas relief in the federal district court with possible appeals to the intermediate federal court of appeal and the U.S. Supreme Court. Under precedents from the 1960s and 1970s and before wrongful convictions were widely recognized, the U.S. Supreme Court stressed that the purpose of federal habeas relief is to vindicate constitutional rights and "the existence merely of newly discovered evidence relevant to the guilt of a state prisoner in not a ground for relief on federal habeas corpus" (*Townsend v Sain* 372 U.S. 293 at 317 (1963)). Under the 1996

Anti-Terrorism and Effective Death Penalty Act (AEDP), factual findings of the state courts are presumed to be correct. A state decision will only be reversed if it was contrary to clearly established federal law as determined by the Supreme Court. In addition, federal habeas can generally be brought only on the basis of facts found in state courts unless the facts could not have been previously discovered through due diligence and would establish "by clear and convincing evidence that but for constitutional error, no reasonable factfinder would have found the applicant guilty" (28 U.S.C. s. 2254(e)). Legislative and judicial restrictions on federal habeas corpus are designed to make a high volume criminal justice system that uses the death penalty more manageable.

Although actual innocence is not a traditional ground for habeas relief, it has been recognized in the innocence era as a gateway that can overcome judicial and Congressional restrictions on the availability of habeas corpus (*Schlup v. Delo* 513 U.S. 298; *House v. Bell* 547 U.S. 518). The Supreme Court has only assumed that a clear showing of actual innocence would render an execution unconstitutional. It has stressed that the burden of proof on the applicant would be "extraordinarily high ... because of the very disruptive effect that entertaining claims of factual innocence would have on the need for finality in capital cases, and the enormous burden that having to retry cases based on stale evidence would place on the States" (*Herrera v. Collins* 506 U.S. 390 (1993)). No court has granted relief on actual innocence grounds (Garrett, 2011: 203). As will be discussed below, the Supreme Court's decision in the Troy Davis case to remand the case back to the federal court to exercise original habeas corpus relief adds yet another potential safeguard. At the same time however, it also requires an applicant to satisfy a high burden of establishing actual innocence. A focus on actual innocence co-exists in the United States with a widespread sense that restrictions must be placed on habeas because the remedy is abused by the factually guilty who assert due process rights and it can result in never ending challenges to guilty verdicts and death sentences.

Under federal law and the laws of most states, there are statutory rights to post-conviction access to material for DNA testing. This appears more generous to the accused than in Canada where there is no such legislation. That said, the federal law requires the prisoner to claim actual innocence under pain of perjury. Most legislation requires that the DNA testing must establish probable innocence and some require even higher standards of clear and convincing evidence. Many DNA laws preclude requests from those who plead guilty, who are not in custody, or who were not convicted of "serious crimes" (Garrett, 2008: 1676–1680). As will be seen, Canadian prosecutors and courts have been willing to give accused who pled guilty access to a wider range of material than DNA. The American approach gives "deserving" accused who can show they are factually innocent the benefit of narrow statutory rules and rights, while the Canadian approach is more flexible in responding to a broader range of miscarriages of justice and is based on an equitable exercise of prosecutorial and judicial discretion.

Brandon Garrett (2011), in his study of the first 250 DNA exonerations, found a 13 percent reversal rate of convictions before DNA evidence was discovered, most in the direct appeal stage. This reversal rate seems high, but was similar to the rate in other murder/sexual assault cases where there were no DNA exonerations. In any event, reversals on appeal resulted in new convictions in every single one of the 15 cases in which the exonerees were given a re-trial (Garrett, 2011: 197). In 38 percent of Garrett's sample, appeal courts found some flaw in the trial, but held that error was harmless or did not cause prejudice to the accused (ibid., 201). The picture that emerges is of a relentless crime control machine that continues to prosecute the innocent (Barry, 2012).

As in Canada, a final safeguard in the United States is an appeal to the executive. The executive, however, typically grants a stay of execution or a pardon. In a recent examination of 873 exonerations, Gross and Shaffer, 2012: 8–9 found 113 pardons from the executive and only 76 acquittals and 11 certificates of innocence, with the remaining exonerations resulting in dismissals of charges. In *Herrera v. Collins* (ibid.) the U.S. Supreme Court emphasized that an actual innocence claim could be presented to the executive and that "clemency is deeply rooted in our Anglo-American tradition of law, and is the historical remedy for preventing miscarriages of justice where judicial process has been exhausted" despite strong arguments in dissent that such a mercy process cannot be relied upon to protect constitutional rights. Garrett reports that 68 of the first 250 exonerees received a pardon from the state executive (Garrett, 2011). It can safely be assumed that the elected executive will only come to the benefit of those with rock solid evidence of actual innocence. Again, the picture that emerges is of an American system that will (reluctantly) recognize overwhelming evidence of actual innocence, but that imposes high standards of proof on the convicted and restricts the use of habeas corpus to vindicate due process.

Summary

This necessarily brief review of the American and Canadian criminal justice systems suggests that a person claiming to be wrongfully convicted has many more formal remedies in the United States than in Canada. The law on the books, however, does not always represent the law in action. One important contextual factor is that the United States prosecutes and imprisons people at seven times the rate of Canada. Another is that most prosecutors and state judges are elected in the United States, whereas all Canadian judges and prosecutors are appointed. Students of wrongful convictions ignore contextual factors of each legal system at their peril.

In an attempt to gain a better understanding of remedies in action for the wrongfully convicted, the rest of this chapter will focus on two recent case studies. The case studies are not randomly selected. The American case study of Troy Davis involves a case where relief was ultimately not obtained, while the Canadian case studies involve a range of cases where a variety of means were used to obtain remedies for those who were wrongly convicted and often pled guilty on the basis of expert testimony from a now discredited pathologist. Although the American case study does not examine an exoneration, it is not atypical of the elaborate processes used in American exonerations. On average, the first 250 DNA exonerations in the United States took 13 years of litigation (Garrett, 2011). Those who have received exonerations in the United States have served, on average, 11 years in prison (Gross and Shaffer, 2012: 8). More work with matched cases should be done and may well reveal more insights, but these case studies provide a current sense of how the different systems are at present dealing with high profile claims of wrongful convictions.

The Troy Davis Case Study

Troy Davis was convicted of a brutal murder of an off-duty police officer who had come to the assistance of a homeless man being attacked by three different men in Georgia in 1989. He was convicted by a jury in 1991 and sentenced to death. He applied for a new trial before the judge who presided at his original trial within the 30-day limitation period provided under Georgia law, but this motion was denied (Hill, 2011: 240). He then brought both a direct appeal against his conviction and a motion for a new trial under Georgia law. The Supreme Court of Georgia denied such relief and stressed the need to defer to the jury's verdict (*Davis v. State*, 263 Ga. 5, 426 S.E.2d 844 (1993)). Davis also brought and lost a request for post-conviction relief in the Georgia courts (*Davis v. Turpin*, 539 S.E.2d 129, 131–134 (Ga. 2000)).

Davis then filed his first federal habeas corpus petition claiming a variety of constitutional violations relating to the presentation of false evidence by the prosecutor, disclosure violations and ineffective assistance of counsel. He also claimed innocence not as a free-standing claim, but as a means to have his constitutional claims heard because they would otherwise not have been heard because Davis had not raised them in his state proceedings. The federal district court and subsequently the 11th Circuit ruled against his constitutional due process claims and, having done so, found that they need not explore his actual innocence claim which could only be raised as a gateway to his otherwise procedurally defaulted habeas claim (*Davis v. Terry*, 465 F.3d 1249 (11th Cir. 2006) cert denied *Davis v. Terry*, 551 U.S. 1145 (2007)). Even though the federal courts have recognized actual innocence as a means to overcome restrictions on habeas corpus, they did not engage with these claims at this point.

Davis then filed a one-time only extraordinary motion under Georgia law for a new trial. He filed affidavits containing new evidence relating to recantations by the witnesses who testified at trial that Davis was the shooter. This motion was denied without a hearing by the judge at first instance largely on the basis that the court deferred to the jury's verdict. This decision was upheld in a divided decision by the Georgia Supreme Court. It would not look with favor on either witness recantations that simply impeach the credibility of the witness or evidence offered only by sworn affidavit. This approach, however, ignored that many of the recanting witnesses explained that they had been pressured by the police to identify Davis as the shooter and had not simply changed their minds. In addition, the court was not sensitive to the cumulative effect of seven of nine witnesses at trials recanting. One of the remaining two eyewitnesses who did not recant was the person who Davis claimed was the real shooter. Dissenters in the Georgia Supreme Court argued that the majority was wrong to rely on categorical rules that excluded from consideration witness recantations and confessions to third parties. The decision also ignored the option of granting an evidentiary hearing so that the recanting witnesses could be subject to cross-examination (*Davis v. State*, 660 S.E.2d 354, 362 (Ga. 2008)). The Georgia Board of Pardons and Parole also denied Davis's application for executive clemency. It is of interest that trial judges, Court of Appeals judges, and Supreme Court judges in Georgia are all elected offices. Having to stand for election may not prevent judges from recognizing innocence, but it may require rock solid evidence of innocence that can if necessary be explained to the electorate.

Davis then requested a second round of federal habeas corpus, raising actual innocence as a free-standing claim, but this request was denied, with the 11th Circuit noting that he could seek habeas corpus directly from the U.S. Supreme Court. Dissenters warned that the case demonstrated "the difficulties in navigating AEDPA's thicket of procedural brambles" and that the Court had lost sight of the dangers of executing a person who, if the affidavits of recanting witnesses were true, was innocent (*Re Davis* 565 F 3d 810 at 827 (11th Cir. 2009)). The U.S. Supreme Court then granted original habeas corpus for the first time in 50 years in August 2009 and remanded the case back to a district court in order to receive testimony and "make findings of fact as to whether evidence that could not have been obtained at the time of trial clearly establishes petitioner's innocence" (*In Re Davis* 130 S.Ct. 1 at 1 (2009)). This was a higher standard than required by dissenters in *Herrera*, who argued that those seeking post-conviction relief should establish probable innocence.

The high standard of proof demanded by the U.S. Supreme Court in *Re Davis* echoed both actual innocence restrictions placed on habeas corpus by Congress and the Supreme Court's previous statement that any actual innocence claim should require a higher standard of proof than the use of innocence as a gateway to otherwise restricted forms of habeas relief (*House v. Bell*, ibid.; Lott, 2011). Thus, to the extent that American courts have recognized actual innocence as a basis for relief, they have imposed a high burden of proof on the prisoner clearly to establish innocence out of deference to the jury's verdict, social interests in finality, Congress's restrictions on habeas corpus relief, and the deference of federal courts to state processes. All of these factors suggest that the context of the American legal system and, in particular, expressive concerns about respecting the decisions of states and juries significantly constrain the ability of the American legal system to recognize the universal value that the innocent should not be executed.

Justice Scalia, with Justice Thomas concurring, dissented in *Re Davis*. He argued that the remand was a "fool's errand" because the District Court would have no power to release Davis because Congress had in the 1996 Effective Death Penalty and Anti-Terrorism Act restricted federal habeas relief either to matters already litigated by the states or to matters that were contrary to clearly established federal law. Justice Scalia accurately noted that the Supreme Court had not clearly established actual innocence as a free-standing ground for habeas relief. In other words, it should not matter if Davis established his innocence because such a claim had not been clearly established in federal law. He also relied on the number of state and federal courts that had already denied relief. Justice Scalia's technical and positivistic approach represents a form of extra-legalism in which the highly technical and prescriptive nature of American law can legitimate extra-legal conduct such as executing the innocent or indeterminate detention (Roach, 2011, ch. 4). Justice Scalia's approach in this and other cases (Finlay, 2011: 1116) represents a form of skepticism about the conviction of the innocent that would not be found in the Canadian judiciary. For example, Justice Scalia expressed reservations in *Herrera* about innocence-based claims in part because they could impose new burdens on the federal courts. In other cases, Justice Scalia has, in the course of defending the death penalty, expressed skepticism about whether the U.S. justice system has ever executed an innocent person and about whether those who have been exonerated are truly innocent (*Kansas v. Marsh* 548 U.S. 163 (2006)).

The District Court then considered Davis's actual innocence claim, but found that he had not established actual innocence by such clear and convincing evidence that no reasonable juror would have convicted him in light of the new evidence. Like the courts before, it stressed that the courts would not generally credit either witness recantation or affidavit evidence. It concluded that while Davis's "new evidence casts some additional, minimal doubt on his conviction, it is largely smoke and mirrors." *In re* Davis, No. CV409-130, 2010 U.S. Dist. LEXIS 87340, at 214 (S.D. Ga. Aug. 24, 2010). The Court stressed the need to defer to juries and state processes by stating that a " federal court simply cannot interpose itself and set aside the jury verdict in this case absent a truly persuasive showing of innocence. To act contrarily would wreck [sic] complete havoc on the criminal justice system" (ibid., 214). Both the 11th

Circuit and the Supreme Court subsequently declined to hear the case. Troy Davis was executed on September 21, 2011.

The Dr. Charles Smith Shaken Baby Case Studies

A recent series of cases in Canada involving the testimony of pathologist Dr. Charles Smith provide an excellent vehicle for examining the remedies that are available for wrongful convictions in Canada. These cases are also significant because they led the provincial government to appoint a public inquiry to make recommendations about the reform of forensic pathology and subsequently to conduct audits of cases involving similar forms of evidence (Goudge, 2008; Roach, 2009). Public inquiries conducted by sitting or retired judges have increased the sensitivity of the Canadian judiciary to the possibility of wrongful conviction.

The first and still best known of the Dr. Smith cases involved William Mullins-Johnson who was convicted of first degree murder in the 1993 death of his four-year-old niece, who had been left in his care. His conviction was upheld by the Ontario Court of Appeal in 1996 as reasonable, but over a strong dissent by a judge who stressed that the trial judge had not adequately instructed the jury about the accused's defense that he did not sexually assault his niece and that she died accidentally (*R. v. Mullins-Johnson*, 1996 112 C.C.C. (3d) 117). Because of the dissent, Mr. Mullins-Johnson was able to appeal his conviction to the Supreme Court of Canada as of right. The appeal was, however, dismissed in a judgment consisting of a single sentence by a five-person panel of the nine-person Court (*R. v. Mullins-Johnson* [1998] 1 S.C.R. 977). The failure to correct the miscarriage of justice on appeal and the Supreme Court's summary handling of the case is disturbing but also consistent with the American cases, which found that appeals did not assist those who were eventually exonerated by DNA.

Mr. Mullins-Johnson applied to the federal Minister of Justice in 2005 to re-open his conviction. Because of related investigations into the work of Dr. Smith, his petition for a new appeal was not decided and granted by the Minister of Justice until 2007. That said, Mullins-Johnson was released and granted bail pending such a decision in 2005. Bail has been granted in several cases, pending decisions by the Minister of Justice, even though there is no explicit statutory jurisdiction for judges to do so. This procedure demonstrates a generous approach to remedies that is sensitive to the merits of claims of wrongful convictions. It also mitigates the delays that often accompany the petitions to the Minister of Justice (Roach, in press).

In 2007, a new appeal was ordered by the Minister of Justice based on new expert evidence from six pathologists that the medical evidence did not support the theory that the niece was sexually assaulted and murdered. Evidence that was originally interpreted as a sign of sexual assault was now interpreted as a post mortem artifact and the experts now said that the cause of death was undetermined. The prosecution consented to the entry of an acquittal and apologized for what had happened. Because Mr. Mullins-Johnson had served 12 years in prison, the Court of Appeal allowed him and one expert to testify. They declined his request that he be declared innocent on the basis that the court had no statutory jurisdiction to do so, but concluded that the Appellant had been the "subject of a terrible miscarriage of justice" and expressed regret for the miscarriage and the time he spent in jail (*R. v. Mullins-Johnson* 2007 ONCA 720 at para 26).

The Mullins-Johnson case illustrates the flexibility of the Canadian system in granting bail pending petitions to the Minister of Justice; ordering new appeals, even though appeals were exhausted; and the willingness of unelected prosecutors in Canada to agree to the quashing of wrongful convictions. Other cases involving Dr. Smith demonstrate flexibility in allowing appeals out of time and re-opening cases where the accused pled guilty in the face of new evidence. Tammy Marquardt was convicted of murder in 1995 for killing her two and a half-year-old-son. She consistently denied killing her son, but was convicted by a jury after a judge refused to allow prospective jurors to be questioned about whether the nature of the charges would affect their impartiality. The main evidence at trial against Ms. Marquardt was the testimony of Dr. Charles Smith, a pathologist who testified that the cause of her son's death was asphyxia and cited petechial hemorrhages and brain swelling as evidence in support of his opinion. The defense called no expert evidence, but relied on the child's history of epileptic seizures. Ms. Marquardt appealed her conviction to the Ontario Court of Appeal, but the appeal was dismissed in 1998 (*R. v. Marquardt*, 1998 124 C.C.C.(3d) 375). Marquardt never appealed to the Supreme Court of Canada because she had been denied legal aid funding. After the Goudge Inquiry had completed its work examining Dr. Smith's testimony and recommending improvements in the delivery of forensic pathology, Marquardt appealed to the Supreme Court in 2009 with notice of fresh evidence relating to the unreliability of Dr. Smith's testimony at trial. The Supreme Court of Canada granted the leave to appeal out of time and remanded the case to the Ontario Court of Appeal to consider the fresh evidence, and the prosecution did not oppose this motion. A judge of the Court of Appeal granted Marquardt bail pending the hearing of appeal, thus releasing her from 13 years of imprisonment. As in the Mullins-Johnson case, the grant of bail was what ultimately freed Tammy Marquardt.

In 2011, the Ontario Court of Appeal considered fresh medical evidence and found that it "shows that Dr. Smith made several significant errors that could have misled the jury and led to a miscarriage of justice" (*R. v. Marquardt*, 2011 ONCA 281 at para 16). The errors included finding asphyxia on the basis of non-specific petechial hemorrhages and stating that the autopsy excluded epilepsy as a cause of death. The Court of Appeal held that in light of the new evidence, the conviction was a miscarriage of justice. Unlike in the Mullins-Johnson case, the Court of Appeal did not enter an acquittal, but instead ordered a new trial. It did so because it did not accept expert evidence that epilepsy was the cause of death because such evidence was outside the scope of the expertise of the two pediatric neurologists who provided the fresh evidence (ibid., at para 21). The Crown subsequently withdrew the murder charge, with the trial judge expressing regret for what had happened (Tyler, 2011).

Another striking feature of the Dr. Smith cases is that the Courts have overturned a number of convictions in which parents and other caregivers pled guilty after the prosecutor agreed to drop murder charges. In one case, Sherry Sherratt-Robinson received a one-year sentence for infanticide of her four-month-old son and agreed to the adoption of her other son in 1999 after Dr. Smith testified at a preliminary inquiry that the child died of asphyxia. An appeal out of time was allowed and fresh evidence admitted with respect to errors in Dr. Smith's diagnosis and an explanation of why the accused pled guilty, with the prosecutor's consent. The Court of Appeal quashed the conviction, entered an acquittal and apologized for the wrongful conviction in 2009 (*R. v. Sherratt-Robinson* 2009 ONCA 886). In 2010, the Court of Appeal, again with the prosecutor's consent, allowed appeals out of time in two other cases in which young mothers had pled guilty to reduced charges, in part on the basis of Dr. Smith's proposed testimony (*R. v. C.M.* 2010 ONCA 690, *R. v. C.F.* 2010 ONCA 691). The Court of Appeal explained in the latter case:

> The appellant applies to have the material gathered as part of the coroner's investigation and the *Goudge Inquiry* and the other expert opinions obtained since then admitted as fresh evidence. She also applies to have her affidavit and the affidavit of her trial counsel admitted on appeal to explain why she entered her guilty plea. The Crown fairly concedes that new expert evidence meets the test for fresh evidence. The Crown also agrees that the affidavits of the appellant and her trial lawyer should be admitted. Crown counsel acknowledged that Dr. Smith's highly respected expertise in the area of pediatric forensic pathology, and his opinion that the appellant committed infanticide, created a very powerful reason for the appellant to agree to plead guilty rather than face trial. The Crown accepts that there has been a miscarriage of justice, that the fresh evidence justifies setting aside the plea and that the appeal must be allowed. We agree.
>
> (Ibid., at paras 12–14)

The behavior of the prosecutors in this case can be contrasted with an American case in which they dropped charges after a new trial was ordered on the basis of the frailties of shaken baby evidence, but nevertheless publicly maintained that the mother was guilty of killing her baby (*State v. Edmunds* 746 NW 2d 590, Finlay, 2011: 1162).

In 2011, the Ontario Court of Appeal allowed two more appeals out of time in other Dr. Smith cases where a parent originally charged with murder pled guilty to lesser charges arising from a child's death. It considered extensive fresh evidence and accepted the joint position of the accused and the prosecutor that the convictions were no longer a reasonable verdict in light of the new evidence. It also stressed that:

> even though an appellant's plea of guilty appears to meet all the traditional tests for a valid guilty plea, the court retains a discretion, to be exercised in the interests of justice, to receive fresh evidence to explain the circumstances that led to the guilty plea and that demonstrate a miscarriage of justice occurred.
>
> (*R. v. Kumar* 2011 ONCA 120 at para. 34,
> *R. v. Brant* 2011 ONCA 362)

The procedural flexibility of Canadian courts is not limited to Ontario. The British Columbia Court of Appeal in 2009 set aside orders that it had made, first in 1984 and then in 1997, to allow a person wrongfully convicted in 1983 to revive his appeal. This was done with the consent of the prosecutor who also consented to the overturning of the conviction in a case that, like the Dr. Smith cases, did not involve DNA (*R. v. Henry* 2009 BCCA 12, 2010 BCCA 462).

At the same time, not every conviction in which Dr. Smith was involved has been overturned as a wrongful conviction. The Court of Appeal has denied a request to re-open a conviction in a case where a man was twice convicted of manslaughter in relation to his grandson's death, in part on the basis of Dr. Smith's testimony. The Court of Appeal considered the new evidence, but concluded that the accused "has not established that his case is a possible wrongful conviction" (*R. v. Simmons* 2012 ONCA 94 at para 17). Consistent with the other cases, however, the Court of Appeal did not let time limits and guilty pleas stand in the way of considering new evidence that might reveal a wrongful conviction and stated: "We would be reluctant to allow an abandoned appeal to stand if the result was a wrongful conviction" (ibid., at para 15).

All of these cases reveal a striking willingness of courts to examine new evidence, even after guilty pleas. They also demonstrate frequent agreement by prosecutors to allow appeals out of time, to admit new evidence, and to overturn convictions. Although prosecutorial behavior in these cases was no doubt influenced by the high profile Goudge public inquiry (Goudge, 2008), there are other Canadian cases where prosecutors have agreed to overturn convictions, including those obtained by guilty pleas on the basis of new evidence (Brockman, 2010). In *R. v. Hanemaayer* 2008 ONCA 580, the prosecutor consented to the entry of the results of a police re-investigation and the overturning of a guilty plea and the Court of Appeal expressed understanding about why the accused pled guilty after he had been subject to a mistaken eyewitness identification. Similarly, the prosecutor consented to the admission of new DNA evidence in a case where a mentally disabled man had falsely confessed and pleaded guilty to a series of sexual assaults (*R. v. Marshall* 2005 QCCA 852).

Too much should perhaps not be made of the actions of Canadian prosecutors in these cases. Professor Garrett reports that prosecutors eventually joined in motions to vacate convictions in 88 percent of the

DNA exonerations (Garrett, 2011: 230). Given the magic bullet of DNA, however, the 12 percent of cases in which the prosecutors opposed the motion is perhaps more telling. Recent data suggests that 8 percent of 873 American exonerations arose in guilty plea cases and these cases bear some similarity to the Canadian Dr. Smith cases. Nevertheless, Gross and Shaffer stress that the 71 exonerations from guilty pleas are "startlingly few for a system in which 95% of felony convictions are the product of guilty pleas" (Gross and Shaffer, 2012: 8). The small number (5) of shaken baby exonerations that they identify (ibid., 70–72) is even more startling. As suggested above, British and Canadian courts have been much more willing to allow new evidence to be admitted to challenge the finality of guilty verdicts in baby death cases than American courts. Indeed, the U.S. Supreme Court has recently summarily reversed an appellate court decision quashing a 1997 conviction in a shaken baby case. The majority stressed the fact that the jury had enough evidence to convict, the need to defer to jury verdicts and state processes, and the ability of the convicted grandmother to seek executive clemency. It found that the appellate court below had erred in reversing a jury's verdict because it found it unreasonable. Justice Ginsberg in dissent argued that "what is now known about shaken baby syndrome (SBS) casts grave doubt" on the conviction. In her view, it did not justify the Court in summarily restoring the conviction without full argument (*Cavazos v. Smith* 132 S.Ct. 1, 9 (2011)). This case stands in stark contrast to the willingness of Canadian courts to re-open many baby death cases on the basis of new evidence.

The Canadian Dr. Smith cases are interesting because remedies were obtained long after lenient sentences had expired. These remedies were facilitated by the systemic response of the public inquiry process (Goudge, 2008). Canadian governments have been more willing than American governments to appoint such commissions (Roach, 2010; Norris et al., 2011: 1355). The fact that Canadian government lawyers have agreed to the reversal of convictions and apologized for wrongful convictions and that Canadian governments so often appoint official inquiries into wrongful convictions suggests that Canada retains some sense of deference to a more benevolent state (Lipset, 1990) in its response to wrongful convictions. In contrast, the American response shows less faith in governments and their lawyers in correcting wrongful convictions. It demonstrates more faith in the volunteerism of the Innocence Projects

(Garrett, 2011) and the processes of adversarial legalism in which lawyers representing the individual assert legal rights and rules to challenge state authority (Kagan, 2001).

Summary

The studies of the Troy Davis case in the U.S. and the Dr. Smith cases in Canada are not representative, but they reveal some of the contextual differences between remedies for wrongful convictions in both countries. Consistent with the idea that the United States embraces adversarial legalism (Kagan, 2001) and that this legalism can take the form of a narrow positivism that resists review of the merits of claims of injustice (Roach, 2011:163–166, 436–438), the Troy Davis case demonstrates how the finality of a guilty verdict can survive multiple adversarial challenges. As each successive challenge to his guilty verdict failed, Troy Davis faced higher burdens of establishing innocence (Lott, 2011: 474) and state prosecutors and multiple state and federal judges seemed to have no reservations about the safety of executing Mr. Davis. His case demonstrates some of the dangers of a factual innocence model that demands high standards of proof that will not be easily satisfied in non-DNA cases (Finlay, 2011). The multiple avenues of appeals extended to the late Mr. Davis are surprising given the high volume of the American criminal justice system. They can, however, perhaps be explained by the seemingly perfunctory nature of much of the reviews that are often offered (Garrett, 2011). The U.S. cases tend to exhibit higher degrees of adversarialism than the Canadian cases. Even after judges have found demanding actual innocence standards satisfied, elected prosecutors in the United States continue to prosecute cases (O'Brien, 2009; Barry, 2012). In contrast, Canadian prosecutors in the Dr. Smith and other cases have consented to the overturning of convictions. A possible explanatory fact is that Canadian prosecutors are appointed, not elected, and they are often career civil servants who are insulated from political pressures.

Conclusion

The Canadian legal system provides far fewer formal remedies for wrongful convictions than the American system. The accused generally has only one appeal as of right and there is no system of collateral review of convictions by habeas corpus. There is also no legislation that guarantees access to

DNA as part of the post-conviction process. Once appeals are exhausted, those claiming to be wrongfully convicted must petition the elected federal Minister of Justice who despite numerous reform recommendations for the appointment of an independent commission as is the case in England and now in North Carolina, still decides whether a new trial or appeal should be ordered on the basis of new evidence (Roach, 2012). Despite these shortcomings, the Canadian system has emerged in this chapter as more flexible and willing to consider new evidence on its merits than the American system. Canadian judges have not allowed due diligence requirements for the discovery of new evidence to stand in the way of the correction of miscarriages of justice. They have creatively granted bail to free the wrongfully convicted pending appeals and petitions to the Minister of Justice. They define wrongful convictions broadly to include not only the conviction of the actually innocent but procedural unfairness and evidence that casts doubt of the safety of guilty verdicts. Unlike many of the American counterparts, they do not require the accused to establish actual innocence as a precondition to relief. In turn, Canadian prosecutors seem to be less adversarial than their American counterparts. They have frequently consented to appeals out of time, the admission of new evidence, and the overturning of wrongful convictions. They have apologized for wrongful convictions. They have collectively produced two major reports detailing the causes of wrongful convictions and the findings of Canadian public inquiries into wrongful convictions (Federal, Provincial and Territorial Heads of Prosecution, 2004, 2011). In turn, the Canadian judiciary has produced seven public inquiry reports on the systemic causes of wrongful convictions (Roach, 2010).

My point in making these comparisons is not to suggest that the Canadian system is better than the American (for my criticisms of the Canadian system see Sangha, Roach, and Moles, 2010; Roach, in press) or that American judges and prosecutors should somehow become more like Canadian ones. The Canadian system is simply different than the American system. It reflects legal and political cultures that are different despite the many similarities between the neighboring states. Canadian appellate judges may be more generous in granting relief because they know that there are few other safeguards in the system. They may pay less deference to the finality of convictions in part because there are many less jury verdicts in Canada and because Canada, even on a per capita basis, has many fewer convictions compared to the United States. Canadian prosecutors can afford to be less adversarial and admit more mistakes because they do not have to stand for elections. All of these contextual factors help explain why the Canadian system has been able to identify a significant number of wrongful convictions while also providing far fewer formal legal remedies than the United States. In turn, cases like the Troy Davis case should be studied in the context of American legal and political culture. The relevant context includes the adversarial, legalistic, and positivistic nature of much of American law (Kagan, 2001; Roach, 2011) and the extraordinarily high use of criminal prosecutions and imprisonment in the United States compared to all other democracies (Statistics Canada, 2009).

One of the many functions of comparative law is to reveal what might otherwise be unquestioned assumptions by those working in only one system. For many working in the American system, habeas corpus review and collateral attack, including the restrictions that courts have placed on such forms of review in terms of limitation periods and actual innocence requirements, may seem natural and inevitable, but understanding the Canadian system may expand the imagination. It may also invite Americans to rethink the degree to which concerns about factual innocence and the protection of the finality of verdicts from an almost endless stream of collateral challenges may paradoxically make it difficult for those convicted in the United States to overturn their convictions on grounds of innocence. American courts have been much more resistant to admitting new evidence in shaken baby cases than Canadian courts in part because of concerns about deferring to jury verdicts and state processes. American prosecutors could learn something from the less adversarial stance of Canadian prosecutors in wrongful conviction cases.

Similarly, those working in the Canadian system may take their system for granted and not always appreciate how courts have relaxed their restrictive appeal structure or how prosecutors have frequently acted in a non-adversarial manner. These mechanisms include generous tests for the admission of fresh evidence, bail pending appeal, or the Minister of Justice's decision on new trial and appeals and appeals out of time, often with prosecutorial consent. The Canadian system can afford to be more generous because the system operates at a significantly lower volume than the American system. Hence, the fear of opening floodgates and undermining the finality of guilty verdicts does not seem as great as in the United States. Canadians should not, however, be complacent. As in the United States, discovered wrongful convictions in Canada are clustered around murder/ sexual assault cases and have disproportionately affected racialized groups, notably Aboriginal people (Roach, in press). Moreover, political and legal culture is not static. Canadian judges and prosecutors could become less generous as the Canadian criminal justice system becomes more punitive and takes on higher volumes of cases. This is especially the case because the comparative flexibility and generosity of the Canadian system depends not on legal rules but the exercise of judicial and prosecutorial discretion. Conventional wisdom is that Canada follows the United States but with a considerable time lag. Time will tell.

The main lesson of this chapter is that even if the causes of wrongful convictions are quite similar across countries, their remedies will reflect the particular legal and political culture of each country. An innocence movement developed in the particular context of the United States should not simplistically be exported to other countries—even countries as similar to the United States as Canada.

References

Barry, Jordan, 2012 "Prosecuting the Exonerated: Actual Innocence and the Double Jeopardy Clause" *Stanford Law Review* 64, 535-588.

Brockman, Joan, 2010 "An Offer You Can't Refuse: Pleading Guilty When Innocent," *Criminal Law Quarterly* 56, 116.

Federal, Provincial and Territorial Heads of Prosecutions, 2004 Report on Miscarriages of Justice (Ottawa: Department of Justice). Available at http://www.justice.gc.ca/eng/dept-min/pub/pmj-pej/pmj-pej.pdf.

Federal, Provincial and Territorial Heads of Prosecution, 2011 *The Path to Justice: Preventing Wrongful Convictions* (Ottawa: Public Prosecutions Canada). Available at http://www.ppsc-sppc.gc.ca/eng/pub/ptj-spj/ptj-spj-eng.pdf.

Finlay, Keith, 2011 "Defining Innocence," *Albany Law Review* 74, 1157–1208.

Friedland, M.L. and Roach, Kent, 1997 "Borderline Justice," *Israeli Law Review* 31, 120–158.

Garland, David, 2001 *The Culture of Control* (Chicago: University of Chicago Press).

Garrett, Brandon, 2008 "Claiming Innocence," *Minnesota Law Review* 92, 1629–1723.

Garrett, Brandon, 2011 *Convicting the Innocent: Where Criminal Prosecutions Go Wrong* (Cambridge: Harvard University Press).

Goudge, Stephen, 2008 *Report on Forensic Pediatric Pathology* (Toronto: Queens Printer,).

Griffin, Lissa 2001 "The Correction of Wrongful Convictions: A Comparative Perspective," *American University International Law Review* 16, 1241–1308.

Griffin, Lissa 2009 "Correcting Injustice: Studying How the United Kingdom and the United States Review Claims of Innocence," *University of Toledo Law Review* 41, 107–152.

Gross, Samuel et al., 2005 "Exonerations in the United States 1989 through 2003," *Journal of Criminal Law and Criminology* 95, 523.

Gross, Samuel and Shaffer, Michael, 2012 "Exonerations in the United States, 1989–2012: Report by the National Registry of Exonerations." Available at http://www.law.umich.edu/special/exoneration/Documents/exonerations_us_1989_2012_full_report.pdf.

Hill, Michael, 2011 "Seen but not Heard: An Argument for Granting Evidentiary Hearings to Weigh the Credibility of Recanted Testimony," *Georgia Law Review* 46, 213–248.

Huff, C.R. (2002) "Wrongful Convictions and Public Policy" *Criminology* 40(1), 1–18.

Kagan, Robert, 2001 *Adversarial Legalism: The American Way of Law* (Cambridge: Harvard University Press).

Lipset, Seymour, 1990 *Continental Divide: The Values and Institutions of the United States and Canada* (New York: Routledge).

Lott, Joshua, 2011 "The End of Innocence? Federal Habeas Corpus Relief After In Re Davis," *Georgia State University Law Review* 27, 443–488.

Medwed, Daniel, 2005 "Up the River with No Procedure: Innocent Prisoners and Newly Discovered Non-DNA Evidence in State Courts," *Arizona Law Review* 47, 655–718.

Norris, Robert, 2011 "'Than One Innocent Suffer': Evaluating State Safeguards Against Wrongful Convictions," *Albany Law Review* 74, 1301–1364.

O'Brien, Sean, 2009 "Mothers and Sons: The Lloyd Schlup Story," *University of Missouri at Kansas City Law Review* 77, 1021–1047.

Roach, Kent, 2009 "Forensic Science and Miscarriages of Justice: Some Lessons from the Canadian Experience," *Jurimetrics* 50, 67–92.

Roach, Kent, 2010 "The Role of Innocence Commissions: Error Correction, Systemic Reform or Both?" *Chicago-Kent Law Review* 85, 89–126.

Roach, Kent, 2011 *The 9/11 Effect: Comparative Counter-Terrorism* (Cambridge: Cambridge University Press).

Roach, Kent, 2012 "An Independent Commission to Review Claims of Wrongful Convictions: Lessons from North Carolina?" *Criminal Law Quarterly* 57, 283–302.

Roach, Kent (in press) "Wrongful Convictions in Canada" *University of Cincinnati Law Review*.

Sangha, Bibi, Roach, Kent and Moles, Robert, 2010 *Forensic Investigations and Miscarriages of Justice: The Rhetoric Meets the Reality* (Toronto: Irwin Law).

Statistics Canada, 2009 "The Daily" December 8, 2009. Available at http://www.statcan.gc.ca/daily-quotidien/091208/dq091208a-eng.htm.

Tyler, Tracey "Murder charges withdrawn against mother wrongfully convicted of killing son, 2" *Toronto Star* June 7, 2011.

Tushnet, Mark 2008 *Weak Courts Strong Rights* (Princeton: Princeton University Press).

Walker, Clive and Campbell, Kathryn (2010) "The CCRC as an Option for Canada: Forwards or Backwards" in Michael Naughton (Ed.) *The Criminal Cases Review Commission: Hope for the Innocent?* (London: Palgrave).

Cases

Cavazos v. Smith 132 S.Ct. 1 (2011).

Davis v. State, 263 Ga. 5, 426 S.E.2d 844 (1993).

Davis v. State, 660 S.E.2d 354, 362 (Ga. 2008).

Davis v. Terry, 465 F.3d 1249 (11th Cir. 2006) cert denied *Davis v. Terry*, 551 U.S. 1145 (2007).

Davis v. Turpin, 539 S.E.2d 129, 131–34 (Ga. 2000).

Herrera v. Collins 506 U.S. 390 (1993).

House v. Bell 547 U.S. 518 (2006).

In re Davis, No. CV409-130, 2010 U.S. Dist. LEXIS 87340, at 214 (S.D. Ga. Aug. 24, 2010).

Kansas v. Marsh 548 U.S. 163 (2006).

Re Davis 565 F 3d 810 (11th Cir. 2009).

Re Davis 130 S Ct.1 (2009).

Re Truscott 2007 ONCA 575.

R. v. A.J. 2011 SCC 17.

R. v. Brant 2011 ONCA 362.

R. v. C.F. 2010 ONCA 691.

R. v. C.M. 2010 ONCA 690.

R. v. G.(B) [2000] 1 S.C.R. 520.

R. v. Hanemaayer, 2008 ONCA 580.

R. v. Henry 2009 BCCA 12, 2010 BCCA 462.

R. v. Kumar 2011 ONCA 120.

R. v. Marquardt 2011 ONCA 281.

R. v. Marshall 2005 QCCA 852.

R. v. Mullins-Johnson 2007 ONCA 720.

R. v. Sherratt-Robinson 2009 ONCA 886.

R. v. Simmons 2012 ONCA 94.

R. v. Unger, 2005 MBQB 238.

Schlup v. Delo 513 U.S. 298 (1993).

State v. Edmunds 746 NW 2d 590 (Wis.Ct. App. 2008).

Townsend v Sain 372 U.S. 293.

United States of America v. Burns and Rafay, [2001] 1 S.C.R. 283.

United States v. Quinones 205 F. Supp 2d. 256 (SDNY 2002).

United States v. Quinones 313 F. 3d. 49 (2d. Cir. 2002).

15

THE ROCKY ROAD TO REFORM

STATE INNOCENCE STUDIES AND THE PENNSYLVANIA STORY

Spero T. Lappas and Elizabeth F. Loftus

The criminal code of every country partakes so much of necessary severity that without an easy access to exceptions in favor of unfortunate guilt, justice would wear a countenance too sanguinary and cruel.

Alexander Hamilton

In 1984, Thomas Doswell was arrested and subsequently acquitted for the rape of Victoria Johnson in Pittsburgh, Pennsylvania. After his acquittal, Doswell remembers that the frustrated and disappointed police detective Herman Wolf warned that he would nonetheless "get him" in the future (*Doswell v. City of Pittsburgh*, 2009, p. 3). When Helen Tokar was raped in 1986 at Pittsburgh's Forbes Health Center, Wolf was assigned to that case too, and he had not forgotten Thomas Doswell. When Ms. Tokar, who is white, described the rapist as a black male of medium height and complexion with short hair, Wolf assembled a photo-array which included Doswell's photograph. His picture, and only his, was marked with a capital "R" which falsely identified Doswell as a convicted rapist. Wolf testified that he used only one "R"-marked photo to facilitate the witness's selection of Doswell's photo. He knew, of course, that Doswell was in fact not a convicted rapist and that the practice of marking photos to ensure selection was unconstitutional (*Doswell v. City of Pittsburgh*, 2009, p. 3). Tokar and another witness, Ore Bolte, who had seen the rapist run away, both identified the pre-marked "R" photo as the perpetrator, Doswell was subsequently and inevitably convicted, and he was sentenced to 26 years.

In 2005, Doswell was exonerated when DNA analysis of rape kit evidence proved that he could not have been the rapist. The District Attorney joined the defense in asking the court to clear Doswell and he was released from prison on August 1, 2005 after serving almost 19 years. When he sued the city and Wolf for malicious prosecution, the eyewitness, Ora Bolte, swore that she had told Wolf that she could not identify the rapist, but that Wolf kept pointing to Doswell's photo in the array and that "the only reason I picked [Doswell] was because Detective Wolf told me to and I was afraid of him" (*Doswell v. City of Pittsburgh*, 2009). The City of Pittsburgh paid Doswell 3.2 million dollars to settle his lawsuit, about $19 for each hour in prison (Time Lost, 2010).

A year after the rape of Helen Tokar, a woman identified in court reports only as LY was abducted and forced into a car in Philadelphia while she walked home from work. Two men drove her away and raped her at gunpoint for over an hour. Several months later, LY saw Vincent Moto walking down a city street and believed him to be one of the rapists. Based substantially on LY's "unwavering" identification, Moto was convicted and sentenced to serve 24 years. He was freed in 1997 when DNA excluded him and the prosecution dismissed the charges, claiming that they could neither find LY nor re-try Moto without her. Moto had served about ten years (*Pennsylvania v. Moto*, 2011). In 2011, the Pennsylvania Supreme Court refused to expunge Moto's rape conviction on the grounds that the DNA evidence did not really "render infirm" LY's identification of Moto. Had Moto been re-tried, "[i]t would have been for the jury to decide if the failure to detect [Moto's] DNA was more compelling than the victim's testimony" (*Pennsylvania v. Moto*, 2011, p. 997).

Both Doswell's conviction and Moto's fall into the increasingly familiar category of cases in which defendants forfeit huge chunks of their lives based on the testimony of eyewitnesses who are sincere and certain and wrong. They implicate the causes of mis-identification, which scientific research and judicial decisions have characterized as Estimator

Variables (mistake provoking aspects of the eyewitness encounter, such as Ms. Tokar's cross-racial identification of a stranger under stressful circumstances, and LY's temporally remote identification during a stray encounter) and System Variables (deficiencies of the police identification procedures, such as Wolf's unconstitutional pre-designation of Doswell's photograph and his coercion of Bolte) (Wells, 1978; *New Jersey v. Henderson*, 2011). Both also find a place in legal controversy as part of the "Pennsylvania Eight" cases in which DNA results freed prisoners after conviction and long confinement. These eight exonerations provoked Professor John Rago's article, "A Fine Line Between Chaos & Creation: Lessons on Innocence Reform from the Pennsylvania Eight" (Rago, 2006) and then the establishment of Pennsylvania's Advisory Committee to Study the Causes of Wrongful Convictions ("the Advisory Committee").

Pennsylvania was certainly not the first state to recognize that hundreds of innocent citizens were being unjustly condemned and to seek a solution. Innocence or evidence commissions had already served California, Connecticut, Florida, Illinois, Louisiana, New York, North Carolina, Texas, and Wisconsin under various mandates and with varying authority. Pennsylvania's Advisory Committee was formed by a state Senate resolution which found that "[a]t least eight individuals have been exonerated in Pennsylvania through post-conviction DNA testing, three of whom were in prison for murder and one of whom was on death row" and which tasked the committee "to study the underlying causes of wrongful convictions . . . [and to] develop a consensus on recommendations intended to reduce the possibility that in the future innocent persons be wrongfully convicted" (Pennsylvania Senate Resolution 381; 2006) By 2006, it was already well known that faulty eyewitness identifications figured in many wrongful convictions (Bedau and Radelet, 1987) and the committee approached its mission informed by research and scholarship which showed how police reforms, better lawyer training and improved judicial procedures could mitigate future risks (Advisory Committee Report, 2011).

In spite of its righteous mission, the Advisory Committee immediately became a battleground where law enforcement members fought for a self-proclaimed moral high ground as part of a wider campaign which currently seeks to de-legitimize the false conviction debate by redefining the very notion of what it means to be innocent. In Pennsylvania and elsewhere, this effort stands on three legs. First, prosecutors present themselves as the only legitimate guardians of the criminal justice system, thus characterizing any opposing views as misinformed or self-serving. Second, they complain that any reform of the status quo is unnecessary or, even worse, dangerous, usually because changes would make it harder to convict people. Third, and certainly most troubling, they try to discredit calls for reform by disputing the validity of exonerations, judging them against Procrustean measures and by contra-legal standards and demands. Here's how it happened in Pennsylvania.

> To vice, innocence must always seem only a superior form of chicanery.
>
> Ouida

Professor Rago's article reached the attention of State Senator Stewart Greenleaf, who introduced Senate Bill 1069 (Sess. of 2006) to establish an Innocence Commission to study the issue in Pennsylvania and recommend reforms. Bill 1069 passed the Senate by a vote of 49–0 and was referred to the more conservative state House of Representatives, where it was never reported out of the Judiciary Committee. The Senate then, acting alone, passed Senate Resolution 381 (2006) which established a committee charged with advising the bipartisan and bicameral research agency of the General Assembly, an agency called the Joint State Government Commission.

Senate Resolution 381 called for a membership of approximately 30 members to be drawn from the bar, the judiciary, law enforcement and corrections authorities, academia, faith-based groups, and other criminal justice experts (SR 381; 2006). Professor Rago was appointed chairman of the committee and its first meeting was scheduled for March 29, 2007.

The committee mission was simple and, one would have thought, inoffensive: People were being convicted by American courts and then conclusively proved innocent. Some lost years or even decades of their lives. Some were Pennsylvanians. If this outrage could be fixed, the advisory committee was tasked to find out how (Lappas, 2011). Most of the committee members expected the effort to be non-controversial; after all, hundreds of people nationwide had been cleared by DNA analysis after being convicted of terrible crimes. Guilty verdicts were returned by conscientious juries, reviewed by experienced judges, affirmed by competent courts, and yet DNA would subsequently reveal that many of those convicted were really innocent. Who could object to efforts to eliminate false convictions? What could be worse than taking innocent citizens, ruining their lives and throwing them in prison for crimes they didn't do? (Lappas, 2006). If there was a way to avoid future similar injustices, SR 381 charged the Advisory Committee to find out how. It sounded non-controversial. It wasn't.

The Pennsylvania District Attorney's Association approached this perceived threat to their supremacy over the state's criminal justice system as if they were prosecuting a trial for felonious obstruction of justice. Their opening statement came in the form of a March 21, 2007, letter to the members of the Joint State Government Commission, in which the president and legislative chair of that association trivialized similar commissions in other states as the darlings of "anti-death-penalty activists, criminal defense attorneys and inmate advocates" (Pennsylvania District Attorneys Association Letter, 2007, p. 1). They described the composition of the Pennsylvania Advisory Committee as a bunch of "the most vocal of Pennsylvania's anti-death-penalty movement, criminal defense ideologues and other activists [with] a strong bias against prosecution and in favor of criminal defendants and inmates seeking to overturn their convictions" (Id., p. 2). As opposed to the letter writers and their prosecutor colleagues who are "honor bound to a system that, by design and practice, protects the innocent" (Id., p. 2), those seeking reform were a "small but vocal minority of critics of the criminal justice system" (Id., p. 3). Worse yet, the letter warned that the reformers had "radical personal agendas" (Id., p. 2).

Not surprisingly, the case for the prosecution continued, the committee was likely to produce a "predetermined ... final report" (Id., p. 4) thus failing in its duty of "objective analysis" (Id., p. 2). The idea that this particular committee could "earnestly deliver an analysis that [was] fair and objective" should be re-considered, advised the prosecutors, lest the Joint State Government Commission "give its imprimatur to a report generated by such a one-sided and predisposed committee" (Id., p. 2).

Exhibit A for the prosecution was the Pennsylvania District Attorneys Association Legislative Staff's "Fact Sheet," which exposed their grievances with Chairman Rago. The "Fact Sheet" called Rago "an advocate on behalf of criminal defendants" who foolishly relied on such dubious authorities as Barry Scheck, David Rudovsky, Scott Turow, and James Liebman[1]

(Pennsylvania District Attorneys Association Fact Sheet, 2007, p. 3). The predisposed Rago had "already firmly made up his mind," and the prosecutors charged that "any product of such a committee cannot reflect well on either the neutrality or the reliability of the Joint State Government Commission" (Id., p. 3).

As the prosecution of the Advisory Committee and its mission proceeded, the court of public opinion heard from James Martin, the president of the District Attorneys Association, whose opinion piece the *Harrisburg Patriot* newspaper published under the headline "State Crime Panel Stacked Against Justice" (Martin, 2007). Martin acknowledged that improvement of conviction accuracy was a goal that "would seem worthy and reasonable" but he argued that it only seems that way "on the surface." In fact, he warned, the committee membership assured that it would "fail to provide Pennsylvania with the kind of objective analysis necessary to preserve the integrity of the state's governmental process and our criminal justice system." The committee was doomed, it seemed, because while four of its members were prosecutors, the rest were attorneys, law professors, prisoner rights advocates, public defenders, "and others determined to tear away at the criminal justice system." While prosecutors promised to "do the right thing for the right reason," the other advisors would use the committee as a "bully pulpit" for their nefarious "biases." This work threatened to deal "a blow to the integrity of the governmental process" and to deliver "injustice to crime victims and their families" (Id.). All this, and the committee had not yet done a single thing.

To address the prosecution's case, the Senate eventually appointed more law enforcement advisors until they made up seventeen out of a total membership of 52. After achieving this numerical supremacy (only 11 advisors were criminal defense lawyers), the prosecutors nonetheless continued to push their arithmetically unsound complaint that they were "outnumbered" and "severely underrepresented" (Minority Report, p. 3).

Over the course of four years and 34 meetings, during which some advisors were replaced, others changed jobs, some left public office, and three died, the committee heard from leading academic and legal experts on the causes of wrongful convictions. Throughout this work, the prosecutors on the committee frustrated any meaningful consensus on even the most basic questions: What is a wrongful conviction? What does it mean to be "innocent?" What was the committee supposed to be doing?

Some prosecutors suggested that the committee should not study exonerations at all but should instead study cases where the defendant's conviction was correct. They argued that the convictions of hundreds of exonerated convicts should take a backseat to a celebration that in other cases, maybe millions of others, the system had got it right. Studying the causes of correct verdicts was not, of course, the committee's mission (SR 381; 2006). When one advisor correctly noted that "we were not charged with patting ourselves on the back for getting 99% of the defendants who were guilty," two prosecutors reproached him for "sarcasm" and "personal attacks" (Advisory Committee, June 7, 2007, audio recording).

As witnesses appeared before the committee, the prosecution put their cross-examination skills to full effect. On June 7, 2007, when Canadian social psychologist Tara Burke described the methodology which she and her colleagues have used to identify the causes of some wrongful convictions, her appearance provoked a blistering prosecutorial attack on everything from her sample set to her acceptance of DNA exclusion as convincing proof of innocence. One Pennsylvania prosecutor demonstrated the prevailing antipathy for innocence determinations by criticizing an inclusion of Chester County, Pennsylvania's Dale Bryson among a sample of exonerees. Bryson had been convicted of rape and then cleared by DNA. He was released and later convicted, apparently correctly, for an unrelated rape. His earlier exoneration was characterized as a mistake, and one that cast doubt on any methodology which would consider Bryson innocent of the first rape. His later rape conviction confirmed his guilt of the earlier one, for which DNA forensics had already cleared him. "His behavior immediately after getting out of prison," the prosecutor claimed, "reinforced *everybody's* belief that he was that rapist because he raped [someone else]" (Advisory Committee, audio recording of June 7, 2007; emphasis added). The fact that he committed a later crime proved that he had committed an earlier one. Despite the DNA, which had excluded him as that rapist, he was "never exonerated" (Id.). Five years later, Professor Burke still recalled the "giant divide between prosecution and defense" which prevailed within the Advisory Committee and noted that the prosecution's "stereotypical" positions "further supported much of the social psychological literature regarding biases (such as confirmation bias) that I was speaking about in the first place" (Burke email, 2012).

When John Jay College of Criminal Justice professor Saul Kassin spoke to the committee, a district attorney representative railed that "sometimes people in your position *can do a disservice to a committee* like this and to the criminal justice system when you create a false impression that our system is so severely broken." When Professor Kassin asked the prosecutor to identify any specific case studies that he disliked, the prosecutor denounced "all of them" (Advisory Committee, August 8, 2008 meeting audio recording). After the chairman criticized the unwarranted *ad hominem* attack, the prosecutor further dismissed Kassin as a mere "defense expert" (Id.):

> "The most fundamental principle of American jurisprudence" is "that an innocent man not be punished for the crimes of another."
> (Advisory Committee Report, 2011, p. 3)

On September 20, 2011, the Advisory Committee completed its work and issued a 316-page report detailing its findings and making recommendations to mitigate the recognized causes of wrong convictions (Advisory Committee Report, 2011). The report correctly stated that "Causes of wrongful convictions are commonly determined to be mistaken eyewitness identifications; false confessions; perjurious informant testimony; inaccurate scientific evidence; prosecutorial and defense lawyer misconduct; and inadequate funding for defense services." Some of these causes are sometimes described by varying terminology, but "at this juncture, the primary causes of wrongful convictions are well understood" (Id., p. 3).

The report went on to acknowledge, but greatly understated, the contention which had prevailed over the previous four years. "While there was some consensus on these recommendations, members remain sharply divided on the advisability of adopting or implementing some or all of these recommendations. Some advisors question whether a foundation has been established to recommend any of these proposals and fear that their implementation could create more injustice" (Id., p. 4). With brave optimism, the report stated that "despite these differences, the advisory committee shares a number of interests central to maintaining public confidence in conviction integrity. Members agree that no innocent person should be punished for a crime he did not commit" (Id.).

This optimism would not survive the prosecution's closing argument. Two short hours after Chairman Rago presented the report to the Pennsylvania Senate, the District Attorneys Association issued a press release titled, "Report Would Create Roadblocks to Justice" (Pennsylvania District Attorneys Association Press Release, 2011). The statement alleged that "Law enforcement and crime victim representatives serving on a legislative commission studying so-called 'wrongful convictions' [internal quotation marks in original] expressed today strong opposition to a final report saying it failed to properly conduct an independent study, contains predetermined conclusions and makes recommendations never considered or voted on by the committee" (Id.). According to the Association's current president, "This report was clearly written for the purposes of public relations, but [the District Attorneys] are deeply concerned that its recommendations have the potential to create roadblocks to justice" (Id.). The Pennsylvania Victim Advocate complained that "this report will create miscarriages of justice for victims by creating more wrongful acquittals of the guilty" (Id.) and the legislative representative for the Fraternal Order of Police was appalled that "this advisory committee and its final report takes the position that we should trust academics and the defense attorneys before we trust citizen juries" (Id.). Indeed, even the fact of exoneration itself was disputed. "[T]he report includes the guilty in its definition of 'innocent'" (Id.).

That same day, a faction of 14 law enforcement advisors released an 83-page document entitled, "Independent Report of Law Enforcement and Victim Representative Members of the Advisory Committee on Wrongful Convictions" (Minority Report, 2011). That report took issue with nearly everything the Advisory Committee had done, from process to result, and charged it with having reached a "result that would primarily benefit the guilty and deny justice to victims." The recommendations were "flawed and one-sided" and would "make [. . .] Pennsylvania less safe" (Minority Report, 2011, pp. 2, 5). The Minority Report called the committee's recommendations "radical" (Id., p. 5), "unconstitutional" (Id., p. 52), "unrealistic" (Id., p. 51), "misleading" (Id., p. 49), "logistically impossible" (Id., p. 47), and "unnecessary," and predicted that they would simply "facilitate gamesmanship" (Id., p. 50). The battle over eyewitness misidentifications exemplifies the discord:

Other causes of wrongful convictions have been recurrently found, but convictions based partly or completely on mistaken eyewitness identifications have been shown to comprise the vast majority of the DNA exoneration cases in the United States. As importantly, this reflects data for the past 100 years as almost every study of wrongful convictions confirms that roughly two-thirds or more involve eyewitness misidentification.

(Advisory Committee Report, 2011, p. 21)

The Advisory Committee heard from five witnesses with various types of expertise in the study and presentation of eyewitness identifications. New Jersey Deputy Attorney General Lori Linskey described the reforms which her state's Supreme Court had instigated with its decision in *New Jersey v. Cromedy* (12 years before the *Henderson* decision which we will discuss further). Detective William Wynn described his handling of over 15,000 live line-ups for the Philadelphia Police Department's Major Crimes Division. Pennsylvania State Police Sergeant Raymond Guth and Captain Bret Waggonner described their department's live and photo identification procedures. Psychologist Gary Wells described his 30 years of research on identification accuracy.

Based on this testimony and a survey of scientific and legal literature, the committee made the following two modest proposals:

A rule of criminal procedure should be amended to require defense counsel in capital cases to be educated on evidence relating to eye-witness identification [and a] statute should require the adminis-tration of lineups and photo arrays to be conducted by a person who does not know either which one is suspected by investigators or which one is being viewed by the witness.

(Advisory Committee Report, 2011, p. 5)

While other recommendations were presented as part of the best practices implemented in other jurisdictions nationwide (Id., pp. 31–38), "blind administration" (i.e., a police procedure in which the detective conducting the photographic or live line-up does not know which of the participants is the police suspect and therefore cannot inadvertently direct the witness's attention to that suspect) was cited, particularly by Professor

Wells, as the most important reform (Id., pp. 5, 49–51; Wells, 1998). The prosecutors were outraged.

First, the very suggestion that faulty eyewitness identifications lead to bad convictions perpetuated the "defense myth that ordinary jurors cannot be trusted to judge for themselves which witnesses are credible and which are not" (Minority Report, 2011, p. 4). The preference for blind administration slandered the integrity of police by "offensively and baselessly presum[ing] that police investigators in Pennsylvania have been obtaining identifications by suggesting to witnesses, either intentionally or through incompetence, which members of lineups and photo arrays are the suspects" (Id., p. 47). This scandalous charge of police "untrustworthiness" rested on nothing more than the ravings of "a committee of law professors, defense attorneys, and defense experts" which could be safely ignored in favor of "plac[ing] our trust in the collective wisdom, experience, and common sense of twelve ordinary jurors" (Id., p.4). Never mind that decades of research had found that honest, and thus credible, witnesses mis-identify defendants, and that psychological studies had established that jurors are falsely convinced by such unreliable factors as witness certainty and immediacy of selection. Those findings, and any proposals that rely on them, may be comfortably disregarded because they "do not reflect true science" at all, describing instead a false "world view" that tells us little about "how the mind operates" (Id., p. 4).

With unintended irony, the Minority Report argued against blind administration stating that "officers who have investigated a case tend to be more successful than outside officers at obtaining identifications [because of] the entirely legitimate reason that the investigating officer has time to develop a relationship with frightened and reluctant witnesses, making the witnesses feel *safe and invested in the identification process*" (Id., p. 47; emphasis added). Invested in the identification process? In Pennsylvania's neighbor to the east, the police practice of making witnesses feel "invested" in the identification-making process provoked a revolution in identification jurisprudence, confirming, for example, the wisdom of the Advisory Committee's recommendations.

The Advisory Committee and Minority Reports were both issued 27 days after the New Jersey Supreme Court's groundbreaking decision in *New Jersey v. Henderson*, which informs the continuing debate about eyewitnesses (*New Jersey v. Henderson*, 2011). In *Henderson*, the New Jersey court carried forward the concerns which it had earlier expressed in *New Jersey v. Cromedy* (1999) and which New Jersey Deputy Attorney General Lori Linskey reported to the Advisory Committee on March 5, 2008. In *Cromedy,* the court addressed the "novel issue" (*Cromedy,* 1999, p. 15) of whether trial courts should give cross-racial identification jury instructions which would "alert the jury through a cautionary instruction that it should pay close attention to a possible influence of race" on a witness's selection of the defendant as the criminal perpetrator (*Cromedy,* 1999, p. 133). After the Court mandated such instructions, Cromedy was exonerated by DNA evidence (Advisory Committee Meeting Summary, March 5, 2008). These developments led to the New Jersey Attorney General's promulgation of statewide "guidelines for best practices" for pre-trial identifications (Id.). Those guidelines, which included blind administration of sequential photo-arrays, in turn led to the New Jersey Court's 2011 recognition in *New Jersey v. Henderson* (2011), that "a vast body of scientific research about human memory has emerged. That body of work casts doubt on some commonly held views relating to memory. It also calls into question the vitality of the current legal framework for analyzing the reliability of eyewitness identifications" (*Henderson,* 2011, p. 217).

The *Henderson* Court, through a special master, reviewed the science of estimator variables and system variables, and ruled for the first time that "when defendants can show some evidence of suggestiveness [in the police identification procedure], all relevant system and estimator variables should be explored at pretrial hearings ... [and] the trial judge should weigh both sets of variables to decide if the [identification] evidence is admissible" (Id., p. 218). In accepting the scientific evidence that police suggestiveness ("system variables") can provoke mis-identification, the *Henderson* Court rejected prosecution arguments, similar to those made in the Pennsylvania Minority Report, that "eyewitness identification science is probabilistic—meaning that it cannot determine if a particular identification is accurate" and that "the legal system should continue to rely on jurors to assess the credibility of eyewitnesses" (*Henderson,* p. 280). The *Henderson* court refused to order pre-trial hearings in all cases or to mandate suppression whenever the Attorney General's guidelines were violated but it did recognize that eyewitness identification evidence "present[s] certain complicated issues requiring careful consider[ation] ... to weed out unreliable identifications" (Id., pp. 292–293). In *Henderson,* the police violation occurred when the investigating detectives took part in the photo-array procedure, thus, encouraging an identification by helping the witness feel "invested" in the process (Id., pp. 223–224).[2]

The need for the sort of eyewitness reforms which *Henderson* mandated and which the Pennsylvania Advisory Committee recommended took on greater urgency with the United States Supreme Court's 2012 ruling in *Perry v. New Hampshire* (2012). There, the defense asked the Court to constitutionalize eyewitness reliability for "all identifications which arise from impermissibly suggestive circumstances and which are very substantially likely to lead to misidentifications." This issue presented the risk of estimator variables in its purest form: where the police do nothing wrong (and so there are no corrupting system variables) can the fact of suggestiveness alone implicate due process concerns? Perry was identified by a witness who saw him in police custody at the crime scene and later failed to identify him at trial (*Perry*, 2012). The Court refused to require trial judges routinely to assess identification reliability ("the Due Process Clause does not require a preliminary judicial inquiry into the reliability of an eyewitness identification when the identification was not procured under unnecessarily suggestive circumstances arranged by law enforcement") (Id., p. 730), resting largely on the "recognition that the jury, not the judge, traditionally determines the reliability of evidence" (Id., p. 719). Or, as Justice Scalia asked at the *Perry* oral argument, "Why is unreliable eyewitness identification any different than unreliable anything else?" (*Perry*, 2011, Transcript of Oral Argument, p. 4).

> Our position is that the logic of this Court's precedents is that there is no right at present to actual innocence.
>
> (Deputy Solicitor General Neal Katyal,
> Oral Argument, *District Attorney v. Osborne*, pp. 24–25)

But beyond arguments about eyewitnesses, committees, and convictions, the present day debate about innocence is an ontological struggle. As the earlier synopses of the *Doswell* and *Moto* cases illustrate, reformers and prosecutors now contend over what it really means to be innocent. Is there a difference between legal innocence and factual innocence? And if so, which one is actual innocence? This problem is not an "example of the legal profession's ability to obfuscate even basic propositions," in Scott

Sundby's memorable phrase (Sundby, p. 459). Rather it asks deep questions about whether the presumption of innocence can ever be revived, and whether it need ever be respected, when a once-convicted defendant is later vindicated. Prosecutors and some courts have used these questions to stake out a new tactic in the war on exonerations: once convicted, they argue, no exoneree can ever again be called innocent.

Although the United States Constitution does not expressly mention the presumption of innocence nor any particular burden of proof, the absence of reasonable doubt has traditionally and unequivocally drawn the line between guilt and innocence in American jurisprudence (*Winship*, 1970). The United States Supreme Court has called the reasonable doubt standard "an ancient and honored aspect of our criminal justice system" but one which "defies easy explication" (*Victor v. Nebraska*, 1994, p. 5). The reasonable doubt standard "provides concrete substance for the presumption of innocence—that bedrock 'axiomatic and elementary' principle whose 'enforcement lies at the foundation of the administration of our criminal law'" (*Winship*, 1970, p. 363). But reasonable doubt creates a dilemma: it requires that proof of guilt must be strong, but allows that it need not be absolute. The government's case need not extinguish all doubts, just those which the law—using any constitutional formulation—considers reasonable. The strange result is that a defendant who is legally guilty beyond reasonable doubt may indeed still be factually innocent. "One cannot have a system of criminal punishment without accepting the possibility that someone will be punished mistakenly" (*Kansas v. Marsh*, 2006, Scalia concurring, p. 199). Prosecutors routinely tell juries, explicitly or implicitly, that they can harbor some doubt about a defendant's guilt and convict nonetheless.

As Pennsylvania has painfully learned, however, after conviction and exoneration, prosecutors translate an earlier and discredited absence of reasonable doubt into a lingering and absolute proof of guilt. When the minority members claimed that the Committee Report "cannot distinguish between the innocent and the guilty" (Minority Report, 2011, p. 40), they rejected acquittals, dismissals of charges, appellate reversals, DNA exclusions, and post-conviction vindications as indicia of wrongful convictions. The Minority cited a prosecutor's article, aptly sub-titled "The Myth of Innocence," to warn against "call[ing] someone 'innocent' when all they managed to do was wriggle through some procedural cracks in the justice system." Such chicanery "cheapens the word and impeaches the moral authority of those who claim that a person has been 'exonerated'" (Marquis, 2005, p. 508). The Minority's analysis of the Pennsylvania Eight exonerations demonstrates their skepticism that factual innocence ever survives a vacated finding of guilt.

As previously noted, the Minority finds Dale Bryson, exonerated by DNA, guilty nonetheless because of his later crimes. Furthermore, the first victim's mistaken identification of Bryson constitutes evidence that "his crimes included the one for which he was supposedly 'exonerated'" (Minority Report, 2011, pp. 25–27).

Thomas Doswell, convicted by rape victim identification and cleared by DNA, does not deserve to be called innocent because "an impartial person in a much better position to know" (the victim) "disagrees with the [Committee] report's claim" of Doswell's innocence (Id., pp. 28–29).

The Minority report describes Bruce Godschalk, convicted of two rapes by a victim identification and his own false confession before he was cleared by DNA, as having been convicted by "overwhelming evidence." Even though the Minority acknowledges a reasonable doubt about his guilt, they call his right to be called innocent "not so clear" (Id., p. 30).

For Vincent Moto, convicted of rape by the victim's identification in spite of an alibi and later cleared by DNA, "the evidence of . . . guilt has always been strong." If the victim had come forward for the court-ordered second trial, prosecutors would have bravely been "more than willing to meet the challenge" of the DNA evidence. When Moto sought to have his wrongful conviction expunged, the Supreme Court refused. Scientific proof of Moto's innocence did not trump the absent victim's mistaken belief in his guilt (Id., pp. 32–34).

Bruce Nelson fares no better in the Minority's consideration. Even though DNA identified Nelson's alleged accomplice as the sole rapist, calling him exonerated "goes too far," in large part because the accomplice, an admitted rapist, "remains adamant to this day that he and Nelson committed the crime together" (Id., pp. 34–36).

Willie Nesmith, convicted of rape and assault before being excluded by DNA after lengthy imprisonment, "was never exonerated in any meaningful sense and the evidence of his guilt remains compelling" (Id., p. 36). The support for this proposition comes, curiously, from the prosecutor's decision to dismiss the case after the DNA exclusion and, like

Bryson, the fact that he later committed other crimes and was suspected of one for which he was never even arrested (Id., pp. 36–37).

Nicholas Yarris was convicted of rape and murder based largely on his false and contradictory confessions. DNA analysis of the victim's fingernail scrapings and rape kit evidence eventually cleared him, but the Minority Report calls his innocence "not conclusively prove[n]" and says that "there is no way to know for sure whether he was convicted of a crime he did not commit" (Id., pp. 37–40).[3]

In each of these cases, the Minority refuses to accept proof of wrongful conviction or to recognize that the overthrow of the guilty verdict reinstates the presumption of innocence. "Innocent until proven guilty" has given way to "never innocent again." Thus do prosecutors and courts try to convince the public that no proof of innocence is good enough. If the jury's earlier mistake remains "compelling proof of guilt," (Minority Report, 2011, p. 36) then no one can be considered exonerated, and it follows that no conviction can ever be wrongful.

This is hardly a new approach. In his concurrence in *Kansas v Marsh*, Justice Scalia complained about the "mischaracterization of reversible error as actual innocence," (*Kansas v. Marsh*, 2006, p. 196) and claimed that "a not guilty verdict expresses no view as to a defendant's innocence" (Id., p. 194). In *Herrera v. Collins* (1993), the United States Supreme Court refused to save a condemnee based on the affidavits of an eyewitness and a judge to whom the real killer had confessed. Herrera had already been convicted after all, and the new evidence of his innocence "must be considered in light of the proof of [his] guilt at trial" (Id., p. 418). In his article "Exoneration Inflation," California prosecutor Ward Campbell contends that acquittals, dismissals, reversals, habeas corpus grants, specific findings of reasonable doubt, and even evidentiary insufficiency don't present "prototypical" examples of actual innocence (Campbell, 2008, p. 54). In "Protecting the Innocent: A Response to the Bedau-Radelet Study," prosecutors Stephen Markman and Paul Cassell criticized the "methodology" of Hugo Bedau and Michael Radelet, who concluded that James Adams, executed by the state of Florida in 1974, was innocent. Not only did Bedau and Radelet have "little evidence" to prove Adams' innocence, but the prosecutors charged that they had ignored the "compelling evidence that convinced a unanimous jury beyond a reasonable doubt" (Markman and Cassell, 1998, p. 131).

In Pennsylvania, as elsewhere, prosecutors often view themselves as the only reliable guardians of virtue. The Minority Report authors call themselves "the committee members most experienced in law enforcement and victim representation" (Minority Report, 2011, p. 2). The District Attorneys Association proclaims them to be "duty bound to a system that is filled with the strictest guidelines, checks and balances, and rights and privileges provided by the law" (Pennsylvania District Attorneys Association Letter, 2007, p. 2). They are "held to the highest professional and ethical standards of any attorneys," (Minority Report, 2011, p. 55) and bear "the overriding duty and responsibility to seek truth in justice, regardless of where the search may lead" (Martin, 2007).

And yet, when it comes to seeking the truth of innocence, our duty bound public servants set the bar impossibly high. Like Procrustes on the ancient road to Athens, they chop and stretch any available proof of innocence until they make it fit their iron bed of guilt. Every test of innocence and each absence of guilty proof falls short, while every whiff of suspicion, piece of discredited evidence, and mistaken verdict represents proof positive that the system casts a narrow and well-aimed net. The fact that Willie Nesmith was suspected of a crime for which he was never even arrested is regarded as supporting the likelihood of his guilt of an unrelated rape of which he had been exonerated (Minority Report, 2011, p. 37).

So all citizens with concerns about wrongful convictions have the right to wonder this: What proof of innocence could ever satisfy the law enforcement establishment? Either some innocent people are convicted or none are. Those who acknowledge the possibility of injustice should work together to mitigate it. Prosecutors must certainly have their say, but reform efforts would go much more smoothly if they could just bring themselves to acknowledge there are at least some false convictions, each of which began as some prosecutor's mistake.

Notes

1 Barry Scheck, a lawyer and law professor in New York City, is one of the founders of The Innocence Project, whose work has exonerated hundreds of falsely convicted prisoners. Scott Turow, the novelist and Chicago attorney, is the author of *Ultimate Punishment: A Lawyer's Reflections on Dealing with the Death Penalty*, 2004. James Liebman, the Simon H. Rifkind Professor of Law at Columbia University School of Law, is a frequent writer and commentator on criminal law issues. David Rudovsky, who practices law in Philadelphia and is also on the faculty of the University of Pennsylvania Law School, was an inaugural member of the Advisory Committee and served as post-conviction counsel for Bruce

Godschalk, one of the "Pennsylvania Eight" exonerees. In 1986, Rudovsky received a Macarthur Foundation Fellowship, the so-called "genius award," for his accomplishments in civil rights law and criminal defense.

2   In *Henderson*, an eyewitness was having difficulty making an identification from a photo-spread administered in the state-mandated double blind fashion. The investigating detectives then became involved in the process, confronted the witness and helped him to become *invested* in the process by demanding that he "just do what you have to do and we'll be out of here." Thus encouraged, the invested witness identified Henderson, leading to a statewide judicial reevaluation and revamping of eyewitness procedures.

3   The one exoneree for whom the Minority acknowledges innocence is Barry Laughman, who was convicted mainly on his false confession and was later exonerated after DNA evidence established his innocence. The Minority Report does not explain why Laughman's DNA exoneration is more compelling than Doswell's, Moto's, Bryson's, Yarris's, Nelson's, Godschalk's, or Nesmith's (Minority Report, 2011, pp. 31–32).

References

Bedau, H. A. and Radelet, M. L. (1987) Miscarriages of Justice in Potentially Capital Cases. *Stanford Law Review*, 40, p. 21.

Campbell, W. A. (2008) Exoneration Inflation: Justice Scalia's Concurrence in Kansas v. Marsh. *IACJ Journal*, Summer 2008, pp. 49–63. Online version retrieved from http://www.cjlf.org/files/CampbellExonerationInflation2008.pdf. Last visited May 15, 2012.

Lappas, S. (2006) The Embarrassment of Innocence. *The Champion*, August 2006.

Lappas, S., Pennsylvania Can Stop Wrongful Convictions. (October 02, 2011) *Harrisburg (Pennsylvania) Sunday Patriot News*. Retrieved from http://www.pennlive.com/editorials/index.ssf/2011/10/pa_can_stop_wrongful_convictio.html.

Markman, S. J. and Cassell, P. G. (1988) Protecting the Innocent: A Response to the Bedau-Radelet Study. *Stanford Law Review*, 41, pp. 121–160.

Marquis, J. (2005) Innocence in Capital Sentencing: The Myth of Innocence. *Journal of Criminal Law and Criminology*, 95, p. 501.

Martin, J. (March 25, 2007) State Crime Panel Stacked Against Justice. Too Many Death Penalty Foes, Activists, Lawyers, are on List. *Harrisburg (Pennsylvania) Sunday Patriot News*. Op-ed page.

Pennsylvania Advisory Committee for the Study of Wrongful Convictions. Audio Recording of the Meeting of the Investigations and Legal Representation Subcommittee, June 7, 2007.

Pennsylvania Advisory Committee for the Study of Wrongful Convictions. Audio Recording of the Meeting of the Investigations and Legal Representation Subcommittee, August 5, 2008.

Pennsylvania Advisory Committee for the Study of Wrongful Convictions (2011). Report of the Advisory Committee on Wrongful Convictions. Retrieved from http://www.innocenceproject.org/docs/2011/PA_WC_Report.pdf. Cited throughout this chapter as "Committee Report."

Pennsylvania Advisory Committee for the Study of Wrongful Convictions (fourteen minority members). Independent Report of Law Enforcement and Victim Representative Members of the Advisory Committee on Wrongful Convictions. (2011). Retrieved from http://www.pdaa.org/images/stories/pdf/law_enforcement_report_final_19_sep_11.pdf. Cited throughout this chapter as "Minority Report."

Pennsylvania Advisory Committee for the Study of Wrongful Convictions. Summary of Proceedings of the Meeting of the Investigations and Legal Representation Subcommittee, March 5, 2008.

Pennsylvania Advisory Committee for the Study of Wrongful Convictions (August 5, 2008). Summary of Proceedings of the Meeting of the Investigations and Legal Representation Subcommittee.

Pennsylvania District Attorneys Association (2007). Fact Sheet: John T. Rago, Esq., Chairman of the Joint State Government Commission's Wrongful Convictions Committee, 2007.

Pennsylvania District Attorneys Association, Press Release, Report Would Create Roadblocks to Justice (2011). Retrieved from http://www.pdaa.org/index.php?option=com_content &view=article&id=139:report-would-create-roadblocks-to-justice&catid=48:press-pdaa& Itemid=64. Last visited on May 15, 2012.

Pennsylvania District Attorneys Association (March 21, 2007). Letter to Selected Members of the Pennsylvania Joint State Government Commission.

Pennsylvania Senate Bill 1069 (Sess. of 2006).

Pennsylvania Senate Resolution 281 of 2006.

Personal Communication, email from Tara Burke, May 1, 2012.

Rago, J. (2006) A Fine Line Between Chaos and Creation: Lessons on Innocence Reform from the Pennsylvania Eight. *Widener Law Review*, 12, pp. 359–440.

Sundby, S., (1989) The Reasonable Doubt Rule and the Meaning of Innocence. *Hastings Law Journal*, 40, pp. 457–510.

Time Lost: What's Fair Compensation for an Innocent Man? (January 5, 2010). *Pittsburgh (Pennsylvania) Post Gazette*. Retrieved from http://old.post-gazette.com/pg/10005/1025737-192.stm#ixzz1v8hxtnrX; http://old.post- gazette.com/pg/10005/1025737-192.stm.

Wells, G., et al. (1998) Eyewitness Identification Procedures: Recommendations for Lineups and Photospreads. *Law and Human Behavior*, 22, p. 603.

Wells, G.L. (1978) Applied Eyewitness-Testimony Research: System Variables and Estimator Variables. *Journal of Personality and Social Psychology*, 36, pp. 1546–1557.

Cases

Doswell v. City of Pittsburgh, 2009 WestLaw 1734199 (W.D. Pa. 2009).

Herrera v. Collins, 506 U.S. 390 (1993).

In re Winship, 397 U.S. 358 (1970).

Kansas v. Marsh, 548 U.S. 163, 126 S.Ct. 2516, 165 L.Ed. 2d 429 (2006).

New Jersey v. Cromedy, 158 N.J. 112, 727 A.2d 457 (1999).

New Jersey v. Henderson, 208 N.J. 208, 27 A.3d 872 (2011).

Osborne v. District Attorney of Anchorage, Alaska, transcript of Supreme Court Oral Argument (2011). Retrieved from http://www.supremecourt.gov/oral_arguments_transcripts/08-6.pdf.

Pennsylvania v. Moto, 23 A.3d 989 (Pa. Supreme Ct. 2011).

Perry v. New Hampshire, 132 S.Ct.716 (2012).

Perry v. New Hampshire, transcript of Supreme Court Oral Argument (2011) retrieved from http://www.supremecourt.gov/oral_arguments/argument_transcripts/10-8974.pdf.

Victor v. Nebraska, 511 U.S. 1, 114 S.Ct. 1239 (1994).

16

EDWIN BORCHARD AND THE
LIMITS OF INNOCENCE REFORM

Marvin Zalman[1]

Edwin Borchard (1932), often cited as the originator of wrongful conviction scholarship, may be viewed as the patron saint of the American innocence movement. Borchard's career has not been studied by wrongful conviction scholars. This paper explores the intellectual and ideological roots of *Convicting the Innocent* and Borchard's activist career in enacting compensation laws. His innocence work was of a piece—intellectually, politically, and strategically—with his other pursuits in international and domestic law and policy before and during his tenure at Yale Law School from 1917 to 1951. His work was rooted in comparative law scholarship and was consistently used to advance progressive policies.

Convicting the Innocent provides early wrongful conviction examples and the first list of "causes," but otherwise does little to advance understanding of innocence issues. Exploring Borchard's career does provide a case study in policy change by the efforts of a determined, astute, and well-connected individual. But there is more to learn from what Borchard did *not* achieve. Burgeoning innocence research and reform today encompasses a dozen major components of criminal justice (Norris, Bonventre, Redlich, and Acker, 2011; Risinger and Risinger, 2012). Borchard's policy prescriptions, to the contrary, were anemic or utopian, with the exception of indemnifying falsely convicted prisoners (Borchard, 1932, pp. xiii–xviv). Some of his ideas were prescient, foreshadowing blind lineups and North Carolina's innovative post-conviction review mechanism (North Carolina, 2011). Nevertheless, except for compensating the innocent, which Borchard almost single-handedly brought into American law, the other proposals were non-starters.

More to the point, Borchard could not have conceived of fundamentally improved police investigation, prosecution, or adjudication processes, necessary for innocence reform, which like any enterprise is embedded in the practices, technologies, structures, and ideologies of its time. Contemporary approaches to innocence reform were not possible before the 1970s, due not simply to the lack of DNA testing, but largely to earlier organizational limitations and the socio-political context of criminal justice. The deep justice system changes called for by innocence reforms are possible today because of significant institutional changes in police departments and law schools, and some changed thinking among prosecutors and judges, that were not part of Edwin Borchard's world.

This thesis harbors a paradox. Most false convictions occur because of systemic criminal justice process flaws. Individual malfeasance is enabled by supervision lapses. Purely "accidental" wrongful convictions do not occur because participants' good faith and subjectively reasonable behaviors mask faulty procedures. Despite this, innocence reforms are feasible, and are being implemented in many jurisdictions today, because criminal justice agencies and institutions have improved significantly in the last 40 to 80 years.

The Progressive and Comparative Law Roots of *Convicting the Innocent*

The motive and ideas underlying *Convicting the Innocent* were found in Borchard's (1913a) early article, "European Systems of State Indemnity for Errors of Criminal Justice," which the book reprinted in its *entirety*. The 1932 book added a draft statute "to grant relief to persons erroneously convicted in courts of the United States" (Borchard, 1932, p. 417), which Borchard originally drafted in 1912 and had introduced in the Senate (Borchard, 1912b). His lobbying activity after the book's publication demonstrates that the motive behind *Convicting the Innocent* was to enact compensation legislation. *Convicting the Innocent*, by establishing the degree to which wrongful convictions were routine, provided the factual basis for enacting compensation legislation.

"European Systems" reviewed medieval and Enlightenment era laws on the subject, and analyzed the compensation statutes of 17 other countries ranging alphabetically from Austria to the Swiss canton of Vaud. An appendix reprinted several. Borchard accused American jurisdictions of avoiding the indemnification of "these unfortunate victims of mistakes in the administration of the criminal law, although cases of shocking injustice are of not infrequent occurrence" (Borchard, 1913a, p. 684). "European Systems" also offers a clue to the case vignette methodology utilized in his later book, a "large collection of cases of unjust executions and sentences of life imprisonment" written by a German attorney and published in Berlin in 1911 (Borchard, 1913a, p. 706 n. 523, referring to Sello, 1911).

By 1913 the 28-year-old Edwin Borchard had risen to prominence in American international law. Raised in a prosperous and cultured environment in New York, he earned a law degree from New York Law School in 1905 and a B.A. from Columbia College. He continued doctoral work at Columbia in international law under John Bassett Moore, the preeminent American international law scholar and a central figure in American diplomacy. He was a staff member of the Library of Congress in Washington, becoming the Law Librarian in 1911. His 1913 dissertation on *The Diplomatic Protection of Citizens Abroad* was published commercially and remains a classic in international law (Borchard, 1915). While on the Library of Congress staff, he advised an American arbitration delegation at The Hague in 1910. From 1911 to 1917 Borchard was Law Librarian of Congress, served as assistant solicitor for the State Department, and practiced law for a year, before being hired by the Yale Law School (Kalman, 1986, pp. 99–103). During his tenure at Yale, Borchard served in a number of official diplomatic posts (Doenecke, 1977; Mayer, 2000).

Several factors explain Borchard's advocacy for wrongful conviction compensation laws in 1913 and his success in shepherding a federal compensation law to existence a quarter-century later. These include deep knowledge of international and comparative law, a progressive ideology, wide-ranging influential contacts, and an indefatigable advocacy style. These strands came together when he received the pen which President Franklin Roosevelt used to sign the federal wrongful conviction compensation law in 1938 ("Edwin Borchard," 1951; Borchard, 1938, June 8).

Borchard, tasked with building up the Library of Congress's foreign law collection, visited western European capitals "to secure, by personal interview, information from lawyers, judges, professors, and law librarians as to the literature of their respective countries" following his mission at The Hague (Putnam, 1911, p. 36). He wrote several bibliographies of foreign laws (Borchard, 1912a; Borchard, 1913b; Borchard, 1917). Borchard thus gained mastery over the corpus of European law. When combined with doctoral dissertation work, it provided the source material for "European Systems." Why Borchard was drawn to the issue of state indemnity for errors of criminal justice in the first place requires some speculation.

First, wrongful convictions were not unknown. Borchard cited the famous Adolf Beck wrongful conviction, leading to England's Court of Criminal Appeals, and other cases (Borchard, 1913a, p. 688, n.1a; Pattenden, 1996). The many cases he later recounted, the yellow press's fixation on crime, and the book on German miscarriages of justice, indicate that wrongful convictions were newsworthy (Borchard 1932; Collins, 2011; Sello, 1911). Yet, availability and notice are different things. Borchard's attention early in his career was influenced by legal and social issues reflective of his progressive ideology.

Borchard's prodigious intellect, strategic acumen, and persistence were focused on three domestic legal issues aside from his primary international law scholarship: abolishing sovereign immunity in tort, adopting the declaratory judgment, and compensating the wrongfully convicted. In each area he grounded analysis of contemporary American law in legal history and political theory concepts of state and citizenship, explored in *Diplomatic Protection*, which was concerned with protecting aliens' rights (Borchard, 1915).

The Progressivism which drew Borchard to these issues placed him to the left of the great ideological divide of his age, between laissez-faire government and the general welfare state (Fine, 1964), and also between radicals and conservatives. Borchard was ten years old when the savage economic depression of 1894 set off widespread suffering throughout the United States as huge secular changes—industrialization, immigration, urbanization—were transforming American life. The effect of these changes on the new middle class generated a progressive ethos that gave its name to the era. Borchard imbibed much of the progressive reform spirit, including a social justice agenda to aid exploited workers. Progressive reform legislation took forms like workers' compensation laws and measures designed to improve the public and much of the private life of workers. It favored settlement-houses and opposed big-city political machines (Chambers, 2000; Jaycox, 2005; Wiebe, 1967).

Borchard expressed the liberal and compassionate side of the Progressive Era's agenda—its emphasis on individual well-being in the context of a caring state and a balanced legal regime—in his dissertation, binding together his views of the state's responsibilities to its citizens abroad and its responsibilities internally:

> The state is not merely an end in itself, nor only a means to secure individual welfare . . . National welfare and individual welfare are indeed intimately bound together. In an impairment of individual rights, the state, the social solidarity, is affected . . .
>
> The assurance of the welfare of individuals, therefore, is a primary function of the state, accomplished internally by the agency of municipal public law, and externally through the instrumentalities of international law and diplomacy. The establishment of the machinery to insure this object constitutes an essential function of state activity—within, protecting every member of society from injustice or oppression by every other member; without, protecting its citizens from violence and oppression by other states.
>
> (Borchard, 1915, p. 31, footnote omitted)

He wore his ideology openly. A letter to progressive Senator Gerald Nye requesting that he introduce a wrongful conviction compensation bill noted, "For your personal information, I may add that I am an old-line Progressive and was happy to be considered a friend of Senator La Follette, Sr." (Borchard, 1929, November 12). Indeed, "European Systems" opens with a paean to progressive values: "In an age when social justice is the watchword of legislative reform, it is strange that society, at least in this country, utterly disregards the plight of the innocent victim of unjust conviction or detention in criminal cases" (Borchard, 1913a, p. 684).

Borchard's early efforts on behalf of the wrongfully convicted was animated by the workmen's compensation issue, perhaps the most prominent progressive cause at that time, and one suited to the interest of a reform-minded lawyer because the tort law system's inefficiency and injustice lay at its core. The problem it addressed, industrial accidents, produced carnage and suffering unimagined and conveniently forgotten today. Speaking to a large audience in 1907, President Theodore Roosevelt addressed the fact that work-related industrial accidents killed or disabled "one worker in 50" with far higher rates in more dangerous industries (Witt, 2004, p. 2). An estimated 35,000 workers were killed and 536,000 injured between 1888 and 1908 (Jaycox, 2005, p. 337).

European countries met industrialization's grisly side effect by social insurance and workers' compensation. The United States, holding to a free labor ideology reflective of early nineteenth century American life, generated legal doctrines that placed the costs of accidents on injured workers rather than on employers (Witt, 2004). Workman's compensation "was the first liability regime that was deployed expressly to provide a viable source of recovery for victims" and expressed Progressivism's social responsibility theme (Abraham, 2008, p. 61). Shifts in social thinking "challenged the dominant nineteenth-century belief in an autonomous and apolitical market system" (Chambers, 2000, p. 136; Wiebe, 1967, p. 181). Workers' compensation was a sea change in tort law.

Thus, just as Edwin Borchard was completing his European law surveys and writing his doctoral dissertation, workmen's compensation grabbed the imaginations of pro-labor advocates, the broader public, and progressive lawyers. Crystal Eastman's recommendations for European-style workman's compensation spread like "prairie fire" and "whirlwind" (Witt, 2004, pp. 126-127). "Over the next decade, forty-two of the forty-eight states followed suit. As one Wisconsin study described it, compensation statutes had arrived with a kind of 'magical rapidity'" (Witt, 2004, p. 127, footnote omitted).

Workmen's compensation stirred legal passions. In 1911 the New York Court of Appeals declared the state's workmen's compensation law unconstitutional (Witt, 2004, pp. 152–186). Conservatives saw the decision as a "dike against the tide of socialism." Most lawyers, scholars, and the populist icon Theodore Roosevelt sharply criticized it. Roscoe Pound wrote that the "artificial reasoning" of the case was "out of harmony with the spirit of the times"; the doctrine of the case was soon "laid to rest by popular consensus" (Witt, 2004, p. 176). A New York constitutional amendment and a second test case resurrected workmen's compensation there and in 1917 the US Supreme Court upheld workmen's compensation statutes under the federal constitution (Witt, 2004, p. 179).

Borchard's reliance on this prominent topic was not a chance reference but reflected his progressive ideology. In "European Systems," workmen's compensation is closely related to the sovereign immunity issue, which answered three theoretical objections to wrongful conviction indemnification. First, a state "assumption of risk" argument was countered with the assertion that state indemnification was more like eminent domain because of "a special sacrifice that is asked of the individual, for which society compensates him." A second argument based on the *lawfulness* of the state's act failed because private tort law had been shifting liability to property owners who were held responsible not to let their property cause injury. Lastly, the tort law rule of no negligence liability without fault was undercut by pointing to the spread of no-fault workmen's compensation laws (Borchard, 1913a, pp. 694–696). Abstracting the risk-spreading philosophy underlying modern tort doctrines and workmen's compensation laws, Borchard concluded, "It requires no further demonstration therefore to show that society rather than the individual should bear the risk of accident in the administration of criminal justice" (Borchard, 1913a, p. 696–697).

Borchard was best known for his support of traditional neutrality and opposition to America's entry into World Wars I and II (Doenecke 1977, 1982; Mayer, 2000). His unwavering liberalism is demonstrated by his American Civil Liberties Union (ACLU) board membership, public support for easing immigration law restrictions to admit refugees fleeing Nazi Germany and public relief bills, and opposition to President Roosevelt's "Court-packing" plan. Never shy of criticizing presidents, Borchard was one of very few academicians to criticize the government openly during World War II for interning Japanese-American civilians. He "signed on to the briefs" in the Korematsu and Endo cases (Ludington, 2011, pp. 397–398). His liberal temperament helps explain his decision to resume the unfinished business of compensating exonerees.

Borchard assiduously pursued two other areas of scholarship—the elimination of sovereign immunity in tort suits and the adoption of the declaratory judgment. A detailed exploration of this work is beyond this chapter's scope. It is enough to note that his prodigious scholarship in each area is cited in law journals today. He reproduced his scholarship in outlets like the *American Bar Association Journal*, to be read by high-level legal policy makers (Borchard, 1924–1925, 1934). He wrote the leading legal treatise and became known as the "father" of the declaratory judgment (Borchard, 1941; U.S. Fidelity, 1939, p. 290; Mayer, 2000). In his memoirs Justice William O. Douglas refers to Borchard being "almost a one-man lobby to push through the federal Declaratory Judgment Act" (Douglas, 1974, p. 167). Many of the lobbying techniques he employed to have the declaratory judgment adopted were borrowed from those used in his campaign to enact wrongful conviction indemnity legislation.

Borchard's success as a publicist was assisted by his stature as a leading and accessible academician and his cultivation of influential people. By the 1930s his circle included a wide variety of influential people. An expert on international law, he was a trusted advisor to many progressive movement leaders, including Hiram Johnson, the populist Republican governor of California and United States senator. He frequently testified before Congress. "He also wrote for such popular periodicals as the *Nation*, *New Republic*, *American Mercury*, *Current History*, and *Saturday Review of Literature*" (Doenecke, 1977).

Borchard's progressive ideology, his deep scholarship grounded in political theory and comparative law, his ability to apply theory and comparative law to specific legal issues, his penchant for drafting model legislation, his influential connections, and his dogged persistence to achieve his goals came together in his innocence compensation campaign.

The Campaign to Pass Indemnity Legislation

Convicting the Innocent was not written simply to establish that false convictions occurred because of justice system errors. Borchard aimed to use the book to establish a foundation for Congressional and state indemnity legislation for the wrongfully convicted. His efforts unfolded in a three-phase campaign. In the first phase, from 1912 to 1914, he drafted a statute specifying the substantive and procedural elements of a workable compensation law, setting maximum relief at $5,000.00 (Borchard, 1913c). "European Systems" accompanied the draft statute, establishing its theoretical basis, along with a supporting editorial by John Wigmore (1913), a prominent law school dean and leading evidence law expert. This three-item package was published first in a Senate Report

(Borchard, 1912b) and later in the *Journal of Criminal Law & Criminology* (Borchard 1913a, 1913c). Borchard enlisted Senator George Sutherland of Wyoming to introduce the bill in Congress. Although the bill did not become federal law, it inspired compensation laws in California and Wisconsin (Borchard, 1914).

In the campaign's second phase, from 1929 to 1932, he wrote *Convicting the Innocent*, with Felix Frankfurter's encouragement and in reaction to the Sacco–Vanzetti case (Borchard, 1929, April 11). Borchard had collected about 35 cases and to complete the project enlisted the assistance of E. Russell Lutz, a former student. He obtained financial support from Yale's Institute of Human Relations. Lutz resided in Washington, D.C. and found wrongful conviction cases in the Library of Congress. Borchard explained his reasons for the book to Lutz: to demonstrate "the dangers of convicting on circumstantial evidence," to "furnish the support necessary to demonstrate the necessity for state indemnification of errors of criminal justice," and to provide fascinating reading (Borchard, 1929, April 15). Borchard's dual dedication of the book to Frankfurter *and* to Dean Wigmore, who had clashed over the notorious Sacco–Vanzetti case, was a subtle way of alerting astute readers that the book was aimed at that trial's unfairness (Urofsky, 1991, p. 24). By not overtly mentioning Sacco–Vanzetti in the book, no ammunition was given to conservative jurists or prosecutors to dismiss it as a polemic (Borchard, 1930, December 26).

The book was designed as ammunition for enacting compensation legislation. It includes the entire text of Borchard's draft statute, the "European Systems" article, and the California and Wisconsin laws. With the book in hand Borchard began the third phase of his campaign, which ended with the 1938 federal law. He wrote to Attorney General Homer Cummings, whose earlier prosecutorial work predisposed him to be concerned about wrongful convictions, and received his support (Borchard, 1934, March 8; Cummings 1924). Special Assistant Attorney General Alexander Holtzoff (1934, December 7) carefully reviewed and improved Borchard's model statute. Borchard was invited to participate in the legislative drafting process. He found congressional sponsors and worked with them to meet objections to the bill. When a weaker Senate version and a stronger House version were passed early in 1934, they turned to Borchard, who recommended that the conference committee pass the House version. President Roosevelt signed the bill into law and the pen used to sign it was forwarded to New Haven (Act, 1938; Borchard, 1938, June 8). Further efforts to have the states enact compensation legislation failed. In a letter to George Soule, editor of *The New Republic*, Borchard revealed an interesting fact. A prosecutor was quoted in the book's preface, saying that "Innocent Men are never convicted. Don't worry about it. Never happens in the world. It is a physical impossibility." The book did not reveal his identity. It turns out that it was the District Attorney in the Sacco–Vanzetti case, and his "dogmatic statement" instigated Borchard to write *Convicting the Innocent* (Borchard, 1938, June 20).

The Limits of Innocence Reform

Innocence Reform

Innocence reform includes legislation, court rulings, or administrative action by police departments, prosecutors, public defenders, forensic science laboratories, courts, and other institutions designed to prevent wrongful convictions and rectify their effects, by modifying practice or creating new offices, such as prosecutors' conviction integrity units (Vance, 2010). Innocence reform is aimed at an open-ended list of wrongful conviction "causes" including eyewitness misidentification; false confessions; forensic science errors; jailhouse snitches; prosecutorial misconduct; inadequate assistance of counsel; and the like (Scheck, Neufeld, and Dwyer, 2000; Garrett, 2011). Borchard was the first to list such causes, including "mistaken identification, circumstantial evidence (from which erroneous inferences are drawn), or perjury" as the most important, and adding others, like coerced confessions and overzealous police and prosecutors (Borchard, 1932, pp. viii, xiv–xix).

Such lists can be expanded or contracted for purposes of exposition, but general categories become less useful when zeroing in on specific reforms. Take the highly touted recommendation to videotape entire police interrogations. It can be adopted by a department's voluntary policy decision or because of a consent decree; by state legislation mandating videotaping or requiring departments to create interrogation regulations; by a state supreme court excluding unrecorded confessions or allowing cautionary instructions to the jury; or by financial subsidies to videotaping departments (Sullivan and Vail, 2009).

A relatively straightforward reform can thus take a variety of institutional paths, each with unique political dynamics. Change must overcome resistance. Each practice area involves routines conducted by experienced practitioners who turn the wheels of justice. Practices are justified, correctly or not, by tradition; inertia; estimates of effectiveness, cost, and efficiency; laws; regulations; constitutional requirements; professional and political ideologies; within-agency and external bargaining; political trade-offs; esprit de corps; prejudice; and necessity. These sunk costs of practice apply to all enterprises and breed skepticism (often healthy) about proposed changes. These general barriers to policy reform are daunting, but reform nevertheless does result from efforts of policy entrepreneurs. Accurately predicting successful reform requires a good understanding of existing conditions, favorable and unfavorable.

Borchard sensed that innocence compensation laws were *feasible*, especially given the sudden popularity of workmen's compensation laws. Aware that justice system flaws generated wrongful convictions and of possible fixes, he also sensed that the likelihood of system-wide reforms was nil. It "is not the main purpose of Professor Borchard in writing [*Convicting the Innocent*] to advocate reforms in criminal judicial procedure" observed a reviewer. "Indeed, in an introductory chapter he says that 'There is not much that the prosecuting or judicial machinery can do to prevent some of these particular miscarriages of justice'" (Taft, 1932). Other reviewers noted the lack of reform prescriptions, but they did not make a convincing case that comprehensive reform was possible (Burnett, 1932; Gifford, 1933; Thompson, 1932).

As a legal scholar, perhaps Borchard focused narrowly on statutory reforms rather than changing police or prosecutors. He knew that suggestiveness, coercion, and perjury permeated his reported cases. Whether Borchard himself could have addressed systemic reforms misses the fact that the 1920s was a "crime commissions" decade—broad-ranging studies of state, local, and national criminal justice systems. Borchard's friend, Felix Frankfurter, co-directed the first and one of the best commissions (Walker, 1977, pp. 109–137). If not Borchard himself, other lawyers, scholars, or activists might have advanced systemic innocence reforms, were they feasible.

Broad-ranging innocence reform was unattainable in the 1930s because justice institutions were administratively undeveloped. Scientific and technological advances unavailable in the 1930s have made innocence reforms feasible, but their implementation depends on institutional capacity to recognize their value and put them into practice. Justice institutions' administrative capabilities have changed over eight decades. One might argue that the organizational structure of criminal justice appears the same in 2012 as in 1932: appellate and trial courts, public prosecution, defense attorneys, police investigators, and even forensic laboratories operated 80 years ago to identify and apprehend offenders. By analogy, cars look fundamentally similar in 1932 and 2012—four wheels, enclosed cabins, steering wheels, internal combustion engines—but no one would think that the new and improved Ford Model B of 1932 is anything like the 2012 Ford Fusion in terms of performance or the materials and technology that go into a contemporary automobile. Driving the car analogy a bit further, the criminal justice system of 80 years ago—especially the slice of criminal justice that apprehends and prosecutes criminals—serves the same function as the criminal justice system today and police work, prosecution, and adjudication seem to operate in the same basic way. What has changed, so to speak, lies under the hood.

Before exploring how police departments, prosecutors' offices, courts, and law schools have changed (and have begun adopting some innocence reforms), recall the paradoxical feature of my thesis. The justice system is bad enough to generate appreciable errors (Zalman, 2012), but is also sufficiently capable to respond effectively to demonstrated errors. The paradox does not mean that justice institutions are ideal. They often fail expected standards of efficiency, effectiveness, and justice, as demonstrated by exonerations. Even if deficient procedures do not lead to wrongful convictions, they raise enough concerns to stimulate reform among otherwise sluggish institutions. Yet, with all their systemic flaws, justice agencies today are mostly capable of adopting and enforcing innocence reforms.

Another preliminary point is that justice agencies have not changed uniformly. Great advances have occurred in police agencies, while prosecutors' offices remained static. The defense role has not fundamentally changed, but their availability in adjudications and the growth of public defenders' offices is a fundamental change since 1932. A nonexistent institution in 1932, the law school clinic, has been critical to the existence and success of the innocence movement.

Public receptiveness to the pathos of false convictions (and even that of agency personnel) may have followed increased social justice consciousness.

The political interference into investigations, prosecutions, and trials of an earlier era is intolerable today. The Justice Department's Public Integrity Section, created after the Watergate scandal, addresses declining tolerance for political corruption (Public Integrity, 1978). Also, despite the ascendancy of conservative politics since Ronald Reagan's presidency, Americans have come to expect more from government even if they are reluctant to pay (Pierson and Skocpol, 2007). Other social changes—declining acceptance of violence (Pinker, 2011), expansion of higher education, shifts in the tone of news coverage (Warden, 2003; Baumgartner, DeBoef, and Boydstun, 2008), and greater demand for procedural justice—support the *rightness* of innocence reform.

Police Departments

In 1933 police reformer August Vollmer wrote about "remarkable changes . . . in the field of police organization and administration during the last quarter of a century. One can scarcely believe that such great advances could be made in so short a time. It is a far cry indeed from the old politically-controlled police department to the modern, scientifically-operated organization" (Vollmer, 1933, p. 161). Positive steps had indeed been taken in a few places where police were civil-service employees rather than political appointees, where police training existed, and where a quasi-military chain of centralized command replaced the power of precinct captains answering to political ward bosses. Record systems, traffic control, and the overriding goal of crime prevention were hallmarks of modern police administration. As for crime investigation, in the past "little or no attention" was paid to "scientific principles." By 1933 Vollmer could list a number of cities that had established scientific crime laboratories applying up-to-date forensic science techniques (Vollmer, 1933, p. 171).

Vollmer was not wrong to assert that positive changes had been made since 1900. Previously, police officials, often "unintelligent and untrained," were appointed because of political connections, patrolled in a hit-or-miss fashion, and lacked adequate means of communication. Record systems were primitive and methods of investigation were obsolete. They "had no conception of the preventive possibilities of the service" (Vollmer, 1933, p. 161; see Walker, 1977, pp. 3–49; Fogelson, 1977, pp. 13–39). His assessment of advances was nevertheless too selective and polemical accurately to reflect the reality about policing quality in general and criminal investigation in particular in the 1930s. The first wave of reform in the Theodore Roosevelt era proved ephemeral (Fogelson, 1977, pp. 67–91; Walker, 1977, pp. 66–75). At the operational level, the "crime lab and the fingerprint system were more important for their public-relations value than for their actual contributions to the apprehension of criminals" (Walker, 1977, p. 73).

To better understand police reform at that time requires examining its political context. Police professionalism was an important issue in the socio-political struggle pitting old stock Protestant, middle-class America against the waves of foreign immigrants who joined poorer whites and African-Americans flocking to urban centers of industrial expansion. The central Progressive Era issue was economic—whether the American political economy would operate under a strict laissez-faire philosophy or as a general welfare state (Fine, 1964). From this central issue flowed a number of other issues shaped by class, region, ethnicity, ideology, and political interests.

City government was dominated by political machines, which managed the disruptions and opportunities brought on by explosive population growth in an era of small, laissez-faire government at the state and federal levels. Far from dissolving before the Progressives' good government prescriptions, political machines grew in power through the 1930s (Wiebe, 1967, pp. 30, 213). Police departments, important to city machines as sources of patronage and control, were not sufficiently independent to pursue policies divorced from politics. Although police departments were "under suspicion" of corruption and political control from the Lexow committee investigation in 1894 through the 1930s (except for interruptions with the election of reform mayors), these patterns continued through the first period of police reform which ended in the 1930s (Fogelson, 1977). The second wave of reform running from the 1930s to about 1970 succeeded in establishing the Progressive era's "professional model" of policing—administrative centralization and modernization; better selection, pay, and training of police officers; and eliminating service functions to focus on law enforcement (Fogelson, 1977, pp. 159–162; Walker, 1977, pp. 167–68). This change did not include concerns about convicting the innocent. Post-Borchard "big-picture" books had no effect on public opinion and generated no political pressure to make error-reduction changes (Gardner, 1952; Frank and Frank, 1957).

Up to the 1960s big-city machines, although in decline, maintained some of their former power (Fogelson, 1977, pp. 150–151). Police recruitment, training, and supervision had not advanced to the stage where police incompetence, corruption, and excessive use of force were things of the past (Fogelson, 1977, pp. 148–149; Westley, 1970). Equally important, the professional model's fatal flaw was its over-reaction to the gross corruption and political interference of Progressive Era policing. Police "officers should not be accountable to elected officials, not even to the degree that the soldiers, to whom the previous generation of reformers had compared them, were answerable to civilian authorities" (Fogelson, p. 158). Tied to this was a false superiority and scientism regarding police crime-solving abilities, and insensitivity to the "uneven impact" that changes in policing would have "on the well-being of urban America's social classes and ethnic groups" (Fogelson, 1977, p. 162). The organizational self-scrutiny that is a prerequisite to innocence reform was lacking.

Most American police departments today are remarkably different, "under the hood," from 1930s police agencies. In 1932 the professional model, advocated by some writers and reform personnel, was not widespread (Fogelson, 1977, pp. 141–145). The professional model's hallmark, bureaucratization, *was* firmly established in sizable departments by 1970 (Walker, 1999, pp. 362–363). But police bureaucracies in 1970 were mostly run by officers unschooled in management techniques and wedded to the insular professional policing model.

Trends in the last 40 years have caused a sea change in American policing. The growth of a sizable criminal justice discipline in higher education positively affected police policy (Walker, 2004). Most police managers and administrators have bachelors' or masters' degrees. The innovative chief, William Bratton, expressed the value of a college education, which he obtained in the 1970s when the trend toward higher education for police was beginning. "At Boston State College, I took some law-enforcement courses, but I also studied urban geography and began to learn the importance of cities and how they develop. I took an American government course ... College taught me to look at things differently than my contemporaries did and to really appreciate what I was looking at. It's good for cops to go to college" (Bratton, 1998, p. 49). A few years later, when Bratton was promoted to sergeant, an innovative police commissioner put his class of sergeants through post-promotion training at Boston University. These first line supervisors were trained in leadership, management-supervision techniques, and how to discipline people. Seminars on anti-corruption and ethics exposed the officers to "things a police officer would never otherwise hear about." Classes on public speaking were required because the new sergeants "were expected to speak persuasively on behalf of the department. The most important effect of our new training was to show" the class "that there were ideas and approaches to policing beyond the narrow confines of the Boston Police Department." The reform commissioner "took us out of the blue cocoon" (Bratton and Knobler, 1998, p. 63). Bratton speaks for other police managers and administrators who were empowered by higher education with the knowledge and the confidence to become effective agency directors, and with skills to effectuate changes where necessary.

Dissatisfaction with professional policing and studies puncturing holes in shibboleths like the deterrent value of routine patrol led to the tectonic shift from the professional policing model to a cluster of contemporary philosophies, encompassing community, problem-solving and evidence-based policing, and administrative accountability models. These new models gave police administrators the *capacity* to respond to community needs and react in measurable ways to perceived problems. For example, when racial profiling became a political issue in 1999, proponents' calls for collecting traffic-stop data led "several hundred law enforcement agencies [to] undertake[...] voluntary traffic-stop data collection. Police chiefs undertook these voluntary efforts to be responsive to the minority communities in their jurisdictions" (Walker, 2004, p. 141). This example demonstrates the capability and the will of many police administrators to impose changes. They comfortably utilized modern technology to monitor the actions of officers who might have been reluctant to change their routines. It suggests that necessary relationships had been developed between police chiefs and mayors, city councils, civic leaders, and organizations, enabling them to take effective action and to generate goodwill for their efforts. This level of leadership, routine among police administrators today, was rare in earlier eras.

A third large change is the "cosmopolitanization" of American policing. Federal involvement in local law enforcement, along with that of such organizations as the International Association of Chiefs of Police, the

Police Foundation, and the Police Executive Research Forum, provide the means for police executives to broaden their horizons via training, reports, forums, and the like. Federal involvement through the research arms of the Justice Department (the National Institute of Justice and the Bureau of Justice Statistics) provides ongoing sources of research support, data, usable information, and forums that allow police administrators to stay current with recent trends. The newly launched Office of Justice Programs website AboutCrimeSolutions.gov (n.d.) describes research-based programs dealing effectively with practical criminal justice issues of interest to program administrators. Examples can be piled up. Perhaps the most impressive illustration of the ability of law enforcement agencies to implement meaningful programs has been crime prevention programs like Operation Ceasefire, which have prevented violent crime while providing the preconditions for channeling potentially violent offenders into law-abiding modes of life (Braga, 2010; Kennedy, 2011; Criminology & Public Policy, 2011)

These "new police" encountered an innocence reform in 1998. At the behest of Attorney General Janet Reno, a Technical Working Group for Eyewitness Evidence was convened. Thirty-four police, prosecutors, defense attorneys, and research psychologists met over 18 months to formulate lineup and witness guidelines based on a quarter-century of groundbreaking eyewitness research. The meetings did not go smoothly. As participant James Doyle (2005) vividly tells it, the scientifically generated ideas for reducing errors during lineup identification ran into buzz saws of opposition from police and prosecutors. But over time the police participants worked through the scientific ideas in practical and feasible ways. The prosecutors called in external political pressure to sink the guidelines. Ultimately, they had the final report's title changed from guidelines to a "guide" (Technical Working Group for Eyewitness Evidence, 1999). The police participants displayed a good deal of administrative savvy and practical intelligence in understanding how the new lineup approaches could improve their work in sorting out guilty from innocent suspects early in the process. Since the *Guide* was adopted, many departments have on their own initiatives undertaken implementation (Fisher, 2008).

This episode exemplifies the broad trend toward contemporary police departments having the capacity to address professional issues in proactive ways, supported by research, abiding by legal requirements, bolstered by politically and community obtained support, utilizing advanced technology, and subjected to program evaluation. To a degree that would have astonished and heartened earlier police reformers, police agencies operate as proficient administrative agencies today (Skogan and Frydl, 2004; Treverton, Wollman, Wilke, and Lai, 2011). With all their problems, police agencies have the capacity to implement innocence reforms.

Prosecutors' Offices

Unlike the police, who saw lineup reform as valuable to their professional work, prosecutors saw only the downside: lineup guidelines as traps that defense attorneys would spring during trials. Their conduct throughout the Technical Working Group meetings was aggressive, rude, confrontational, and obstructive. They were eventually maneuvered into not walking out of the process by a few concessions and by the fear that guides constructed by police and researchers would create even more restrictions (Doyle, 2005, pp. 172–185). A broad conclusion to be drawn from the Technical Working Group's experience was that "[f]ollowing routine procedures is a fundamental part of police culture." To the contrary, "from the prosecutors' vantage point, anything resembling standardized procedures represents a potential danger" (Doyle, 2005, p. 176).

The question regarding prosecutors and innocence reform is less a matter of their capacity to effect change and more their willingness to do so. Unlike police departments, which were organizationally deficient in 1932, prosecutors' offices were and are led by and staffed by lawyers, whose education has not fundamentally changed. Raymond Moley's (1929) detailed examination of American prosecution eight decades ago essentially describes prosecution today. The prosecutor then and now has virtually uncontrolled discretion to charge or dismiss cases; controls the grand jury; and disposes of most cases after plea-bargaining, during which some charges are dismissed, or the defendant pleads to a lesser included offense, or lenient sentencing recommendations are made (Moley, 1929, pp. 48–54, 149–192; compare with Davis, 2007, pp. 19–60). The prosecutor's unreviewable power and immunity from civil suit led observers to conclude that the prosecutor was the most powerful actor in the courts (Moley, 1929, p. 48; Davis, 2007, p. 5). Then and now appellate cases show many examples of "legal malpractice" by prosecutors (Moley, 1929, pp. 54–55; Weinberg, Gordon, and Williams, 2003).

What has changed since 1932 is better pay, allowing a larger number of people drawn to the profession to become career prosecutors (Moley, 1929, pp. 66–68). This might make things worse regarding wrongful convictions as more ADAs become infused with a "prosecutorial complex" (Medwed, 2012, p. 3). Also, local political party bosses or "machines" no longer supply assistant district attorneys nor interfere directly in prosecutions, eliminating pressure to railroad political enemies (Moley, 1929, pp. 74–94). Nevertheless, most prosecutors are elected and the politics of prosecution causes many to emphasize conviction rates and publicity in notorious crime cases over the evenhanded appraisal of cases (Davis, 2007, pp. 166–169; Medwed, 2012, pp. 78–79; Moley, 1929, pp. 76–79).

Although scholars emphasize the problems in American prosecution, a careful reading suggests that authors believe that most prosecutors are honest, competent, adhere to professional standards, and that most convicted defendants are guilty (Davis, 2007; Medwed, 2012). They show, nevertheless, that prosecutors' practices help convict a significant (if quantitatively indeterminate) number of innocent defendants because of violations of due process, standards of practice, and canons of ethics (Gershman, 2007). More worrisome is the conclusion that the prevailing legal rules of practice appear to generate wrongful convictions (Davis, 2007; Medwed, 2012).

One change is the greater amount of scholarly attention given to prosecution and plea-bargaining. Scholars have proposed a raft of workable changes in legislation, constitutional rulings, court rules, and prosecution practice. These include clarifying the canons of ethics; strengthening prosecutor's discipline internally and externally (by official disciplinary bodies or bar associations); modifying evidentiary charging standards; internal charging and plea negotiation review committees; effective open-file policies; prosecutor training about wrongful conviction and psychological biases; reducing the sentence-length for defendants with strong cases who go to trial and are found guilty; and improving or eliminating the election of prosecutors (Davis, 2007, pp. 179–194; Medwed, 2012). The most visible reform has been establishing conviction integrity units in a handful of jurisdictions. They review past cases to ensure that convicted prisoners were not actually innocent (Vance, 2010; Medwed, 2012, pp. 139–142).

While this is a hopeful step from the innocence perspective, the larger question is whether knowledge of wrongful convictions, academic reform proposals, and a few initial reforms have changed the greater part of prosecution culture in America. It is unlikely. As Medwed (2012, p. 140) notes, even in Dallas, where the conviction integrity unit was initiated, the response "within the . . . prosecutors' office has been more mixed. Some employees view the Conviction Integrity Unit as a type of Internal Affairs Bureau and treat it with commensurate scorn." Medwed hopefully comments that although the Bureau staff endure "social ostracism," what "matters is that the unit is an accepted and respected office fixture." Perhaps, but in light of the fierce resistance exhibited by many prosecutors to DNA testing of prisoners (Medwed, 2012, pp. 158–165), it seems safer to surmise that in the main, prosecution culture today is hostile to innocence reform and can be expected to resist it.

Courts

Trials, appellate procedures, public defenders' offices, and the requirement that all defendants be represented, have not prevented or reversed wrongful convictions (Garrett, 2008; Garrett, 2011, pp. 145–212; Findley, 2009). Trial procedure has not fundamentally changed since Borchard's era. Perhaps the gross unfairness characterizing the Sacco–Vanzetti trial is impossible today (Frankfurter, 1927). Fewer trials proportional to all adjudications are held today. Trials are longer and seem to be burdened by more procedural and evidentiary rules, although very low appellate reversal rates suggest that trial regulations have not stopped a working railroad. Detailed explorations of how courts actually function present troubling pictures of too many haphazard processes that lean heavily in favor of prosecutors and produce wrongful convictions (Tulsky, 2006; Bach, 2009).

Empirical research about trial operations and outcomes conducted since the 1970s has also studied reforms designed to make jury trials more accurate, which have been implemented in a few jurisdictions. A massive review concluded:

> *Reforms that promote juror comprehension.* Existing research on juror and jury comprehension of legal instruction highlights the need

for prescriptive research concerning ways to improve jury performance. In particular, future research should examine the effects of the following: (a) using court-appointed experts, (b) pre-instructing jurors, (c) providing jurors with written copies of judicial instructions, (d) revising/simplifying judicial instructions, (e) allowing jurors to take notes and/or ask questions during the trial, (f) having judges and/or attorneys provide summary comments on the evidence, and (g) using verdict forms that include interrogatories. It is clear from this review, as well as considerable research conducted with mock jurors, that jurors are often uncertain or confused about their task, a condition only slightly lessened by discussing the judge's instructions with other jurors during deliberation. Most of these areas have received some initial attention, but the results so far have been modestly encouraging, certainly not overwhelming. Much more work is needed.

(Devine et al., 2001, p. 712).

Such reforms have not been implemented in such large numbers as to profoundly change the trial process.

Perhaps judges could become a leading force for policy change. State supreme court justices have shown some leadership in raising awareness and stimulating action favoring innocence reform. An early and effective effort by former Chief Justice I. Beverly Lake of North Carolina (Mumma, 2004) seems to have fallen into abeyance. A more recent effort spearheaded by Chief Judge Jonathan Lippman of New York has established a permanent state Justice Task Force (New York, n.d.) which advocates the passage of most of the reform measures designed by the Innocence Project (n.d.) and has entered the political fray in New York (Editorial, 2012). It is too early to tell whether many state supreme courts will follow such leads. The New York and North Carolina experiences suggest that much depends on the ideology and leadership abilities of particular judges rather than institutional imperatives.

Law Schools

As a thought experiment, suppose that DNA testing was available in 1932 but that justice institutions and society were no different. Could the justice system in 1932 have marshalled resources to defend suspects? Not all defendants had lawyers in those days; indigent defense was superficial or shoddy; and public defenders' offices hardly existed (Borchard, 1932, p. xx). The third-degree was prevalent and anti-immigrant and racial prejudice was toxic. While wrongful convictions were shocking injustices, Borchard's book did not spark deep reform. Society did not see false convictions as a major problem. Nothing changed a generation later in the prosperous 1950s when "Perry Mason's" creator, Erle Stanley Gardner (1957), could not excite major public outrage with his "Court of Last Resort," even when televised. Given such limitations, who had the resources to advocate for post-appeal petitioners seeking DNA testing in 1932? Who does so in 2012?

The thought experiment, of course, has an element of unreality since all inventions are embedded in the social as well as the technological matrix of their times. Yet, it raises the question of whether the innocence movement would have taken its present shape were it not for the innovation of legal clinical education in law schools in the 1970s. Reviewing convictions in order to determine if they were factually wrongful requires prodigious labors. The U.K.'s Criminal Cases Review Commission (CCRC), touted by some as a desirable American reform, has not fulfilled its mandate adequately to review cases, in large part because of limited staff (Naughton, 2010). It is worth noting that the American reform that most closely parallels the CCRC, the North Carolina Innocence Inquiry Commission, is authorized by its "Rules and Procedures" to avail itself of law student labor (North Carolina, 2011, Art. 4 (E)).

The Innocence Project was originally a law school clinical class, and most innocence projects take that form (Findley, 2006). Law school clinics provide a major "engine" for the innocence movement, and without this resource, which has grown from one Innocence Project to more than fifty in the United States (Innocence Network, n.d.), it is unlikely that the innocence movement could have achieved its present stature. Scheck et al. (2000) utilized an institution that was "at hand," so to speak, and adapted this pedagogical innovation to the purpose of exonerating prisoners. Clinical education, as a reaction to the case method, was first proposed by a noted "legal realist", Jerome Frank (1933). It is significant for my thesis that Frank, who was before his time in recommending clinical education for lawyers, did not mention it at all in his "big-picture" book on wrongful convictions (Frank and Frank, 1957).

Conclusion

DNA testing has powerfully affected the advance of innocence reform, making it easy to overlook the complex of ideas and institutions that makes innocence reform possible. The story of Borchard's single-minded efforts to enact a compensation law is stirring but, by negative implication, demonstrates the limited capacity of justice agencies in Borchard's time to generate innocence reform. Many extraordinary advances in cognitive psychology research regarding eyewitness identification, false confessions, and child witnesses helped make innocence reform possible (Leo, 2005). Broad changes in socially acceptable thinking may have made wrongful convictions less palatable and helped bend the news media from a pro-prosecution position to an innocence orientation (Pinker, 2011; Warden, 2003; Baumgartner, DeBoef, and Boydstun, 2008). Included in these broader changes, the expansion of law school clinics provided a necessary foundation for the innocence movement. Of central importance, improvements in policing make the adoption of innocence reforms reasonably likely among a significant number of law enforcement agencies. I am less sanguine about the potential for real change in prosecutors' offices and in the judiciary. Nevertheless, some innocence reforms are likely to occur even there. This exploration barely scratches the surface of the question posed by this chapter. Innocence reform involves complex changes in dozens or perhaps scores of practices from the handling of confidential informants to charging defendants to the intricacies of post-conviction review. Reforms can take the form of rules, regulations, administrative orders, legal doctrines, and statutes. These changes must result in changed practices to ensure compliance. And to become effective in any meaningful way, they will have to be implemented in approximately 14,000 law enforcement agencies; more than 3,000 prosecutor's offices; courts in more than 3,000 counties; in all fifty states, and in federal jurisdictions; and in other agencies such as forensic science laboratories. Given the decentralized nature of the American polity, meaningful innocence reform will require changes in professional and institutional cultures.

Having specified some historical trends that have made the current level of innocence reform feasible, and having specified some of the parameters of significant innocence reform, further speculation as to the general likelihood of innocence reform is foolhardy. Better estimates of reform likelihood should focus on specific reform areas rather than on global innocence reform.

Note

1 The author thanks the Humanities Center, Wayne State University, for its support.

References

AboutCrimeSolutions.gov (n.d.). Accessed http://www.crimesolutions.gov/about.aspx.

Abraham, K. S. (2008). *The liability century: Insurance and tort law from the progressive era to 9/11.* Cambridge, MA./London: Harvard University Press.

Act (1938, May 24). An act to grant relief to persons erroneously convicted in courts of the United States, Public Law No. 539, Statutes at Large 52, 438.

Bach, A. (2009). *Ordinary injustice: How America holds court.* New York: Metropolitan Books/ Henry Holt.

Baumgartner, F. R., DeBoef, S. L. and Boydstun, A. E. (2008). *The decline of the death penalty and the discovery of innocence.* Cambridge, NY: Cambridge University Press.

Borchard, E. M. (1912a). *Guide to the law and legal literature of Germany.* Washington: United States Government Printing Office.

Borchard, E. M. (1912b). State indemnity for errors of criminal justice. Senate Document No. 974, 62d Cong., 3d Sess. Washington: United States Government Printing Office.

Borchard, E. M. (1913a). European systems of state indemnity for errors of criminal justice. *Journal of the American Institute of Criminal Law and Criminology,* 3, 684–718.

Borchard, E. M. (1913b). *The bibliography of international law and continental law.* Washington: United States Government Printing Office.

Borchard, E. M. (1913c). For relief to persons erroneously convicted. *Journal of the American Institute of Criminal Law and Criminology,* 3, 772–795 [draft statute].

Borchard, E. M. (1914). State indemnity for errors of criminal justice. *Annals of the American Academy of Political and Social Science,* 52, 108–114.

Borchard, E. M. (1915). *Diplomatic protection of citizens abroad, or, the law of international claims.* New York: Banks Law Publishing Company.

Borchard, E. M. (1917). *Guide to the law and legal literature of Argentina, Brazil and Chile.* Washington: United States Government Printing Office.

Borchard, E. M. (1924–1925). Government liability in tort. *Yale Law Journal,* 34, 1–45, 129–143, 229–258.

Borchard, E. M. (1929, April 11). Letter to Felix Frankfurter. April 11, 1929. Edwin M. Borchard Papers, MSS Group #670, Box 111, Folder 1065, Yale University Archives.

Borchard, E. M. (1929, April 15). Letter to E. Russell Lutz. April 15, 1929. Edwin M. Borchard Papers, MSS Group #670, Box 111, Folder 1065, Yale University Archives.

Borchard, E. M. (1929, November 12). Letter to Gerald P. Nye. November 12, 1929. Edwin M. Borchard Papers, MSS Group #670, Box 111, Folder 1065, Yale University Archives.

Borchard, E. M. (1930, December 26). Letter to Felix Frankfurter. December 26, 1930. Edwin M. Borchard Papers, MSS Group #670, Box 111, Folder 1067, Yale University Archives.

Borchard, E. M. (1932). *Convicting the innocent: Errors of criminal justice.* New Haven: Yale University Press [with the collaboration of E. Russell Lutz].

Borchard, E. M. (1934, March 8). Letter to Homer S. Cummings. March 8, 1934. Edwin M. Borchard Papers, MSS Group #670, Box 109, Folder 1050, Yale University Archives.

Borchard, E. M. (1934). State and municipal liability in tort—Proposed statutory reform. *American Bar Association Journal,* 20, 747–752, 793–794.

Borchard, E. M. (1938, June 8). Letter to John Wigmore. June 8, 1938. Edwin M. Borchard Papers, MSS Group #670, Box 109, Folder 1051, Yale University Archives.

Borchard, E. M. (1938, June 20). Letter to George Soule. June 20, 1938. Edwin M. Borchard Papers, MSS Group #670, Box 109, Folder 1051, Yale University Archives.

Borchard, E. M. (1941). *Declaratory judgments, revised and rewritten, second edition.* Cleveland: Banks-Baldwin Law Publishing Co.

Braga, A. A. (2010). *Problem-oriented policing and crime prevention, second edition*. Boulder, CO: Lynne Rienner.

Bratton, W., with Knobler, P. (1998). *Turnaround: How America's top cop reversed the crime epidemic*. New York: Random House.

Burnett, A. (1932, November 27). Circumstantial evidence is often WRONG [book review]. *Washington Post*, p. SM5.

Chambers, J. W., II. (2000). *The tyranny of change: America in the Progressive Era 1890–1920, second edition*. New Brunswick, NJ: Rutgers University Press.

Collins, P. (2011). *The murder of the century: The gilded age crime that scandalized a city and sparked the tabloid wars*. New York: Broadway Paperbacks.

Criminology & Public Policy (2011). Special policy issue: imprisonment and crime. *Criminology & Public Policy*, 10(1), 1–206.

Cummings, H. S. (1924). The State v. Harold Israel. *Journal of the American Institute of Criminal Law and Criminology*, 15, 406–434.

Davis, A. J. (2007). *Arbitrary justice: The power of the American prosecutor*. Oxford, NY: Oxford University Press.

Devine, D. J., Clayton, L. D., Dunford, B. B., Seying, R., and Pryce, J. (2001). Jury decision making: 45 years of empirical research on deliberating groups. *Psychology, Public Policy, and Law*, 7(3), 622–727.

Doenecke, J. D. (1977). "Edwin Montefiore Borchard." *Dictionary of American Biography*, Supplement Five: 1951–1955. New York: Scribner's.

Douglas, W. O. (1974). *Go east, young man: early years: The autobiography of William O. Douglas*. New York: Vintage Books.

Doyle, J. M. (2005). *True witness: Cops, courts, science, and the battle against misidentification*. New York: Palgrave Macmillan

Editorial (2012, February 25). DNA and reform. *New York Times*, A18.

"Edwin Borchard, Law Expert, Dead," (1951, July 23) *New York Times* [obituary].

Findley, K. A. (2006). The pedagogy of innocence: Reflections on the role of innocence projects in clinical legal education. *Clinical Law Review*, 13, 231–278.

Findley, K. A. (2009). Innocence protection in the appellate process. *Marquette Law Review*, 93, 591–638.

Fine, S. (1964). *Laissez Faire and the General-Welfare State: A study of conflict in American thought, 1865-1901*. Ann Arbor: University of Michigan Press.

Fisher, S. Z. (2008, July). Eyewitness identification reform in Massachusetts. *Massachusetts Law Review*, 91(2), 52–66.

Fogelson, R. M. (1977). *Big-city police*. Cambridge, MA and London: Harvard University Press.

Frank, J. (1933). Why not a clinical lawyer-school? *University of Pennsylvania Law Review*, 81, 907–923.

Frank, J. and Frank, B. (1957). *Not guilty*. Garden City, NY: Doubleday & Co.

Frankfurter, F. (1927). *The case of Sacco and Vanzetti: A critical analysis for lawyers and laymen*. Boston: Little, Brown.

Gardner, E. S. (1952). *The court of last resort*. New York: W. Sloane.

Garrett, B. L. (2008). Judging innocence. *Columbia Law Review*, 108, 55-141.

Garrett, B. L. (2011). *Convicting the innocent: Where criminal prosecutions go wrong*. Cambridge, Mass., London, Eng.: Harvard University Press.

Gershman, B. L. (2007). *Prosecutorial misconduct, second edition*. St Paul, MN: Thompson-West.

Gifford, J. P. (1933). Convicting the innocent [book review]. *Political Science Quarterly*, 48(1), 127–129.

Holtzoff, A. (1934, December 7). Letter to Edwin M. Borchard. December 7, 1934. Edwin M. Borchard Papers, MSS Group #670, Box 109, Folder 1050, Yale University Archives.

Innocent Network (n.d.). Retrieved from http://www.innocentnetwork.org/.

Jaycox, F. (2005). *Eyewitness history: The progressive era*. New York: Facts on File.

Kalman, L. (1986). *Legal realism at Yale: 1927-1960*. Chapel Hill and London: University Of North Carolina Press.

Kennedy, D. M. (2011). *Don't shoot: One man, a street fellowship, and the end of violence in inner-city America*. New York: Bloomsbury.

Leo, R. A. (2005). Rethinking the study of miscarriages of justice: Developing a criminology of wrongful conviction. *Journal of Contemporary Criminal Justice*, 21(3), 201–23.

Ludington, S. H. (2011). The dogs that did not bark: The silence of the legal academy during World War II. *Journal of Legal Education*, 60(3), 396–432.

Mayer, M. S. (2000). Borchard, Edwin Montefiore. Accessed: http://www.anb.org/articles/11/11-00081.html; American National Biography Online Feb. 2000. American Council of Learned Societies; Oxford University Press.

Medwed, D.S. (2012). *Prosecution complex: America's race to convict and its impact on the innocent*. New York and London: New York University Press.

Moley, R. (1929). *Politics* and *criminal prosecution*. New York: Minton, Balch & Co.

Mumma, C. C. (2004). The North Carolina Actual Innocence Commission: Uncommon perspectives joined by a common cause. *Drake Law Review*, 52, 647–656.

Naughton, M. (Ed.) (2010). *The Criminal Cases Review Commission: Hope for the innocent?* Basingstoke, Hampshire; New York: Palgrave Macmillan.

New York (n.d.). New York State Justice Task Force. Accessed http://www.nyjusticetaskforce.com/index.html.

Norris, R. J., Bonventre, C. L., Redlich, A. D. and Acker, J. R. (2011). "Than that one innocent suffer": Evaluating state safeguards against wrongful convictions. *Albany Law Review*, 74(3), 1301–1364.

North Carolina (2011). The North Carolina Innocence Inquiry Commission Rules and Procedures, Revised September 9, 2011. Accessed: http://www.innocencecommission-nc.gov/rules.html.

Pattenden, R. (1996). *English criminal appeals, 1844-1994: Appeals against conviction and sentence in England and Wales*. Oxford: Clarendon Press.

Pierson, P. and Skocpol, T. (2007). *The transformation of American politics: Activist government and the rise of conservatism*. Princeton and Oxford: Princeton University Press.

Pinker, S. (2011). *The better angels of our nature: Why violence has declined*. New York: Viking.

Public Integrity (1978). Report to Congress on the activities and operations of the Public Integrity Section for 1978, United States Department of Justice. Accessed June 14, 2012 http://www.justice.gov/criminal/pin/.

Putnam, H. (1911). *Report of the Library of Congress*. Washington: Government Printing Office; House of Representatives, 62d Congress, 2d Session, Doc. No. 147.

Risinger, D. M. and Risinger. L. C. (2012). Innocence is different: Taking innocence into account in reforming criminal procedure. *New York Law School Law Review*, 65, 869–909.

Scheck, B., Neufeld, P. and Dwyer, J. (2000). *Actual innocence: Five days to execution, and other dispatches from the wrongly convicted*. New York: Doubleday.

Sello, Justizrat Dr. E. (1911). *Die Irrtümer der Strafjustiz und ihre Ursachen* [The errors (mistakes/falsities) of criminal justice (law) and their causes]. Berlin: R. V. Deckers Verlag. [Title translated by Lisa Hoch].

Skogan, W. and Frydl, K. (Eds.) (2004). *Fairness and effectiveness in policing: The evidence*. Washington, DC: National Academies Press.

Sullivan, T. P. and Vail, A. W. (2009). Recent developments: The consequences of law enforcement officials' failure to record custodial interviews as required by law. *Journal of Criminal Law & Criminology*, 99, 215–228.

Taft, H. W. (1932, May 7). Miscarriages of justice [book review]. *Saturday Review of Literature*, 8(42), 712.

Technical Working Group for Eyewitness Evidence (1999, October). *Eyewitness evidence: A guide for law enforcement*. Washington, DC: National Institute of Justice, NCJ 178240.

Thompson, W. G. (1932). Convicting the innocent [book review]. *Columbia Law Review*, 32, 1460–1462.

Treverton, F. G., Wollman, M., Wilke, E. and Lai, D. (2011). *Moving toward the future of policing*. Santa Monica, CA: Rand Corporation.

Tulsky, F. N. (2006, January). Tainted trials, stolen justice [series], *San Jose Mercury News*. Accessed http://www.nlada.org/DMS/Documents/1138373597.07/index.html.

U.S. Fidelity & Guaranty Co. v. Koch, 102 F.2d 288 (1939).

Urofsky, M. I. (1991). *Felix Frankfurter: Judicial restraint and individual liberties*. Boston: Twayne Publishers.

Vance, C. R., Jr. (2010). A conviction integrity initiative. *Albany Law Review*, 73, 1213–1217.

Vollmer, A. (1933). Police progress in the past twenty-five years. *American Institute of Criminal Law & Criminology*, 24, 161–175.

Walker, S. (1977). *A critical history of police reform: The emergence of professionalism*. Lexington, MA: Lexington Books/D.C. Heath & Co.

Walker, S. (1999). *The police in America: An introduction, third edition*. Boston, MA McGraw-Hill College.

Walker, S. (2004). Science and politics in police research: Reflections on their tangled relationship. *Annals of the American Academy of Political and Social Science*, 593, 137–155.

Warden, R. (2003). The revolutionary role of journalism in identifying and rectifying wrongful convictions. *UMKC Law Review*, 70, 803–846.

Weinberg, S., Gordon, N. and Williams B. (2003). *Harmful error: Investigating America's local prosecutors*. Washington, DC: Center for Public Integrity.

Westley, W. A. (1970). *Violence and the police: A sociological study of law, custom, and morality*. Cambridge, MA and London: MIT Press.

Wiebe, R. H. (1967). *The search for order: 1877-1920*. New York: Hill and Wang.

Wigmore, J. H. (1913). Editorial: The bill to make compensation for persons erroneously convicted of crime. *Journal of the American Institute of Criminal Law and Criminology*, 3, 665–667.

Witt, J. H. (2004). *The accidental republic: Crippled workmen, destitute widows, and the remaking of American law*. Cambridge, MA and London: Harvard University Press.

Zalman, M. (2012). Qualitatively estimating the incidence of wrongful convictions. *Criminal Law Bulletin*, 48(2), 221–279.

17

WRONGFUL CONVICTIONS, MISCARRIAGES OF JUSTICE, AND POLITICAL REPRESSION

CHALLENGES FOR TRANSITIONAL JUSTICE

C. Ronald Huff

A great deal of discussion has focused on the definition of "wrongful conviction." One important definition, by inference, can be found in the Council of Europe's (1998) Convention for the Protection of Human Rights and Fundamental Freedoms:

> Protocol No. 7, Article 3, Compensation for Wrongful Conviction
> When a person has by a final decision been convicted of a criminal offence and when subsequently his conviction has been reversed, or he has been pardoned, on the ground that a new or newly discovered fact shows conclusively that there has been a miscarriage of justice, the person who has suffered punishment as a result of such conviction shall be compensated according to the law or the practice of the State concerned, unless it is proved that the non-disclosure of the unknown fact in time is wholly or partly attributable to him.

In a previous publication, we said the following: "Convicted innocents . . . are people who have been arrested on criminal charges . . . who have either pleaded guilty to the charge or have been tried and found guilty; and who, notwithstanding plea or verdict, are in fact innocent" (Huff, Rattner, and Sagarin, 1996: 10). We excluded those cases in which a conviction was overturned but did not result in a clear showing of innocence because a "not guilty" finding does not necessarily mean that the person was actually innocent. In recent years, that conservative definitional approach ("actual innocence") has become easier to establish in cases where biological evidence is available for testing, due to advances in the use of DNA tests. For example, according to the Innocence Project's database (www.innocenceproject.org/know/), there had been 301 post-conviction DNA-based exonerations in the U.S. as of December, 2012. Among those cases:

- Eighteen people had been sentenced to death before DNA proved their innocence and led to their release.
- The average sentence served by DNA exonerees has been 13.6 years.
- About 70 percent of those exonerated by DNA testing are people of color.
- In almost 50 percent of DNA exoneration cases, the actual perpetrator has been identified by DNA testing.
- Exonerations have been won in 35 states and Washington, D.C.

Many of those cases have been described by Scheck, Neufeld, and Dwyer in their book, *Actual Innocence: When Justice Goes Wrong and How to Make It Right* (2003).

Of course, DNA-based exonerations represent only the proverbial "tip of the iceberg." According to the recently launched National Registry of Exonerations database (http://www.law.umich.edu/special/exoneration/Pages/about.aspx), there have been more than 2,000 known exonerations in the U.S. since 1989. The Registry, a joint project of the University of Michigan Law School and Northwestern University's Center on Wrongful Convictions, profiles more than 1,000 of those exonerations, with searchable data and summaries of the cases. It represents both the largest collection of such cases ever assembled and the best sample of different types of cases, including both DNA-based exonerations and those not based on DNA; state and federal cases; and a variety of violent and non-violent, as well as white collar, crimes. Recent research has produced valuable insights into the factors associated with such wrongful convictions in the U.S. and in many European cases, as well (see, for example, the discussions by Gross, Chapter 3; Garrett, Chapter 5; Petro and Petro, Chapter 6; Brants, Chapter 9; and Lappas and Loftus, Chapter 15).

DNA profiling, which has been so valuable in producing exonerations in the U.S., was first used in forensic science in a criminal case in the U.K. in the 1980s and its use for this purpose has been expanding rapidly in many nations. It has become the "gold standard" for proving that someone could not have committed the crime for which he was convicted or charged. It is enormously useful in dealing with the injustices associated with wrongful conviction. (For more information concerning the use of DNA and issues concerning forensic science, see the discussions by Cole and Thompson in Chapter 7, and Vuille, Taroni, and Biedermann in Chapter 8.)

But there are other kinds of injustice for which DNA profiling cannot help. There are the 90 percent or so of criminal cases in which no biological evidence exists, thus ruling out DNA testing even though the accused/convicted may be innocent. But there are still other kinds of injustice. In fact, from a broader intellectual perspective, cases of proven wrongful conviction based on a standard of actual innocence represent only one important type of miscarriage of justice. What about those who have been convicted of "crimes" that were crimes only because they were defined as such by politically repressive governments? Such convictions, while not technically qualifying as wrongful convictions since they were based on actual violations of existing law, can certainly be viewed as miscarriages of justice since the laws that were broken were unjust. For the sake of clarity, these can be considered to be "convictions based on political repression" and classified as another type of miscarriage of justice, rather than a wrongful conviction per se, reserving the latter category for convictions that occur despite actual innocence.

To be certain, many criminal convictions that have occurred under repressive regimes involve "ordinary crimes"—major crimes such as homicide, robbery, burglary, and rape and less serious crimes such as petty theft that would also be considered crimes in liberal democratic societies. Convictions for those offenses are not included in this conceptualization of convictions based on political repression. What are some examples of the latter? Such examples would include convictions under existing laws for engaging in behaviors perceived by repressive regimes as anti-government (e.g., organizing protests; publishing materials or making public comments that are critical of the repressive government; engaging in behavior that is perceived as threatening the existing economic or social order; or possession of weapons if the weapons were needed to defend oneself against the repressive regime or to overthrow it). Following democratization, many issues arise concerning how to address the violations of human rights and other abuses of power that occurred under earlier, repressive regimes. One such challenge is what to do about criminal convictions based solely on political repression:

> (T)here has been a remarkable movement in various regions of the world away from undemocratic and repressive rule towards the establishment of constitutional democracies. In nearly all instances, the displaced regimes were characterized by massive violations of human rights and undemocratic systems of governance ... As all these countries recover from the trauma and wounds of the past, they have had to devise mechanisms not only for handling past human rights violations, but also to ensure that the dignity of the victims, survivors, and relatives is restored. In the context of this relentless search for appropriate equilibria, profound issues of policy and law have emerged.
>
> *Nelson Mandela, 1995*

The Impacts of Wrongful Conviction

Citizens, and nation states, should care deeply about these errors for a number of reasons. First, they involve the conviction, and often incarceration and even execution, of innocent persons. Imagine the trauma of being in prison for something you didn't do. Such injustices damage not only the wrongfully convicted person but also, in many cases, his family, as shown by Westervelt and Cook in Chapter 13. One of the best studies of the psychological impact of wrongful conviction was carried out by Adrian Grounds (Grounds, 2005), a forensic psychiatrist at the Institute of Criminology at Cambridge. Grounds completed clinical assessments of eleven wrongfully convicted men, five of whom were victims of injustice in the notorious British cases known as "the Birmingham Six" and "the Guildford Four."

In October 1974, the IRA bombed two "pubs" in Guildford, England, causing the deaths of five Army recruits. Three young Irishmen and a 17-year-old English woman were wrongfully convicted and sentenced to life imprisonment. They were released in 1989, having spent 15 years in prison for a crime they did not commit.

Just seven weeks after the Guildford bombings, the IRA bombed two "pubs" in the center of Birmingham, England, resulting in the deaths of 21 people and injuries to 162 others. Six Irishmen who lived in Birmingham were convicted of the 21 murders and sentenced to life imprisonment. After serving more than 16 years in prison, they were freed when it was discovered that the prosecution's principal case had rested on false and coerced confessions, misleading testimony, and withheld exculpatory evidence concerning a chemical test for explosives. This case was later featured in the powerful movie, *In the Name of the Father*. These two cases, following a number of other errors over the years that had been documented by Ludovic Kennedy, led to a crisis in public confidence in the criminal justice system, and on the day following the release of the Birmingham Six, the British government announced the formation of a Royal Commission to review the operation of the criminal justice system.

Grounds followed up on 11 wrongfully convicted men who served prison terms ranging from 4 to 16 years (mean = 12 years, median = 13 years). They were, on average, 30 years old when incarcerated and about 42 when released. As he put it, "Those who had been in . . . longest had lost a generation of family life. Parents had died and children had grown up. Young men who entered prison as fathers of young children were released as middle-aged men with grandchildren."

Grounds acknowledges that he "didn't expect to find much," based on the absence of prior histories of mental illness and the general findings in the research literature, which implied that there was little solid evidence of psychological deterioration in long-term imprisonment. What Grounds discovered, he said, was "wholly unexpected." His assessments revealed a pattern of severe disabling symptoms and psychological problems that were comparable in all 11 cases. He returned to the research literature and found striking similarities in symptomatology in documented cases involving hostages and the victims of natural disasters. In 10 of the 11 cases, the personality change could be classified as "enduring" and included estrangement, loss of capacity for intimacy, moodiness, inability to settle, and loss of a sense of purpose and direction. Indicative of these symptoms was one mother's comment to Dr. Grounds concerning her son: "He is like a stranger … He always used to be affectionate. Now he can't express emotion, he can't sit and talk. He jumps about, he is unsettled. Prison has changed him. His personality has changed."

Eight of the men were diagnosed as having post-traumatic stress symptoms, generally related to specific threats or violence they experienced following arrest or while in prison; three had made false and coerced confessions; 10 of the 11 reported being terrified of being assaulted or killed; and three of them suffered serious violence (two were sexually assaulted and one was stabbed). Some reported experiencing violence and abuse by prison staff. Several said that they had learned to be "highly aggressive and intimidating as a form of self-protection." They also suffered in their social adjustment following their sudden release from prison. They could not cope with ordinary tasks such as shopping, operating mechanical controls, using credit cards or ATM machines. One of the men told Grounds that he felt humiliated by his lack of ability and the need to ask his wife to teach him basic skills. "It's like when someone has a stroke; you have to be taught how to do things again," he said.

Some children of the wrongfully convicted, having suddenly lost their fathers, developed significant psychological problems. Some had to cope with sudden poverty and hunger, as well. Families were shunned because they were related to the men who had been arrested and because they were Irish. A mother was physically attacked several times. One woman told Dr. Grounds that she and her children were sworn at, spat at, had their house vandalized, a noose hung on their gate, and graffiti painted on the house that said "Hang Irish Bastards" and "Scum." The women became seriously depressed, and one considered using her gas oven to kill herself. They used alcohol to cope with their depression and stress, leading one of the children to say, "She turned to drink. I hated her for it … As young children, we blamed her. She didn't have any more to give us."

In addition to the psychological consequences of serving time in prison for a crime that one did not commit, we know that there are many other negative consequences that occur. A detailed analysis and discussion concerning many of those challenges and consequences is provided by Westervelt and Cook in Chapter 13.

A second reason for concern relates to public safety. Wrongful convictions allow the actual criminal to go free, unless he has been incarcerated for a different offense. While he remains free, he may commit many more crimes. How many violent crimes, for example, might occur during the years when an innocent person is in prison? And how much more difficult will it be to convict the real criminal as years go by, witnesses' memories fade or they pass away, and other leads disappear?

Third, wrongful convictions undermine the public's confidence in the criminal justice system, which was also noted by Forst in Chapter 2. In those cases involving jury trials, juries may be more reluctant to convict actual offenders when they distrust the system. And certainly, convictions based solely on political repression violate the public's trust in both the ruling government and its criminal justice system.

State Obligations Regarding Wrongful Conviction

The problem of wrongful conviction is a problem that democratic nations are obligated to address. This is not just an option, but is a mandate. For example, the International Court of Justice, in a case decided in 1970,[1] stated: "With regard more particularly to human rights ... it should be noted that these also include protection against denial of justice."[2]

Growing concern in the United States led to the enactment of the Innocence Protection Act, which was incorporated in the Justice for All Act in 2004.[3] That Act included a number of reforms designed to reduce wrongful convictions of the innocent. The Act calls for greater access to DNA testing, better quality legal representation in death penalty cases, and compensation for those who are wrongfully convicted and imprisoned, among other reforms.

Transitional Justice: Multiple Challenges

The term "transitional justice" (sometimes referred to as "retrospective justice") generally refers to the policies and procedures (governmental and non-governmental, criminal and civil in nature) that newly democratic societies adopt to address the human rights violations, atrocities, and other abuses of power that occurred during the preceding repressive regimes. The public often associates transitional justice with truth commissions, the Nuremberg Trials, the trial of former Yugoslavian President Slobodan Milošević, and other high profile criminal prosecutions, but the meaning of transitional justice is much broader, encompassing many aspects of the newly democratizing society's transition and its attempts to "deal with the past." This discussion will focus solely on the criminal justice issues that occur during such periods.

Much of the attention in the scholarly literature has focused on how the perpetrators have been dealt with. As one scholar notes, for example:

> The debate over transitional criminal justice is marked by profound dilemmas: Whether to punish or to amnesty? Whether punishment is a backward-looking exercise in retribution or an expression of the renewal of the rule of law? Who properly bears responsibility for past repression? To what extent is responsibility for repression appropriate to the individual, as opposed to the collective, the regime, and even the entire society?
>
> *Teitel, 2000: 27*

Less attention has been paid to the victims and how they might be exonerated and, ideally, compensated for the injustices that they suffered. In part, this is undoubtedly due to the fact that there were far more victims than perpetrators, making it much easier and perhaps more feasible (given financial and practical constraints) to address the perpetrators and attempt to hold them accountable. The practical problems involved in identifying these victims (often exacerbated by missing or inaccurate or altered official files and records) and the financial limitations on emerging democratic societies (often exacerbated by the economic devastation caused by war) have generally resulted in far less than satisfactory resolutions of this problem. The problem itself is generally referred to as "reparatory justice." Several important documents address the obligation of states and successor states (those democracies that emerge following repressive regimes) to provide redress, compensation, and/or some form of rehabilitation for such victims of injustice. These include the *Declaration of Basic Principles of Justice for Victims of Crime and Abuse of Power* (United Nations, General Assembly, 1985); the *Study Concerning the Right to Restitution, Compensation, and Rehabilitation for Victims of Gross Violations of Human Rights and Fundamental Freedoms* (United Nations Economic and Security Council, 1993); and the *Recommendation on No. R (84) 15 on Public Liability* (Council of Europe, 1984).

These important documents have helped establish the principle, generally accepted in international law, that successor state governments are responsible for attempting to help correct the injustices of the past. As one prominent human rights proponent and author noted, societies faced with a legacy of human rights violations must strive to fulfill four obligations that the state owes to the victims and to society. One of those obligations, he said, "is to grant reparations to victims in a manner that recognizes their worth and their dignity as human beings. Monetary compensation . . . is certainly a part of this duty, but [this also should include] nonmonetary gestures that express recognition of the harm done to them (Mendez, 1997: 12). Edwin Borchard would certainly concur!

Transitional Justice in Poland

"It is better to leave a guilty man unpunished than to convict an innocent man."
>   English translation of an inscription appearing on the
>   Supreme Court building, Republic of Poland

This admonition is deeply ingrained in the evolution of many democratic societies and their judicial systems, as well as in philosophy. Voltaire (1747) wrote, "It is better to risk saving a guilty person than to condemn an innocent one." Two decades later, Sir William Blackstone proclaimed, "It is better that ten persons escape than one innocent suffer" (Blackstone, 1765). Of course, both Type I and Type II errors are serious problems for justice and for public safety and both are to be avoided (see the discussion by Forst, Chapter 2). Convictions based solely on political repression constitute one kind of Type I error, not because the convicted person is necessarily innocent of violating extant law but because some laws are based solely on such political repression. From the perspective of political philosophy, such systems of "justice" violate the tenets of social contract theory as set forth in more recent history by Rawls (1971) and by earlier philosophers such as Rousseau (1762) because they certainly do not reflect the consent of the governed.

One example of a nation that has undertaken a critical period of transitional justice is the Republic of Poland. As noted in an earlier publication on wrongful conviction in Poland (Plywaczewski, Gorski, and Sakowicz, 2008), Poland has adopted two different approaches to "dealing with the past" with respect to wrongful convictions. One approach involves what is known as "extraordinary revision" and it includes several different procedures, one of which is via the Ombudsman, who has the authority to become engaged in cases involving violations of human rights, for example. The other (and historically remarkable) approach occurred with the passage of the Rehabilitation Act—a special law that invalidates some categories of former politically based convictions by courts and special commissions.

In the Rehabilitation Act of 1991, any sentences meted out against people in connection with their activities in favor of the independence of Poland,[4] were declared void. Declaring a verdict invalid automatically implies *declaring the defendant not guilty*. This approach solves the formal as well as the moral side of the problem. The Rehabilitation Act declares void any rulings by Courts made between January 1, 1944 and the end of the year 1956 (when the first political change occurred in Poland). The law was not limited to court judgments only. It included the decisions of "special commissions" that, despite their role in political procedures, cannot be regarded as courts (Plywaczewski, Gorski, and Sakowicz, 2008: 276–277).

In operationalizing this Act, the Polish Supreme Court later stated that only by analyzing the intention of the convicted person (that is, the defendant's will) would it be possible to determine whether the conduct that led to the conviction fit within the legislative intent reflected in the Rehabilitation Act. For example, if someone was convicted of possessing illegal weapons, did that person have the weapons in order to help overthrow the communist regime or was he simply a common criminal? A recent interview conducted with the 1st President of the Supreme Court of Poland confirmed that each case brought to the Court's attention had to be considered based on the detailed facts of the case, including the individual's motivation at the time, and that this necessitated a great deal of time for each case in order to ensure a fair consideration of the facts (Gardocki, 2010).

The Rehabilitation Act wisely included decisions made by special commissions, whose jurisdictions included such "crimes" as inflicting economic damage on the socialist state. Such commissions provided none of the safeguards associated with fair trials and operated with a general presumption of guilt rather than innocence in its verdicts (Plywaczewski,

Gorski, and Sakowicz, 2008: 277). Section 8 of the Rehabilitation Act also provided the opportunity to award victims both material and moral compensation for the damages caused by a wrongful verdict. In addition, Poland is a party to the European Convention of Human Rights, which also affirms a right to compensation. Finally, the role of the Ombudsman in Poland has been a critical one, and that office has paid special attention to wrongful convictions that occurred under the communist regime. During the last period for which data are available (1992 to 2003), the annual compensation paid to victims of wrongful conviction averaged about €200,000 (Plywaczewski, Gorski, and Sakowicz, 2008: 279–281).

Transitional Justice in Hungary

A final example of an attempt to address the "wrongs of the past" can be seen in the nation of Hungary. Law No. 11 (1992), passed by the National Assembly, stated:

> (A)n adjudicative practice in conflict with the basic principles contained in the then effective Constitution, and repugnant to generally recognized principles and rules of human rights and to society's system of moral values, has prevailed . . . The National Assembly condemns this legal practice and intends to provide moral satisfaction to all those who suffered as a result.
>
> *National Assembly of Hungary, 1992*

That Law declared null and void convictions that took place between April 5, 1963, and October 15, 1989, for a number of criminal acts, including conspiracy; insurrection; incitement; conspiracy or insurrection against another socialist state; offending an authority or an official person; offending the community; incitement against a law or action by the authorities; abuse of the right to associate with others; prohibited border crossing; refusal to return to Hungary; crime against the people's freedom; misdemeanors violating rules governing the press; and others "provided that the commission of the crime constituted an exercise of the basic rights enumerated in the International Covenant on Civil and Political Rights proclaimed by Decree With the Force of Law No. 8 of 1976, or the realization of the principles and goals contained therein" (National Assembly of Hungary, 1982). In separate public laws, the National

Assembly also provided for the compensation of those whose convictions were nullified by Law No. 11 and for those whose private property was violated by the State under the prior regime.

Conclusions

Countless individuals in numerous nations have suffered criminal convictions based solely on political repression, often accompanied by long periods of confinement and even torture. While the field of criminology has paid increasing attention to the problem of wrongful convictions and public attention has been increased due to highly publicized DNA-based exonerations, little attention has been paid to the problem of convictions based on political repression and how such convictions might be conceived as a subtype of wrongful conviction—"wrongful" in the sense that they are unjust. Such convictions have victimized countless individuals in nations that were formerly controlled by communist regimes, such as Poland and Hungary, and also in nations that were formerly characterized by other repressive regimes, such as that which practiced apartheid in South Africa for nearly five decades. Convictions based on political repression pose multiple challenges for transitional justice following the democratization of formerly repressive governments. Both Poland and Hungary serve as examples of how transitional democracies can confront the injustices of the past and, through democratic legislative and judicial processes, allow for the nullification of unjust convictions and appropriate compensation for victims where appropriate. This issue may become increasingly timely in the near future, given the recent revolutions and protests in a number of Middle Eastern nations characterized by repressive regimes.

Notes

1   Barcelona Traction Light and Power Company case [Belgium v. Spain, 1970], International Court of Justice, Rep. 44, as cited by Knoops, 2006: 6–8.
2   Id., para 47, as cited by Knoops, 2006: 8.
3   Public Law No. 108–405, 108th Congress, 2nd Session, 2004.
4   One example involves one of the author's colleagues, a professor at a U.S. university who was originally from Poland. He was convicted and incarcerated in Poland for publishing-related activities in support of the Solidarity Movement for Polish independence.

References

Blackstone, Sir William, *Commentaries on the Laws of England*. Book IV:27. London: Strahan (15th edition), 1765.

Council of Europe, *Recommendation on No. R (84) 15 on Public Liability* (adopted on September 18, 1984).

Council of Europe, *Protocol No. 7 to the Convention for the Protection of Human Rights and Fundamental Freedoms, as amended by Protocol No. 11* (adopted on November 1, 1998).

Gardocki, L. (1st President, Supreme Court of Poland). Interview notes, C. Ronald Huff, May 21, 2010, Warsaw.

Grounds, A. "Understanding the Effects of Wrongful Imprisonment." Pp. 1–58 in M. Tonry (ed.), *Crime and Justice: A Review of Research (Volume 32)*. Chicago: University of Chicago Press, 2005.

Huff C. R., Rattner A., and Sagarin E., *Convicted but Innocent: Wrongful Conviction and Public Policy*, Thousand Oaks, CA and London: Sage, 1996.

Innocence Project, "Innocence Project Case Profiles." (www.innocenceproject.org/know). Retrieved on July 9, 2012.

Knoops, G-J. *Redressing Miscarriages of Justice: Practice and Procedure in National and International Criminal Law Cases*. Ardsley, NY: Transnational Publishers, 2006.

Mandela, N. "Foreword." P. xiii in N. J. Kritz (ed.), *Transitional Justice: How Emerging Democracies Reckon with Former Regimes* (Volume III: Laws, Rulings, and Reports).Washington, DC: United States Institute of Peace Press, 1995.

Mendez, J. E. "In Defense of Transitional Justice." Pp. 1–26 in A. J. McAdams (ed.), *Transitional Justice and the Rule of Law in New Democracies*. Notre Dame, IN: University of Notre Dame Press, 1997.

National Assembly of Hungary. *Law No. 11* (adopted on February 19, 1992).

National Registry of Exonerations, "Exonerations in the United States, 1989–2012." (http://www.law.umich.edu/special/exoneration/Pages/about.aspx). Retrieved July 12, 2012.

Plywaczewski, E. W., Gorski, A., and Sakowicz, A., "Wrongful Convictions in Poland: From the Communist Era to the Rechtstaat Experience." Pp. 273–283 in Huff, C. R. and M. Killias (eds.), *Wrongful Convictions: International Perspectives on Miscarriages of Justice*. Philadelphia: Temple University Press, 2008.

Rawls, J., *A Theory of Justice*. [1971]. Cambridge, MA: Harvard University Press, (revised edition) 1999.

Rousseau, J.-J., *The Social Contract*. [1762]. In P. D. Jimack, *The Social Contract and Discourses*. (revised edition). Rutland, VT: Charles E. Tuttle, 1993.

Scheck, B., Neufeld, P., and Dwyer, J., *Actual Innocence: When Justice Goes Wrong and How to Make It Right*. New York: New American Library, 2003.

Teitel, R. G., *Transitional Justice*. New York: Oxford University Press, 2000.

United Nations, General Assembly. *General Assembly Resolution 40/34* (adopted on November 29, 1985).

United Nations, Economic and Security Council. *Study Concerning the Right to Restitution, Compensation, and Rehabilitation for Victims of Gross Violations of Human Rights and Fundamental Freedoms: Final Report*. July 2, 1993.

Voltaire, *Zadig*. Chapter 6. [1747] New York: Signet, (reissue) 1961.

PART III

WRONGFUL CONVICTIONS AND MISCARRIAGES OF JUSTICE

CONCLUSIONS AND RECOMMENDATIONS

18
WRONGFUL CONVICTIONS AND MISCARRIAGES OF JUSTICE – WHAT DID WE LEARN?

Martin Killias and C. Ronald Huff

At the end of an edited book, it is not the editors' job to simply summarize the preceding chapters, but instead it is generally expected that they will offer some "take-away" messages. To comply with our readers' expectations, what messages can we offer? We shall try to review:

(1) what we understand by "wrongful" in this context;
(2) the size of the problem;
(3) current knowledge about major sources of wrongful convictions, including errors in forensic science;
(4) the role of prosecutors and other key players in criminal justice procedure;
(5) the role of procedural systems;
(6) the consequences of wrongful convictions beyond exoneration;
(7) possible remedies.

Ideally, we would prefer to base our conclusions on the model of a meta-analysis that might produce quantitative statements on the respective merits of competing explanations and possible remedies. Unfortunately, research in this area is rarely quantitative but is predominantly descriptive, and although we have made an effort to adopt a comparative approach in this volume, as well as in a preceding book (Huff and Killias, 2008), we are far from the kind of clear-cut conclusions that truly comparative studies can produce. The main reason for this shortcoming is not simply the lack of quantitative data but also the fact that there is no set of independent variables—such as reliance on witnesses rather than forensic science, the way witnesses are interviewed in court, the way key players' roles are shaped in several systems, and so forth—whose importance could be assessed through a comparative analysis. Keeping these limitations in mind, we shall, nevertheless, try to summarize what we believe can be learned about the seven issues identified above as critically important in advancing the study of miscarriages of justice.

What Kinds of Judicial Errors Should We Care About?

Brian Forst (Chapter 2) reminds us that miscarriages of justice go far beyond what is at the center of our attention, in this book and in general—namely the conviction of factually innocent defendants. Another serious error is the failure to convict the guilty offender. This sort of miscarriage of justice frustrates the victim and jeopardizes public safety since the offender is typically free (unless incarcerated for another offense) to continue victimizing other citizens. This outcome can be produced by errors at trial or during the preceding stages of the criminal justice process, but it can also occur when victims fail to report offenses to the police.[1] As Forst points out, this type of error is probably the most common among all errors, although it cannot necessarily be attributed to courts or to other agents of the criminal justice system. There are also other errors, such as the arrest, prosecution, and indictment of factually innocent defendants who, despite being acquitted in the end, may suffer considerable financial losses and damage to their reputations. Worse, as Campbell (Chapter 11) reminds us, innocent persons may be subjected to long pretrial detention without adequate legal redress, especially if they are considered to be terrorists or proxies for terrorist organizations. They may be denied immigration and deported or, if their name appears on any of the "blacklists" that have been created during the post-9/11 years, they may have their assets seized.

This problem has grown considerably—both quantitatively and qualitatively—in the aftermath of post-9/11 legislation when (particularly in the United States) the decision was taken to approach the threat of terrorism not under the umbrella of criminal law, but as a foreign policy issue to be dealt with in military terms (see Campbell, Chapter 11). Ironically, terrorists – and not only those held at Guantanamo Bay—are deprived not only of the rights they would have under the Geneva Conventions as military personnel of an enemy force, but also of the rights protecting defendants in ordinary criminal cases. As Campbell observes, it seems that Canada has found solutions that are more respectful of civil rights than what has been the U.S. policy in this respect. In Europe, the European Convention of Human Rights and Fundamental Freedoms (now known as the European Convention on Human Rights), along with the control of national governments by the European Human Rights Court, have tempered legislative attempts to restrict civil rights in the name of fighting terrorist threats.

Miscarriages of justice also include errors of misinterpretation of substantive criminal law by the courts. Such errors occur when a defendant is convicted for what is not an offense or when he is acquitted despite the fact that his act would have been legally punishable. These kinds of errors are often, but not always, redressed through appeals, given that higher courts, almost everywhere, are entitled to review issues related to the interpretation of law. Finally, miscarriages of justice can also arise from violations of procedural rules and standards of due process. Along with Forst (Chapter 2), one can question, however, whether such errors are equally serious—at least if they do not translate into erroneous outcomes. In a world where lawyers are extremely nervous about violations of procedural rules, it may be salutary to be reminded that, in the end, outcomes matter more than just the rules of the game. Forst's assertion that wrongful convictions (in the sense used throughout this book) can only be avoided if there are no longer any convictions is thought-provoking, but the challenge remains for us to figure out how to reduce "false positives" (wrongful convictions) without increasing the proportion of "false negatives" (wrongful acquittals).

While we attempt to provide some answers to this later in this chapter, we are also acutely aware that the world is always more complex than theories, or policy reforms, suggest. For example, even if we restrict our concern to the convictions of factually innocent defendants, Aebi and Campistol (Chapter 10) remind us that there are also errors (wrongful convictions) that are due to the willful manipulation of the criminal justice system by defendants who accept (or even seek) being convicted of crimes they never committed in order to protect others—perhaps even members of criminal or terrorist groups. In Chapter 17, Huff describes yet another type of miscarriage of justice—convictions based solely on political repression. Drawing on the experiences of such nations as Poland, Hungary, and South Africa, Huff includes in this category cases of people who were either (1) convicted of common crimes that they actually did not commit but were found guilty because police, prosecutors, and courts deferred to political pressures or (2) convicted because they violated laws that were enacted to restrict human rights as a result of politically repressive regimes.

How Many Innocent Defendants are Convicted?

If we stick to the narrow definition of "wrongful conviction" that prevails across the chapters of this book, the question arises as to how many defendants end up being convicted, after exhausting all appeals, even though they never committed the offenses of which they are found guilty. As Zalman (2012) points out, it is really not feasible to estimate reliably the incidence of wrongful convictions, since there is no way to know how many convictions might be erroneous out of all verdicts in a given jurisdiction per year. Taking known exonerations as a lower bound, Gross (Chapter 3) arrives at a minimum rate of 1.5 percent of defendants who were wrongly sentenced to death. However, this rate is probably not the final word, since new exonerations continue to be added to the list. It certainly does not reflect the full story, since death sentences disproportionately concern cases of homicide and/or rape, where DNA analysis can more efficiently be used to assess innocence even after a long time has elapsed (see also Cole & Thompson, Chapter 7).[2] In other cases, the odds of finding new evidence that may lead to exoneration are obviously far more limited. On the other hand, around half of homicide cases go to trial, as Gilliéron (Chapter 12) points out, whereas plea bargaining is the rule in more than nine out of ten cases in other areas. And since errors are probably more frequent in cases handled through plea bargains and summary proceedings than in those that go to trial, one might expect the rate of errors to be lower than average in murder (and, especially, capital) cases (but see Liebman et al., 2000, for an analysis of error rates in capital cases). Thus, the rate of 1.5 percent of wrongfully convicted death row inmates may be a conservative estimate. Indeed, estimates of wrongful convictions in rape cases, based on a sample of old cases from Virginia, as reported by Gross in Chapter 3, are slightly above 5 percent. Estimates for Germany, France, Switzerland, and the Netherlands fall far short of such proportions, even after adjusting for population and for the number of convictions (Killias, 2008). Even in the Netherlands, the four cases reported by Brants (Chapter 9), spanning roughly two decades, suggest fewer exonerations in that country. According to data from the *European Sourcebook of Crime and Criminal Justice Statistics* (2010, Table 3.2.5.1/ p. 255), about 50 defendants per year are sentenced to more than 10 years[3] in the Netherlands. Thus, the proportion of exonerations would be about one case every second year or at least 10 such cases in 20 years. Whatever the frequencies actually may be, it should be clear that, in the United States and some other countries, the proportion of innocent people receiving long sentences is unacceptably high. Later, we shall consider possible causes in a comparative perspective.

How often do defendants intentionally accept (or even "volunteer") to be convicted for offenses committed by fellow offenders or members of the same gang, terrorist group, or ethnic clan? The study by Aebi and Campistol (Chapter 10) suggests that there are some indications that this problem exists among juvenile and Roma groups in Spain, although the frequency with which this occurs may have been exaggerated in the public's perception. However, there is no indication that members of terrorist groups (and especially of the Basque terrorist organization ETA) or offenders belonging to criminal organizations have ever used this tactic to protect fellow members who were not under suspicion or prosecution. Therefore, this phenomenon may not have reached a sufficient level to justify its being considered a significant type of wrongful conviction (except insofar as it corresponds to false confessions in general).

Prominent Causes of Wrongful Convictions

Garrett (Chapter 5) identifies three major sources of errors during trial: the use of jailhouse informants (combined with prosecutorial misconduct), contaminated confessions, and eyewitness misidentification. According to the rates reported by Garrett, each of these causes contributes to a very substantial proportion of errors. Informant statements, including those made by cellmates, co-defendants, and cooperating witnesses played a role in 20 percent of the first 250 exonerations based on newly available DNA evidence in the United States. Confessions obtained through unfair interview methods accounted for 26 percent of exonerations in that sample. We also know, based on many studies, that eyewitness misidentification plays a major role in wrongful convictions, particularly in cases of rape, where the central issue at trial is the identity of the actual offender. It may be that DNA testing has, in more recent years, helped limit the role of eyewitnesses in identifying the suspect. Even if DNA evidence simply raises new concerns, this trend certainly is an improvement over relying so heavily on eyewitness testimony that is subject to so much cognitive and physiological distortion.

The decreasing reliance on witnesses is a direct result of the increasing role of forensic science in establishing guilt or innocence. As Cole and Thompson (Chapter 7) point out, exonerations were greatly assisted by the generalization of DNA testing. As they note, the notion that there is a wrongful conviction "problem" and that this notion has by now assumed the status of "common knowledge" is largely a product of forensic science— especially DNA testing. Perhaps more than one-third of all exonerations thus far can be attributed, at least in part, to DNA testing. However, as Cole and Thompson caution us, forensic science has also emerged as a major contributor to several high-profile wrongful convictions—for example, in the notorious wrongful convictions related to the Irish Republican Army bombing cases. Although classical methods of forensic science, such as serological testing, microscopic hair comparisons, and fingerprints are more often associated with miscarriages of justice, DNA testing is not beyond suspicion. One of the leading causes of errors in forensic expertise is inadequate statistical inferences based on the materials available, leading to exaggerated statements about the strength of the evidence[4]. Another source of error, according to forensic scientists interviewed by Schiffer (2009), was incompetent recovery of evidence from the crime scene. These and related errors were also prominently represented in the Amanda Knox case in Italy, which Vuille, Biedermann, and Taroni (Chapter 8) used as an illustration of errors in forensic science. For example, the expert failed to inform the court that the machine had warned her that the level of DNA was too low to be relied upon. There were also problems related to the recovery of objects at the crime scene. The officers were wearing gloves, but did not change gloves after touching an object and before touching another one. They also walked from one room to the next without changing their shoe protections. But the most serious problems were related to the interpretation of the materials and the tests that were performed. Rather than offering the court, as requested by the judges, "a degree of proof," the experts failed to consider the findings in light of the competing versions of events presented by the prosecution and the defense. Indeed, scientific findings can have only a gradual discriminative capacity for distinguishing between propositions. As Vuille, Biedermann, and Taroni conclude, it is not the scientist's role to decide for the judge, but to allow the court, in an intelligible and adequate language, to consider the competing versions of the truth presented by both parties and to assess their relative probabilities.

The Roles of Prosecutors, Defense Counsels, Witnesses, and Other Key Players

In addition to experts who may fall short of professional standards, other key players may commit more or fewer fatal errors during the trial process. Witnesses may err not only by misidentifying offenders. They may occasionally lie and invent stories that never occurred. Defense lawyers may be lazy in searching for exculpatory evidence, or they may miss opportunities to cite violations of procedural rules. Unfortunately, there is no obvious answer concerning how such sources of error might be eliminated. The only possible way may be to reduce the importance of human beings—for example, by assigning higher priority, whenever possible, to forensic or material evidence rather than to oral statements by witnesses. Regarding the defense, it may be possible to increase the emphasis on finding the truth and on holding prosecutors and judges more accountable for doing so. As a result, defense counsels may become less critically important in the prevention of wrongful convictions, as is generally the case under continental Europe's inquisitorial systems (see Killias, Chapter 4). While that would be highly controversial in the U.S., such a shift in emphasis must be considered in the context of severe declines in funding and greatly increased workloads for public defenders, as well as the widespread problems associated with inadequate counsel in an adversarial system that assumes (nearly always incorrectly) that in a battle of equals, the truth will emerge. Given the reality of current constraints, the adversarial system's "battle" analogy too often devolves into a fight between an armed and an unarmed man, in which the truth may not emerge.

And then there is the role of the prosecutor. As Petro and Petro (Chapter 6) report, prosecutorial misconduct occurs far too often in the United States and has been associated with a substantial number of wrongful convictions that later led to exonerations. Even in the face of strong exculpatory evidence, prosecutors sometimes defend wrongful convictions rather than seeking the truth, as evidenced by the materials presented in Chapter 6. Worse, courts later seem more than reluctant to blame prosecutors, even for blatant misconduct. According to data presented by Petro and Petro, only about 1 percent of prosecutorial misconduct led to any disciplinary action by state bar associations in some 600 cases in which the courts found evidence of misconduct. "Tunnel thinking" and "confirmation bias" make actors resist recognizing new evidence that does not fit into the "story" they have come to believe. These cognitive distortions predispose all actors, in any system, uncritically to accept any new piece of information that seems to confirm pre-existing views and to overlook or reject new information that conflicts with those views. This is certainly not limited to American prosecutors. Evidence for similar attitudes has been found in the Netherlands (see Brants, Chapter 9), in Germany (Peters, 1970–1974), and in Switzerland (Killias, 2008). The cases presented by Petro and Petro in Chapter 6, however, go far beyond simple "tunnel vision" and the common human resistance to changing one's view. In disturbingly many cases, American prosecutors have not only ignored or failed to disclose some contradictory pieces of evidence, but have even produced forged evidence in court (see the examples cited by Garrett in Chapter 5) in a way that comes close to perjury, as Petro and Petro rightly observe. Although instances of serious prosecutorial misbehavior are not unknown in other jurisdictions, prosecutors whose misconduct was discovered have not always escaped sanctions in some of those jurisdictions (see the examples cited in Killias, 2008), as has generally been the case in the United States, as documented by the Center for Public Integrity (2003) and other studies. This must be kept in mind with respect to possible remedies.

In discussing prosecutorial misconduct and miscarriages of justice, it should be kept in mind that Garrett (Chapter 5) and Petro and Petro (Chapter 6) refer primarily to exonerations after trials. As Gilliéron (Chapter 12) points out, however, the vast majority of defendants are not convicted in court but instead enter guilty pleas sometime before the case goes to trial. Taking into account European data on wrongful convictions (see Gilliéron, Chapter 12; Killias, 2008), there is good reason to believe that most miscarriages of justice do not occur in a trial court, but in plea negotiations behind closed doors. In an open trial with considerable public attention and many key players present, one may assume that prosecutors, defense counsels, judges, witnesses, and experts all do their best to avoid exposing themselves to blame. There is very limited information on how fair plea negotiations behind closed doors actually are. Do prosecutors disclose, at this stage, possibly exculpatory evidence to defense lawyers? Do the rules about disclosure even apply at this stage? As reported by Brants (Chapter 9), under the European inquisitorial procedures, witnesses and experts are usually heard (by the prosecutor or an examining magistrate, "*juge d'instruction*") during the investigation but in the presence of the defendant and his counsel[5] who have full access to the prosecution's complete file. Thus, a defense lawyer who negotiates any plea (and sentence) with the prosecutor does so with knowledge of the essential information on the merits of the case. Most importantly, however, European continental law allows plea bargaining only in very limited circumstances (see Killias, Chapter 4; Gilliéron, Chapter 12). As a general rule, entering a guilty plea (and accepting a "verdict" and a sentence) is possible only in minor offenses, those not calling for a sentence beyond about six months[6] or a fine. American procedural rules, however, also allow plea bargaining in very serious cases—and without the safeguards that exist during the investigative stage under continental inquisitorial systems.

The Role of Procedural Rules

Complete analyses of exonerations, like those conducted in Germany in the 1960s (Peters, 1970–1974) and in Switzerland (Killias, Gilliéron, and Dongois, 2007), included several hundred exonerations over the course of a decade. However, the great majority of those miscarriages of justice concerned relatively trivial cases, such as traffic offenses, that were dealt with through penal orders (the European equivalent of plea bargaining in cases involving petty offenses). The reason, obviously, is that in summary proceedings, the rights of the defense are often not respected or are waived (in exchange for a milder sentence and/or a more rapid settlement without media coverage), and evidence, if collected at all, is often evaluated very summarily. These simplifications (largely at the cost of the defense) are acceptable, under continental European legal doctrine, as long as the defendant (1) is charged with a minor offense that can only result in a short prison sentence (if any) not exceeding a few months, (2) not only enters a guilty plea but admits having committed the offense[7] and (3) retains the right to require a full trial without risking, if convicted, a much longer sentence (Gilliéron, Chapter 12). None of these safeguards apply under America's adversarial system. Therefore, it comes as no surprise that both wrongful convictions and exonerations appear to be far more frequent in the United States than in Western Europe, even when taking into account the respective populations and numbers of convictions in each nation.

Beyond summary proceedings and their vulnerability to miscarriages of justice, there are a number of critical differences between America's adversarial and continental Europe's inquisitorial systems. The most critical difference, in our judgment, is the responsibility of courts, under the inquisitorial system, to find the "truth," independent of whatever the prosecution and the defense may present, or fail to present, at trial. The courts' responsibility in seeking the truth helps compensate for the poor performance of defense counsels due to lack of resources, poor training, ineffectiveness, and/or incompetence. The prosecution (or, in some countries, "examining magistrate" or "*juge d'instruction*") is charged with the responsibility to direct a neutral investigation, to which the defense is entitled to contribute from the beginning—or at least from a relatively early stage of the proceedings. Prosecutors and police officers who conceal or manipulate critical evidence are liable for criminal prosecution (Killias, Chapter 4). Thus, the relative impunity of American prosecutors, as reported by Petro and Petro (Chapter 6), Garrett (Chapter 5), and the Center for Public Integrity (2003), is hardly imaginable in Europe. As a result, relatively few cases come to court wherein the central facts of the case are still contested. As a general rule, guilty defendants usually confess during the investigation once the prosecution's case becomes strong enough. In the United States, defendants faced with strong evidence generally enter guilty pleas, but in Europe, guilty pleas do not help settle the case, given the limited sentencing options that are available within prosecutors' "penal orders." Thus, many cases that are settled out of court in the United States go to "trial" in Europe, although the essential facts are not contested. The real issue is the sentence and whether or not the court will suspend it in consideration of the defendant's cooperation[8].

How, then, do pitfalls like those described by Brants (Chapter 9) occur? As she explains, there is an inherent tendency toward "tunnel vision" among police officers, prosecutors, and judges and we suggest that this human tendency extends far beyond the Netherlands, to the rest of Europe and beyond. However, these cases should not be interpreted to mean that procedural rules do not matter. Certainly, those four exonerations represent a far lower rate than what has been found in the United States over the last few decades, but this quantitative aspect is far less significant than is a qualitative difference. Indeed, none of the exonerations in the Netherlands concerned a case where prosecutors or police officers had intentionally manipulated (or even "created") evidence. If prosecutors and police officers escaped criminal sanctions, it was precisely because they had acted in good faith, albeit very unprofessionally. More critical, perhaps, is the performance of the Netherlands Forensic Institute (NFI), whose staff was aware that the prosecution was misinterpreting the evidence in the Schiedam Park case (Brants, Chapter 9) but never disclosed their doubts to the court or to the defense. This may be a matter of hierarchical subordination of forensic scientists under the authority of the government, although the NFI[9] is relatively autonomous compared to similar labs in other countries that often are incorporated into police departments. As Brants explains, the poor performance of the NFI staff may have been a side effect of the "culture," which emphasized the importance of not contradicting prosecutors, rather than the competing (and, legally, superordinate) value of seeking the truth.

In sum, all procedural systems are vulnerable to confirmation bias and unwillingness on the part of criminal justice staff to reconsider their vision of a case when presented with conflicting new evidence. On the other hand, making police officers, prosecutors, and judges accountable (even under criminal law) for misconduct certainly can work as a deterrent against the blatant manipulation of evidence. Requiring prosecutors and police officers to conduct balanced investigations, to collect and disclose evidence that may be favorable to the defendant, and to interrogate the defendant in a fair, "information-seeking" manner, rather than in an accusatorial way (Killias, Chapter 4), may help reduce the incidence of wrongful convictions.

It is a matter of choice whether one considers the opportunity to appeal a verdict as a means of redress or as a way to prevent wrongful convictions. In any case, it should be obvious that higher courts that often overturn decisions by lower courts may exercise a preventive effect not only directly, by correcting miscarriages of justice before they reach the stage of a final decision, but also indirectly, by pushing lower courts to respect due process rights more carefully and review evidence more critically. It seems that higher courts in Germany and Switzerland are more apt to quash lower courts' decisions than are courts of appeal in France (Dongois, 2008) and in the Netherlands (Brants, Chapter 9). As it appears in the Netherlands, where daily routine and a climate of excessive consensus seem to have paralyzed well-intended legal mechanisms of judicial review, the mere existence of rules may not necessarily result in better protection of defendants and better outlooks for redress.

Roach (Chapter 14) offers compelling illustrations of this in his comparison of appeals and exonerations in Canada and the United States. Whereas ways to obtain legal redress, especially under the form of collateral attacks based on *habeas corpus*, are undoubtedly more numerous in the American system, Canadian prosecutors and courts seem considerably more willing to accept appeals or grant new trials than are their counterparts in the United States. For example, in the face of new evidence, Canadian prosecutors quite often agree to grant a new trial, as do the courts, without insisting on requirements of due diligence, "adversarial legalism" (Roach, quoting Kagan, 2001), and other obstacles to exoneration. Roach offers several explanations for this difference in legal culture. Magistrates are not elected in Canada. The caseload, even after adjusting for population, is significantly lower in Canada. Juries are far less involved in Canadian trials than is the case in the United States. It is interesting to note that similar differences can be found across Europe. For example Germany, the Netherlands, and Switzerland[10] seem to offer exonerations (and new trials) rather generously, whereas instances of judicial "generosity" in recent decades can be counted on one hand in France (Dongois, 2008) or in Israel (Rattner, 2008).

Although Canadian rules may be more in line with European than with American standards, the same differences across Europe should come as reminders of the importance of what we term, with an obvious lack of precision, "legal culture." Even among countries with similar legal traditions, the relative focus on material truth or on the respect for formal rules (including the "respect" for final court decisions) may differ considerably across national boundaries. Roach (Chapter 14) offers explanations that are intuitively appealing, such as the lower caseload in Canada, where magistrates can more easily afford to be "generous"; the fact that juries are less involved; and the fact that a "new trial" does not imply the same sacrifice of resources. These explanations also apply widely to Europe. However, contrary examples exist. For instance, Swiss prosecutors and judges are also elected, either in a general election or by local parliaments, not unlike U.S. judges, but their reaction to demands for a new trial is far less "adversarial" than that of their counterparts in the U.S. and more like their peers in Canada. Thus, democracy, in this respect, may not be as bad (or as important a variable) as many critics of the U.S. system tend to assume. In any event, this detail reminds us of how important it is, in conducting comparative research, to widen our perspective to include a larger array of countries.

Beyond any doubt, it seems that the standards required to obtain exonerations are higher in the United States since, as Lappas and Loftus (Chapter 15) observe, courts and prosecutors tend to insist that the innocence be clearly proven. In Canada and in Europe—at least in those countries where exonerations are granted more "generously"—the laws on exonerations do not require such a severe standard; a new trial is granted if the new evidence, had it been known to the court at the time of the first trial, seems "apt" to have affected the outcome (acquittal or a less severe punishment)[11]. In this connection, it should be kept in mind that most European nations allow double jeopardy and that new evidence can, occasionally, also lead to the reversal of an acquittal (or to a harsher penalty).

The Aftermath of Exonerations: Lasting Damages

Westervelt and Cook's (Chapter 13) compelling accounts help us better understand how rarely is exoneration the end of the story—and even if it is, it certainly almost never comes as a happy ending. This is to a large degree inevitable—lost years, partners having gone their ways, children left as babies having grown to young adults. In addition to all that come post-traumatic stress disorders after release (see Huff, Chapter 17, citing Grounds). All these outcomes are related to long-term separation.[12] As Westervelt and Cook illustrate, however, American exonerees often leave prison totally unprepared. They have to find their way back to ordinary life and to rebuild their social networks. But they face more than just emotional and relational problems. They must find housing, work, and financial resources, but with a criminal record that is not expunged, all these efforts are likely to be frustrated. For European observers, it is one of the most astonishing aspects of American exonerations that criminal records are not automatically expunged, as the examples given by Westervelt and Cook (Chapter 13) and by Lappas and Loftus (Chapter 15) show.

Beyond the amendment of criminal records, a further difference between U.S. and European criminal justice systems concerns the damages paid to exonerees. In Europe, article 3 of Protocol 7 to the European Convention of Human Rights and Fundamental Freedoms, adopted in 1984 by the Council of Europe and ratified by all 43 member states, stipulates that all persons exonerated have to be paid reasonable compensation (as noted by Huff, Chapter 17). This is not generally true in the United States, since victims of wrongful convictions, as Petro and Petro (Chapter 6) illustrate, have to seek compensation primarily by filing lawsuits. In doing so, they face two major obstacles—prosecutorial immunity and the requirement to establish evidence of intentional misconduct. Under European law, there are also statutes awarding officials (including prosecutors) personal immunity against civil lawsuits. However, although the state does not allow citizens to sue its officials, as a substitute it allows its citizens to claim compensation from the government which, in cases of serious misconduct, may require the officer to pay a portion or all of the compensation. Under this system, exonerees do not need to prove that prosecutors or police officers were guilty of serious misconduct. The mere fact that, acting as an agent of the government, an official made an error which led to material or immaterial damages is sufficient to obtain compensation.

When, under the influence of Edwin Borchard, President Roosevelt signed the federal wrongful compensation law in the U.S. in 1938, the European model of compensation laws was obviously influential (Zalman, Chapter 16). Indeed, it adopted an approach not unlike social security, where the inherent risk in a state's activity—in this case, administrating justice—is at the core of the idea that victims of any errors in the pursuit of this task should be compensated. A similar philosophy was behind workmen's compensation statutes that also were "imported" from Europe.

Interestingly, American elites and the legal profession were, at the beginning at least, rather hostile to such statutes, inspired by the tort law rule that no negligence liability should be admitted without fault. Unfortunately, efforts to expand wrongful conviction compensation laws to states have had mixed results, with some states having adopted statutes and increased financial compensation while others offer little or nothing to exonerees. This is especially unfortunate since most exonerations concern state courts, not the federal system.

Possible Ways to Reduce the Incidence of Wrongful Convictions

For obvious reasons, the risks of convicting innocent defendants should not be reduced simply by reducing the proportion of guilty verdicts over acquittals, since this would, as Forst (Chapter 2) reminds us, simply increase the "false negatives"—that is, the proportion of guilty defendants who are not convicted and who may then continue to pose threats to public safety and undermine public respect for the justice system. Careful consideration of recommendations for reform leads us to a less pessimistic assessment of risks, however. Indeed, reducing one type of error (convicting innocent defendants) should not automatically result in increasing the acquittals of guilty defendants. Other than in statistical inference, these two types of errors are not mechanically interdependent, in the sense that decreasing one necessarily increases the other one. To the contrary, convicting innocent defendants often has the side effect that the real offender remains free to continue committing crimes (thereby causing both Type I and Type II errors in the same case). Petro and Petro (Chapter 6) offer a tragic illustration of this by referring to a case where a child rapist committed similar crimes against three more children while the first crime was falsely ascribed to an innocent defendant (Clarence Elkins). Beyond this, clearing innocent defendants at an early stage of investigations can help redirect resources to identify other, possibly guilty, suspects.

In this final section, let us consider some of the recommendations that are derived from among the chapters in this book and our own prior research.

Reforms in Police Investigations

Zalman (Chapter 16) describes how investment in the education of police officers improved their professional performance. It is interesting to note that police officers reacted far more constructively than have prosecutors to some of the recommendations coming out of the innocence movement, according to Zalman's accounts of debates among police and criminal justice practitioners. For example, police officers accepted rather easily proposals to improve eyewitness identification by making lineups "double-blind."[13] Further, videotaping interviews with defendants may eliminate, or at least reduce, doubts about the conditions under which confessions may have been obtained. This would apply to defendants who, in the United States, waive their rights under *Miranda*, and in Europe to interrogations without the defense counsel being present.[14] A further important step that would not require legal change would be to adopt more neutral methods of interrogation (the "information-gathering approach"). Such methods, when compared to traditional American "accusatorial styles" of interrogation, pose less risk of eliciting false confessions, but are more efficient because they appear to elicit more true confessions. Meissner et al.'s (2012) systematic review suggests that police work could only benefit from such a change in police culture. Eliminating the wrong suspect(s) at an early stage and obtaining valid confessions goes beyond the important goal of protecting civil rights. It will also make the police more efficient.

Quality Control Among Forensic Scientists

Some thought has been given to whether or not police forensic labs should become independent labs that would not be subordinate to police departments and their priorities or ingrained in their organizational cultures. There is some plausibility in this approach, although private firms can become just as dependent on "big clients" as are labs that are integrated into a police or a government organization. A more important goal is the creation of a culture of independence that might be backed by statutes protecting forensic scientists who tell the court "the whole truth and nothing but the truth," whether or not it fits with the case presented by the prosecution. Errors by forensic scientists are generally not the result of intentional misconduct but usually result from incompetent collection or treatment of materials at crime scenes or inadequate statistical interpretation (see Vuille, Biedermann, and Taroni, Chapter 8). Proposals to improve the quality of forensic science focus on creating a culture of error management, as it has emerged in the medical field in recent decades (see, for example,

Schiffer, 2009). One useful reform might involve using "blind" procedures for interpreting results and delegating to a case manager the collection and treatment of materials at the crime scene (see Cole and Thompson, Chapter 7). Taking some inspiration from medical models, one could also envisage systematically requiring a second lab's expert opinion (using a blind procedure, of course) whenever the analysis of some materials is crucial for the outcome of a trial, as in the Amanda Knox case (see Vuille, Biedermann, and Taroni, Chapter 8), or whenever the defendant persists in contesting his presence at the crime scene[15]. Finally, materials should never be destroyed, as they still are in France and in many other European countries (Killias, 2008) once a case is definitively settled in court. They should, instead, be conserved and remain available for re-examination long beyond the final ruling. A possible reason for the relatively rare exonerations involving DNA tests in Europe may simply be that the genetic materials are often destroyed, and thus unavailable for testing, once the case is definitively settled. Such respect for one legal value (the "finality of the law") is inconsistent with another legal value ("the search for the truth"). In our judgment, the latter value should be given greater weight and deference at all times.

Restrict Plea Bargaining or Increase Internal Controls

If trials are increasingly going to be the exception, given the caseloads of most jurisdictions, the question arises as to how we can make plea negotiations more fair and more respectful of the defendant's rights. Most importantly, this would imply that the prosecution must disclose to the defense all possibly exculpatory evidence since, otherwise, no "informed consent" can logically be given to any agreement (see Gilliéron, Chapter 12). In order to make negotiations less "coercive" and "vindictive," it would also be necessary to review the practice of "punishing" defendants for insisting on a trial by threatening them with far longer sentences than those they would receive by pleading guilty—even if such forms of extortion do not violate U.S. Constitutional principles (*Bordenkircher v. Hayes*, 1978). Another possibility might be to consider adopting the European "solution"—to restrict plea bargaining to relatively minor cases. This, however, may not be an option in the United States because the alternative would be a heavy and lengthy trial, "American style," rather than a short and "easy" court hearing, as usually occurs in Europe. However, it might not be so unimaginable to have the judge directly supervise, or even preside over, plea negotiations in order to ensure that fairness principles are respected.

Make Prosecutors' Culture More "Balanced" and Require Full Access to Prosecution Files

As reported by Lappas and Loftus (Chapter 15) and Zalman (Chapter 16), American prosecutors seem to have resented the "innocence movement" as an attack on their credibility, and resistance against even moderate and seemingly uncontroversial proposals (such as "blind" line up procedures) was fierce and aggressive in a few instances. One could hardly imagine similar attitudes among European prosecutors, simply because they conceive of their role differently, as illustrated by their often active role in exonerations (Killias, 2008). Perhaps by altering the training provided in law schools (see Petro and Petro, Chapter 6; Zalman, Chapter 16) and/or by establishing a culture of balanced assessment of the evidence, promoted by codes of ethics, it should be possible to reduce the excessively confrontational, adversarial culture (Pizzi, 1999) that seems to have prevailed in many prosecutors' offices in the U.S. In their internal discussions of cases, for example, it may be very helpful regularly to require internal debate (as some prosecutors' offices now do), especially in highly contested cases lacking unequivocal evidence. Roles can be assigned in such debates, so that arguments are presented for and against charging a suspect with a crime, based on all known facts. We also recommend that defense counsels should have full access to prosecution files, as occurs already in some jurisdictions. Such access could go a long way in avoiding *Brady* violations by unethical prosecutors who withhold potentially exculpatory evidence from the defense.

These changes in prosecution culture might also make it less provocative and unacceptable to adopt statutes or internal regulations that make prosecutors personally accountable for intentional misconduct. Such statutes could also extend to police officers and forensic experts who suppress potentially exculpatory evidence, or who press defendants to confess, using unacceptable methods of interrogation. Criminal law provisions of this sort exist in most European countries. They play a non-trivial role in helping keep police practices in line with professional standards. And speaking of professional standards, bar associations at the local, state, and national levels must become far more active in disciplining lawyers who violate ethical standards, some with impunity and some on multiple occasions.

Make Appeals Work

Appeals—including those based on factual matters—are an important way to prevent lower courts from violating due process and convicting defendants in doubtful cases. An important pre-condition for such deterrence, however, is that appeals must exist not only on the books, but must offer meaningful redress in a reasonable proportion (and not just a handful) of cases. Roach (Chapter 14) and Zalman (Chapter 16) have both pointed to current deficiencies in this regard.

Offer Exonerations Beyond "Proof" of Innocence

As noted elsewhere in this volume (see, for example, Roach, Chapter 14; Lappas and Loftus, Chapter 15), U.S. prosecutors and courts are often highly resistant to granting a new trial, even in the face of strong new evidence, such as DNA analysis excluding the convicted person as the actual perpetrator of the crime for which he/she was convicted. In Canada (Roach, Chapter 14), the Netherlands (Brants, Chapter 9), Switzerland or Germany (Killias, 2008), to cite just a few examples, exonerations are granted relatively "generously," probably because prosecutors and court staff alike do not want to face the kind of public criticism that is often unavoidable in such instances. Granting a new trial is, under such circumstances, often the best way of "damage control." For those convicted of a crime which they obviously could not have committed, not obtaining a new trial is an additional frustration that is hard to live with. It should be standard practice to grant an exoneration (or at least a new trial) whenever new evidence raises serious doubts about the first trial—that is, whenever the new evidence is "apt" to make a reasonable observer conclude that the court would have decided otherwise had it known about the new evidence at the time of the conviction.

Offer Compensation to the Victims of Wrongful Convictions

An obvious, but widely unrealized, reform would be to expunge criminal records once exoneration is granted. Beyond this, exonerees should be assisted in finding their way back to normal life. This implies not only helping them in re-engaging with their personal networks but also to find jobs, housing, and adequate financial resources. A further option that might be considered would be to offer them a new identity in order to avoid stigmatization. This is, after all, frequently offered to some victims and witnesses via relocation programs. Why should the victims of wrongful conviction not be given similar consideration when necessary to ensure their successful reintegration into society? Finally, they should be entitled to adequate compensation from the government (see related discussions by Zalman, Chapter 16, and Huff, Chapter 17), through statutory language that includes reasonable levels of compensation and does not impose unrealistically restrictive barriers. Their hopes for adequate compensation should not depend on the need to file civil lawsuits against prosecutors (who often have absolute immunity) or other individuals who may have contributed to their wrongful conviction through misconduct (see Petro and Petro, Chapter 6). Exonerees almost always lack the resources to pursue such remedies and have a need for immediate financial and other assistance, which is typically far too delayed in the U.S. Prosecutors, police officers, forensic experts, and other actors may, and should, be held personally accountable under criminal or disciplinary statutes. Compensation, however, should remain the responsibility of the government in whose name the person was convicted.

Concluding Remarks

Studying wrongful convictions across many different nations with various criminal justice systems is a promising strategy that can lead to new insights. What at first seems unique to any place or system may be a more general pattern that can be observed in very different countries. On the other hand, some seemingly obvious explanations, such as the popular election of prosecutors and judges in the U.S., may not be responsible for all defects of the U.S. criminal justice system since similar modes of election exist in Europe without the same side effects being apparent. Obviously, there is a need to develop more comparative—and especially more quantitative—data across nations. What are, for example, the comparative proportions of cases dropped by prosecutors? How many rulings by lower courts are overturned in the course of the appeals process? How many cases are settled out of court? How long do investigations and trials (and criminal procedures in general) take? But, first of all, we should work to develop better data on how many miscarriages of justice actually occur under different systems. How many defendants are exonerated, often after long years of incarceration? What is the relative importance of several sources of error under different systems? An interesting thought exercise, even if not (in pragmatic terms) amenable to implementation, is how one might design a new, "hybrid" criminal justice system that would combine the best aspects of both the adversarial and the inquisitorial systems.[16] Short of actually implementing such a new system, we can at least learn from each other how best to reduce our errors.

Our list of remedies, based on the research presented in this volume and our own prior studies, should not be misunderstood as a list of European recipes to "fix" American ills. The solution is not the wholesale adoption of the inquisitorial system in America or the adversarial system in Europe. Instead, it is important to identify the strengths and weaknesses of each system and design relevant reforms that can and should be made within both systems (also see van Koppen and Penrod, 2003). Certainly, much of what has been said here about improvements in the areas of forensic science, eyewitness identification, police work, and appeals concerns European systems as much as those in the United States. However, it is clear to us that the European Convention of Human Rights and Fundamental Freedoms has reshaped criminal procedure throughout Europe in many significant ways over the last 60 years. It is not without some irony, it seems to us, that reforms in Europe were often inspired by American innovations achieved under the Warren Supreme Court. Importing many of these principles from the U.S. has certainly contributed to making criminal procedures in Europe much more fair than they had been in the past. Why, then, should criminal law reform be a one-way street? We are convinced that U.S. police departments, prosecution offices, and courts could, along with the American public, benefit from some fresh ideas found in "old" Europe. Many ideas that are regularly expressed in American writings on wrongful conviction have been standard practices in some European countries. Why not devote a bit more attention to how these ideas have worked in those nations and what we might continue to learn from each other—and from our mistakes that produce wrongful convictions and other miscarriages of justice?

Notes

1 Based on the most recent National Crime Victimization Survey conducted by the Bureau of Justice Statistics, more than half of the nearly 3.4 million violent offenses committed in the U.S. between 2006 and 2010 were not even reported to the police, often due to fear of retaliation or fear of getting the offender in trouble (Bureau of Justice Statistics, 2012). The International Crime Victimization Surveys (reproduced in the *European Sourcebook of Crime and Criminal Justice Statistics*, 2010) show very similar patterns across Europe.

2 Thus, exonerations are not a random sample of all cases handled by the courts. A sample of exonerations obtained because the true offender has been identified in the meantime (for whatever reason) may be less biased. To our knowledge, no study has ever used such a sample.

3 Life sentences are not frequently meted out on the European continent.

4 A related problem is the misunderstanding that proving the "identity" of materials left at the crime scene or on an object does not necessarily imply the suspect's guilt. A good illustration is the case of Brigitte D. in Switzerland, an 18-year-old woman found dead after having had sexual intercourse. After many years, a suspect's DNA (in a totally unrelated case) matched the DNA (from sperm) found in the victim's vagina but not that found under her nails. This suspect claimed to have had a romantic affair with that woman and that they had had intercourse earlier that day. Questioned as to why he never came forward to tell this to the police, he explained that he could not do this at the time since he was just about to marry a different person. After a long period in pretrial detention, he was cleared after systematic DNA testing on all prison inmates. As it turned out, the young woman had encountered, later that same day, a man (incarcerated for a different case of rape-murder) whose DNA matched materials found under the victim's nails.

5 This is required by article 6 (par. 3-d) of the European Convention of Human Rights and Fundamental Freedoms.

6 The limits vary among Europe's legal systems, but generally the upper limit is 6 months. This must be seen in the context of continental Europe's relatively mild sentences (on sentences in Europe, see *European Sourcebook of Crime and Criminal Justice Statistics 2010*, Table 3.2.5.1/p. 255).

7 This outlaws so-called "Alford pleas" (*North Carolina v. Alford, 1970*) where the defendant, despite pleading guilty, continues to claim that he is innocent.

8 It should be remembered that, throughout Europe, the verdict and the sentence are usually decided in the same hearing.

9 Given its status as an independent institute under the authority of the Ministry of Public Security and Justice.

10 A substantial proportion of exonerations in Switzerland (usually after "penal orders") are initiated by prosecutors rather than defense counsels (Killias, 2008, and Chapter 4).

11 The lower frequency of exonerations in Europe, as observed above, must also be assessed against softer legal requirements that should be expected to increase the likelihood of exonerations.

12 As Huff has noted elsewhere, "(W)hile prison sentences are based on a linear calculation of time, with each year being weighted equally, societal change . . . is decidedly nonlinear. The innocent inmate, upon release, has fallen even further behind—socially, psychologically, and economically—than might be implied even by a lengthy sentence" (Huff, 2002: 10).

13 "Double-blind" means that the officer who stands next to the witness while observing a physical lineup or presents an array of photographs in a photo lineup procedure does not know who the actual suspect is.

14 Some countries allow the defense counsel to be present from the first interview at the police station, whereas others (as, for example, in the Netherlands; see Brants, Chapter 9) allow attorneys to be present only at a later stage of the investigation.

15 An illustration is offered by the case mentioned in Note 4. The fact that the sperm and the materials under the victim's nails did not originate from the same person should have allowed the authorities to clear the suspect at an earlier stage of the investigation.

16 See, for example, Huff and Zalman, 2010; Zalman, 2011.

References

Bureau of Justice Statistics, U.S. Department of Justice. (August 9, 2012). Advance press release (http://www.bjs.gov/content/pub/press/vnrp0610pr.cfm).

Center for Public Integrity. (2003). "Harmful Error." Washington, D.C.: Center for Public Integrity.

Dongois N. (2008). "Wrongful Convictions in France: The Limits of 'Pourvoi en Révision.'" Pp. 249–261 in C.R. Huff and M. Killias (Eds.), *Wrongful Conviction. International Perspectives on Miscarriages of Justice*, Philadelphia: Temple University Press, 249–261.

European Sourcebook of Crime and Criminal Justice Statistics (2010). 4th edition. The Hague: Boom Juridische Uitgevers. www.europeansourcebook.org.

Huff, C.R. (2002). "Wrongful Conviction and Public Policy: The American Society of Criminology 2001 Presidential Address," *Criminology* 40 (1): 1–18.

Huff, C.R. and M. Killias (Eds.) (2008). *Wrongful Conviction. International Perspectives on Miscarriages of Justice*, Philadelphia: Temple University Press.

Huff, C.R. and M. Zalman (2010). "Legal Systems: An Integrated Justice Model." Pp. 66–67 in M. Jolicoeur, *International Perspectives on Wrongful Convictions*, Washington, D.C.: National Institute of Justice, International Center.

Kagan, R. (2001). *Adversarial Legalism: The American Way of Law*, Cambridge: Harvard University Press.

Killias, M., G. Gilliéron, and N. Dongois (2007). A Survey of Exonerations in Switzerland Over Ten Years (Report to the Swiss National Science Foundation), Universities of Lausanne and Zurich (Switzerland).

Killias, M. (2008). "Wrongful Convictions in Switzerland: The Experience of a Continental Law Country." Pp. 139–155 in C.R. Huff and M. Killias (Eds.), *Wrongful Conviction. International Perspectives on Miscarriages of Justice*, Philadelphia: Temple University Press.

Liebman, J.S., J. Fagan, V. West, and J. Lloyd (2000). "Capital Attrition: Error Rates in Capital Cases, 1973–1995," *Texas Law Review*, 78 (7): 1839–1866.

Meissner, C.A., A.D. Redlich, S. Bhatt, and S. Brandon (2012). "Interview and Interrogation Methods and Their Effects on True and False Confessions." www.campbellcollaboration. org.

Peters, K. (1970–1974). *Fehlerquellen im Strafprozess. Eine Untersuchung der Wiederaufnahmeverfahren in der Bundesrepublik Deutschland. (Sources of Errors in Criminal Proceedings. A Study of Cases of Successful Petitions of Revision in the Federal Republic of Germany.)* 3 volumes, Karlsruhe: C.F. Müller 1970, 1972, 1974.

Pizzi, W. T. (1999). *Trials without Truth*, New York/London: New York University Press.

Rattner, A. (2008). "The Sanctity of Criminal Law: Thoughts and Reflections on Wrongful Conviction in Israel." Pp. 263–271 in C.R. Huff and M. Killias (Eds.), *Wrongful Conviction. International Perspectives on Miscarriages of Justice*, Philadelphia: Temple University Press.

Schiffer, B. (2009). "The Relationship between Forensic Science and Judicial Error: A Study Covering Error Sources, Bias and Remedies." University of Lausanne: PhD dissertation.

Van Koppen, P.J. and S.D. Penrod (2003). "Adversarial or Inquisitorial? Comparing Systems." Pp. 1–19 in P.J. van Koppen and S.D. Penrod (Eds.), *Adversarial versus Inquisitorial Justice. Psychological Perspectives on Criminal Justice Systems*, New York/Boston/Dordrecht/London/Moscow: Kluwer Academic.

Zalman, M. (2011). "An Integrated Justice Model of Wrongful Convictions," *Albany Law Review* 74: 1465–1524.

Zalman, M. (2012). "Qualitatively Estimating the Incidence of Wrongful Convictions," *Criminal Law Bulletin* 48 (2): 221–277.

Cases

Bordenkircher v. Hayes, 434 U.S. 357 (1978).

Brady v. Maryland, 373 U.S. 83 (1963).

North Carolina v. Alford, 400 U.S. 25 (1970).

ABOUT THE CONTRIBUTORS

Marcelo Aebi is Professor of Criminology and Vice Director of the School of Criminal Sciences at the University of Lausanne, Switzerland. He is also Visiting Professor at the Autonomous University of Barcelona, Spain. His main research topics include comparative criminology; prisons; methodology; juvenile delinquency; drugs and crime; and victimization and self-reported delinquency studies. He is author or co-author of more than 100 scientific publications. After his studies at the Universities of Buenos Aires, Argentina, (M.A., Law) and Lausanne, (M.A. and Ph.D, Criminology) he was a Visiting Fellow at the Rutgers School of Criminal Justice and at the Max Planck Institute for Foreign and International Criminal Law (Freiburg, Germany), as well as Vice Director and Professor of Criminology at the Andalusian Institute of Criminology at the University of Seville, Spain. He is also a consultant to the Council of Europe and the United Nations Office on Drugs and Crime, a member of the European Sourcebook Group, and Executive Secretary of the European Society of Criminology.

Alex Biedermann received his first degree in forensic science from the University of Lausanne in 2002. From 2003 to 2010, he worked as a co-ordinating forensic scientist within the Federal Department of Justice and Police (Federal Office of Police) in Bern, Switzerland. Parallel with this activity, he collaborated closely in research and casework with the Forensic Science Institute at the University of Lausanne. His Ph.D. (University of Lausanne, 2007) focused on graphical models and probabilistic inference for evaluating scientific evidence in forensic science. Currently, he works as an Assistant Lecturer and Maître Assistant at the

Forensic Science Institute, University of Lausanne. His current research and teaching focus on concepts, methods, and techniques—in particular graphical modeling—for evidential reasoning and decision making in forensic science. He has co-authored two monographs and a series of papers on these topics.

Chrisje Brants is Professor of Criminal Law and Criminal Process at the Willem Pompe Institute for Criminal Law and Criminology, University of Utrecht. She is a member of the Académie Internationale de Droit Comparé and the Association for International Criminal Justice and a fellow of the European Law Institute. Her main interests, in which she combines a multidisciplinary background in law and criminology, are international criminal justice; comparative studies on different aspects of criminal procedure; and crime, criminal justice, and the media. Her most recent book is *Issues of Convergence: Inquisitorial Prosecution in England and Wales* (Wolf Legal Publishers, 2011).

Kathryn M. Campbell is Associate Professor of Criminology at the University of Ottawa. Her teaching and research interests span the area of social justice. This includes exploring the perspectives of victims of errors of the criminal justice system and examining the limitations of policy and law in addressing miscarriages of justice. Additional areas of her research focus include writing about the challenges presented in recognizing the rights of children and young persons generally and, more recently, investigating the sentencing of Aboriginal peoples in Canadian criminal law, as well as judicial perspectives on the role of victims in the criminal justice process.

Claudia Campistol is Researcher at the Autonomous University of Barcelona, Spain, and Visiting Researcher at the University of Lausanne, Switzerland. After her studies at the University of Barcelona (M.A., Psychology), she worked for four years in the Juvenile Justice Department of Catalonia, Spain. She later moved to Lausanne, where she obtained an M.A. degree in Criminology and is completing her Ph.D. degree. She is also a member of the European Sourcebook Group.

Simon A. Cole is Associate Professor of Criminology, Law and Society at the University of California, Irvine. He is the author of *Suspect Identities:*

A History of Fingerprinting and Criminal Identification (Harvard University Press, 2001) and *Truth Machine: The Contentious History of DNA Fingerprinting* (University of Chicago Press, 2008, with Michael Lynch, Ruth McNally, and Kathleen Jordan). He has written and spoken widely about forensic evidence and miscarriages of justice.

Kimberly J. Cook lives in Wilmington, North Carolina. She is Professor and Department Chair of Sociology and Criminology at the University of North Carolina Wilmington. Her areas of interest include capital punishment, restorative justice, violence against women, and social justice. Her earlier work includes *Divided Passions: Public Opinions on Abortion and the Death Penalty* (1998). In her spare time, she enjoys hanging out with her son Greg; major domestic renovations; going to the beach; birding; pottery; shopping with Saundra; and chasing turtles with Drew, Saundra, and Van.

Brian Forst is Professor of Justice, Law and Society at American University in Washington, D.C. He is the author of eight books and scores of refereed articles and book chapters, mostly on matters of criminal justice policy. His primary areas of research interest include errors of justice; the exercise of discretion in prosecution and sentencing; policing; criminal justice legitimacy; terrorism; and the deterrent effect of the death penalty. He is a senior member of the editorial board of the Oxford Bibliographies – Criminology (since 2009) and an associate editor of the *Journal of Quantitative Criminology* (since 2008). He also served recently as an associate editor of *Justice Quarterly* (2006–2009). He was a voting member of the Sentencing and Criminal Code Revision Commission of the District of Columbia from 2004 through 2010.

Brandon L. Garrett is the Roy L. and Rosamond Woodruff Morgan Professor of Law at the University of Virginia School of Law. He joined the law faculty in 2005. His scholarly and teaching interests include criminal procedure; wrongful convictions; forensic science; habeas corpus; corporate crime; civil rights; civil procedure; and constitutional law. His recent research includes studies of DNA exonerations and organizational prosecutions. In 2011, Harvard University Press published his book, *Convicting the Innocent: Where Criminal Prosecutions Go Wrong*, examining the cases of the first 250 people to be exonerated by DNA testing in the U.S. He attended Columbia Law School, where he was an articles editor of the Columbia Law Review and a Kent Scholar. After graduating, he clerked for the Hon. Pierre N. Leval of the U.S. Court of Appeals for the Second Circuit. He then worked as an associate at Neufeld, Scheck & Brustin LLP in New York City. He is currently working on a new book, in contract with Harvard University Press, examining prosecutions of corporations.

Gwladys Gilliéron received a Ph.D. in Law from the University of Zürich and an LL.M. in Criminal Justice from the University of Lausanne. Her work has centered on wrongful convictions in several nations, the examination of prosecution services in Europe and the United States, and randomized controlled trials on new criminal sanctions. She formerly served as a Research Fellow at the University of Minnesota's Institute on Crime and Public Policy and at the Max Planck Institute for Foreign and International Criminal Law in Freiburg. She is currently teaching criminal law at the Distance Learning University in Switzerland and working for a law firm in Zurich as part of her traineeship for the bar.

Samuel Gross is the Thomas and Mable Long Professor of Law at the University of Michigan, where he teaches evidence, criminal procedure, and courses on false criminal convictions. He has litigated test cases on jury selection in capital trials, racial discrimination in the use of the death penalty, and the constitutionality of executing defendants in the face of a substantial known risk of factual innocence. Professor Gross has published works on eyewitness identification; evidence law; pre-trial settlement and the selection of cases for trial; racial profiling; the death penalty; and the use of expert witnesses. For the past several years his work has focused on false convictions and exonerations. He is the editor of the *National Registry of Exonerations*.

Spero T. Lappas has practiced criminal and constitutional law in Harrisburg, Pennsylvania since 1977. He has served as lead counsel in hundreds of major civil, criminal, and civil rights actions, including some of Central Pennsylvania's most important criminal and civil trials. He has been a member of the Pennsylvania Joint State Government

Commission's Senate Advisory Committee to Study the Causes of Wrongful Convictions and has been appointed to the Pennsylvania legislative advisory committee to study the Commonwealth's death penalty. He was among the nation's youngest attorneys to be named in the first edition of *The Best Lawyers in America* and has been listed in numerous *Who's Who* publications. He graduated with honors from Allegheny College and received his J.D. degree cum laude from the Dickinson School of Law (now the Dickinson School of Law of the Pennsylvania State University), where he won two American Jurisprudence awards; was named to the Editorial Board of the *Dickinson Law Review*; was a member of the National Trial Moot Court Team; and was later named to Dickinson's Woolsack Society. He has served on the adjunct faculty of Widener University School of Law and the Harrisburg Area Community College and is now a Ph.D. candidate in the American Studies Program at The Pennsylvania State University, Harrisburg, where he studies the intersections of American law and culture.

Elizabeth Loftus is Distinguished Professor at the University of California, Irvine. She holds faculty positions in three departments (Psychology and Social Behavior; Criminology, Law, and Society; and Cognitive Sciences) and in the School of Law, and is also a Fellow of the Center for the Neurobiology of Learning and Memory. She received her Ph.D. in Psychology from Stanford University. Since then, she has published 22 books (including the award winning *Eyewitness Testimony*) and nearly 500 scientific articles. Over the last 30 years, her research has focused on the malleability of human memory. She has been recognized for this research with six honorary doctorates from universities in the U.S., Norway, the Netherlands, Israel, and the U.K. She was elected to the Royal Society of Edinburgh, the American Philosophical Society, and the National Academy of Sciences. She is Past President of the Association for Psychological Science, the Western Psychological Association, and the American Psychology-Law Society.

Jim Petro is Chancellor of the University System of Ohio. A graduate of Denison University and Case Western Reserve University School of Law, he has litigated cases in legal venues from Mayor's Court to the United States Supreme Court and has been elected to serve Ohioans as Rocky

River Council Member and Director of Law; State Representative; Cuyahoga County Commissioner; Auditor of State; and Attorney General. He was the first state attorney general to intervene on behalf of an Innocence Project client and later became a pro bono lawyer for the Ohio Innocence Project (OIP). He worked with OIP Director Mark Godsey on Ohio's criminal justice reform law, enacted in 2010. He received the 2010 Innocence Network Champion of Justice Award. He co-authored (with Nancy Petro) *False Justice—Eight Myths that Convict the Innocent* (Kaplan 2011).

Nancy Petro, a Phi Beta Kappa graduate of Denison University, retired from a communications and business career before focusing in 2008 on writing and advocacy relating to wrongful conviction and criminal justice reform. She co-authored (with Jim Petro) *False Justice—Eight Myths that Convict the Innocent* (Kaplan 2011), which earned a 2011 Constitutional Commentary Award from the Constitution Project and the 2012 Media Award from the Northern California Innocence Project. She has written for *InBrief*, The Magazine of Case Western Reserve School of Law; the Ohio Innocence Project's *Annual Review 2011;* and, as a contributing editor, for the *Wrongful Convictions Blog*, an international forum.

Michael L. Radelet is Professor, Department of Sociology, University of Colorado-Boulder. He completed his Ph.D. at Purdue University in 1977 and post-doctoral training in psychiatry at the University of Wisconsin Medical School, then spent 22 years at the University of Florida before moving to Boulder in 2001. From 1996–2001, he served as chair of the Department of Sociology at the University of Florida, and from 2004–2009 was chair of the Sociology Department at Boulder. Radelet's research focuses on capital punishment, especially the problems of erroneous convictions, racial bias, and ethical issues faced by health care personnel who are involved in capital cases and executions. His work on erroneous convictions (with Hugo Adam Bedau) is widely credited with introducing the "innocence argument" into contemporary death penalty debates. In 2002, at the request of Illinois Governor George Ryan, he completed a study of racial biases in the death penalty in Illinois that Governor Ryan used in his decision in 2003 to commute 167 death sentences. Radelet has testified in approximately 75 death penalty cases, before committees of both the U.S. Senate and the House of Representatives, and in legislatures in seven states. He has worked with scores of death row inmates and gone through "last visits" with 50 of them, and he also works closely with families of homicide victims in Colorado. His awards include a Distinguished Alumni Award from Purdue University (2011), the William Chambliss Award for Lifetime Achievements in Law and Society from the Society for the Study of Social Problems (2011), and one of three campus-wide awards for distinguished research from the Boulder Faculty Assembly (2012).

Kent Roach is Professor of Law at the University of Toronto, where he holds the Prichard Wilson Chair in Law and Public Policy. He is the author of 12 books, including *The 9/11 Effect: Comparative Counter-Terrorism* (Cambridge, 2011) and *Forensic Science and Miscarriages of Justice* (Irwin Law, 2010). He has also written several articles on miscarriages of justice that have been published in both Canada and the United States. He acted for the Association in Defence of the Wrongfully Convicted in the Morin Inquiry and served as Research Director for the Goudge Inquiry into forensic science.

Franco Taroni is Professor of Forensic Statistics at the University of Lausanne (Faculty of Law and Criminal Justice, School of Criminal Justice, Forensic Science Institute). He received his Ph.D. in forensic science in 1996 from the University of Lausanne. He was awarded two European Community Grants for Training and Mobility of Researchers for a collaboration with Colin Aitken of the Department of Mathematics and Statistics of the University of Edinburgh. He spent four years as a research project manager at the Institutes of Forensic Medicine of the Universities of Lausanne and Zürich (Switzerland). His main areas of research, casework, and teaching include forensic statistics, Bayesian networks, and Bayesian decision-theoretic data analyses. He has authored or co-authored several books on these topics and is editor of the journal *Law, Probability and Risk* (Oxford University Press).

William C. Thompson is Professor of Criminology, Law and Society at the University of California, Irvine (UCI). He has a joint appointment in UCI's School of Law, where he has taught Evidence. He received a Ph.D.

in psychology from Stanford University and a J.D. from the University of California, Berkeley. He has published extensively on the use and misuse of scientific and statistical evidence in the courtroom and on jurors' reactions to such evidence, focusing particularly on forensic DNA analysis. Although primarily an academic, Thompson occasionally practices law, representing clients in cases involving novel scientific and statistical issues. He has also consulted on forensic science issues with government agencies and law firms in several nations and has assisted in journalistic investigations of crime labs, including the investigation that exposed problems in the notorious Houston Police Department Crime Laboratory. Thompson served as Reporter for an American Bar Association Study Group on DNA Evidence and was a member of the Task Force that drafted the ABA's Standards on DNA Evidence. He also served on the California Crime Laboratory Review Task Force, a body created by the state legislature to recommend ways of improving forensic science in California.

Joëlle Vuille received a law degree and a Ph.D. degree in criminology from the University of Lausanne (Switzerland), where she worked as a researcher for five years, mainly in the fields of forensic science, sentencing, and drug legislation. She is currently a postdoctoral scholar at the University of California, Irvine, on a grant from the Swiss National Science Foundation. Her main research interests focus on the judiciary's use of expert and scientific evidence. She has authored and co-authored many book chapters, articles, and scientific reports on the admissibility of scientific evidence and its evaluation by the courts and on the use of probabilities in the judicial context.

Saundra D. Westervelt lives in Greensboro, North Carolina, with her husband, Van, and their son, Drew. She is Associate Professor of Sociology at the University of North Carolina Greensboro. Her broad areas of interest include criminology and the sociology of law, but her more recent work has focused on miscarriages of justice. She is the author of *Shifting the Blame: How Victimization Became a Criminal Defense* (1998) and co-editor of *Wrongly Convicted: Perspectives on Failed Justice* (2001). Together, she and Kimberly Cook have recently completed *Life after Death Row: Exonerees' Search for Community and Identity* (2012), which examines life after exoneration for 18 death row exonerees. In her spare time, she enjoys traveling with her family and chasing turtles with her son.

Marvin Zalman is Professor of Criminal Justice at Wayne State University. He has written on criminal procedure (including articles on *Miranda* rights, the Fourth Amendment, and venue); criminal justice policy; wrongful convictions; civil liberties; and judicial sentencing. His recent publications include "Wrongful Conviction" in *Oxford Bibliographies Online* (Fall, 2012); "Qualitatively Estimating the Incidence of Wrongful Convictions" (*Criminal Law Bulletin*, 2012); "An Integrated Justice Model of Wrongful Convictions" (*Albany Law Review*, 2011); and *Criminal Procedure: Constitution & Society* (Prentice Hall, 2011, 6th edition).

INDEX

A

American Bar Association (ABA) 94, 336

ABC newspaper 199

abortion, changes in law on 7, 200, 205

AboutCrimeSolutions.gov 345

acceptance on return to society, lack of 270–1, 277

accountability 20, 25, 29, 69–70, 276–8, 390–1

accreditation 126–7, 148–9

accusatorial methods of police interrogation 63

actual innocence: acceptance, lack of 270; Canada 284; crime control culture 284; definition of wrongful convictions 11, 358–9; DNA evidence 117, 358; political repression, convictions based on 11, 359; prosecution resistance to relief 10, 321–2, 324; United States 227, 284–6, 288, 290–6, 304–5, 324

Actual Innocence: When Justice Goes Wrong and How to Make It Right. Scheck, B., Neufeld, P. and Dwyer, J. 358

Adams, James 324

adversarial systems: Canada 212, 218, 305; confirmation bias, tunnel vision and belief perseverance 7, 176, 178; culture 390; exculpatory evidence, disclosure of 176; forensic science 154; independence of expert evidence 179–80; Netherlands 6–7, 162–3, 167–70, 176–80, 186–9; prosecutors' misconduct 94; recording of interviews 177; remedies for wrongful convictions 4, 11, 69–73, 238, 284, 303, 305, 393; terrorist suspects, treatment of 212, 218; United States 7–8, 176, 212, 238–9, 256, 284, 303, 305 *see also* adversarial systems and inquisitorial systems, comparison between

adversarial systems and inquisitorial systems, comparison between 4, 61–74; accountability 69–70; appeals 71; confirmation bias, tunnel vision and belief perseverance 162–3, 170; death penalty cases 61; defense counsel, role of 4, 63–4, 69, 70, 379, 381–2; disclosure of evidence before trial 64; DNA evidence 138; Europe 4, 6–7, 61–74, 162–3, 238, 381–2;

European Convention on Human Rights 62, 63; exculpatory evidence, suppression of 70; false confessions 4, 62–4, 68–9, 70–1; forensic science 71–2; functions of trials 4, 63–4; judge and jury, role of 238; material truth versus procedural justice 4, 62–4, 69–70, 384–5; mixed systems 238, 393; mitigation 63, 65; penal orders 8, 64–7, 381–3; plea bargains 4, 8, 64–7, 69, 70, 74, 381–3; police interviews/interrogations 4, 63, 67–8, 70–1, 74, 388; prosecutors, role of 238–9;risk reduction 4, 11, 69–73, 238; sentencing 63–4, 70, 74, 381–2; standard of proof 62; statistics 61–2; statute of limitations, removal of 72–3; summary proceedings 8, 67, 70, 74, 381–2; Switzerland 61– 2, 66–7, 71–2, 381–2; United States 4, 61–74, 382

Aebi, Marcelo F. 7, 375–6, 377

Afghanistan 215, 217, 222, 226–7

alcohol use 274–5

Alford pleas 66, 254

Almalki, Abdullah 221

Almrei, Hassan 215, 217

alternatives to trials 237–56; adversarial systems in United States 8, 238–9, 256; Europe 2, 8, 237–56, 381; inquisitorial systems in Europe 8, 238–51, 256; prosecutor, role of 239, 255–6; statements of guilt in Europe 237; Switzerland 239, 244–7, 249–51, 255–6; truth 237–8; United States 2, 8, 237, 239, 250–1 *see also* penal orders in Europe; plea bargaining; summary proceedings

Amenábar, Alejandro 201

American Bar Association (ABA) Journal 336

American Bar Association (ABA) Standards of Criminal Justice 94

Andalusian Association of Terrorist Victims (AAVT) 202

Anderson, Ken 104–5

appeals: adversarial systems and inquisitorial systems, comparison between 71; Austria 71; Canada 285–9, 297–301, 304–5, 384; executive 292–3, 295, 297–8, 304; France 384; Germany 71, 248, 250, 384; interpretation of law 375; Italy 71; Netherlands 71, 170, 175, 185; penal orders 240; plea bargains 248, 250–1; quality control 71; remedies for wrongful convictions 62, 284–92, 297–305, 384, 391; social costs 30; Switzerland 71, 246, 384; United States 251, 284, 289–90, 292, 303

Arar, Maher 221

arrest 17, 22–3, 37, 213

Association for the Right to Die with Dignity *(Derecho a Morir Dignamente)* 201

Austria 71, 331

avoidance approach after release 272–5

B

Bagram Air Force Base, Afghanistan 227

bar associations 94, 390–1

Barkow, R.E. 255

Beck, Adolf 332

Bedau, Hugo 30, 49, 324

belief perseverance *see* confirmation bias, tunnel vision and belief perseverance

benign sources of miscarriages of justice 19–21

Beyer, M. 197
bias: adversarial systems 138;
    contextual bias 128; DNA evidence
    128, 143; forensic science 112,
    122–3, 125, 128, 138–9; hindsight
    bias 164; inquisitorial systems 138;
    interpretations 112, 122–3, 125,
    128, 138–9; Knox, Amanda, case of
    143, 148–9; Netherlands 167–8;
    outcome bias 164; penal orders 240
Biedermann, Alex 6, 378–9
Birmingham Six 360–1
bitemarks 116, 121, 127
Bittner, Egon 23–4
Blackstone, William 19, 22, 23, 365
blind procedures 87–9, 128–9, 318–20,
    330, 388–90
blood analysis 67, 79, 102, 121, 144
Bloodsworth, Kirk 88, 263, 270–1,
    273, 275
Bolte, Ora 310–11
Borchard, Edwin: background 331;
    causes of wrongful convictions 338;
    comparative law 330–6, 386–7;
    compensation for wrongful
    convictions, campaign for 329–33,
    335–9, 351, 365, 386–7; *Convicting
    the Innocent* 10, 48–9, 163, 329–36,
    338–9; declaratory judgments 332,
    335–6; *Diplomatic Protection* 331–2;
    European Systems 330–7; innocent
    movement 10, 329–39, 348, 350–1;
    Library of Congress 331–2, 337;
    Progressivism 330–6; sovereign
    immunity 332, 335–6; workmen's
    compensation 333–5, 339, 386–7
border controls 213–14
Bradley, John 104–5
Brady violations 5, 390
Brants, Chrisje 6–7, 381, 383
Bratton, William J. 29, 343–4

Brissette, James 17
Brown, Shabaka 272–3
Bryson, Dale 315, 323–4
Bucklo, Elaine 103
Buffalo Creek mining disaster and
    flood 272
bullet lead analysis 117, 123, 127
bureaucratization 343
Burke, Tara 315
Bush, George W. 212, 224–7, 231
Butler, Sabrina 263, 277

C

Campbell, Kathryn M. 8, 374–5
Campbell, Ward 324
Campistol, Claudia 7, 375–6, 377
Canada: actual innocence 284;
    adversarial systems 212, 218, 305;
    Charter of Rights and Freedoms
    213, 217, 222, 287; jurors 284,
    286–7, 297–8, 302–6, 384; race
    214–15, 306; return to free society
    262 *see also* remedies for wrongful
    convictions in Canada; terrorist
    suspects in Canada, treatment of
capital punishment *see* death penalty
    cases
Cassell, Paul 324
Center for Public Integrity 380, 382
certification 126–7
Chamberlain, Lindy 185
Champod, C. 112
changes in law, false confessions to
    pressure for 7, 199–201, 205
Charkaoui, Adil 217–18
children and families, impact of
    wrongful convictions on 11, 23, 362,
    385–6
Clinton, Bill 228–9
Code, M. 220
Cole, Simon A. 5–6, 230, 378

collateral attacks on verdicts 290–1, 303, 305, 384

commissions: Canada 289, 304; Criminal Cases Review Commission (UK) 189, 284, 289, 304, 350; independence 126, 187, 284, 289, 304; military commissions, use of 228–9, 231; Netherlands, introduction in 187–8; Poland, transitional justice in 366–7; prosecution resistance to relief 10, 312–18; remedies for wrongful convictions 289, 304

community policing 25, 27, 29

compensation: accountability 392; Borchard, Edwin 329–33, 335–9, 351, 365, 386–7; European Convention on Human Rights 11, 367, 386; immunity 386; Poland, transitional justice in 367; prosecutors' misconduct 386; return to free society 276–7, 391–2; serious errors are detected, whenever 72; workmen's compensation 333–5, 339, 386–7

confessions 244–6, 248, 250 see also false confessions

confinement model 36

confirmation bias, tunnel vision and belief perseverance 6–7, 161–6; adversarial systems 7, 162–3, 170, 176, 178; definition of confirmation bias 94–5; definition of tunnel vision 163–5; disclosure 189–90; DNA evidence 378; false confessions 7, 166; groupthink 181; hindsight bias 164; inquisitorial systems 7, 162–3, 170; institutional pressures 162–3, 170, 175–90, 381, 383; judges 162–3, 165–6, 383; Netherlands 6–7, 161–6, 175–88;

outcome bias 164; police incompetence and misconduct 7, 161–2, 165–6, 383; predisposing circumstances 183–6; prosecutors 91–107, 380, 383; public opinion, pressures of 183–4; repeating proof 173, 182; Scotland 190; systemic flaws 176–83

Connick Sr, Harry 102–3

contamination of evidence 143–6, 150–1, 378–9

context 15–37, 128

continuing legal education 106

Convicted but Innocent: Wrongful Conviction and Public Policy. Huff, C. Ronald, Rattner, Arye and Sagarin, Edward 194

Convicting the Innocent. Borchard, Edwin 10, 48–9, 163, 329–36, 338–9

Convicting the Innocent. Garrett, Brandon L. 77, 89

conviction integrity units, establishment of 347–8

Cook, Kimberley J. 8, 360, 385–6

Cook, R. 150

coroners 72

correctional officials/prisons 35–6

corruption 17, 28–9, 81, 120–1, 252, 341–4

cosmopolitanization 344–5

counsel *see* defense counsel

Court of Last Resort, the. Gardner, Earle Stanley 49

courts, reforms to 338, 340, 348–9, 351

crime scenes, errors at 120, 143–6, 389

Criminal Cases Review Commission (CCRC) (UK) 189, 284, 289, 304, 350

Criminal Justice Abstracts 199

Croakley, Marion 114
Crombag, H.F.M. 180–1
Cromedy, McKinley 85–8
Cudmore, Byron 103
culture: adversarial systems 390;
  Canada 284, 304, 306, 384; forensic
  science 127, 388–9; institutional
  culture, changes in 10–11, 330,
  349–51; political culture, changes in
  10–11, 341; remedies for wrongful
  convictions 284, 304–5, 306, 384;
  United States 284, 305, 384
Cummings, Homer 337
curbside justice 28

D

dangerousness designation 211, 230
Darden, Christopher 32
Davis, Troy 227, 285, 291, 293–7, 303,
  305
de Berk, Lucia 173–4, 177, 181–2,
  185
death penalty cases: adversarial
  systems and inquisitorial systems,
  comparison between 61; Death
  Penalty Information Center 49, 278;
  DNA evidence 30; due process,
  without 17; extradition 287;
  frequency of wrongful convictions,
  estimates of 3, 45–6, 51–4, 376–7;
  guilty pleas 196; remedies for
  wrongful convictions 287, 290,
  293–7; resistance to relief 313;
  resources 53–4; return to free
  society 9, 262–78; social costs 30;
  statistics 30, 52–3, 56–7; United
  States 49, 61, 196, 262–78, 287,
  290, 293–7
Death Penalty Focus 274
decline in crime 34–5
declaratory judgments 332, 335–6

defending convictions see prosecution
  resistance to post-conviction relief
defense counsel: adversarial systems 4,
  63–4, 69, 70, 379, 381–2; causes of
  wrongful convictions 4, 89, 379; fair
  hearing, right to a 187; false
  confessions 69, 187; forensic science
  125; incompetence and misconduct
  4, 89, 74, 379; inquisitorial systems
  4, 63–4, 69, 70, 379, 381–2; material
  truth versus procedural justice 63;
  Netherlands 168–9, 177, 187;
  remedies for wrongful convictions
  62; resources 70
definition of wrongful convictions 11,
  357–9, 376
deportation 8, 212, 215–17, 221–2, 225
detention see preventive detention
  without charge
deterrence 18, 33–5
Diallo, Amadou 17
Diplomatic Protection. Borchard,
  Edwin 331–2
disclosure 64, 129, 189–90, 210–11,
  218–19
discretion 16, 20, 29, 33–4
discrimination 121 see also race
DNA evidence: accreditation 148–9;
  actual innocence 117, 358;
  adversarial systems 138; bias 128,
  143; Canada 218, 287–8, 297, 301;
  cause of wrongful convictions, as
  4–5, 77–81, 84, 87–90, 113– 17,
  121–4, 129, 131, 377–8;
  confirmation bias, tunnel vision and
  belief perseverance 378;
  contamination 143–6, 150–1; data
  sets 116–17; death penalty 30;
  destruction 389; eyewitness
  identification 87–9, 379; failures to
  convict 22; frequency of wrongful

convictions, estimates of 3, 49, 54–6, 376; immunity 101; inferences 6, 140, 150, 152, 154; innocent projects 49, 137, 278, 358; inquisitorial systems 138; Knox, Amanda, case of 6, 140–55, 378–9; law schools 105, 349–50; levels of propositions 150–2; low-template DNA (LT-DNA) 142–3; National Registry of Exonerations 278, 358; Netherlands 171–3, 179; overclaiming 121; post-conviction exonerations 113–17, 123–4; probability 140, 151–3; probative value 140, 145–6, 149, 152; profiles 139–40; prosecutors 91–3, 96, 101, 104–7, 310–12, 315, 318, 322–4, 348; rape and rape-murder cases 51–7, 77, 80, 92–3, 113, 116, 290, 310, 315, 323– 4, 376–8; remedies for wrongful convictions 285, 287–93, 297, 301, 303–4; resistance to relief 310–12, 315, 318, 322–4; robbery 51–2; standards 148–9; stains versus profiles 146–7; statistics 116, 292–3; statute of limitations, removal of 73; stuttering 147–8; SWGDAM guidelines 128; United Kingdom 359; United States 285, 288, 289–93, 303–4, 349–51, 363; validation research, lack of basic 123; wrongful arrests 22–3

Doswell, Thomas 309–11, 321, 323
double jeopardy 385
Douglas, William O. 336
Doyle, James 345
"drug kingpin" laws 20, 34–5
drug use 52, 198, 274–5
due diligence 287–8, 304, 384
Duty, Jana 105
Dwyer, J. 358

E

Eastman, Crystal 334
economic needs on release 262, 276–8, 392
education and training: continuing legal education 106; DNA 105; forensic science 127; law school clinics 330, 340, 349–51; police 20, 28, 343–4, 387–8; return to free society 266; use of force 28
El Maati, Ahmad 221–2
election of prosecutors 30, 106–7, 286, 290, 293, 295, 385
Elkins, Clarence, case of 5, 93, 95–6, 390
emerging democracies and transitional justice 11, 360, 363–9
emotional toll of wrongful convictions 266–76, 361–2, 385–6
employment: return to free society 265–6, 276, 392; workmen's compensation 333–5, 339, 386–7
Endo, Mitsuye 335
enemy combatants 210, 223, 225–7
epistemic hardness 113
error management systems 21–2, 37, 62, 368
errors of impunity 18
escapes from prison 35
ETA (*Euskadi ta Askatasuna* (Basque Homeland and Liberty)) 7–8, 202–3, 205, 377
Europa Press 199
Europe: adversarial systems 4, 6–7, 61–74, 162–3, 238, 381–2; alternatives to trials 2, 8, 238–56, 381; double jeopardy 385; false confessions 171–4, 177–81, 186–7, 193–205, 361, 390–1; inquisitorial systems 4, 6–8, 61–74, 162–3, 238–51, 256, 381–2; personal

accountability 390–1; plea bargains 195–7; sentencing 63;statements of guilt 237 *see also* individual countries; penal orders in Europe; summary proceedings in Europe

European Convention on Human Rights: adversarial systems and inquisitorial systems, comparison between 62, 63; compensation, right to 11, 386; definition of wrongful convictions 357; fair hearing, right to a 66, 68, 187, 240–1; terrorism 375; United States 386, 393

European Systems. Borchard, Edwin 330–7

euthanasia, false confessions to force changes in law on 7, 200–1, 205

everyday life, problems of 264–6

evidence: compulsion, obtained by 213; hearsay 168; Netherlands 168, 169–89, 388; terrorist suspects, treatment of 8, 210, 212–13, 215–21, 225–6, 228–30; torture, obtained by 217 *see also* DNA evidence; exculpatory evidence, suppression of; expert evidence; eyewitness identification; forensic science; new evidence; witnesses

exculpatory evidence, suppression of: adversarial systems 70, 176; *Brady* violations 5, 390; Guildford Four and Birmingham Six 361; inquisitorial systems 70, 176; Netherlands 176–7, 179; plea bargains 29–30, 250; prosecutors, misconduct by 97, 99–100, 102–6, 380; social costs 29–30; statistics 30

executive, appeals to the 292–3, 295, 297–8, 304

Exonerations in the United States, 1989 Through 2003. Gross, Samuel R. 252

expert evidence: independence 71, 125–6, 179–80, 183–4, 383, 389; IRA cases 180; Netherlands 179–80, 183 *see also* DNA evidence; forensic science

extradition 287

extraordinary rendition 210

eyewitness identification: blind administration 318–20; Canada 301; causes of wrongful convictions 85–9, 377; cross-racial identification 86–7, 310–11, 320; curbside justice 28; DNA evidence 87–9, 116, 379; Estimator Variables 310–11, 320–1; false negatives and false positives 27; guidelines 87–9; inducements 27; intimidation 27; juries 87–8, 319–21; Netherlands 177–8; police 25, 27–8, 309–10, 318–21; pre-trial hearings 88; prosecution resistance to relief 309–11, 318–21, 323; rape cases 85–6, 323; remedies for wrongful convictions 301; robbery 51; social costs 25, 27–8; suggestive procedures 86, 88–9; System Variables 311, 320; Technical Working Group for Eyewitness Evidence 345; time between event and identification 27; United States 87–9, 319–20; violent crimes 27 *see also* lineups

F

factual innocence 270, 303, 321–3

failures to convict 3–4, 15–19, 22–5, 31–2, 37

Fain, Charles 263, 264, 277

fair hearing, right to a 66, 68, 187, 240–1, 244

Fallis, David S. 27–8

false confessions: accountability 390–1; adversarial systems 4, 7, 62–4, 68–71; changes in law, voluntary confessions to pressure for 7, 199–201, 205; classification of confessions 194–5, 198–9; coerced-compliant confessions 194–5, 198; coerced-internalized confessions 194–5; coerced-persuaded confessions 195; coerced-reactive confessions 195, 198; confirmation bias, tunnel vision and belief perseverance 7, 166; contaminated confessions 4, 82–5, 89, 377; defence counsel, role of 69, 187; definition 194–6; detention, to avoid 198; drug intoxication 198; Europe 171–4, 177–81, 186–7, 193–205, 361, 390–1; forensic science 111; groups, loyalty to 7, 199, 202; Guildford Four and Birmingham Six 361; inquisitorial systems 4, 7, 62–4, 68–71; intangible benefits, for 7, 194, 196–205; juveniles 7, 84–5, 197–202, 205, 377; loyalty 197–202, 205–6, 375–6, 377; mental disabilities 84–5; penal orders 241, 243; plea bargains 195–7; protection of actual offenders 7–8, 197–9, 201–6, 375–6, 377; punishment, to obtain a milder 193, 195; recording interviews 69, 83–4, 85, 388; remedies for wrongful convictions 62; research 194, 197–206; Roma 7, 200, 203–6, 277; Spain 7, 194, 199–206; statistics 84; stress-compliant confessions 195; tangible benefits 193–4; terrorist suspects 7–8, 200, 202–3, 210, 375, 377; United States 7, 205, 210;

videotaping interrogations 69, 83–4, 388; women 7, 203–5; voluntary confessions 2, 7–8, 193–206, 375–6, 377

false negatives and positives 3, 18, 22, 25–7, 375, 387

families, impact of wrongful convictions on 23, 362, 385–6

Farruquito (Montoya, Juan Manuel Fernández) 204

fatal shootings 17, 27–8

finality of verdicts 284, 289–90, 295, 302–6

Findley, Keith 94–5, 163–4, 175, 177–8, 183, 186–7

fingerprints 72, 116, 121, 123, 127–8, 224, 342, 378

fishing expeditions 25–6

forensic science 2, 5–6, 111–31; accreditation 126–7; adversarial systems 71–2, 154; biased interpretations 112, 122–3, 125, 128, 138–9; blind procedures 128–9, 389; Canada 287–8, 297–9; cause of wrongful convictions, as a 4, 89, 111–12, 114–31, 378; certification 126–7; commissions, creation of independent 126; competition between labs 126; contextual bias 128; corrupt analysts 120–1; courts 124–5; crime scenes, errors at 120, 389; culture 127, 388–9; data sets 116–18; disclosure and information sharing 129; discrimination 121; education and training 127; epistemic hardness 113; error management 62; exclusion of evidence 130; false confessions 111; features of contributions to wrongful convictions 120–5; frequency studies 123; halo effect

113; incompetence or misconduct 4, 89, 111–31, 120–1, 378, 389; independence 71, 125–6, 179, 383, 389; innocence movement 112–13; inquisitorial systems 6, 71–2, 154; IRA cases 114, 378; Knox, Amanda, case of 6, 389; masking or blinding 122; Netherlands 171–6, 179–80, 388; "no-crime" cases 117; overclaiming 121, 123; pathology 117; police 341–2; policy recommendations 125–30; quality assurance/quality control 71–2, 126–7, 388–9; reform 6, 130, 387–93; remedies for wrongful convictions 62, 287–8, 297–9; reporting, standardization of 129; resources and funding 129–30; second opinions 389; sequential unmasking, proposal for 128–9; shaken baby syndrome 117, 285, 297–303, 305; statistics 113, 116–19, 378, 388; truth, association with 112, 138– 9; United Kingdom 114; United States 111–14, 125–7; validation research, lack of basic 123, 127 *see also* DNA evidence

Forst, Brian 2–4, 363, 374–5, 387

"Forty Two" gang 202

frameworks for assessing miscarriages of justice 21–2

France: adversarial systems and inquisitorial systems, comparison between 61–2, 72; appeals 384; frequency of wrongful convictions, estimates of 61–2, 376–7; new trials 384; penal orders 240, 242; plea bargains 196–7

Frank, Barbara 49

Frank, Jerome 49, 163, 350

Frankfurter, Frank 337, 339

frequency of wrongful convictions, estimates of 3–4, 45–57, 61–2, 376–7

Fyfe, James 28

G

Gardner, Earle Stanley 49, 350

Garrett, Brandon L. 4–5, 77, 89, 116–17, 131, 292, 301–2, 377–8, 380–1

Gauger, Gary 263, 265, 269–71, 275

Gell, Alan 263, 267, 273

Geneva Conventions 226–7, 375

Germany: adversarial systems and inquisitorial systems, comparison between 61–2, 66–7, 71–2, 381; alternatives to trials 247–51; appeals 71, 248, 250, 384; frequency of wrongful convictions, estimates of 61–2, 376–7; penal orders 240, 242, 381; plea bargains 66, 196, 247–51; retrials 384, 391; risk of wrongful convictions 249–50; sentencing 238, 249–50

Gilliéron, Gwladys 8, 67, 376, 380–1

Ginsburg, Ruth Bader 102–3, 302

Givelber, D. 74

Godschalk, Bruce 323

Godsey, Mark 92–3

Goudge Inquiry 298–9, 301–2

graphology 174–5

Greenleaf, Stewart 312

grief 268–9

Griffin, Lissa 284

Gross, Samuel R. 3–4, 49, 61, 116–17, 252, 292, 302, 376–7

Grounds, Adrian 360–2

group exonerations 49

groups, loyalty to 7, 199, 202

groupthink 181

Guantánamo Bay detainees 212, 222, 226–8
Gudjonsson Confession Questionnaire (GCQ) 198
Gudjonsson, G.H. 197–8
Guede, Rudy 141
Guildford Four 360–1
guilty pleas: alternatives to trials 239; Canada 285, 299, 301; death penalty cases 196; false confessions 193, 196; penal orders 382; plea bargains 8, 65, 250–4, 382; rape cases 196, 252; remedies for wrongful convictions 285, 299, 301–2; United States 8, 239, 250–4, 302, 382
Gulet, Mohamed 229
Guth, Raymond 318

H

habeas corpus 80–1, 223, 225–7, 285, 290–1, 293–6, 303–5, 384
hair evidence 111, 116, 121, 124, 128, 131, 171–2, 378
halo effect 113
Al-Hamzi, Albadar 225
Hand, Learned 48–9
Harper, Stephen 221
Harrington, Terry 100–1
Harrisburg Patriot 314
health care needs 266, 276
hearsay 168
Heath, Brad 31
Hellmann, Claudio Pratillo 141
Herman, J.L. 275
Hernández, G. 203
Herrera, Leonel 324
hindsight bias 164
Holtzoff, Alexander 337
homicide cases *see* death penalty cases
housing on release 264–5, 266, 392

Howard, Tim 263, 277
Huff, C. Ronald 11, 49, 120, 194
human rights *see* European Convention on Human Rights; Human Rights Watch (HRW)
Human Rights Watch (HRW) 225
Hungary, transitional justice in 11, 367–8, 376

I

identification *see* eyewitness identification
identity, offers of a new 392
immigration policies in Canada 8, 210, 213–14, 219, 229
immunity: absolute immunity, doctrine of 91, 100–2, 106; compensation 386; constitutional violations 104; DNA evidence 101; police 386; prosecutors 5, 91, 99–106, 386; sovereign immunity 332, 335–6
impact of wrongful convictions: children and families, impact on 23, 362, 385–6; emotional toll of wrongful convictions 266–76, 361–2, 385–6; false coerced confessions 361; Guildford Four and Birmingham Six 360–1; personality changes 361–2; political repression, convictions based on 360–3; post- traumatic stress disorder 362, 385–6; public confidence in criminal justice system 11, 361, 363; public safety 11, 363, 387; social costs 2–3, 15, 18, 23–36 *see also* return to free society
impartiality *see* bias
impunity 18, 32, 382, 391
In the Name of the Father (movie) 361

incompetence or misconduct: accountability 20, 25, 29, 69–70, 276–8, 390–1; correctional officials 35–6; defense counsel 4, 89, 74, 379; forensic science 4, 89, 111–31, 120–1, 378, 389; judges 4–5, 162–3, 165–6, 374–6, 383; juries 33, 47, 138, 295–6, 319, 348–9; plea bargains 30–2, 65–7, 99, 188, 249–55, 346–8, 376, 381, 389–90; witnesses 379 *see also* police misconduct or incompetence; prosecutorial misconduct or incompetence

incorporation approach after release 272–6

independence: commissions 126, 187, 284, 289, 304; expert evidence 71, 125–6, 179–80, 183–4, 383, 389; forensic science 71, 125–6, 179, 383, 389; penal orders 240

informants *see* jailhouse informants

innocence, definition of 311, 313–15, 317, 321–5

innocent movements/projects: Borchard, Edwin 10, 329–39, 348, 350–1; DNA evidence 49, 137, 278, 358; forensic science 112–13, 358; law school clinics 330, 340, 349–51; North Carolina Innocence Inquiry Commission 350; prosecutors, misconduct by 92–3, 96, 102–5, 338; United States 10–11, 285, 302–3, 306, 329–51, 388, 390

innocence, presumption of 8, 66, 210, 322, 324

inquisitorial system: alternatives to trials 8, 238–51, 256; confirmation bias, tunnel vision and belief perseverance 7, 176, 178, 183–6, 381; Europe 4, 8, 61–74, 238–51, 256, 382; fair hearing, right to a 244; forensic science 6, 154; instruction, principle of 244; Knox, Amanda, case of 6, 154; legality, principle of 244; Netherlands 166, 180, 183, 186–9; plea bargains 239, 244–51, 255, 381; remedies for wrongful convictions 4, 11, 69–73, 238, 393; truth 238; United States 255, 381 *see also* adversarial systems and inquisitorial systems, comparison between institutions: confirmation bias, tunnel vision and belief perseverance 183–6, 381; culture, changes to 10–11, 330, 339–51; Netherlands 183–6; pressures, from 183–6; United States 10–11, 330, 339–51

instruction, principle of 244

internal controls, increase in 389–90

International Court of Justice (ICJ) 363

International Covenant on Civil and Political Rights (ICCPR) 367–8

intimacy problems after release 264, 267–9

intimidation of witnesses 27

IRA cases 114, 180, 210, 360–1, 378

Iraq 211, 226

Italy 66, 71, 196–7 *see also* Knox, Amanda, case of

J

jailhouse informants: causes of wrongful convictions 4, 78–82, 89, 377–8; guidelines 82; incentives offered 78–82

James, Gary 263, 264

James, William 165

Japanese people, internment of 214, 335

Johns, Margaret 101
Johnson, Hiram 336
Johnson, Victoria 309
Journal of Criminal Law &
    Criminology 337
judges: adversarial systems and
    inquisitorial systems, comparison
    between 238; causes of wrongful
    convictions 4–5, 162–3, 165–6,
    374–6, 383; confirmation bias,
    tunnel vision and belief
    perseverance 162–3, 165–6, 383;
    elections 286, 290, 293, 295, 363;
    errors 374–6; incompetence and
    misconduct 4–5, 162–3, 165–6,
    374–6, 383; Netherlands 167–8,
    175, 179–84, 188; public safety 374;
    sentencing, discretion on 33–4;
    social costs 32–4; Switzerland 385;
    United States 349
juries: bullying by one juror 33; Canada
    284, 286–7, 297–8, 302–6, 384;
    comprehension, promoting 348–9;
    eyewitness evidence 87–8, 319–21;
    finality of verdicts 284, 289–90,
    295, 302–6; incompetence and
    misconduct 33, 47, 138, 295–6, 319,
    348–9; note-taking 33; rape cases 77;
    remedies for wrongful convictions
    284, 286–7, 294, 296–8, 302–6, 384;
    scientific and legal evidence, lack of
    understanding of 33; social costs
    32–3; standard of proof, warnings on
    22; United States 287, 294, 296,
    302–6, 348–9; warnings 22, 87–8
juveniles, false confessions by 7, 84–5,
    197–202, 205, 377

K

Kassin, Saul 194–5, 198, 316
Keaton, Dave 263, 279

Keine, Ronald 265
Kennedy, Ludovic 361
Kercher, Meredith 140–1
Khadr, Omar 222
Kiger, A. 120
Killias, Martin 4
Kitchen, Ronald 103
Knox, Amanda, case of 140–55;
    accreditation 148–9; Appeal Brief
    141; bias 143, 148–9; contamination
    of evidence 143–6, 150–1, 378–9;
    Conti & Vecchiotti Report 141,
    143; DNA evidence 6, 140–55,
    378–9; evaluation versus
    interpretation 149–50; facts of case
    140–2; forensic science 6, 140–55,
    378–9, 389; inferences 6, 140, 150,
    152, 154; inquisitorial systems 6,
    154; Laboratory DNA Report 141;
    Massei Judgmemt 141; Rinaldi &
    Boemia Report 141; scientific
    standards 148–9; stains versus
    profiles 146–7; stuttering 147–8
Koppl, Roger 126
Korematsu, Fred 335
Krane, D.E. 128
Krzewinski, L.M. 197

L

Lake, Beverly 349
Lappas, Spero T. 10, 385–6, 390
law schools: clinics 330, 340, 349–51;
    DNA evidence 105
lawyers *see* defense counsel; judges,
    prosecutors
legal innocence 321–2
legal needs on release 276–8, 386, 392
legality, principle of 244
legislators 32–5
legitimacy, asymmetry of 23–4
Leibman, James 313–14

Leipold, Andrew D. 176
Leo, R.A. 194–5
Lexow committee investigations 342
Liebman, James 175
limitation periods 72–3, 289, 293–4, 301, 305
Lindbergh baby kidnapping 196
lineups: double blind lineups 87–9, 330, 388, 390; false positive and false negatives 27; guidance 87–8, 320, 345–6; police misconduct 27, 86–9, 319; prosecutors 318–19, 390; reforms 87–8, 97–9, 320, 330, 345–6, 388, 390; resistance to relief 318–19; Technical Working Group for Eyewitness Evidence 345
Linskey, Lori 318, 320
Lippman, Jonathan 349
literacy 242–3
Loftus, Elizabeth F. 10, 385–6, 390
Logan, Charles 35–6
loyalty and false confessions 197–202, 205–6, 375–6, 377
Lucas, Henry Lee 196
Lukanich, Mark 103
Lutz, E. Russell 337

M

Macfarlane, Bruce A. 165, 177, 183, 185
Madigan, Lisa 104
Madison, Ronald 17
malignant sources of miscarriages of justice 19–21
Mar Adentro/The Sea Inside (movie) 201
Markman, Stephen 324
Marquardt, Tammy 298–9
Marquis, Joshua 50, 52
Marshall, Donald 219
Martin, Dianne 163–4

Martin, James 314
masking or blinding 122
material truth 4, 62–5, 69–70, 384–5
material witness warrants 224–5, 230
McCann, J.T. 195
McCoy, Kevin 31
McDade, Joe Billy 103
McFatridge, Michael 104
McGhee, Curtis 100–1
media 50, 62, 93, 106, 124, 173–5, 183–5, 209, 276, 351
Medwed, D.S. 348
Meissner, C.A. 67, 70–1, 388
Melendez, Juan 263, 264–5, 269
mental illness 66–7, 84–5, 196, 243, 262, 266, 276, 361–2, 385–6
mercy, royal prerogative of 289
Middle East 11, 368
Milgaard, David 218
military commissions 228–9, 231
Milosevic, Slobodan 363–4
Miranda warnings 74, 83, 84–5, 388
miscarriages of justice, contextual framework of 15–37; assessment of miscarriages, framework for 21–3; definition of miscarriages of justice 16; discretion, exercise of 16, 20; failures to convict 3, 15–16, 18–19, 22–5, 31–2, 37; false positives and negatives 3, 18, 22, 375; mindful management of wrongful convictions 3, 36–7; reporting offences 16–19, 25, 37, 374; social costs 2–3, 15, 18, 23–37; sources of miscarriages 19–21; Type I errors 2–3, 22, 387; Type II errors 2–3, 22, 387; types of miscarriages of justice 2–3, 16, 22, 374, 387
misconduct *see* incompetence or misconduct; police misconduct or

incompetence; prosecutorial
misconduct or incompetence
mitigation 63, 65, 245
Mohammed, Khalid Sheikh 228
Moley, Raymond 346
monopoly of state to use force 23–4
Moore, John Bassett 331
Morton, Michael 104
Moto, Vincent 310, 321, 323
Mullins-Johnson, William 297–8, 299
El Mundo 199
murder *see* death penalty cases
*Murder, Errors of Justice, and Capital
Punishment*. Bedau, Hugo 49
Murphy, Patrick 28–9

N

National Institute of Forensic Science
(NIFS), proposal for 126
National Registry of Exonerations 3,
49–51, 97, 278, 358–9
National Research Council (NRC)
122, 125–7, 129–30
Nelson, Bruce 323–4
Nesmith, Willie 323–4, 325
Netherlands 166–90; actors in
criminal justice process 167–8;
adversarial systems 6–7, 162–3,
167–70, 176–80, 186–9; appeals 71,
170, 175, 185; case studies 170–9,
181–3, 185–6, 388; commission of
investigations, introduction of
187–9; confirmation bias, belief
perseverance and tunnel vision 6–7,
161–6, 170, 175–90, 383; criminal
justice process 162, 166–90; de
Berk, Lucia, case of 173–4, 177,
181–2, 185; defense counsel during
investigation, lack of right to 168–9,
177, 187; DNA evidence 171–3,
179; dossiers 168–9, 180–1, 185,

187; evidence 168, 169–89, 388;
exculpatory evidence, disclosure of
176–7, 179; experts, independence
of 179–80, 183; eyewitness
identification 177–8; false
confessions 171–2, 174, 177,
179–81, 186–7; forensic evidence
171–6, 179–80, 388; frequency of
wrongful convictions, estimates of
61–2, 376–7; improvements to
system, policy and legislation on
186–90; inquisitorial system 6–7,
162–3, 166, 180, 183, 186–9;
institutional pressures 183–6; judges
167–8, 175, 179–84, 188; media
183–5; new evidence 170, 172, 174,
182–3, 188; police misconduct or
incompetence 6–7, 167–78, 183–4,
186, 388; Post, Ina, case of 174–5,
177–8, 183; predisposing
circumstances 183–6; pre-trial
investigations 167–8, 176–85;
prosecutors 105–6, 166–80, 183–8,
380, 388; public opinion, pressures
of 183–5; Putten Murder case
171–2, 176–9, 181, 183; recording
of interviews 177, 186–7; retrials
170, 172–3, 175, 179, 182, 185, 188,
384; review procedure, introduction
of 187–8; safeguards against
wrongful convictions 162, 169–70,
186–8; Schiedam Park Murder
172–3, 177, 179, 185– 6, 388;
systemic flaws 176–83; third party
review 186; tunnel vision 170,
175–90, 383; witnesses 168, 170,
177–8, 185, 187
Neufeld, Peter 113–14, 137, 358
new evidence: Canada 287–8, 299–
302, 305, 385; definition 172, 174,
182; Netherlands 170, 172, 174,

182–3, 188; remedies for wrongful convictions 284, 290–1, 295–6, 305, 385; United States 284, 290–1, 295–6, 305, 385

new identity, offers of a 392

new trials *see* retrials

"no crime" cases 117

No-Fly List 221, 229

nolo contendere pleas 239, 254

Not Guilty. Frank, Jerome and Frank, Barbara 49

numbing strategies on release 275–6

Nureddin, Muayyed 221–2

Nye, Gerald 333

O

Obama, Barack 226–9, 231

O'Connor, Sandra Day 33

Office of Justice Programs 345

Ofshe, R.J. 194–5

ombudsman 366, 367

Operation Ceasefire 345

organizational structures, changes to 340

organized evaluation 186

overclaiming 121, 123

P

El País 199

paper trials 168

pardons 292–3

penal orders in Europe 2, 239–43; adversarial systems and inquisitorial systems, comparison between 8, 64–7, 381–3; appeals 240; definition 239; fair hearing, right to a 240–1; false confessions 241, 243; France 240, 242; Germany 240, 242, 381; guilty pleas 382; independence and impartiality 240; mental disabilities,

persons with 243; objections, raising 240–3; plea bargains 64–7, 241; police 238, 241–2; prosecutors 239–42; risk of wrongful convictions 241–3; sentences 239–41, 243; statistics 243; Switzerland 239–40, 242–3, 381; time limits for opposition 242–3; types of offences 239

"Pennsylvania Eight" 311, 323

Pennsylvania, prosecution resistance to post-conviction relief in 9–10, 309–25

personality changes 361–2

Petro, Jim 5, 8, 380–2, 386, 387

Petro, Nancy 5, 8, 380–2, 386, 387

Phillion, Romeo 218

Pitchfork, Colin 137

plea bargaining 2, 244–56; abridged proceedings 244–6; advantages 249, 250–1; adversarial systems and inquisitorial systems, comparison between 4, 8, 64–7; *Alford* pleas 66, 254; appeals 246, 248, 250–1; charges 244–5, 248, 251; coercion 245, 249–51, 253, 255; confessions 195–7, 244–6, 248, 250; consent 244; definition 251; exculpatory evidence 31, 250; fact bargaining 251, 253; fair hearing, right to a 244; forms of plea bargains 66–7; France 196–7; frequency of wrongful convictions, estimates of 376; Germany 66, 196, 248–51; guilty pleas 8, 65, 239, 250–4, 382; implicit plea bargaining 251; incompetence or misconduct 30–2, 65–7, 99, 188, 249–55, 346–8, 376, 381, 389–90; informal agreements 247–50; inquisitorial systems 244–51, 255, 381; instruction, principle of 244; legality, principle of 244; *nolo contendere* pleas 239, 254; penal orders 64–7; presumption of innocence 66; prosecutors 5, 30–2, 65–7, 99, 188, 249–55, 346–8, 376, 381, 389–90; remedies for wrongful convictions 389–90; resources 31, 251; restrictions 389–90; risk of wrongful convictions 249–55; sentences 244–6, 248, 249, 250–4; social costs 31; statistics 30, 252; summary proceedings 66, 70; Switzerland 66, 198, 244–6, 249–51; United States 2, 8, 30–2, 237, 239, 250–5, 347–8, 381–2, 389–90

Poland: plea bargains 197; transitional justice 11, 365–7, 368, 376

police: accountability 25, 29; accusatorial methods of investigation 63; adversarial systems and inquisitorial systems, comparison between 4, 63, 67–8, 70, 74, 388; Canada 213; community policing 25, 27, 29; corruption 28–9; culture 388; deception in interrogations 68; ethnic and racial profiling 25–7; eyewitness identification 25, 27–8; forensic experts, independence of 71; interrogations 4, 63, 67–8, 70, 74, 388; methods of information-gathering 66–8, 70–1, 388; neutral methods of interrogation 66, 70–1, 388; penal orders 238, 241–2; social costs 24–9; terrorist suspects, treatment of 213; United States 63; use of force 25, 27–9 *see also* false confessions; police misconduct or incompetence

police misconduct or incompetence: brutality 17, 27–8, 37; causes of wrongful convictions and miscarriages of justice 4, 20–1, 89, 378; city government 342–3; confirmation bias, tunnel vision and belief perseverance 7, 161–2, 165–6, 383; cosmopolitanization 344–5; education and training 20, 28, 343–4, 387–8; fatal shootings 17, 27–8; forensic science 341–2; group exonerations 49; higher education 343–4; immunity 386; inducement to witnesses 27; lineups 27, 86–9, 319; Netherlands 6–7, 167–78, 183–4, 186, 388; Police and Criminal Evidence Act 1984 (UK) 177; professional model 387–8, 390–1; prosecution resistance to relief 309–10, 318–21; public opinion 20; remedies for wrongful convictions 330, 338–46, 387–8; sanctions 37

political culture, changes to 10–11, 341

political pandering and pressures 20–1, 184, 187, 303, 342, 345, 376

political parties 200, 347

political repression, convictions based on 2, 357–68; actual innocence standard 11, 359; examples 359–60; Hungary, transitional justice in 11, 367–8, 376; impacts of wrongful convictions 360–3, 385–6; Middle East 11, 368; Poland, transitional justice in 11, 365–7, 368, 376; South Africa 369, 376; transitional justice 11, 360, 363–9

politicization 34, 184–5

Portugal 198

Post, Ina 174–5, 177–8, 183

post-traumatic stress disorder (PTSD) 362, 385–6

Pound, Roscoe 334–5

presumption of innocence 8, 66, 210, 322, 324

prevalence of wrongful convictions, estimates of 3–4, 45–57, 61–2, 376–7

Preventable Error: A Report on Prosecutorial Misconduct in California 1997–2009 98–9

preventive detention without charge: Canada 8, 212, 213, 216–17, 221–2, 230, 374; *habeas corpus* 223, 225–7; terrorist suspects, treatment of 8, 212, 213, 216–17, 221–7, 229–30, 374–5; United States 8, 212, 222–7, 229–31, 374–5

prison population, explosion in 34–5, 107

product defects 3

professional model of policing 342–3

professional standards 105–6, 342–3, 387–8, 390–1

profiling 25–7, 215, 344

Progressive Era 330–6, 342–3

prosecution resistance to post-conviction relief: actual innocence 10, 321–2, 324; Advisory Committee 311–20; blind administration 318–19; Canada 9–10, 287–9; causes of wrongful convictions 316; death penalty cases 313; DNA evidence 310–12, 315, 318, 322–4; eyewitness identification 309–11, 318–21, 323; factual innocence 321–2; incompetence and misconduct 5, 9–10, 93, 104–5, 380, 348, 380, 390–1; Innocence Commission, proposal to establish a 10, 312–18; innocence, what constitutes 311, 313–15, 317, 321–5; Joint State Government Commission (US) 312–18, 322; legal innocence 321–2; Minority Report 317– 20, 322–4; Pennsylvania 9–10, 309–25; "Pennsylvania Eight" 311, 323; police misconduct 309–10, 318–21; presumption of innocence 322, 324; public safety, dangers to 10; redefining innocence 10, 311; United States 9–10, 93, 104–5, 309–25, 380, 390–1

prosecutorial misconduct or incompetence 91–107; ABA Standards of Criminal Justice 94; absolute immunity, doctrine of 91, 100–2, 106; accountability 390–1; adversarial systems 94, 390; bar associations 94, 390–1; Brady violations 5, 390; causes of wrongful convictions 4, 78–82; compensation 386; confirmation bias, tunnel vision and belief perseverance 94–5, 380, 383; continuing legal education 106; conviction integrity units, establishment of 347–8; culture more balanced, making 390–1; death penalty 30; disciplinary action 64, 97–9, 105, 347, 380, 391–2; DNA evidence 91–3, 96, 101, 104–7, 348; Elkins case 93, 95–6; exculpatory evidence, failure to share 5, 97, 99–100, 102–6, 380, 390; immunity 5, 91, 99– 106, 386; Innocence Projects 92–3, 96, 102–5, 338 ; jailhouse informants 4, 78–82, 89, 377–8; lineup reform 346, 388, 390; Netherlands 166–80, 173–8, 380, 388; plea bargains 5, 30–2, 65–7, 99, 188, 249–55, 346–8, 376, 381, 389–90; politicization 185; professional standards 105–6; public

pressure 94, 97–8; remedies for
wrongful convictions 5, 105–7,
330, 338–41, 346– 8, 351, 380, 388,
390–1; research 347–8; rightful role
of Public Prosecutor 93–6; statistics
96, 98, 106; Switzerland 380; truth
93–4, 105; United States 5, 91–107,
330, 338–41, 346– 8, 351, 338, 380,
390
prosecutors: accountability 69–70;
adversarial systems and inquisitorial
systems, comparison between
238–9; alternatives to trials 239,
255–6; elections, provision of
information for 106–7; files, full
access to 390–1; oversight, lack of
239, 255; penal orders 239–42;
sentencing 239–40; social costs
29–32; Switzerland 239; United
States 253 *see also* prosecution
resistance to post-conviction relief;
prosecutorial misconduct or
incompetence
protect actual offenders, false
confessions to 7–8, 197–9, 201–6,
375–6, 377
psychology: anomalous psychological
processes 196; emotional toll of
wrongful convictions 266–76,
361–2, 385–6; false confessions 84,
196; rational psychological processes
196
public confidence in criminal justice
system 4, 9, 11, 16, 18, 26–7, 32,
182–4, 316, 361, 363
public inquiries 297, 302, 304
public opinion 20–1, 94, 97–8, 104,
183–5
public safety, risks to 10–11, 18–19,
363, 374, 387
publicity in high-profile cases 62

punishment, false confessions to
obtain a lesser 193, 195
Putnam, Constance 49
Putten murder case 171–2, 176–9,
181, 183

Q

al Qaeda 221–2, 227
quality control 71–2, 126–7, 388–9
quantitative data 373–4, 392–3

R

race: Canada 214–15, 306;
community relations 27; eyewitness
identification 86–7, 310– 11, 320;
legitimacy of criminal justice system
26–7; police 25–7, 344; racial
profiling 25–7, 215, 344; remedies
for wrongful convictions 306;
screening 26–7; terrorist suspects,
treatment of 214–15; United States
86–7, 111, 306, 311, 320, 344, 350
Radelet, Michael 30, 49, 324
Radin, Edward. *Innocent* 49
Raeder, Myrna 163–4
Rago, John 311–13, 317
Rakoff, Jed S. 287
rape cases: DNA evidence 51–7, 77,
80, 92–3, 113, 116, 290, 310, 315,
323–4, 376–8; eyewitness
identification 85–6, 323; frequency
of wrongful convictions 3, 46, 51,
54–7; guilty pleas 196, 252;
jailhouse informants 78–80; jurors
77; Netherlands 171–2, 176–9, 181,
183; resistance to relief 309–10,
323–5
rational choice theory 196
Rattner, Ayre 49, 194
Rawls, John 365

Razack, S. 215
Reagan, Ronald 228, 341
recognizances and peace bonds 213
recording interviews 69, 83–5, 177, 186–7, 338–9
reducing incidence of wrongful convictions *see* remedies for wrongful convictions
reform *see* remedies for wrongful convictions
relationships on release 264, 266–9
release from prison *see* return to free society
relief *see* prosecution resistance to post-conviction relief; remedies for wrongful convictions
remedies for wrongful convictions 387–93; adversarial systems 4, 11, 69–73, 238, 284, 303, 305, 393; alternatives to trials 237; appeals 62, 284–92, 297–305, 384, 391; arrests, inducements to improve quality of 37; commission for investigations, proposal for 187–8; courts, reform to 338, 340, 348–9, 351; defence counsel 62; false confessions 62; forensic science 62, 125– 30, 388–9; inquisitorial systems 4, 11, 69–73, 238, 393; institutional culture, changes in 10–11, 330, 339–51; internal controls, increase in 389–90; jurors 284, 286–7, 294, 296–8, 302–6, 384; law school clinics 330, 340, 349–51; lineups 87–8, 97–9, 320, 330, 345–6, 388, 390; Netherlands 162, 169–70, 186–90; new trials 391; organizational structure of criminal law justice 230; organized evaluation 186; plea bargains, restrictions on 251–5, 389–90;

police 330, 338–46, 387–8; political culture, changes in 10–11, 341; proof of innocence, exonerations beyond 391; prosecution files, full access to 390–1; prosecutors, misconduct by 5, 105–7, 330, 338–41, 346–8, 351, 380, 388, 390–1; recording interviews 186–7; review procedure, introduction of 187–8; serious errors are detected, allowing exonerations whenever 72; summary proceedings, restrictions on 62, 70; third party review 186 *see also* compensation; prosecution resistance to post-conviction relief; remedies for wrongful convictions in Canada; remedies for wrongful convictions in United States; retrials
remedies for wrongful convictions in Canada 283–306; adversarial systems 305; appeals 285–9, 297–301, 304–5, 384; Charter of Rights and Freedoms 287; commission, proposal for a 289, 304; culture 284, 304, 306, 384; DNA evidence 287–8, 297, 301; due diligence 287–8, 304, 384; eyewitness identification 301; executive, appeals to the 289, 297–8, 304; extradition to United States in death penalty cases 287; flexibility 9, 292, 298, 300, 304; forensic science 287–8, 297–9; guilty pleas 285, 299, 301; *habeas corpus* 304; jury trials 286–7, 297–8, 302, 305–6, 384; jury verdicts, finality of 284, 302; mercy, royal prerogative of 289; new evidence 287–8, 299–302, 305, 385; public inquiries 297, 302, 304; race 306; retrials 219, 289, 299, 384–5, 391; reviews 285–6; shaken baby

syndrome cases 285, 297–303, 305;
United Kingdom 284, 289, 304;
United States, comparison with
9–10, 283–93, 302–6, 384
remedies for wrongful convictions in
United States 283–306; actual
innocence 285–6, 288, 290–6,
304–5; adversarial systems 284,
303, 305; appeals 284, 289–90,
292, 303; Canada, comparison
with 9–10, 283–93, 302–6, 384;
collateral attacks on verdicts 290–1,
303, 305, 384; culture 284, 305,
384; Davis, Troy, case of 285, 291,
293–7, 303, 305; death penalty
cases 287, 290, 293–7; DNA
evidence 285, 288, 289–93, 303–4;
election of prosecutors and judges
286, 290, 293, 295; executive,
appeals to the 292–3, 295; guilty
pleas 302; *habeas corpus* 285, 290–1,
293–6, 303–5, 384; Innocence
Projects 285, 302–3, 306; jury
trials 287, 294, 296, 302, 305–6;
new evidence 284, 290–1, 295–6,
305, 385; pardons 292–3; race 306;
retrials 102, 289, 293–4, 300, 304–5,
391; shaken baby syndrome cases
302, 305; state law 286–7, 289–91,
296–7; statistics 292
Reno, Janet 345
reporting offences 16–19, 25, 37, 374
reporting, standardization of forensic
129
repressive regimes *see* political
repression, convictions based on
resistance to relief *see* prosecution
resistance to post-conviction relief
resources and funding 53–4, 70,
129–30, 251, 350
restorative justice 35

retrials: Canada 219, 289, 299, 384–5,
391; France 384; Germany 384,
391; Netherlands 170, 172–3, 175,
179, 182, 185, 188, 384;
Switzerland 391; United States 102,
289, 293–4, 300, 304–5, 391
retributive justice 34
return to free society 2, 9, 261–78;
acceptance, lack of 270–1, 277;
accountability of state 276–8;
avoidance approach 272–5;
biographical details 263; children
and families, impact on 11, 23, 362,
385–6; compensation, lack of
276–7, 391–2; coping with
aftermath 271–6; death row
exonerees 9, 262–78; drugs and
alcohol 274–5; economic needs 262,
276–8, 392; education 266;
emotional toll 266–76, 361–2,
385–6; employment 265–6, 276,
392; everyday life, problems of
264–6; grief 268–9; health care
needs 266, 276; housing 264–5,
266, 392; incorporation approach
272–6; intimacy 264, 267–9; legal
needs 276–8, 386, 392; mental
health issues 266, 276; new identity,
offers of 392; post-traumatic stress
disorder 362, 385–6; public
confidence, impact on 361, 363;
public safety 363; reintegration and
restoration 276–8; re-victimization
9, 261–2; ruptured relationships
266–8; social and economic
exclusion 262, 278; space,
negotiating 266; state help, lack of
265, 276–8; stigma 261–2, 266, 276,
392; survivor guilt 269–70, 275;
survivor mission, adopting a 273–4;
trust 262, 268–9; United States

262–78, 385–6; withdrawal and numbing strategies 275–6

re-victimization on release 9, 261–2

Reynard, Charles 103

Richardson, G. 197–8

right to a fair hearing 66, 68, 187, 240–1, 244

Risinger, Michael 54, 128

Roach, Kent 8, 209, 220, 227, 229, 384–5, 391

robbery 51–2, 359

Robertson, B. 154

Roma, false confessions by 7, 200, 203–6, 277

Roosevelt, Franklin D. 331–2, 335, 337–8, 386–7

Roosevelt, Theodore 334, 342

Rousseau, Jean-Jacques 365

royal prerogative of mercy 289

Rudovsky, David 313–14

S

Sacco-Vanzetti case 337–8, 348

safeguards against wrongful convictions *see* remedies for wrongful convictions

safety *see* public safety, risks to

Sagarin, Edward 49, 194

Sampedro, Ramon 201

Scalia, Antonin 50, 52, 296, 322, 324

Schalken, T.M. 189

Scheck, Barry 105, 113–14, 137, 313–14, 350, 358

Schiedam Park Murder 172–3, 177, 179, 185–6, 388

Schiffer, B. 112, 378

Scotland 190

Scott, Michael A. 163, 175, 177–8, 183, 186–7

screening 26–7, 32, 37, 85

second opinions 389

security certificates 212, 214–21, 230

Seitz, Bill 92

self-regulation 124, 126

sentencing: adversarial systems and inquisitorial systems, comparison between 63–4, 70, 74, 381–2; deterrence 33–5; discretion 33–4; false confessions to obtain a lighter sentence 193, 195; Germany 248, 249, 250; guidelines 34; lenient sentences 19, 193, 195; mitigation 63; penal orders 239–41, 243; plea bargains 244–6, 248, 249, 250–4; politicization 34; prison population, explosion in 34–5, 107; prosecutors 31, 239–40; restorative justice 35; retributive justice 34; social costs 31, 33–5; Switzerland 244–6, 250–1; tough-on-crime laws 20, 34–5, 99, 107; United States 250–4

September 11, 2001 terrorist attacks 8, 209–31

sequential unmasking, proposal for 128–9

serious errors, exonerations whenever there are 72

serology 79, 111, 115–16, 121–2, 124, 131, 378

Shaffer, Michael 116–17, 292, 302

shaken baby syndrome 117, 285, 297–303, 305

Sherratt-Robinson, Sherry 299–300

shoe prints 116, 121, 141

Short, Elizabeth (Black Dahlia) 196

Sigurdsson, J.F. 197–8

Simpson, O.J. 32

Skolnick, Jerome 28–9

Smith, B. 120

Smith, Charles 297–303

Smith, Juan 103

social and economic exclusion 262, 278

social contract 365

social costs 2–3, 15, 18, 23–36

Sollecito, Raffaele 141–2, 145, 153

Souk, James 103

Soule, George 338

Sourcebook of Crime and Criminal Justice Statistics 377

sources of miscarriages and wrongful convictions *see* causes of wrongful convictions and miscarriages of justice

South Africa, transitional justice in 369, 376

sovereign immunity 332, 335–6

space on release, negotiating 266

Spain 7–8, 194, 198–206, 377

standard of proof 21–2, 24, 31, 62, 170, 210–11, 229

statements of guilt in Europe, use of 237

statute of limitations 72–3, 289, 293–4, 301, 305

Steidl, Gordon "Randy" 104

stereotyping 216

Sterling, Frank 82–5

stigma 261–2, 266, 276, 392

summary proceedings in Europe 237–43; adversarial systems and inquisitorial systems, comparison between 8, 67, 70, 74, 381–2; bureaucracy 67; defense, rights of the 8, 381; frequency of wrongful convictions, estimates of 376; mental illness 66–7; plea bargains 66, 70; prosecutors, powers of 70, 246–9, 255–6; remedies for wrongful convictions 62, 70 *see also* penal orders in Europe

Sundby, Scott 321–2

survivor guilt 269–70, 275

survivor mission, adopting a 273–4

Sutherland, George 30

Switzerland: abridged proceedings 244–6; adversarial systems and inquisitorial systems, comparison between 61–2, 66–7, 71–2, 381–2; alternatives to trials 239, 244–7, 249–51, 255–6; appeals 71, 246, 384; confessions 245–6; exculpatory evidence, disclosure of 250; frequency of wrongful convictions, estimates of 61–2, 377; judges, election of 385; literacy 242–3; mitigation 245; penal orders 239–40, 242–6, 249–51, 381; plea bargains 66, 198; prosecutors 239, 380; retrials 391; risk of wrongful convictions 249–50; sentences 244–6, 250–1; Swiss National Science Foundation 243; United States, plea bargains in 250–1

systemic flaws 4, 20–1, 176–83, 330, 339–40

T

Taliban 227

Taroni, Franco 6, 378

Taylor, Scott 263, 267, 269, 273

terrorism: European Convention on Human Rights 375; false confessions 7–8, 200, 202–3, 375, 377; IRA cases 114, 180, 210, 360–1, 378; police investigations, false confessions ending 7–8 *see also* terrorist suspects in Canada, treatment of; terrorist suspects in United States, treatment of

terrorist suspects in Canada, treatment of 209–22; adversarial systems 212, 218; Anti-terrorism Act 213; border controls 213–14; Charter of Rights and Freedoms 213, 217, 222; compulsion, evidence obtained by 213; definition of terrorism 213; deportation following unsubstantiated allegations 8, 212, 215–17; designation of terrorist organizations 213; disclosure 210–11, 218–19; evidence 8, 210, 213, 215–21, 229–30; false confessions 210; Guantánamo Bay detainees 222; immigration polices 8, 210, 213–14, 219, 229; individual rights 8, 209–21, 229–31, 375; intelligence, reliance on 212, 215, 217–18, 220–2, 229–30; police powers 213; presumption of innocence 8, 210; preventive arrest 213; preventive detention without charge 8, 212, 213, 216–17, 221–2, 230, 374; profiling 215; racism 214–15; recognizances and peace bonds 213; rights of suspects 8, 210–12; security certificates to exclude non-citizens 212, 214–21, 230; September 11, 2001 terrorist attacks on the United States 8, 209–22, 229–31; special advocates, role of 219–21; standard of proof 210–11, 229; stereotyping 216; torture 212, 217, 221–2; UN Security Council Resolution 1373 213; unreliable evidence 8, 210, 212, 215–17, 229–30; war on terror 209–10

terrorist suspects in United States, treatment of: adversarial systems 212; Bail Reform Act 223–4; definition of terrorism 223; deportation 8, 225; disclosure 210–11; Enemy Alien Act 224; enemy combatants, designation as 210, 223, 225–7; evidence 210, 225–8; extraordinary rendition 228–9, 231; false confessions 210; Guantánamo Bay detainees 212, 222, 226–8; *habeas corpus*, suspension of 223, 225–7; immigration round-up after 9/11 223–4; indeterminate military detention 225–7; individual rights 8, 209–12, 222–31, 375; investigative detention 224–5; material witness warrants 224–5, 230; military commissions, use of 228–9, 231; No-Fly List 221, 229; Patriot Act 223–4; presumption of innocence 8, 210; prevention of further terrorist acts 211; preventive detention without charge 8, 212, 222–7, 229–31, 374–5; registration program 224; rights of suspects 8, 210–12; September 11, 2001 terrorist attacks on the United States 8, 209–12, 222–31; standard of proof 210–11, 229; torture 225–8; war on terror 209–10, 222, 229, 375

third party review 186
Thomas, Clarence 296
Thompson, John 102–3, 105
Thompson, William C. 5–6, 378
"three-strikes-and-you're out" laws 20, 34–5
Tibbs, Delbert 263, 274
time limits 72–3, 289, 293–4, 301, 305
Tokar, Helen 309–11
"Toronto 18" 230
torture 212, 221–2, 226–8
Totenberg, Nina 102
tough-on-crime laws 20–1, 34–5, 99, 107

training *see* education and training

transitional justice 11, 360, 363–9

transparency 32

Trotter, G. 209

trust issues 262, 268–9

truth: alternatives to trials 237–8; forensic science 112, 138–9; law schools, teaching in 105; material truth 4, 62–4, 69–70, 384–5; procedural justice 4, 62–4, 69–70, 384–5; prosecutors, misconduct by 93–4, 105; summary proceedings 237–8

tunnel vision *see* confirmation bias, tunnel vision and belief perseverance

Turow, Scott 313–14

Tushnet, Mark 283–4

Tyler, Tom 18

Type I errors 5–6, 22, 112, 365, 387

Type II errors 5–6, 22, 112, 365, 387

U

United Kingdom: Criminal Cases Review Commission 189, 284, 289, 304, 350; disclosure rules 189–90; DNA evidence 359; forensic science 114; Guildford Four and Birmingham Six 360–1; IRA cases 114, 180, 210, 360–1, 378; Police and Criminal Evidence Act 1984 177;

United States: actual innocence 227, 284–6, 288, 290–6, 304–5, 324; adversarial systems 4, 7, 61–74, 176, 382; Borchard, Edwin, career of 10, 329–39, 348, 350–1; causes of wrongful convictions 77– 90, 338–40, 377–9; Constitution 322; courts, reform to 338, 340, 348–9, 351; death penalty cases 49, 61, 196,

262–78, 287, 290, 293–7; DNA testing 349–51, 363; European Convention on Human Rights 386, 393; extradition 287; eyewitness identification 319–20; false confessions 7, 205; forensic science 111–14; frequency of wrongful convictions, estimates of 46–57, 377; impunity 382; innocence reforms 10–11, 329–51, 388, 390; Innocence Protection Act 363; inquisitorial systems 4, 61–74, 382; institutional culture, changes in 10–11, 330, 339– 51; juries 287, 294, 296, 302–6, 348–9; Justice for All Act 363; law school clinics 330, 340, 349–51; limits of reform 338–50; *Miranda* warnings 74, 83, 84–5, 388; organizational structure of criminal justice system 340; plea bargains 2, 8, 30–2, 237, 239, 250–5, 347–8, 381–2, 389–90; police 25, 27–8, 63, 330, 338–40, 341–6, 387–8; political culture, changes in 10–11, 341; proof of innocence, exonerations beyond 391; prosecutors 5, 29–31, 91– 107, 330, 338–41, 346–8, 351, 380, 388, 390; race 86–7, 111, 306, 311, 320, 344, 350; reform 10–11, 329–51, 388, 390; remedies for wrongful convictions 9–10; resistance to relief 9–10, 93, 104–5, 309–25, 380, 390–1; retrials 391; return to free society 262–78, 385–6; social costs 29–31; United States 287; video recording of interviews 388; Watergate scandal 341 *see also* remedies for wrongful convictions in United States; terrorist suspects in United States, treatment of use of force: police 25, 27–9; state's monopoly on violence 23–4

V

validation research, lack of 123, 127
validity of exonerations, challenging 10, 312
Van Koppen, P.J. 181, 189
Vanzetti, Bartolomeo 337–8, 348
victimization survey 46
victims, social costs to 23
videotaping interrogations 69, 83–4, 338–9
vigilantism 120
Vignaux, G. A. 154
Vollmer, August 341
Voltaire 365
voluntary false confessions 2, 7–8, 193–206, 375–6, 377
Vuille, Joëlle 6, 378–9

W

Waggonner, Bret 318
Walker, C. 210
war on terror 209–10, 222, 229, 375
Ward, Judith 180
Warden, Rob 101
Warner, Mark 55
warnings: false confessions 69; eyewitness identification, jury warnings on 87–8; *Miranda* warnings 74, 83, 84–5, 388
Warren, Earl 74, 393
waterboarding 228

Watergate scandal 341
Watkins, Jerry 78–82
Weber, Max 23–4
Westervelt, Saundra D. 8, 360, 385–6
Whitlock, Craig 27–9
Whitlock, Herb 104
Wigmore, Dean 337
Wigmore, John 336–7
Wilhoit, Greg 263, 267, 271, 273
withdrawal and numbing strategies 275–6
Witness to Innocence 274
witnesses: material witness warrants 224–5, 230; misconduct 379; Netherlands 168, 170, 177–8, 185, 187; social costs 23 *see also* eyewitness identification
Wolf, Herman 309–11
women, false confessions by 7, 203–5
workmen's compensation 333–5, 339, 386–7
Wrightsman, L.S. 194–5, 198
wrongful arrests 17, 22–3, 37
Wynn, William 318

Y

Yagüe, C. 203
Yarris, Nicholas 324
young offenders, false confessions by 7, 84–5, 197–202, 205, 377

Z

Zalman, Marvin 10–11, 57, 61, 120, 376, 387–8, 391

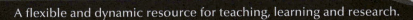

THE SOCIAL ISSUES
COLLECTION™

Finally, it's easy to
customize materials for your sociology course

Choose from a collection of 250 readings from Routledge and other
publishers to create a perfect anthology that fits your course and students.

1 Go to the website at
socialissuescollection.com

2 Choose from 250
readings in sociology

3 Create your complete
custom anthology

Readings from The Social Issues Collection are pre-cleared and available at reduced permission
rates, helping your students save money on course materials. Projects are ready in 2 weeks for
direct e-commerce student purchases.

For over 25 undergraduate sociology courses including:

Criminology	Globalization	Social Inequalities
Cultural Sociology	Sociology of Work and Economy	Sociology of Media and Communication
Environmental Sociology	Marriage and Family	Sociology of Place
Gender	Race and Ethnicity	Sociology of Religion

Contact us to learn more about our services

3970 Sorrento Valley Blvd. Ste 500, San Diego, CA 92121 | info@universityreaders.com | 800-200-3908 x 501

University Readers is an imprint of Cognella, Inc. ©1997-2012